EMINENT DOMAIN

The taking of private property for development projects has caused controversy in many nations, where it has often been used to benefit powerful interests at the expense of the general public. This edited collection is the first to use a common framework to analyze the law and economics of eminent domain around the world. The authors show that seemingly disparate nations face a common set of problems in seeking to regulate the condemnation of private property by the state. They include the tendency to forcibly displace the poor and politically weak for the benefit of those with greater influence, disputes over compensation, and resort to condemnation in cases where it destroys more economic value than it creates. With contributions from leading scholars in the fields of property law and economics, the book offers a comparative perspective and considers a wide range of possible solutions to these problems.

ILJOONG KIM is Professor of Economics at Sungkyunkwan University. He is a leading expert in the field of law and economics in Korea where his research activities have ignited the scholarly interest in the field.

HOJUN LEE is a Fellow at the Korea Development Institute (KDI). His academic research topics include mechanism design in public sectors, law and economics of property rights, and public finance of regional development. He is a former Director of the Public Private Partnership Division at KDI.

ILYA SOMIN is Professor of Law at George Mason University. His research focuses on constitutional law and property law. He is the author of *The Grasping Hand: Kelo v. City of New London and the Limits of Eminent Domain* (2015) and *Democracy and Political Ignorance*, 2nd edn (2016).

The use of the eminent domain power is common throughout democracies in both the developed and developing world. The exercise of that power, so necessary for sustainable growth, is also fraught with great peril. This timely and instructive volume fills a major gap in the literature by examining the ups and downs of eminent domain in a comparative context, with special emphasis on the law of South Korea, which has been the home to some of the most important takings conflicts in recent years.

— Richard Epstein, *Laurence A. Tisch Professor of Law, New York University*

In *Eminent Domain: A Comparative Perspective*, Ilya Somin, Hojun Lee, and Iljoong Kim have assembled a panoramic view of the law of eminent domain across nations as diverse as Germany, the United States, Korea, and Taiwan. Providing an exceptionally complete yet concise summary of each regime, this volume also provides an extraordinarily useful framework for understanding how and why each system succeeds or fails in safeguarding fundamental rights to retain what one owns in the face of eminent domain. It is an essential volume for anyone studying or defending the right to private property.

— Roderick M. Hills, Jr., *William T. Comfort, III Professor of Law, New York University*

This volume is a superb analysis of eminent domain at a genuinely global level. The organization is systematic in that the authors faithfully follow a unified analytic framework to overcome the difficulty of making meaningful inter-jurisdictional comparisons. As a judge who has experienced different stages of development in my own country, I am certain that professional and lay readers alike can benefit from this wide-ranging and learned book.

— Soon-il Kwon, *Honorable Justice, Supreme Court of Korea*

EMINENT DOMAIN

A Comparative Perspective

ILJOONG KIM

Sungkyunkwan University, Seoul

HOJUN LEE

Korea Development Institute, Sejong

ILYA SOMIN

George Mason University, Virginia

CAMBRIDGE UNIVERSITY PRESS

KDI Korea Development Institute

CAMBRIDGE
UNIVERSITY PRESS

University Printing House, Cambridge CB2 8BS, United Kingdom

One Liberty Plaza, 20th Floor, New York, NY 10006, USA

477 Williamstown Road, Port Melbourne, VIC 3207, Australia

4843/24, 2nd Floor, Ansari Road, Daryaganj, Delhi – 110002, India

79 Anson Road, #06–04/06, Singapore 079906

Cambridge University Press is part of the University of Cambridge.

It furthers the University's mission by disseminating knowledge in the pursuit of education, learning, and research at the highest international levels of excellence.

www.cambridge.org
Information on this title: www.cambridge.org/9781107177291
DOI: 10.1017/9781316822685

First published 2017

A catalogue record for this publication is available from the British Library.

Library of Congress Cataloging-in-Publication Data
Names: Kim, Iljoong, editor. | Lee, Hojun, editor. | Somin, Ilya, editor.
Title: Eminent domain : a comparative perspective / edited by Iljoong Kim, Hojun Lee, Ilya Somin.
Description: New York : Cambridge University Press, 2017.
Identifiers: LCCN 2016059566 | ISBN 9781107177291 (hardback)
Subjects: LCSH: Eminent domain. | Eminent domain – Korea (South)
Classification: LCC K3511 .E45 2017 | DDC 343/.0252–dc23
LC record available at https://lccn.loc.gov/2016059566

ISBN 978-1-107-17729-1 Hardback
ISBN 978-1-316-62833-1 Paperback

CONTENTS

CONTRIBUTORS

ANNE VAN AAKEN is Professor of Law and Economics, Legal Theory, Public International Law and European Law at the University of St. Gallen, Switzerland. Before that she was a Senior Research Fellow at the Max Planck Institute for the Research of Collective Goods as well as at the Max Planck Institute for Comparative Public Law and International Law. She holds a Masters in law from the University of Munich, a Ph.D. in law from the University of Frankfurt/Oder, and a Masters degree in economics from the University of Fribourg, Switzerland. She was admitted to the bar in Germany.

YUN-CHIEN CHANG is Associate Research Professor at Institutum Jurisprudentiae, Academia Sinica, Taiwan, and serves as the Deputy Director of its Empirical Legal Studies Center. He was a Visiting Professor at the Law Faculty at the Hebrew University of Jerusalem and Haifa University in 2011 and 2015, respectively. In 2016, Professor Chang was appointed as Law and Economics Fellow at the University of Chicago Law School. His current academic interests focus on economic, empirical and comparative analysis of property law and land use law, as well as empirical studies of the judicial system. He received his J.S.D. and LL.M. degree from New York University School of Law. He also earned LL.B. and LL.M. degrees at the National Taiwan University and passed the Taiwan bar.

BYUNGKOO CHO is a judge at the Supreme Court of Korea. He has been working as a judge for about 14 years. He passed the Korean bar in 1994 and completed a two-year course from the Judicial Research and Training Institute of Korea. Then, he was appointed as a judge at the Seoul Central District Court in 2002. He was a visiting scholar at the Max Planck Institute, Germany, in 2007 and a Professor at the Judicial Research and Training Institute of Korea and Adjunct Professor at the Law School of Hankook University of Foreign Studies from 2010 to 2012.

He then worked as a judge at the Seoul Administrative Court and was appointed as a presiding judge of the Jinju Branch Court from 2012 to 2015. He received his LL.B. from Seoul National University and completed an LL.M. degree at Seoul National University.

KLAUS DEININGER is Lead Economist in the rural development group of the Development Research Group at the World Bank. His areas of research focus on income and asset inequality and its relationship to poverty reduction and growth; access to land, land markets and land reform and their impact on household welfare and agricultural productivity; land tenure and its impact on investment, including environmental sustainability; and capacity-building (including the use of quantitative and qualitative methods) for policy analysis and evaluation, mainly in the Africa, Central America and East Asia regions. He is a German national with a Ph.D. in Applied Economics from the University of Minnesota, an M.A. in Agricultural Economics from the University of Berlin and an M.A. in theology from the University of Bonn.

THEA HILHORST is the Global Coordinator of the World Bank's Land Governance Assessment Framework. She previously served as a senior staff member at the Royal Tropical Institute of the Netherlands and a research associate at the International Institute for Environment and Development in the United Kingdom. She has served as a consultant on land development issues for numerous governments in the developing world and has published articles on a variety of land development issues. She holds an M.Sc. degree from the Agricultural University, Wageningen, in the Netherlands.

KISANG JUNG is a Judge at the Eastern Branch of Busan District Court of Korea. He was appointed as a Judge in the Seoul Western District Court in 2009 after he passed the Korean bar in 2003. He was a Judge at the Seoul Administrative Court from 2011 to 2013 and handled many cases of expropriation and compensation. He has conducted research on expropriation and compensation as well as on the issue of taxation and has published several articles in scholarly journals. He holds LL.B. and LL.M. degrees from Seoul National University.

DUOL KIM is Professor of Economics at Myongji University. Prior to his current position, he conducted academic and policy-oriented research and taught at the University of California Davis, Korea Development Institute (KDI) and KDI School of Public Policy and Management. His research focuses on economic history (Korea, East Asia and the United States), economic development, law and economics, institutional economics and industrial organization. He was formerly the editor of the *Korean Journal of Law and Economics* and currently an editorial board member of the *Korean Journal of Economic Studies*. He studied economics at Seoul National University (B.A. and M.A.) and the University of California Los Angeles (Ph.D.).

ILJOONG KIM is Professor of Economics at Sungkyunkwan University where he was also appointed as the Dasan Economics Chair. Professor Kim is known as a frontrunner in the field of law and economics in Korea where his research activities have ignited the scholarly interest in the field, as recognized by the Wiegong Prize and other awards. He served as the President and the Vice President of the Korean Law and Economics Association, the editor of the *Korean Journal of Law and Economics*, and the Director of the study/research forum, "Law and Economics with Courts". He has also published many books on property rights and criminal justice policy and about 100 articles in journals worldwide, such as *Public Choice, International Review of Law and Economics*, and the *Journal of Institutional and Theoretical Economics*. He received a B.A. in economics from Yonsei University and an M.Sc. and Ph.D. in economics from Florida State University in 1990.

HOJUN LEE is a Fellow of KDI. From 2014 to 2016, he served as the Director of the Public Private Partnership division of the Public and Private Infrastructure Investment Management Center at KDI. His academic research topics include mechanism design in public sectors, law and economics of property rights, and public finance of regional development. He also has conducted policy research to help the Korean government formulate budget plans and build social and economic policies. He has published numerous academic articles in Korean academic journals as well as policy advisory documents to the Korean government in various forms. He holds a B.A. and an M.A. in economics from Seoul National University and a Ph.D. in economics from the University of Wisconsin Madison.

JONATHAN LINDSAY is Lead Counsel for Land and Natural Resources at the World Bank. He is also a member of the Environment and

International Law practice group of the Legal Vice Presidency, supporting the World Bank's operational and analytical work on application of the World Bank safeguard and related policies, and natural resource management and related environmental issues. He has written extensively on property and natural resources law in developing nations. He holds a J.D. from the University of California Berkeley and a B.A. from Yale University.

SUNGKYU PARK is a Fellow at the Korea Real Estate Research Institute (KRERI) since 2001. At KRERI, he has conducted research on the issues of property rights, takings and real estate valuation and published widely on those topics. He also helped, in varying capacities, the Ministry of Land, Infrastructure and Transportation of Korea formulate land policies (e.g. land use regulation, compensation and appraisal), the Korean Association of Public Appraisers and other public corporations. He has been an Adjunct Professor at Soongsil University since 2012. He holds B.A., M.A., and Ph.D. degrees in economics from Soongsil University.

HANS-BERND SCHÄFER is Professor of Law and Economics at Bucerius Law School in Hamburg. He is also Professor Emeritus at the University of Hamburg. His main publications are on the economic analysis of civil law and on law and development. His writings are well known to have influenced the scholarship of law and economics in Europe. He has also taught at several foreign universities including George Mason University, University of Toronto, University of St. Gallen, University of Haifa and the Indira Gandhi Institute in Mumbai. Dr. Schäfer was co-founder and director of the Institute of Law and Economics at the University of Hamburg and of the Ph.D. program of the institute. He was long-serving editor of the *International Review of Law and Economics*, Director of the European Masters Program in Law and Economics and President of the European Association of Law and Economics. He studied economics and business administration in Cologne and received his Ph.D. in economics from the University of Bochum.

ILYA SOMIN is Professor of Law at George Mason University School of Law. His research focuses on constitutional law, property law and the study of popular political participation and its implications for constitutional democracy. He is the author of *The Grasping Hand: Kelo v. City of New London and the Limits of Eminent Domain* (2015) and *Democracy and Political Ignorance: Why Smaller Government is Smarter*

(2016). His work has appeared in numerous scholarly journals, including the *Yale Law Journal, Stanford Law Review, Northwestern University Law Review, Georgetown Law Journal, Critical Review* and others. He has served as a Visiting Professor at the University of Hamburg, Germany, the University of Torcuato Di Tella in Buenos Aires, Argentina, and Zhengzhou University in China. Professor Somin earned his B.A., *summa cum laude*, at Amherst College, his M.A. in political science from Harvard University, and his J.D. from Yale Law School.

ACKNOWLEDGEMENTS

We are grateful to many people who have helped make this volume possible. First and foremost, we would like to thank the scholars from around the world who contributed chapters. We are very grateful to Joe Ng and Chloe Harries of Cambridge University Press for their excellent handling of this project, from start to finish.

Our sincere appreciation goes to Dr. Joon-Kyung Kim, President of Korea Development Institute (KDI) who has strongly supported the publication of this book, as well as the March 2015 KDI conference on "Shifting the Paradigm for Sustainable Development: Eminent Domain and Property Rights," which gave rise to the book. We are also indebted to Honorable Justice Yi-Su Kim of the Constitutional Court of Korea who gave invaluable congratulatory remarks at the conference and Honorable Justice Soon-il Kwon of the Supreme Court of Korea who participated and gave indispensable comments during the conference. The active involvement of these Justices in the conference readily showed the importance of such a subject and how much attention is being paid to the issue of eminent domain as a major constitutional matter in Korea.

Numerous colleagues and friends also deserve credit for their invaluable assistance. Professor Jinsu Yune of the Seoul National University and Professor Wonhyuk Lim of the KDI School of Public Policy and Management served as wonderful moderators at the conference. Dr. Yonghyen Yang of KDI and Professor Yifat Holzman-Gazit of the College of Management Academic Studies in Israel contributed excellent presentations and comments. Presiding Judge Hwansoo Kim of the Patent Court of Korea and the KDI fellows, particularly Dr. Dongseok Kim, Dr. Dongchul Cho, Dr. Jay-Hyung Kim, and Dr. Kangsoo Kim, provided a variety of useful suggestions. We would also like to thank Ms. Soojung Kim and Ms. Sujin Kim for their excellent administrative support.

Three anonymous referees who reviewed our initial proposal submitted to Cambridge University Press offered criticisms and editorial suggestions which helped improve this volume.

Introduction

ILJOONG KIM, HOJUN LEE AND ILYA SOMIN

In 1795, United States Supreme Court Justice William Paterson famously called eminent domain "a despotic power," but also one that necessarily "exists in every government."[1] The use and abuse of eminent domain has caused conflict and controversy in nations around the world. Condemnation is sometimes a useful tool for acquiring property for important development projects. But this potentially valuable institution also has flaws. Coercive acquisition of property can undermine private property rights, which themselves play a vital role in development. Moreover, condemning authorities in many countries often abuse their power by taking property for the benefit of politically influential interest groups at the expense of the politically weak and the general public.

While there have been many works that describe and assess the use of eminent domain in the United States and other individual nations,[2] this volume is the first that uses a common framework to analyze the law and economics of eminent domain in many countries at once.

Debates over the use and abuse of eminent domain have arisen in both advanced and developing countries in recent years. The United States Supreme Court's controversial ruling in the 2005 case of *Kelo v. City of New London*,[3] upholding the use of eminent domain for private "economic development," led to a massive political backlash in that country which has resonated elsewhere around the world.[4] The need for a comparative analysis of eminent domain policy has never been

[1] *Vanhorne's Lessee v. Dorrance*, 2 U.S. (2 Dall.) 304, 311 (1795).

[2] For recent surveys of eminent domain law and policy in the United States, see, e.g., Ilya Somin, *The Grasping Hand: Kelo v. City of New London and the Limits of Eminent Domain* (University of Chicago Press, 2015); and Thomas Miceli, *The Economic Theory of Eminent Domain; Private Property, Public Use* (Cambridge University Press, 2011).

[3] *Kelo v. City of New London*, 545 U.S. 469 (2005).

[4] For an overview of the political reaction to *Kelo*, see Somin, *Grasping Hand*, chs. 5–6, and Chapter 2 of the present volume.

greater. Yet, few attempts have been made to fill this crucial gap in the literature.[5]

This volume provides a comparative perspective on the law of eminent domain in various countries around the world. Each author assesses the law and economics of the use of eminent domain in their respective nations, from the standpoint of six common issues that arise in any legal system that gives the state the power to condemn private property.

The chapters in this volume build upon the papers originally presented at an international conference on "Shifting the Paradigm for Sustainable Development: Eminent Domain and Property Rights," hosted by the Korea Development Institute (KDI) in Seoul on March 4, 2015

The Six Pillars of Eminent Domain

Given the varied histories and legal cultures that give rise to the eminent domain systems of each country, it is often hard to make meaningful comparisons. To make the task more tractable, we have sought to apply a unified analytical framework to all of the nations covered in the book. That will make it easier to identify important differences and commonalities, and to begin to make useful generalizations.

Consequently, a key distinctive feature of this volume is that all the contributors focus on six common institutional aspects of eminent domain law and policy, which we refer to as the "Six Pillars" of takings law: (1) public interest criteria for takings; (2) subjects of takings (the entities authorized to use the power to condemn); (3) just compensation; (4) due process in takings; (5) the distribution of the development surplus; and (6) the dispute resolution system.

[5] The previous work most similar to this one is probably Gregory Alexander, *The Global Debate over Constitutional Property: Lessons for American Takings Jurisprudence* (University of Chicago Press, 2006). Alexander considers constitutional property rights jurisprudence in several countries and attempts to extract lessons for American takings jurisprudence. However, Alexander only focuses on eminent domain relatively briefly, devoting most of his analysis to other takings issues. Moreover, his comparative analysis focuses mostly on Germany and South Africa. He does not give significant attention to the many other countries covered in this book, including EU nations other than Germany, South Korea, Taiwan, and a variety of developing countries. Perhaps most importantly, Alexander's book was published in 2006, only about a year after the US Supreme Court's controversial decision in *Kelo v. City of New London* (2005). He thus was not able to give much consideration to the massive debate over takings that the decision sparked not only in the United States but in other countries.

Public interest criteria for takings (known as "public use" in the United States) limit the range of purposes for which the government may condemn private property. Such restrictions are needed to prevent abusive and economically harmful takings that undermine property rights and potentially destroy more economic value than they create. Public interest constraints on takings exist in many countries, but there is considerable variation in how restrictive they are. In many nations, there are fierce controversies over whether such restrictions should be tightened or loosened.

Eminent domain systems also vary as to which public and private entities are authorized to use the power to condemn, thereby becoming "subjects of takings," in our terminology. Eminent domain is often conceptualized as a power exclusively held by the state. Yet, many governments have, at times, delegated its use to private firms, such as railroads and public utilities.

Virtually all eminent domain systems offer "just compensation" to owners of condemned property. But there is considerable disagreement and controversy over the question of how much compensation is enough. While many countries use the "fair market value" standard, critics argue that it fails to account for a variety of important losses suffered by displaced property owners. This has led some jurisdictions to require additional compensation of various kinds.

The use of eminent domain typically requires some form of procedural due process. Most nations, at the very least, require some form of advance notice to owners, and some form of legal process by which owners can challenge the legality of the condemnation, or the amount of the compensation award. But there is considerable variation beyond this bare minimum.

There is also variation over how different jurisdictions deal with the "development surplus" created by takings: the extra economic value that officials hope will be created by the condemnation. It is often argued that some of this value should be given to the former owners of the condemned land, though few jurisdictions assign them more than a very modest share of this surplus.

Finally, it is almost inevitable that the use of eminent domain generates disputes over the legality of the various aspects of the process. Different legal systems provide a variety of approaches to resolving such disputes.

Overview of the Book

The book is organized into two parts. Part I analyzes the use of eminent domain in a variety of legal systems around the world, assessing each from the standpoint of the Six Pillars framework.

In Chapter 1, Hans-Bernd Schäfer considers the use of eminent domain in Germany. He argues that Germany's relatively stringent public interest criteria effectively constrain most potential abuses, but suggests that the nation's procedural structure for takings has a number of shortcomings.

Chapter 2, written by Ilya Somin, focuses on eminent domain in the United States. Somin emphasizes that it is difficult to generalize about takings in that country, because most condemnations are initiated by state and local governments, and there is wide variation between the 50 states on many key aspects of eminent domain law and policy. Nonetheless, he explains that, during the twentieth century, both the federal Supreme Court and many state courts loosened "public use" constraints on takings, which has resulted in numerous questionable practices, including the forcible displacement of many hundreds of thousands of people and businesses. In recent years, there has been a strong public and judicial reaction against such abuses, particularly in the wake of the Supreme Court's unpopular decision in the *Kelo* case.

In Chapter 3, Anne van Aaken assesses eminent domain in the European Union, particularly the role of the European Convention on Human Rights, which provides a backstop to the varied protections offered by the laws of the individual member nations. She concludes that this multilevel system of constitutional rights provides useful protection for property owners against potentially dubious takings.

Yun-chien Chang's Chapter 4 focuses on Taiwan. Recent reforms in that country, enacted in 2012, have tightened public interest criteria for takings, increased compensation for property owners, and provided new procedural protections. Nonetheless, Chang suggests that these reforms have done little to curb abuses or restrict the use of eminent domain on the ground, in part because judges have continued to defer to the decisions of condemning authorities. He suggests that future reform efforts might usefully take a different approach from that enacted in 2012.

In Chapter 5, Jonathan Lindsay, Klaus Deininger, and Thea Hilhorst provide an overview of the use of eminent domain in developing countries. Many such nations have resorted to extensive takings for the purpose of promoting economic growth. These practices have sometimes led to abuses, which are extremely difficult to forestall.

Compulsory acquisition in developing economies poses enormous challenges. While a number of countries have adopted remarkably bold and innovative approaches to eminent domain reform, the authors emphasize the need for further research, so as to minimize the risks created by takings and implement policies that contribute to enhanced social welfare in the long term.

Part II provides a comprehensive analysis of the Korean eminent domain system. Each of its six chapters is devoted to in-depth examination of one of the Six Pillars in South Korea. Korea is a nation that has condemned vast amounts of land over several decades. The KDI conference was originally inspired by the two Korean co-editors' ongoing observation of the use of eminent domain in their country, which have begun to cause serious conflict between condemners and condemnees in recent years.

Korea is one of the several East Asian nations, including China, Taiwan, and others where there has been extensive controversy over takings in recent years. Because of the cultural and political similarities between these countries, the Korean case is likely to be of special interest to audiences in those countries, and scholars who study their legal systems. The in-depth examination of the Korean case in Part II will be of interest to scholars and other interested readers around the world as well as those in Korea itself.

Moreover, Korea has interesting features because it is one of the many countries that has experienced conflict between development-oriented institutions that made extensive use of eminent domain and an increasing awareness of the importance of property rights. Until the late 1980s, Korea was an authoritarian state, and government-led development was a high priority. Citizens, at the time, rarely resisted development policy, even when their rights were severely infringed. Since the late 1980s, Korea has rapidly democratized, and people have begun to take a more skeptical view of government policies. Consequently, public awareness of property rights issues has reached a much higher level, while the legal system of the past persisted.

In order to continue to promote sustainable development, Korea may need a paradigm shift in its eminent domain system. Similar issues have arisen, and likely will continue to arise, in other nations that have experienced rapid economic growth. In the current environment where many types of social media have become available, people in these countries are more exposed to contending opinions on property rights originating from the West and elsewhere. For these and other reasons, we believe that the Korean experience has important relevance for other countries, particularly developing nations.

In Chapter 6, Hojun Lee reviews the state of public interest limits on takings in Korea. He contends that such limits are often insufficiently enforced, and argues that Korea should adopt reforms that limit abuses more effectively.

Iljoong Kim's Chapter 7 focuses on the subjects of eminent domain in Korea, particularly the extensive delegation of condemnation authority to private entities. He concludes that this policy has led to serious problems and abuses, and advocates tightening restrictions on the use of eminent domain by private parties.

In Chapter 8, Byungkoo Cho provides an overview of takings compensation in Korea. He suggests that the present system often fails to adequately compensate for important losses, and thereby exacerbates the social costs of eminent domain, particularly "demoralization costs."

Chapter 9, authored by Kisang Jung, assesses Korean eminent domain procedure, and concludes that procedural restrictions on takings are often inadequate, especially in assessing the "public necessity" of proposed takings.

In Chapter 10, Sungkyu Park explains how and why Korean law – like that of many other countries – forbids giving displaced property owners a share of the development surplus created by takings. He contends that this rule is ill-advised, because it incentivizes abusive and inefficient practices by developers.

Finally, Chapter 11, authored by Duol Kim, examines the Central Land Tribunal of Korea (CLT), the leading dispute resolution body adjudicating eminent domain cases. He suggests that the CLT's current practices have significant flaws. Many cases receive only cursory examination, and often little is done to prevent abusive practices. Kim concludes reforms are urgently needed to ensure thorough and just consideration of takings cases.

We hope that readers of this volume will be able to use it to compare the key characteristics of eminent domain systems across countries and assess their implications. For example, there is much to be learned from the variation in the strictness of public interest constraints on takings. In his chapter on the German system, Hans-Bernd Schäfer argues that its relatively tight restrictions on condemnations have effectively curbed many potential abuses. In the United States, the federal Supreme Court's broad interpretation of public use allows more discretion to governments, but that has begun to be questioned by many people since the controversial *Kelo* decision. Some state courts have taken a tougher line.

In both Korea and Taiwan, in spite of an otherwise strong legal framework, very broad discretion is often given to government officials, leading to numerous questionable condemnations. The developing nations covered in Chapter 5 often face even more severe challenges in regulating the use of eminent domain.

We hope and expect that this book will be a useful resource for economists, legal scholars, jurists, public officials, and others interested in the use of eminent domain around the world.

1

Taking Law from an Economic Perspective with Reference to German Law

HANS-BERND SCHÄFER

I Market Economy, Planned Economy and Eminent Domain Power

The institution of private property assigns the use, the appropriation of the fruits and the voluntary transfer of a resource to an individual or a private person. It protects the owner against anybody, including the state. It is also widely though not universally considered a human right.[1] Having its roots in Roman law rather than in the laws and institutions of traditional communities or tribes, property is not an investiture or privilege which a ruler can assign or withdraw. Many scholars[2] criticized Roman property law as cold, unbrotherly and capitalistic. In fact, this concept became strongest in those areas which embraced the market economy. Historically, it replaced or crowded out other forms of property rights like the commons or the commandries, which reflected traditional community values rather than individualism and market capitalism. Strongly protected, well-defined and undiluted property rights are a prerequisite for well-functioning markets.

In many developing countries, and in countries like Korea which have recently accumulated substantial wealth, private property is less well protected against the state than in western countries. The reasons for this are partly economic and partly cultural.

One important economic reason was the influential theory of state-led economic development, which dominated development economics from the 1950s to the 1980s. From the 1940s onwards the newly independent

[1] In all 47 countries of the Council of Europe property is a human right. India is a counterexample. It does not include private property in the list of fundamental rights stipulated in part 3 of its constitution.

[2] For an overview see J. Q. Whitman, "The moral menace of Roman law and the making of commerce. Some Dutch evidence," *Yale Law Journal*, 105(7) (1995), 1841–89.

countries of Africa and Asia implemented various types of socialism. Within this political environment, development economics emerged as an academic discipline. In the 1940s and 1950s, many of its most prominent scholars taught that developing countries needed state leadership of the economy.[3] These theories maintained that a market economy might be good for rich countries, but that in poor countries free markets would lead to so many departures from the workable market model that the state should lead the economy. Development theory diagnosed a whole Olympus of market failures in poor countries. These ranged from increasing returns to scale and natural monopoly via unbalanced growth. They were also attributed to linkages between firms not internalized by prices, as well as dualistic economies with wages differing from the opportunity costs of labor. These considerations favored the demand for a strong hand on the part of the government to plan the economy. Within a planned or mixed economy private property must necessarily be less well protected by the law than in a market economy. The state must have planning capacity and the taking of private property by the state must be relatively easy in order to promote economic development. Development economics has ceased to be the dominant paradigm pertaining to developing countries, yet the legal structures supporting a planned or mixed economy still exist. However, the shift of the sustainable development paradigm from state-led growth with a strong hand from above to a decentralized market economy will also tend to change the laws of eminent domain in favor of enhanced private property protection.

In East-Asian countries a cultural Confucian influence supports taking laws with ample discretion for the state. Ginsburg argues in an article on constitutional judicial review in Korea and Taiwan that this tradition emphasizes social order over individual autonomy as well as responsibilities over rights.[4] Ideally the state organs would form a harmonious unity under a strong leadership which is to be constrained by a community-oriented

[3] The economist and Nobel Laureate Gunnar Myrdal captured the spirit of development economics in the 1950 with the following words: "The most important change in state policies in underdeveloped countries is the common understanding that they should each and all have a national economic development policy . . . Indeed it is also universally urged that each of them should have an overall, integrated national plan. All underdeveloped countries are now attempting to provide themselves with such a plan, except a few that have not yet been reached by the Great Awakening." G. Myrdal, *Economic Theory and Underdeveloped Countries* (Duckworth, 1957), p. 79.

[4] T. Ginsburg, "Confucian constitutionalism? The emergence of constitutional review in Korea and Taiwan," *Law and Social Inquiry*, 27(4) (2002), 763–690.

ethic. They are traditionally not seen as organizations monitoring and controlling each other. Yet Ginsburg also shows how innovative legal systems in these two countries have developed in recent years by introducing constitutional judicial review and protecting individual rights, including property, against the administration and parliament.

Both development economics and culture favored taking without an elaborated due process, with ample discretion of the bureaucracy, with outsourcing the taking decisions from the state to private firms, with no temporary relief, without constitutional review and with damage compensation often much lower than a damage award in civil law cases. This chapter deals with some basic problems of expropriation from a law and economics perspective. It makes reference to German rules pertaining to takings. It focuses on the following Six Pillars of eminent domain: just compensation and distribution of surplus, public interest or common good, due process and dispute resolution and, finally, the subjects of eminent domain power.[5]

II Compensation for Taking in Comparison to a Civil Liability Damage Award

1 Compensation for Taking is Systematically Lower than a Damage Award under Civil Liability

An individual who loses property is faced with a loss or disutility, thus placing her on a lower ranked indifference curve. Full compensation would require providing the individual with those goods or the money required to buy them, such that she is back on the original indifference curve, possibly endowed with a different basket of goods. Legal orders do not fully meet this economic requirement for full compensation, even in cases of tort liability in which an unlawful act triggers damage compensation. In many countries including Germany damage compensation is conceptualized by the so-called differential method.[6] According to this method, a court compares the actual wealth of the claimant against her hypothetical wealth assuming the wrongful act which led to the damage

[5] Korea Development Institute (KDI), International Conference on Shifting the Paradigm for Sustainable Development: Eminent Domain and Property Rights, KDI paper, 7pp (2015).

[6] N. Birch, "Comparative compensation," in S. W. Schill (ed.), *International Investment Law and Comparative Public Law* (Oxford University Press, 2010: published at Oxford Scholarship Online, 2011), pp. 2–31.

had not occurred. The difference between these two numbers defines the damage award. As a result, the original wealth is restored. This way of damage assessment includes all future expectation, the goodwill, interest and losses from currency devaluation or any other loss of wealth. However, in many countries – including Germany – it does not include sentimental value, mental stress or other non-financial damages. Some countries, like France, compensate non-financial damages. From an economic view the exclusion of non-financial damages economizes on the costs of the judicial procedure but leads to under-compensation and possibly under-deterrence. It then does not fully restore the utility level which would have existed without the wrongful act.

In the law of eminent domain, a precise formula leading to the damage award by way of deduction, such as the differential method, is missing. Instead, one finds a large number of definitions which are often vague and have to be substantiated by jurisdiction. However, almost all of these definitions have one thing in common. They might lead to a damage award, which is below the level of compensation in a tort law case under the differential method. Before turning to the question of whether this is in any way defendable from an incentive perspective or fairness point of view, let me provide some examples.

In international law the damage award might be calculated according to the differential method, whenever the act of expropriation occurred in violation of international law.[7] A Korean investor, whose foreign-owned land is taken by the foreign state, might be awarded full damages under international law, provided the act of taking violates a bilateral investment treaty.[8] If, however, the act of taking was legal under international law, very different formulas are applied in order to describe the damage award. The frequently used Hull formula requires

[7] Birch, "Comparative compensation." Birch mentions the case of a group of Irish famers in Zimbabwe whose farms were expropriated. This was regarded as a violation of international law. The International Centre for Settlement of Investment Disputes calculated a damage award according to the differential method. It seems, however, unclear whether there is a clear calculation prescription. See T. Wälde and B. Sabahi, "Compensation, damages and valuation in international investment law," in P. Muchlinski, F. Ortino and C. Schreuer (eds.), *The Oxford Handbook of International Investment Law* (Oxford University Press, 2008), p. 1049.

[8] The investor is not obliged to file for restitution in this case but can directly go to damage compensation. A. van Aaken, "Primary and secondary remedies in international investment law and national state liability: a functional and comparative view," in S. W. Schill (ed.), *International Investment Law and Comparative Public Law* (Oxford University Press, 2010), p. 721.

a "prompt, adequate and effective" compensation, meaning compensation without unreasonable delay, covering the fair market value and being transferable. This amounts to a lower damage award than under the differential method. Developing countries use the term "just compensation" from a UN resolution on the "New International Economic Order"; a damage award which is again lower than according to the Hull formula and would allow the government to take into account instances of colonialism when calculating damages and thus potentially reduce the award to a nominal compensation. The Korean Constitution also uses the term "just compensation" (Art. 23.3). The term "fair market value" is also subject to dispute since it could be viewed as the actual market value, the discounted future income stream or the book value. Different views also exist on the date of valuation. Should this be the value at the time of the decision on a public project, the taking decision, or at the time of judgment? In the latter case compensation would be higher because the subsequent increase of the value resulting from the taking would be included in the compensation. However, the general practice of international law is to disregard this surplus value when calculating the damage award.[9] Current practice of international law follows the Hull formula, which leads to an award higher than according to other formulas but lower than under the differential method.[10]

In Germany compensation for expropriation is regulated by the constitution (Art. 14 Abs. 3)[11] and by many sub-constitutional laws, which are often not federal but state laws. The constitution does not require full compensation but rather a compensation which balances the interests of society and of the individuals affected. The constitution requires that taking must be regulated by sub-constitutional laws, for instance, regional planning laws, energy laws etc., and that these laws must describe the compensation formula. Any taking which cannot be substantiated by means of sub-constitutional law is unconstitutional. This also applies to cases in which sub-constitutional law does not regulate or is too imprecise with regard to the level of compensation. The constitution does not force but allows the sub-constitutional

[9] On compensation, see especially Yun-chien Chang, *Private Property and Takings Compensation: Theoretical Framework and Empirical Analysis* (Edward Elgar, 2013).

[10] Birch, "Comparative compensation."

[11] "Such compensation shall be determined by establishing an equitable balance between the public interest and the interests of those affected." Art. 14(3), Basic Law of the Federal Republic of Germany, www.gesetze-im-internet.de/englisch_gg/englisch_gg.html #p0079.

legislator to fix a damage award below a civil liability award. The constitution rules out a purely nominal compensation; it allows but does not require full damage compensation. Usually, the market value is compensated but, if circumstances require, less than the market value may be paid as compensation (reduction clauses). Chances and expectations which are not reflected in the price are not protected in sub-constitutional taking laws. The rationale for this in legal dogma is that a civil liability award is to compensate the consequences of an unlawful tortious act, whereas a taking is considered to be lawful and in the interests of the public. It may imply that the citizen affected by the taking decision has to make some contribution and sacrifice some personal wealth for the pursuance of the common good for which the taking decision was made. It may also require that the damage award is further reduced if the citizen not only loses property and wealth but also gains wealth by the taking decision.

What is the difference between compensation for taking and compensation in a tort case if the market value is the underlying standard for both rules? This complicated matter cannot be dealt with in substantial detail,[12] but rather be illustrated as follows.

(1) If as a result of a tortious act or breach of contract a business must be relocated to a different location and the owner can show that the expected income to be earned is below the income level of the old location, the owner must be compensated with the present value of these losses, assuming that the market value for both locations is identical. This would be an award over and above the market price of the old location. In Germany compensation for taking would be constitutional if the sub-constitutional law rules out or limits compensation for this additional loss.

(2) Under tort law, a tenant of the owner who is forced to use new premises which are less profitable has a claim for compensation of these losses. Compensation for taking might either exclude him from compensation of these losses or grant a payment of only a quota of them.

Overall takings systematically lead to lower compensation for a lawful expropriation than civil liability. This does not only apply to socialist countries or such countries with a weak legal system but also to

[12] See, for more detailed information, B. Pieroth, B. Schlink, T. Kingreen and R. Poscher, *Grundrechte, Staatsrecht II* (C.F. Müller Publ., 2014), p. 249, and W. Leisner, "Eigentum," in J. Isensee, and P. Kirchhof (eds.), *Handbuch des Staatsrechts* (C.F. Müller Publ., 2010), vol. VIII: Grundrechte: Wirtschaft, Verfahren, Gleichheit, pp. 301–93.

international law and to states with a democratic rule of law such as Germany. Is this efficient in terms of deterrence and is it fair?[13]

2 *Incentive Effects of Full Compensation for the State and for Owners of Property*

a The Level of Damage Compensation Cannot Provide Foreseeable Incentives for the State

Taking is an involuntary transaction. A theory of taking is therefore part of the theory of involuntary transactions which dates back to the seminal article of Calabresi and Melamed on property versus liability rules.[14] These authors argued that if a right or entitlement is protected by an injunction which excludes any involuntary transfer of title, this guarantees that resources flow to the highest valued user by voluntary transactions. It also guarantees that any such transaction is beneficial to both parties. However, this result is dependent on low transaction costs, which also includes the absence of free-rider and hold-up positions. Therefore, some legal entitlements should be transferred by force if transaction costs are very high. A typical example in corporate law would be squeeze-out rules which allow the majority owner of between 90 and 95 per cent of a company's shares to take the other 5 per cent against compensation.[15] This would save the huge costs of informing the public about the state of the company as it would then be owned by one person only. The minority shareholders then lose their hold-up position which might make a voluntary transfer difficult or even impossible. If compensation covers all losses, a forced transaction is argued to be efficient in the sense of a Pareto improvement.

Can this argument be extended to a taking on the part of the state? For the sake of argument, we hypothetically disregard all critique in the broad literature on the Calabresi-Melamed proposition. Specifically, this critique includes the fact that often not all damages are covered by compensation rules and that many recoverable damages cannot be

[13] P. Niemann and P. Shapiro, "Efficiency and fairness, compensation for takings," *International Review of Law and Economics*, 28 (2008), 157–65. These authors work with a budget-maximizing bureaucracy which is, however, a special case.

[14] G. Calabresi and A. D. Melamed, "Property rules, liability rules and inalienability: one view of the cathedral," *Harvard Law Review*, 84(6) (1972), 1085–128. G. Calabresi, "An introduction to legal thought: four approaches to law and to the allocation of body parts," *Stanford Law Review*, 55(6) (2003), 2113–51. G. Calabresi, "Toward a unified theory of torts," *Journal of Tort Law*, 1(3) (2007), 1–11.

[15] I. Martineza and S. Serveb, "The delisting decision: the case of buyout offer with squeeze-out," *International Review of Law and Economics*, 31(4) (2011), 228–39.

sufficiently proven e.g. the value of "goodwill" or a patent. Moreover, the critique is extended by the claim that judges are outside observers and hence cannot know the parties' subjective valuation which thus tends to result in under-compensation despite a full damage award under civil liability. Ultimately, this would question the proposition that a forced transaction with damage compensation be a Pareto improvement. Hence, assuming that all damages were compensated, would full state liability lead the state to only expropriate property if it becomes more valuable in the hands of the new owner?

The literature on state liability shows that this view must be rejected outright. Authors who transfer models of civil liability to the state are mistaken. In an early article Cohen wrote: "The critical assumption behind such recommendations [of state liability] is that the government reacts to liability rules as a private actor would."[16] This observation, which Cohen related to wrongful acts of government officials, is even more important when parliaments or governments act. Cohen goes as far as to question the rationale of state liability in general: "We might better direct our efforts to designing effective "political" markets instead of attempting to use economic signals to influence state and bureaucratic action."[17]

Models used in civil law to determine liability for damages are not suitable for the state. Parliaments are not profit-oriented like private firms.[18] Rather, the effect of liability on voting behavior of members of parliament is most relevant and must be analyzed. Parliaments engage in rent-seeking activities; they are dependent on voters in their constituency. Whether liability can change the median voting behavior in parliament is an open question. Bureaucrats might maximize their budget,[19] as analyzed by Miceli and others.[20] It is difficult to model the effects of liability rules on administrations and even

16 D. S. Cohen, "Regulating regulators: the legal environment of the state," *University of Toronto Law Journal*, 40 (1990), 213–70.

17 Ibid.

18 H.-B. Schaefer, "Can member state liability for the infringement of European law deter national legislators?," in T. Eger and H.-B. Schaefer (eds.), *Research Handbook on the Economics of European Union Law* (Edward Elgar, 2012), 82–95, and G. Dari-Mattiacci, N. M. Garoupa and F. Gomez-Pomar, "State liability," *European Review of Private Law*, 18 (4) (2010), 773–811.

19 For an analysis in Korea, see J. Cho and I. Kim, "An economic analysis of takings in Korea: endogenous probability and announcement effects," *International Review of Law and Economics*, 22(3) (2002) 331–46.

20 Such compensation shall be determined by establishing an equitable balance between the public interest and the interests of those affected.

more so to model them on parliaments. I have shown elsewhere that state liability pertaining to state decisions is highly unpredictable in its direction and that it may even lead to the perverse outcome that more liability leads to more unwanted or unlawful state activity.[21]

Comparable observations apply to bureaucrats, who might want to increase their budgets or engage in empire-building and many other activities not related to the common good. State liability, whose costs can be passed on to the general taxpayer, can by no means guarantee that members of parliament and bureaucrats do what they should do. Unlike for the income-maximizing individual or a profit-maximizing firm, the incentive effects of state liability are unclear even in their direction and no robust models exist, unlike in the literature for civil liability. The level of compensation, be it full compensation, reduced compensation or no compensation at all, provides little information on how parliaments and bureaucracies decide. Therefore, liability as such has no predictable incentive effect on the state. Very little can be said on whether full compensation would deter a public organization from taking land unless the social value of the land were to increase. The argument of fiscal illusion becomes problematic if compensation costs can be easily shifted and spread around to the general taxpayer and if the benefit of taking goes to a small and highly motivated group. Full compensation for taking is no safeguard against rent-seekers demanding taking decisions from the state.

b The "Suffer Injustice and Cash in" Problem

Full liability can even lead to the perverse effect that the state engages in more unconstitutional takings in the private interest of oligarchs or lobby groups which are ultimately against the constitution and detrimental to the economy. This can be shown with a thought experiment. Assume that a government plans a whole series of takings of which half are constitutional and pursue the interests of the public whilst the other half are the result of lobbyism, only in the private interest and unconstitutional. Assume also that courts are independent, law-abiding and protective towards the constitution. Assume further that compensation for taking is below full compensation, for instance, 70 per cent. Then all affected owners have a strong incentive to go to court and demand

[21] H.-B. Schäfer and Claus Ott, *Lehrbuch der ökonomischen Analyse des Zivilrechts*, 5th edn (Springer, 2012).

restitution rather than compensation, since restitution is more valuable to them. Half of them will get their land back and the other half gets 70 per cent compensation whilst all takings permitted by the courts will be constitutional. In other words, this rule would prevent unconstitutional government activity. Assume now that the rule is not 70 but 100 per cent including all non-financial damages plus a small epsilon. Then no affected citizen will go to court for restitution but file for compensation and the government would get away with all constitutional as well as with all unconstitutional takings. Therefore, as long as the judiciary is loyal to the law, a rule stipulating less than full compensation has the tendency to curb unlawful taking decisions of an administration. It avoids an attitude of citizens not to fight for the restitution of their property and thus to check unlawful acts of the government with the help of courts.

c Full Compensation for Taking if the New Owner is a Profit-Maximizing Firm

Many countries, including Korea, the United States and Germany allow taking in favor of a private investor. Sometimes, as in Korea[22] but not in Germany, the state can even entitle the private investor to take the land. The *Kelo* case on which Ilya Somin wrote a thought-provoking book, shows how easily a US investor can get the land even without showing that the taking leads to a better or higher-valued use.[23] In such cases of taking in favor of a private for-profit company, the fiscal illusion argument applies. Even if the state and not the private investor is legally obliged to pay the compensation, these payments will ultimately be incurred by a private business for which profit maximization is the reasonable standard assumption. A private investor burdened with less than the full damage has an incentive to get the land whenever he values it higher than the damage award. This is fully compatible with a taking decision leading to a lower rather than a higher value of the land as compared to its value for the present owner.

One can argue that compensation should cover all sentimental value in such cases when residential land is taken. The sentimental value of land is sometimes reflected in the market price, e.g. a scenic view from the house, but often it is not, e.g. the number of friends in the

[22] Iljoong Kim and Sungkyu Park, "Are private takings efficient?: An empirical investigation," unpublished manuscript, 35 pp.

[23] I. Somin; *The Grasping Hand:* Kelo v. City of New London *and the Limits of Eminent Domain* (University of Chicago Press, 2015).

neighborhood or the feeling of being at home. Consequently, even full compensation for all financial damages cannot guarantee that taking transfers the land to the highest-valued user. Therefore, economic arguments indicate that taking in favor of a private profit-oriented firm should lead to a full damage award according to the differential method and that taking of residential land in favor of a profit-oriented company should include compensation of sentimental value which does not become part of the market price. This would lead to higher costs of the legal procedure and possibly even to willful decisions if good information on the sentimental value is missing. This problem has led many countries – including Germany – to restrict damage awards to financial damages. However, the example of French courts shows that the latter can successfully develop routines for the compensation of such damages. For instance, it might be possible to calculate sentimental damages as a function of years a person has lived in a particular neighborhood. This would be similar to the golden handshake for a dismissed worker who has accumulated firm-specific capital which is worth nothing in a new job. This compensation is often linked to the number of years employed by the company.

d Full Compensation and Investor Decisions before the Land is Condemned

A seemingly obvious argument for full compensation is the observation that less than full compensation reduces the investment level. If, at the time of investment, the investor can fully trust that he will receive full compensation in the event of a taking, the expected return on investment is comparatively higher and, consequently, the profit-maximizing investment level will also be higher than without full compensation. However, the argument crucially depends on whether the taking is within the interests of the public and whether it would lead to a socially enhanced use of the land.

Assume as an extreme case a country in which the interests of the ruling oligarchy, rent-seeking, corruption or public choice constellations lead the government to grab land in the private interest and that courts are not able to monitor this because the legal system remains weak. Land-owners will take this possibility into account and if they get little or no compensation they will invest little or nothing. Then the country suffers not only from the economically adverse effects of willful taking decisions, which are not in the interests of the public, but also from a general underinvestment level. If, however, the state credibly commits itself to full compensation by passing the costs of its willful decisions on to the general tax payer, the underinvestment can be avoided. Full compensation for taking is therefore a reasonable strategy for a state, which is continuously executing taking decisions in favor of private and against public interests whilst still aiming to maintain a high level of private investment and thereby promote economic development. Full compensation is therefore a second-best solution for states with a weak legal system.

Now consider the other extreme case of a perfect rule of law state in which substantive and procedural taking law, judicial independence and swift law enforcement guarantee that takings always pursue the interests of the public and lead to a better social utilization of the condemned property. In that case, private property is well protected and taking decisions will not lead to an inefficient low level of investment. On the contrary, public investment then increases the profitability of private investment. Several authors, notably Blum and Rubinfeld,[24] have even argued that under such conditions full compensation might even lead to a socially wasteful overinvestment on the later condemned land. Under this condition, a risk-neutral investor gets the right incentives for her investment level if no compensation is paid as, by assumption, the taking leads to a socially higher-valued use and the investor should discount the future income stream from her investment with the probability of a taking. She has an incentive to do so only if she receives no compensation at all. The picture changes if the investor is risk averse. The entitlement to compensation is then an insurance of the risk-averse investor by the risk-neutral state. However, even then the optimal amount of compensation would be below full compensation in order to preserve incentives against overinvestment. This would induce the investor to take the possibility of a welfare-increasing taking decision into account and avoid socially wasteful overinvestment.

Now take yet a third and more realistic view; namely, a government which is dependent on interest groups and often attempts to realize takings that do not pursue the public interest. But assume also that the courts are loyal to the law. Then less than full compensation incentivizes owners to fight illegal acts and claim restitution. Provided that every owner were to pursue this strategy and provided that courts were to make

[24] L. Blum and D. Rubinfeld, "Compensation for takings: an economic analysis", *California Law Review*, 72(4) (1984), 569–628. R. Epstein, "Takings," in *The New Palgrave Dictionary of Economics and the Law* (Palgrave, 1989) vol. 3, p. 561; Schäfer and Ott, "Lehrbuch", p. 617.

no mistakes, this would guarantee that takings were only made for the interests of the public.

The less courts can guarantee that takings can effectively be controlled by the law, the more reasonable full compensation would be. And the better courts can guarantee that taking decisions are in the public interest and are otherwise uplifted, the less convincing full compensation becomes. Under such conditions a less than full compensation incentivizes filings for restitution rather than for damages and thus avoids the "suffer and cash in effect"[25], which is socially undesirable as it increases the number of unlawful takings.

3 *Full Compensation for Takings that Pursue the Public Interest Can Be Unfair*

Is full compensation always fair? This is also questionable if one regards fairness as equal treatment by the law.

a Winners and Losers from Takings

If a piece of land is expropriated, full compensation can reinstate people's original wealth or utility level in some cases but in other cases it might privilege them. Assume the discovery of a well-preserved 2000-year-old Roman mosaic in a south-German village. There is no doubt that the taking of this land and the preservation of the mosaic in a local museum as a tourist attraction are in the interests of the public. Should the landowner get full compensation if he is the owner of a neighboring restaurant whose business is flourishing because of the many busloads of tourists visiting the site? It would be in line with fairness considerations not to fully compensate him. There would be no reason to criticize norms in taking laws on fairness grounds which would allow a court to make deductions from full compensation in such a case.

An economically far more important extension of this insight pertains to takings with the aim of building an infrastructure in the interests of the public. Assume that the agricultural hinterland of a large metropolitan Asian megacity is undeveloped and that this leads to prohibitively high transportation costs from farms to the city. Agricultural markets remain scattered, local and cannot contribute

[25] In German, "Dulde und liquidiere". Some of the taking rules of German law are especially designed to incentivize citizens to take action against willful takings and not to accept compensation instead. Leisner, "Eigentum", pp. 397–98 and Pieroth et al., *Grundrechte*, p. 261.

much to the nutrition of the city population. Food is imported. Now assume that the state develops the traffic infrastructure in the southern but not in the northern hinterland of the city. Transportation becomes less costly, connects the agricultural region with the city markets and leads to opulence among farmers in the southern hinterland. Food prices drop in the city, land prices increase steeply in the southern hinterland and decrease somewhat in the northern hinterland which remains poorly connected with the city. This public investment project and the related takings make people in the city better off but makes landowners in the northern hinterland somewhat worse off. They have to accept this as members of a community with rights and duties. No law in the world entitles them to compensation. It also makes farmers in the southern hinterland much better off. Those who lost part of their land to road and irrigation systems are still better off than before but less so than other farmers in the southern hinterland. Should courts be entitled to consider these effects when calculating the damage award which has to be financed by all taxpayers? This would be fair and the compensation could be higher than a nominal compensation but lower than full compensation without violating the principle of just, fair and effective compensation. Expropriation laws which take this into account by way of balancing gains and losses of such takings would not violate but rather underline fairness considerations.

b Full Compensation Might Lead to Unequal Treatment

The state often imposes some costly duties for the common good on its citizens. I refer to a much debated German case about a statutory law imposing a duty on all publishers to send a free copy of every published book to a central library. This serves cultural purposes. The constitutional court decided in this regard that this rule of sub-constitutional law is not taking but a "definition of private property" which may include some sacrifice for the public good. However, it also defined limits to this rule. In the present case the claimant was a publisher of reprints of bibliophile rarities, for instance, of an exact reprint of Martin Luther's medieval Bible. These books were sold at high prices, for example €1000, in small editions of perhaps 50 copies. The constitutional court ruled that an owner might have some costly duties. None can, however, be forced to an outstanding or special sacrifice (so called "*Sonderopfer*"). It ruled that this so-defined group of publishers were entitled to compensation. Parliament or courts must set the price limit above which the delivery of one book to the central library has to be compensated.[26] Assuming that this price limit is €300, if the price is €300 the loss of the book is not compensated and if it is €301 it is compensated. But full compensation would not be fair. Laws regulating the rules of compensation should give discretion to judges to take such aspects into account. The same logic applies to laws aimed at preserving buildings of national or historic importance. According to legal dogma, this would not be considered a taking but rather law's definition of private property which the owner must accept without any compensation but not beyond a certain threshold.

c Taking and Prior Subsidies

Full compensation for taking might be unfair if a private firm gets huge subsidies and is later expropriated. Consider the following simplified example. After the Lehman crisis many private banks in Europe would have collapsed without state intervention and their owners would have lost their equity capital. To avoid conflagration in the financial sector many European states set up rescue plans and heavily subsidized such banks to keep them running as a going concern. Their market capitalization remained positive merely because they were saved with taxpayers' money. If later the state takes over the bank to restructure it and reintroduces it to the market after such a successful restructuring, would it then be fair to pay the full market price per share which would otherwise have been worthless without the heavy subsidies?

d The Different Consequences of Taking and Regulatory Taking

Some contribution of the citizen, whose property is rightfully taken in the interests of the public is defendable on grounds of fairness. Otherwise a huge gap would open between the legal consequence of taking and the legal consequence of regulatory taking. Parliaments and courts continuously change the content of property rights and consequently change their value. Ideally, these new laws increase a nation's wealth or welfare. However, they also continuously produce winners and losers among owners. The losers do not lose the title of ownership but some of the wealth which the ownership represented under the previous set of rules. The winners among the citizens enjoy the gains. The losers have to live with the losses, usually without any compensation. Assume, for instance,

[26] Bundesverfassungsgericht (BVerfG E58, 137/150).

that in an attempt to promote public health a new regulatory law sets new and higher standards for medical x-ray machines which makes some old machines valueless without taking the ownership titles. The law will probably not regard this as a taking but rather as a redefinition of property which may lead to no compensation at all. Without any contribution to the common good in case of a lawful taking that pursues the public interest the gap between the legal consequences of lawful taking and regulatory taking or redefinition of property would become even wider than it actually is.

4 How Should the Surplus Be Distributed?

Often the *ex post* value of expropriated land is higher than the *ex ante* value. Should the old owner participate in this surplus value? With regard to providing incentives to the state to abstain from unlawful takings, the above arguments apply. The extent and range within which a state can be incentivized to avoid activism in the private interest through higher damage awards is not generally known. Takings, decisions to nationalize industries, privatize or renationalize utilities, are often of overriding political importance at both local and national levels. They are often forged by political parties and powerful interest groups. This makes the taking decision relatively independent from the exact amount of compensation, especially since its costs can be passed on to millions of taxpayers. It is not necessary to repeat in detail the insights of Mancur Olson's seminal book on *The Logic of Collective Action*.[27] Therefore one should not be too optimistic with regard to the incentive effects of more compensation on the part of the state to avoid such takings which are not in the interests of the public. It is always possible that an overriding public interest is not within the interests of the government and vice versa. To prevent takings that do not pursue the public interest is the task of constitutional and sub-constitutional legal norms, as well as those courts which adjudicate the norms.

It is also questionable whether the compensation of the surplus should be divided on grounds of fairness.

(1) No parallel exists in private contract law, which protects the surplus value from a higher-valued use in favor of the buyer. A private buyer

[27] M. Olson, *The Logic of Collective Action: Public Goods and the Theory of Groups* (Harvard University Press, 1965, 20th reprint 2002).

who is aware of the fact that a piece of land would be worth much more than the seller's perceived value e.g. because the land could be used in a more profitable way, has no legal obligation to disclose this private knowledge to the seller. This rule implies that the buyer might reap all gains from the better use of the land which are not already reflected in the market price. This is efficient because a disclosure rule would shift the surplus value from the better use of the resource to the seller and destroy the incentives on the part of potential buyers to heavily invest in finding superior ways of using resources which are owned by others.[28] One can argue that this argument does not apply for the state, whose investment decisions are based not on valuable and profitable private knowledge but on public knowledge. Taking laws, which regulate the involuntary transfer of titles, are therefore not necessary to incentivize the state in the same way as a private profit-maximizing investor who buys land. And yet compensation for the surplus in taking laws would create a rift between the outcome of voluntary transactions in markets regulated by contract law and the outcome of takings by the state that pursue the interests of the public. It would also distribute some of the public benefits to private persons.

(2) Also, as public investments are made on public information, often some of the surplus will in any case be appropriated by the old owner. Assume, for instance, that in the vicinity of Seoul a new international airport is to be built. This plan initially triggers lengthy public and political debates. The information generated from such debates will increase the market value of the land on which the airport is to be built long before the date of the actual taking or planning decision. These dates are often used for calculating the fair market price for the damage award.

(3) In Germany most sub-constitutional taking laws are in line with these considerations. The Federal Construction Law (Bundesbaugesetz, BbauG) which stipulates rules for taking and compensation, explicitly states that for the calculation of the damage award the date of the taking decision and the market

[28] H.-B. Schäfer and C. Ott, *Economic Analysis of Civil Law* (Edward Elgar, 2004), ch. 16, p. 375.

value at that date are decisive.[29] It even explicitly excludes from compensation all increases of the value of the land caused by the imminent expectation of the taking decision. The Bavarian taking law contains similar provisions.[30] These are only two of a whole range of examples of federal or state laws which explicitly exclude compensation of most of the surplus value by fixing an early date for assessing the value of the land.

Compensation: Conclusion

In civil liability the differential method precisely defines damage compensation and leads to full compensation. The compensation rules pertaining to takings often lead to a damage award which is much higher than a nominal compensation but somewhat lower than full compensation. The rationale of full compensation as an incentive mechanism to ensure the higher-valued use of a resource after an involuntary transfer of title holds only if the condemned property is transferred to a private profit-maximizing investor. It does not hold for the state, which might take property for many political reasons not reflecting the public interest and which can pass on the cost of compensation to the tax payers.

Full compensation is not an optimal incentive for owners either. It might induce them not to fight against takings that do not pursue the public interest. Generous compensation would thus not lead to filings for restitution but rather for damages. It is, however, in the interests of the public to incentivize citizens to fight unconstitutional takings. Also, fairness considerations often lead to a departure from full compensation.

Full compensation is – with exceptions – not a strategic instrument in states with a highly developed rule of law. It is only recommendable for countries with a weak legal system where it would generate more private investment without reducing the government's willfulness. The strategic instruments to avoid unlawful and unconstitutional takings are to be found in constitutional and sub-constitutional substantive and procedural legal norms.

[29] §95(1) BbauG: "Maßgebend ist der Verkehrswert in dem Zeitpunkt, in dem die Enteignungsbehörde über den Enteignungsantrag entscheidet."

[30] Art. 10, Bavarian Taking Law, Bayerisches Gesetz über die entschädigungspflichtige Enteignung (BayEG).

III Ensuring that Takings Pursue the Public Interest: Examples from German Substantive Law

1 The Subjects of Power to Specify the Rationale for Takings (the Requirement of Federal or State Bills, Subject to Constitutional Review)

Governments, parliament or administrative agencies can pursue goals of their own that are incompatible with the "public good". Provided they are free to define this term, they might inflate its use to such an extent that a taking decision can be made whenever they assert that the state or a private investor can utilize a resource better than its owner. The legal system can react to this danger in different ways. In a German context this reaction would comprise a combination of constitutional and sub-constitutional rules and safeguards.

- The rationale for the taking must be substantiated in a specific federal or state law.
- The law must specify how the compensation is calculated and the taking must be necessary.
- Takings that pursue the interests of private persons need to pass an additional test.

German agencies or municipalities cannot execute takings based on their interpretation of "common good" according to Art. 14 of the German constitution, despite the fact that such an interpretation would be controlled by courts. The subjects of power to define what justifies a taking for the "common good" are the federal parliament, the state parliaments and the constitutional court. As private property is a fundamental constitutional right, laws regulating property and takings are subject to constitutional judicial review. The constitutional court has therefore the power to reject the reasoning provided in the law on grounds of vagueness or because the extent of it being in the interests of the public is not large enough to justify such an infringement of a fundamental right. The German constitutional court ruled that a specific public interest must be accurately defined in either a federal or state law. A municipal zoning law or any other statute of a municipality does not have the qualification of a law in this regard. Any administrative decision that is based on a (municipal) zoning law would therefore be considered unconstitutional. The constitutional court has two channels of control at its disposal. If the rationale of the taking decision cannot be found in either a federal or state law, the taking is unconstitutional. If it is contained in a law, it must be specific and describe a severe public interest. Not every common good rationale would justify a taking, as this would destroy the freedom-preserving function of private property.

Sometimes it is difficult or even impossible to formulate the rationale of certain takings in an abstract way. Constitutional law then requires a specific law containing the rationale for the taking in a single case. This guarantees that the taking decision is not based on a purely bureaucratic decision but on a majority decision of a democratically elected parliament. An example is a taking law in favor of Airbus Industries in Hamburg. For the construction of the big Airbus 380 the existing runway had to be extended. The parliament of the city state of Hamburg passed a specific law for the taking of land in favor of Airbus Corporation, describing in detail the importance of a longer runway on the premises of the firm for the economy of the city state. This law led the courts to accept the taking decision.[31]

In a landmark decision (BVerfGE 74, 264 – *Boxberg.*), the federal constitutional court decided that the state of Baden-Württemberg violated the federal constitution by taking farm land for the construction of a test track for Mercedes Company. The court rejected the view that the taking was legal as it was based on municipal zoning law because municipal law does not qualify as a law in the constitutional sense and that municipalities are no subjects of power in this matter. It also rejected the government's view that the taking could be based on a state law regulating consolidation and reallocation of farm land. The reasons according to this law did not contain the purpose of the specific taking, namely, to create about 600 jobs outside agriculture in an underdeveloped and remote area of the state. The constitutional court left unanswered whether or not the criterion of a strict public interest was sufficiently fulfilled if this rationale had been explicitly included in the state law. However, the court raised doubts on whether such a general description of the purpose of taking would pass the precision test and the strict public interest test.

Federal and state parliaments must substantiate the criterion of severe public interest in statutory laws. It is legally undisputed that taking rationales described in sub-constitutional laws are both constitutional and in the interests of the public, provided they serve the construction of electric lines, railway tracks, canals, roads, public airports and, with some further specifications, also schools and sports facilities. The creation and

[31] Enteignungsgesetz für die Erweiterung des Werkflugplatzes in Hamburg-Finkenwerder (Werkflugplatz-Enteignungsgesetz) vom 18. February 2004.

preservation of jobs is disputed and its constitutionality would largely depend on the number of jobs created or preserved. More profitable use of the land or higher tax income[32] do not justify takings from a constitutional point of view.[33] This is reasonable since higher tax income is not per se within the interests of the public. This leads to another remark on the *Kelo* case, as described by Ilya Somin.[34] In this case the US Supreme court decided in a 5:4 decision to allow the taking of residential land in favor of a private developer on the ground of generating higher tax income. In Germany the *Kelo* taking would be considered unconstitutional as raising tax income would not qualify the strict pursuance of public interest. This insight came as a surprise. The United States is the motherland of both free market capitalism and strong protection of private property. Germany is a "social and democratic rule of law state" (Art. 20, Abs.1 of the constitution), yet it seems to protect private property in a more libertarian way than the United States.[35]

2 *The Necessity Condition*

Provided the realm specifying the conditions for the common good does allow takings, the decision has to meet a second condition, namely, "necessity" (so-called "*Erforderlichkeit*"). This criterion is derived from the principle of proportionality which is generally applied in German administrative and constitutional law.[36] In this context necessity implies that takings are the mildest form of violation of a right with the aim of reaching a policy target. The criterion is not fulfilled if a voluntary purchase is both possible and reasonable, or if more land is taken than would be necessary for the underlying purposes. Moreover, it would also not be fulfilled if the public purpose could also be reached on pre-existing public ground or if a milder form of taking such as an easement would also sufficiently serve the public purpose. The necessity criterion does not require the state to prove that a project such as a rail track cannot be built somewhere else because often many alternatives to realize a project in the

32 Somin; *The Grasping Hand.*

33 Taking for fiscal reasons is unlawful. Leisner, "Eigentum," p. 386.

34 Somin, *The Grasping Hand.*

35 T. J. Miceli, K. Segerson and T. F. Sirmans, "Tax motivated takings," *National Tax Journal*, LXI(4) Part 1 (2008), 579–91. The US Supreme Court ruled that the spillover effect of a private project in terms of jobs and tax income justified the taking of residential land in the *Kelo* Case, p. 580.

36 Pieroth et al., *Grundrechte*, p. 3.

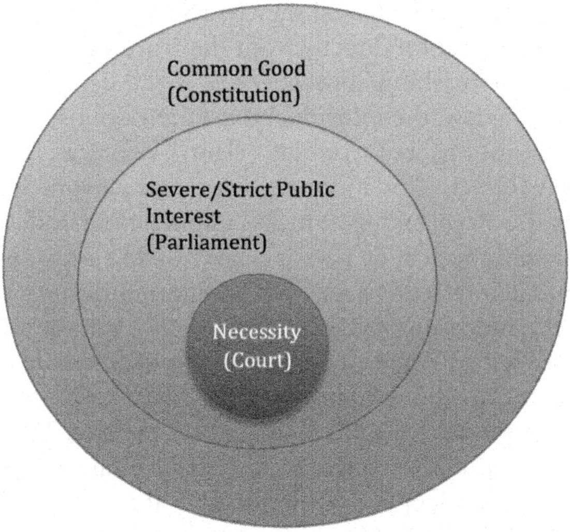

Figure 1.1. Shrinking the eminent domain by constitutional rules in Germany

interests of the public do in fact exist. Yet it requires a "substantial contribution"[37] on the part of the project towards the interests of the public. As an example, a second or third slip road from a city to a highway might not always qualify as a strict public interest.

The rules thus described require that any project for the common good that induces takings must make a considerable contribution to the public interest. This subset of projects further reduces lawful takings to such projects for which takings are necessary as defined by the courts. This is illustrated by Figure 1.1.

3 *Specifying the Compensation and the Public Interest in One Law with a Link*

Art. 13, para. 3, of the German constitution states that takings are possible only to promote the common good and only on the basis of a law specifying the public interest as well as the compensation. The way in which compensation is paid must be explicitly stated in the taking law. Without the existence of a link between the exact rationale for a taking and its associated compensation within the same law, a taking would be unconstitutional. Administrative courts are neither allowed to create

[37] Pieroth et al., *Grundrechte*, p. 255.

a missing link by means of analogy, nor would they be allowed to derive principles of just and fair compensation directly from the wording of the constitution. This does have far-reaching consequences. If the described link is missing in the underlying law, the individual must fight against the unlawfulness and for restitution but cannot claim damages as a consequence of this unlawful act. This incentivizes private persons to focus all efforts on avoiding the illegal taking. It makes impossible a "suffer and cash in" mentality of the affected. It also incentivizes the state to clearly regulate both the public interest and its compensation in the same law. If no such link exists, the state cannot realize the project. It cannot be ransomed from the unlawful act by way of compensation and thus hold on to the taken property if the law did not contain both the rationale for taking and the rule of compensation. It would then have to restitute. This link rule also deters sub-constitutional courts from simply establishing a missing link between the specific public interest and the scope of compensation within the same law, since such courts are not given the competencies to derive such rules by way of analogy, interpretation or interpolation. Hence sub-constitutional courts cannot obstruct the power of the constitutional court to declare such a violation as unconstitutional.

4 *Takings in Favor of Private Persons*

Expropriation in favor of a private person, for instance, a company, poses a special problem. A profit-maximizing private person legally acts within the realm of its private autonomy, whilst a public agency is bound by legally defined policy targets in the interests of the public. Public law provides the citizen with safeguards in case the public agency fails to do so. A private investor might utilize the taken land differently when circumstances change and make a different use more profitable. A public administration that is directly mandated by government tasks regulated by the law certainly works differently. Consider the following illustrative example. A private investor who runs a private school is legally free to close the school and use the building as e.g. a hotel or for any other arbitrary purpose. A municipality which runs a public school does not have this freedom of choice. It is bound by the law to serve a specific public interest and can only close the school or sell its buildings as regulated by public law. This does not imply that takings in favor of private persons pose any conceptual problems. However, a profit-oriented private person serves the specific public purpose indirectly through the profit motive and the market mechanism. Therefore, expropriation laws which cause an involuntary transfer of property to a private person should include safeguards that the specific public purpose on which the taking decision is based will be reached. German law stipulates two specific rules pertaining to takings in favor of a private person.

First, the state must show and convince the court that the private investor will use the land in pursuance of the specified public purpose for the long run. The state is free to implement any instruments in order to ensure the investor's credibility. This could either be in the form of a contract between the private investor and the state which defines the specified use of the land, or a collateral or any other legal obligations on the part of the private investor that would ensure its credibility. Otherwise the taking would be unlawful. The much debated *Kelo* taking in the United States would probably have been unconstitutional in Germany for this reason as well. The residential land was transferred to a development company for a large project. The owners were evicted and it turned out that the company did not have the financial resources for the planned investment. The land remains idle to this day. In Germany a future investment would have to be made credible, for instance, by means of a finance guarantee through a bank and a contractual obligation.

Second, the taking decision should not be outsourced to an investor driven by the profit motive. If compensation is not full in the sense of replacing the affected individual on his indifference curve prior to the taking decision, this could not even guarantee that the property moves to a higher-valued user. The taking decision should be an administrative act of a public administration and fully governed by administrative and constitutional law. This applies in Germany where taking decisions are allowed in favor of a private person but may not be executed by a private person.

Public Interest: Conclusion

In rule of law states the strategic instrument pertaining to takings is a set of rules which can guarantee that the taking is in the interests of the public. In Germany this is achieved by the requirement that every taking decision must be based on a specific sub-constitutional federal or state law. Neither an administration nor a court is allowed to derive the specific public interest freehandedly from the constitution or through interpretation of the constitution. A taking not based on such a law is per se unconstitutional. The constitutional court also monitors whether the rationale for taking given in the law is precise enough and requires a severe public interest. Also, taking must be the mildest instrument applied to reach the described policy target. Incentives are given to the citizen to file for restitution and not to "suffer and cash in". These special rules regulating takings are hardly questioned in German scholarship which is in line with economic reasoning. If the level of compensation as such can contribute little to guarantee that the takings pursue the interests of the public, the law must establish high hurdles of substantive law. It must channel government decisions directly by means of legal requirements and tight judicial control in order to make the state observe the constitution. It must also motivate citizens to fight for their rights and to file claims for restitution. The procedural hurdles for takings are much more disputed and subject to critique than the rules of substantive law.

IV Elements and Problems of Due Process in German Taking Law

1 Preliminary Injunctive Relief

Due process is time-consuming and costly. A tradeoff exists between due process and a speedy decision in favor of the public good. In Germany this tradeoff is reflected in a set of different rules protecting the interests of the private owner and the public interest: for instance, the rule of preliminary injunctive relief aimed at protecting the private owner, or the rule of temporary putting into possession which pursues the interests of the public.

A taking decision is lawful only if the state authority has made serious but unsuccessful prior attempts to buy the property. The later taking decision of the state entitles the affected to objection. A court would then decide in an urgent decision whether the objection has a chance of success. Only if this urgent decision is in the negative and even a quick look indicates that the taking is lawful can the state take possession of the condemned land. Otherwise the owner remains the possessor until the legal proceedings in the main action come to an end. In the meantime, the project is bound to stand still. This is a strong protection as it postpones many projects in the public interest until a final and binding decision is taken. The plaintiff can move the case up to the federal administrative court and finally to the constitutional court. The final decision might take several years and only after the final and binding decision can the new owner take possession of the land and start with the investment project.

2 *The Right to Participate in a Planning Decision*

Many taking decisions are embedded in a long and complex planning process on zoning and land use. Take the construction of a large international airport, which might require takings of agricultural, residential and farm land, or the production of brown coal by daylight mining, which might require the removal of whole villages and the taking of almost all land in their vicinity. The planning decisions for such projects predetermine to a large extent which parcels of land must later be taken. At the outset of the planning process alternative options still exist. During this stage of planning a procedure of due process should include an explicit balancing of public and private interests. Hence landowners and possibly associations of civil society, such as environmental groups, must be heard during the planning process and their views on alternatives have to be considered in the decision-making process.

In Germany the planning of brown coal production displaced 7000 residents from their land and homes. As a result, the constitutional court strengthened the participation rights of the affected (*Garzweiler* decision 2013). The constitutional court in Germany also strengthened the participation rights of landowners in the planning process of such projects and imposed additional duties of balancing interests on the planning authorities.[38]

3 *Temporary Putting into Possession*

Federal or state laws, for instance, the Construction Law (BauGB), entitle the taking authority to transfer not ownership but possession to the new investor before courts have finally decided on the lawfulness of the underlying taking. This decision requires an urgent public interest. The new possessor can start her investment on the land. She has to compensate the owner for all losses during the temporary possession, especially if they do not form part of the general compensation. If the final court decision regards the taking as unlawful, the land must be restituted and any damages incurred must be compensated. The investment on the land is therefore at the investor's risk since the land must potentially be returned.

It would go beyond the scope of this chapter to review in detail the procedural rules which might lead to or prevent takings in Germany.

[38] www.bundesverfassungsgericht.de/SharedDocs/Entscheidungen/DE/2013/12/rs20131217_1bvr313908.html

They are arcane, numerous and vary between different types of projects. Often even experienced and specialized legal practitioners in government agencies fail to meet all of them. They consist of a thicket of rules, exceptions and exceptions from the exceptions. Some of them prolong the planning procedure; others can shorten it. Some violations of the procedural rules have far-reaching legal consequences whilst others do not. It is questionable whether the German combination of procedural rules strikes the balance between the protection of individual rights and economic development well. And, although it seems that the rules of substantive expropriation law in Germany are well designed, this might not hold true for the procedural rules. The thicket of these rules has led to countless complaints about an overly lengthy planning duration of large projects, such as a waterway or an international airport. The planning procedures were even criticized as a substantial cause of the economic stagnation of the German economy. These complains culminated after the German reunification in the early 1990s when the partly ailing and partly underdeveloped East-German infrastructure was to be upgraded with public construction projects. This subsequently led to the introduction of new laws to speed up planning procedures. The wave of critique, which the very long planning procedures faced in the 1980 and 1990, has somewhat ebbed away.[39]

V Conclusions

This article analyzes the Six Pillars of taking law from an economic point of view with specific reference to German law. Many constitutions, including those of Korea (Art. 23) and Germany (Art. 14), protect private property and allow takings only in the interests of the public and against fair or just compensation. This implies that in countries with judicial review like Korea or Germany the supreme court or the constitutional court has the power to review sub-constitutional norms regulating taking decisions. The constitutional safeguards alone cannot, however, protect owners sufficiently. Governments, parliaments and bureaucracies might take property for purely political purposes, for campaign goodies, or to comfort powerful industries and lobby groups, or to maximize budgets and build bureaucratic empires. Yet they might still be in the position to

[39] Bernhard Stüer, "Bürgerbeteiligung und Rechtsschutz im Bau- und Fachplanungsrecht," in Jan Ziekow (ed.), *Beschleunigung von Planungs- und Genehmigungsverfahren* (Duncker und Humblot, 1998), 141–70.

hide their intentions under the veil of the "common good". In the United States the famous *Kelo* case has shown how far practice can deviate from protecting private property as a fundamental right. It is therefore highly desirable not to allow a public agency or bureaucracy to freehandedly specify the meaning of "common good". German constitutional law requires that the precise specification of the public interest for any taking be stipulated in a federal or state statutory law. These specifications are subject to judicial review of the constitutional court and might be rejected for vagueness or for not per se pursuing the public interest. Thus "raising taxes" would violate the latter and "economic development" the former criterion. "Preserving energy safety" is, however, a constitutional rationale for taking. The numerous precise sub-constitutional laws describing a "severe public interest" can therefore only define a subset of the broad term "common good." This subset shrinks further by the necessity requirement according to which the state must show that the taking is the mildest available way to realize the underlying project. These two restrictions lead to an effective protection of private property. They principally allow takings, yet they are submitted to a tight and far-reaching judicial control. The rules effectively monitor the "grabbing hand" phenomenon, which can be observed in many countries.

From this it follows that there exist three subjects of power in German law. Parliaments must specify precisely the "severe public interest" under which a taking decision is constitutional. This guarantees that the specific rationale for takings is subject to a democratic decision in parliament. Bureaucracies take the decision without having much discretion with regard to the interpretation of the reasons given in the law and the decisions are subject to judicial control by administrative courts and constitutional review.

Takings in favor of private persons and profit-seeking firms pose no particular conceptual problems. A profit-maximizing firm can promote public interests to the same extent as a bureaucracy: the latter directly, the former indirectly. However, differences do exist. Unlike a public agency a profit-maximizing firm acts within the realm of private autonomy. Whenever it seems to be advantageous, it might deviate the utilization of the land towards purposes other than the specific public interest that legitimizes the taking. Safeguards should therefore guarantee that the expropriated property is used for its intended purpose in the long run. In Germany a taking in favor of a private person is unlawful, provided the administration cannot show that the new investor has made a credible commitment to guarantee this. This problem does not arise for state agencies, whose policy targets are defined by the law.

In many legal orders including Germany compensation for taking has to be prompt, adequate, fair and effective. This is normally somewhat less than a damage award under civil liability, which applies the much more precise differential method and which fully restores either the claimant's wealth or even utility.[40]

This can be justified by way of economic reasoning in rule of law states. The state cannot be incentivized and deterred by a damage award which is equal to the damage in the same way as a private actor. The economic analysis of state liability therefore differs from the analysis of civil liability. Unlike a private actor, the state can spread the compensation payment among millions of taxpayers regardless of whether the compensation is full or somewhat less. Full damage compensation can therefore not guarantee that a taking leads to the higher-valued use of a resource, unlike in the cases for involuntary transactions in civil liability. The question of an appropriate level of compensation must be answered not with regard to incentives for the state, but with regard to incentives for property owners. Hence, one would have to differentiate between two different legal and political environments.

In the case of a government that continuously violates the constitution and engages in willful takings within a weak legal system with no judicial independence, a low level of compensation could seriously affect the level of private investment in the country. Investors would potentially fear the grabbing hand of the government knowing that they would not be able to rely on the judiciary when filing law suits for restitution of their property. If this pattern cannot be changed in the short run, a full and generous compensation could still maintain a high level of private investment in such a country. However, this is only a second best solution.

Provided courts abide by the law and constitution in a system with swift law enforcement, full compensation according to the differential method would have adverse effects. Full compensation would remove incentives from private investors to proceed against takings and file claims for restitution, since the latter would not be worth more than a damage award. Owners would then develop an attitude of "suffer injustice and cash in" rather than taking action against illegal or unconstitutional government acts. It is, however, in the interests of the public

40 For an overview, see Anne van Aaken, "Direct expropriation: the multi-layered legal protection in Europe," this volume.

that citizens defend themselves against unlawful acts of their government rather than settle down as a result of generous compensation. Compensation which is somewhat lower than a full damage award motivates citizens to fight for their rights i.e. for restitution of the land. They will do so if restitution is worth more to them than damage compensation. This guarantees that courts sort out the taking decisions which are not in the public interest and restitute the land to the affected. Less than full compensation thus helps to achieve an important policy target, namely, to prevent effectively unconstitutional takings which do not pursue the public interest. The rules on taking, which allow for some deduction from full compensation and some contribution to the lawful taking in the public interest, find a justification in economic considerations of giving the right incentives to citizen and making them guardians of the law. Some of those rules even explicitly try to destroy a "suffer and cash in" attitude among the affected.

Full compensation using the differential method can also not always be recommended on grounds of fairness. Takings might also lead to gains and they might follow huge subsidies. Both can justify a reduction of the damage award. Also, the consequences of takings and regulatory takings are different, the latter leading to a damage award only in exceptional cases. This rift would be widened in the case of a legal taking in the interest of the public with no participation at all being required on the part of a citizen.

Not only substantive law but also a fair procedure, which includes hearings and participation in planning decisions of large projects, committee meetings and procedures, contribute to the justice of a taking decision. Extending those procedural rights will prolong planning procedures. If these procedural rights do not exist, planners might even lack the information to make right decisions. The information coming from land-owners in a planning process is valuable even though it emanates from a group pursuing their own specific interests. If procedural rights are overstretched or become too complex to handle, they might lead to very lengthy and costly planning procedures and possibly even result in frustration, especially for large public investment projects. A tradeoff exists between the target of effectively protecting a citizen's right and that of economic development. It is not certain that the thicket of German procedural rules properly strikes the balance between these two goals.

2

Eminent Domain in the United States

ILYA SOMIN*

Introduction

The use of eminent domain to take private property has been the object of extensive debate throughout almost the entire history of the United States. At least since the early nineteenth century, some Americans have argued that aggressive use of eminent domain is needed to address social and economic problems, while others have decried the practice as an unjust infringement on property rights. That longstanding debate was reinvigorated by the Supreme Court's controversial 2005 decision in *Kelo v. City of New London*,[1] which ruled that the US Constitution permits government to take property from one private owner and give it to another for purposes of promoting "economic development." The ruling generated a widespread negative reaction among many who believe it authorized abusive condemnations that victimize ordinary people for the benefit of politically connected interest groups.[2]

This chapter provides an overview of the use of eminent domain in the United States, and the continuing debate it has generated. Part I focuses on "public use" constraints on eminent domain. The Fifth Amendment to the US Constitution and similar provisions in nearly all of the 50 state constitutions permit the government to condemn property only if it is for a "public use."[3] But there is a longstanding disagreement about exactly

* For helpful suggestions and criticisms, I would like to thank Hojun Lee, Iljoong Kim, Hans-Bernd Schäfer, and participants in the Korea Development Institute conference on eminent domain.

1 545 U.S. 469 (2005).

2 For a detailed discussion of the *Kelo* case and the debate it triggered, see Ilya Somin, *The Grasping Hand:* Kelo v. City of New London *and the Limits of Eminent Domain* (Chicago: University of Chicago Press, 2015).

3 U.S. Const., Amend. V. In the United States, each state has its own constitution and body of statutory law, which bind state and local government officials, but usually not the federal government. For an overview of the history of state constitutions, see John J. Dinan, *The American State Constitutional Tradition* (Lawrence: University Press of Kansas, 2006).

what that restriction means, and how tightly it should be enforced by courts. Before the *Kelo* case, many experts believed that the debate had been definitely resolved in favor of a broad definition of public use under which the government can take private property for almost any purpose it wants. But the negative public and elite reaction to *Kelo* has shattered that seeming consensus.

Part II discusses the issue of compensation for takings. Longstanding United States Supreme Court precedent holds that property owners are entitled to "fair market value" compensation for property taken by eminent domain, defined as the price that the asset would bring if it were sold on the open market.[4] But critics have long argued that this standard often fails to compensate owners for the full extent of their losses. Some also contend that the owners of condemned property should be entitled to a part of the "surplus value" created by the taking, which is rarely done under current policy. On the other hand, a few economists have contended that providing any compensation at all creates inefficiencies.

Part III briefly surveys procedural constraints on eminent domain. Property owners are entitled to a variety of constitutional and statutory procedural rights before their land can be taken. For example, they must be notified of the condemnation in advance and offered an opportunity to contest it in court. Most jurisdictions also require many types of condemnations to be undertaken only as part of a specially structured planning process. In recent years, the US Supreme Court has in some ways strengthened enforcement of procedural protections for property owners. Whether these procedural rights provide effective protection against abuses is a subject of debate. This debate also impacts the closely related issue of whether disputes over eminent domain should be resolved by courts, or by other government agencies. It is similarly relevant to the question of whether and how eminent domain authority should be delegated to private enterprises.

On many of the issues covered in this chapter, there is considerable diversity in the policies and legal doctrines adopted by individual states. Because the vast majority of uses of eminent domain in America are undertaken by state and local authorities rather than by the federal government, there is really no one nationwide eminent domain policy. Instead, we have numerous different policies, often widely variant ones.

4 See, e.g., *Kirby Forest Industries Inc. v. United States*, 467 U.S. 1, 10 (1984); *United States v. General Motors Corp.*, 323 U.S. 373, 378 (1945).

Part IV of the chapter briefly discusses the implications of American federalism for eminent domain. Some scholars and judges contend that America's diversity is an argument for leaving eminent domain issues to the decisions of state governments, with little judicial review by federal courts. But diversity can also potentially justify the exact opposite conclusion.

Finally, the Conclusion notes some tentative lessons of the American experience with eminent domain, especially for foreign observers. Many of the issues covered in the American debate over takings have counterparts abroad. Although the United States is often – with considerable justice – viewed as a nation with a strong commitment to property rights, it also has a disturbing history of permitting serious abuses of eminent domain, particularly those that victimize the poor and the politically weak. Both Americans and foreigners should try to learn from that experience, and avoid committing similar errors in the future.

The organizational structure of this chapter differs somewhat from the "Six Pillars" framework that is the organizing principle of this volume. I have chosen to deviate from the framework in certain respects because some sections would otherwise be vastly longer than others. In addition, much of what is said in one section would often overlap greatly with another. However, for readers needing to quickly find discussions of any of the Six Pillars, I would note that Part I covers "public interest criteria" (referred to as "public use" in US jurisprudence), and some aspects of the "dispute resolution system" (as it applies to the separation of authority between courts and political branches of government). Part II addresses "just compensation" and "distribution of development surpluses." Part III considers "due process" and the "subjects of the eminent domain power." Part IV discusses the relevance of America's system of federalism, whose diversity is relevant to all six issues.

I The Debate over Public Use

The Takings Clause of the Fifth Amendment to the US Constitution states: "nor shall private property be taken for public use without just compensation."[5] The reference to "public use" in the Amendment is usually referred to as the "Public Use Clause." Nearly every state constitution has a similar provision.

It is theoretically possible to interpret this language as simply requiring that property owners be compensated for takings, with no mandate that

[5] U.S. Const., Amend. V.

the taking be for a public use. A few modern scholars have adopted this view.[6] But for some two hundred years, courts have held otherwise, consistently concluding that the Public Use Clause imposes at least some substantive limitation on the scope of permissible takings, even if only a modest one. This judicial consistency may be partly due to the fact that the opposite approach would lead to the seemingly absurd result that takings for a "private" use need not be compensated, thereby imposing fewer restrictions on them than on public use condemnations.[7]

The Conflict between the Broad and Narrow Views of Public Use

There has been a longstanding debate between advocates of what may be called the "broad" and "narrow" interpretations of public use.[8] The broad definition holds that a public use is anything that might potentially benefit the public in some way. This view places few if any limits on the power of eminent domain, since almost any private enterprise can claim that giving it more property might benefit the public in some way. By contrast, the narrow definition counts as a public use only the transfer of condemned property to government ownership, or to a private entity that has a legal obligation to serve the entire public, such as a public utility or a common carrier.

The protection of private property rights was one of the main objectives of the Founding Fathers who drafted the US Constitution in 1787.[9] At the Constitutional Convention, future Secretary of the Treasury Alexander Hamilton claimed that "one great obj[ect] of Gov[ernment] is the personal protection and security of property."[10] In "Federalist 10", James Madison – often called "the father of the Constitution" – famously wrote that "the first object of government" is the "protection of different and unequal faculties of acquiring property."[11]

6 See, e.g., Jed Rubenfeld, "Usings," 102 (1993) *Yale Law Journal* 1077, 1078–80.

7 For a more detailed discussion of this issue, see Somin, *Grasping Hand*, 71–72.

8 For an extensive discussion of the two definitions of "public use" and the history of the debate over them, see ibid, ch. 2.

9 On the Founding Fathers' emphasis on the importance of property rights, see, e.g., James W. Ely, Jr., *The Guardian of Every Other Right: A Constitutional History of Property Rights*, 3rd edn (New York: Oxford University Press, 2008), 42–59; Jennifer Nedelsky, *Private Property and the Limits of American Constitutionalism* (Chicago: University of Chicago Press, 1990).

10 Max Farrand, *The Records of the Federal Convention of 1787*, Vol. 1 (New Haven: Yale University Press, 1937), 534.

11 James Madison, "Federalist 10," in Alexander Hamilton, James Madison, and John Jay, Clinton Rossiter (ed.), *The Federalist Papers* (New York: Mentor, 1961), 58.

Nonetheless, there was relatively little discussion of the meaning of "public use" at the time of the enactment of the Fifth Amendment in 1791, in part because the Amendment then applied only against the federal government, and the dominant view at the time held that the federal government did not have the power of eminent domain within territory controlled by the states.[12] But numerous state courts did address the issue in the early to mid-nineteenth century, in the context of interpreting their state constitutions – most of which included public use clauses very similar to the federal one.[13]

Throughout the nineteenth century, there was considerable division between those states where courts enforced a narrow definitions of public use and those that endorsed the broad one.[14] The decisions that most often tested the limits of public use were the Mill Act cases, which ruled on the constitutionality of state laws enabling private owners of power mills to acquire property by using eminent domain. Unlike grist mills of the sort that were more common in the eighteenth and early nineteenth centuries, power mills were usually purely private businesses that were not required to serve all comers, as public utilities.

Other controversial nineteenth-century public use cases included the use of eminent domain for private roads and for irrigation and mineral extraction in the newly established states of the western United States. Meanwhile, state governments continued to use eminent domain for less controversial purposes permissible even under the narrow definition of public use. These included takings for public roads and common carriers, including railroads (which were required by law to serve the entire public).

Neither side in the nineteenth-century debate achieved a total victory. But by the time the Fifth Amendment and the rest of the Bill of Rights became applicable to state governments as a result of the enactment of

[12] See William Baude, "Rethinking the federal eminent domain power," 122 (2013) *Yale Law Journal* 1738.

[13] For discussions of these decisions, see, e.g., Somin, *Grasping Hand*, 43–49; Eric R. Claeys, "Public-use limitations and natural property rights," (2004) *Michigan State Law Review* 877; Lawrence Berger, "The public use requirement in eminent domain," 57 (1977) *Oregon Law Review* 203, 207–12; and Philip Nichols, "The meaning of public use in the law of eminent domain," 20 (1940) *B.U. Law Review* 615. For an important and influential nineteenth-century account, see John Lewis, *A Treatise on the Law of Eminent Domain in the United States* (Chicago: Callaghan & Co., 1888), 235–82.

[14] This account of nineteenth-century debates over public use is based on material discussed more fully in Somin, *Grasping Hand*, 43–55.

the Fourteenth Amendment in 1868,[15] a clear majority of state supreme courts had endorsed the narrow view, as did many leading jurists and treatise writers of the era.[16]

Most courts and jurists rejected the broad view in part because it seemed to give government virtually unlimited power to take private property. Any transfer of property to a private entity could potentially benefit the public in some way. As an 1884 Supreme Court of Ohio ruling put it, "[t]he prosperity of each individual condues, in a certain sense, to the public welfare, but this fact is not a sufficient reason for taking other private property to increase the prosperity of individual men."[17] In addition, the broad view threatened to make the phrase "public use" superfluous. John Lewis, author of the leading nineteenth-century treatise on eminent domain argued that "[t]o give these words any effect, they must be construed as limiting the power to which they relate . . . [and] it is evident that the words *public use*, if they are to be construed as a limitation, cannot be equivalent to the general welfare or public good."[18]

But the narrow view never completely routed the opposition.[19] And its dominance began to erode in the early twentieth century. During that period, the left-wing Progressive movement – which achieved considerable influence in both politics and legal circles – argued that strong judicial protection for property rights was misguided because it blocked beneficial government policies, and benefited the wealthy at the expense of the poor.[20]

15 For a long time, many scholars denied that the Fourteenth Amendment was intended to "incorporate" the Bill of Rights against state governments. But incorporation has now become the dominant view among constitutional law specialists. See Akhil Reed Amar, *The Bill of Rights: Creation and Reconstruction* (New Haven: Yale University Press, 1998), chs. 7–12; Michael Kent Curtis, *No State Shall Abridge: The Fourteenth Amendment and the Bill of Rights* (Durham: Duke University Press, 1986); and Kurt T. Lash, *The Fourteenth Amendment and the Privileges and Immunities of American Citizenship* (Cambridge University Press, 2014). It has also largely been endorsed by the Supreme Court, which has now applied all but a few small parts of the Bill of Rights to the states. For the most recent major decision in this field, see *McDonald v. City of Chicago*, 561 U.S. 742 (2010), which incorporated the Second Amendment right to bear arms, one of the last parts of the Bill of Rights that had not been incorporated previously.

16 For a detailed account, see Somin, *Grasping Hand*, 47–55.

17 *McQuillen v. Hatton*, 42 Ohio St. 202, 204 (Ohio 1884).

18 Lewis, *Treatise on Eminent Domain*, 221.

19 For a skillfully argued prominent nineteenth-century state supreme court decision endorsing the broad view, see *Dayton Gold and Silver Mining Co. v. Seawell*, 11 Nev. 394 (1876).

20 See e.g., Morton J. Horwitz, *The Transformation of American Law, 1870–1960: The Crisis of Legal Orthodoxy* (Cambridge: Harvard University Press, 1992) chs. 2, 5; Barbara Fried,

The Triumph of the Broad View

In the early twentieth century, some state courts gradually began to move towards the broad interpretation of public use.[21] This movement gained further impetus during the Great Depression of the 1930s, which helped discredit judicial protection of property rights and economic rights more generally in the eyes of much of the public, especially the political and legal elite. During this period, the Supreme Court also gradually began to interpret the Public Use Clause of the federal Constitution in a more deferential way.[22]

The Supreme Court decisively endorsed the broad view of public use in the 1954 case of *Berman v. Parker*.[23] Writing for a unanimous Court, Justice William O. Douglas concluded that "[t]he role of the judiciary in determining whether [eminent domain] is being exercised for a public purpose is an extremely narrow one."[24] If the "legislature has spoken, the public interest has been declared in terms well-nigh conclusive."[25] The fact that the condemned property was to be transferred to another private owner was deemed essentially irrelevant.[26] The *Berman* opinion also emphasized the need for courts to defer to experts in the other branches of government, who are better positioned than judges to determine whether a given taking genuinely benefits the public interest or not. As Justice Douglas put it, the Court must defer to the wisdom of "experts [who] concluded that if the community were to be healthy, if it were not to revert again to a blighted or slum area, as though possessed of a congenital disease, the area must be planned as a whole."[27] This

The Progressive Assault on Laissez-Faire: Robert Hale and the First Law and Economics Movement (Cambridge: Harvard University Press, 2001); and James W. Ely, Jr., "The Progressive Era Assault on Individualism and Property Rights," 29 (2012) *Social Philosophy and Policy* 255.

21 For a more detailed discussion of early twentieth-century developments in public use law and the decline of the narrow view, see Somin, *Grasping Hand*, 55–58; see also Nichols, "The meaning of public use"; and Comment [anonymous], "The public use limitation on eminent domain: an advance requiem," 58 (1949) *Yale Law Journal* 599.

22 See Somin, *Grasping Hand*, 55–58. The early twentieth-century Supreme Court also took a relatively deferential approach to takings reviewed under the Due Process Clause of the Fourteenth Amendment, which was the only available vehicle to challenge state government takings in federal court in a period when the Supreme Court had not yet ruled that the Public Use Clause of the Fifth Amendment applied to state governments. Many years later, the majority opinion in the *Kelo* case created confusion by misinterpreting these Due Process Clause cases as public use precedents. For a discussion of this issue, see Somin, *Grasping Hand*, 123–26. Justice John Paul Stevens, the author of the *Kelo* majority opinion, eventually admitted that he had erred on this point. Ibid. 125–26.

23 348 U.S. 26 (1954). 24 Ibid., 32. 25 Ibid. 26 Ibid., 33–34. 27 Ibid., 34.

emphasis on the need for deference to expertise was, and still remains, a common theme of advocates of the broad definition of public use.[28]

Berman was probably the most important eminent domain decision in the history of the United States. In addition to establishing the dominance of the broad view of public use in the federal courts, it also had an enormous effect far beyond the judicial system. The urban renewal and blight condemnations it ultimately permitted in many states resulted in the forcible displacement of hundreds of thousands of other people, most of them also poor minorities.[29] The taking upheld in *Berman* was part of an urban renewal project that forcibly displaced some 5000 African-Americans and transferred the condemned land to private real estate developers.[30]

Legal historian Wendell Pritchett emphasizes the tragic irony that a ruling that "enabled institutional and political elites to relocate minority populations and entrench racial segregation ... was decided just six months after *Brown v. Board of Education*,"[31] by the very same Court, including almost all the same justices. By 1980, some three million people had been forcibly displaced by takings similar to the one permitted in *Berman*, most of them poor minorities.[32] Blight condemnations continue in most states to this day, though on a much reduced scale relative to the 1950s and 1960s.[33]

Over the 15 years following *Berman*, most state supreme courts adopted *Berman* as a guide to the interpretation of their state constitutions' public use clauses.[34] The federal Supreme Court unanimously reaffirmed the highly deferential *Berman* approach to public use in its next major ruling on the subject, *Hawaii Housing Authority v. Midkiff* (1984).[35] For decades after *Berman*, most experts believed that the broad view had decisively prevailed, and that there was a virtual consensus about its correctness. As one 1996 article put it, "[t]oday, in *Berman's* wake, the broad view [of public use] holds the field completely."[36]

Yet even at the height of the dominance of the broad view – between the 1950s and the 1970s – several state supreme courts still rejected it,

[28] See Somin, *Grasping Hand*, 86, 119–20. [29] Ibid., 86–90, 100–02. [30] Ibid., 87–88.

[31] Wendell E. Pritchett, "The 'Public Menace' of Blight: Urban Renewal and the Private Uses of Eminent Domain," 21 (2003) *Yale Law and Policy Review* 1, 6.

[32] Somin, *Grasping Hand*, 87. [33] Ibid., 88. [34] See ibid., 59–60.

[35] 467 U.S. 229 (1984).

[36] Buckner F. Melton, Jr. "Eminent Domain, 'Public Use,' and the Conundrum of Original Intent," 36 (1996) *Natural Resources Journal*, 59, 62. For citations to other similar statements, see Somin, *Grasping Hand*, 60.

imposing significant public use constraints on takings even if they did not fully embrace the narrow view.[37] Outside the courts, critics of blight condemnations argued that they victimized minorities and the poor, undermined neighborhood cohesion, and destroyed more economic value than they created.[38] Critics also noted that, while blight condemnations initially focused on areas that were genuinely dilapidated, over time many states began to define blight so broadly that almost any area can be declared blighted and condemned for transfer to influential business interests.[39]

In the 1981 *Poletown* case, the most high-profile public use case since *Berman*, the Michigan Supreme Court ruled that the state constitution did not forbid the forcible displacement of over 4000 people by eminent domain in order to build a General Motors auto factory that would promote "economic development" in the city of Detroit.[40] Tragically, the takings probably destroyed far more wealth than they created, as the new factory created only a fraction of the anticipated job growth.[41]

The *Poletown* decision drew forceful dissents by two of the state Supreme Court justices, and also resulted in widespread public protest on both the left and the right.[42] Even the majority opinion held that condemnations that transferred property to private owners in order to

[37] See, e.g., *Baycol, Inc. v. Downtown Development Authority*, 315 So.2d 451, 457 (Fla. 1975) (holding that a "'public [economic] benefit' is not synonymous with 'public purpose' as a predicate which can justify eminent domain"); *Owensboro v. McCormick*, 581 S.W.2d 3, 8 (Ky. 1979) ("No 'public use' is involved where the land of A is condemned merely to enable B to build a factory"); *Karesh v. City of Charleston*, 247 S.E.2d 342, 345 (S.C. 1978) (striking down taking justified only by economic development); *City of Little Rock v. Raines*, 411 S.W.2d 486, 495 (Ark. 1967) (private economic development project not a public use); *Hogue v. Port of Seattle*, 341 P.2d 171, 181–91 (Wash. 1959) (denying condemnation of residential property so that agency could "devote it to what it considers a higher and better economic use"); Opinion of the Justices, 131 A.2d 904, 905–06 (Me. 1957) (condemnation for industrial development to enhance economy not a public use).

[38] For important early critiques of this kind, see, e.g., Jane Jacobs, *Death and Life of Great American Cities* (New York: Random House, 1961), 270–90, 311–14; and Martin Anderson, *The Federal Bulldozer* (Cambridge: MIT Press, 1964).

[39] For a discussion of this issue, see Somin, *Grasping Hand*, 84–86.

[40] *Poletown Neighborhood Council v. City of Detroit*, 304 N.W.2d 455, 457, 459 (Mich. 1981), overruled by *County of Wayne v. Hathcock*, 684 N.W.2d 765 (Mich. 2004). For a detailed analysis of *Poletown* and its eventual reversal in 2004, see Ilya Somin, "Overcoming Poletown: County of Wayne v. Hathcock, Economic Development Takings, and the Future of Public Use," (2004) *Michigan State Law Review* 1005.

[41] See Somin, "Overcoming *Poletown*," 1015–18.

[42] See Jeannie Wylie, *Poletown: Community Betrayed* (Urbana: University of Illinois Press, 1989).

promote economic development should get "heightened scrutiny" from state courts,[43] a far less deferential approach than that adopted by the federal Supreme Court in *Berman*. The uproar was an early sign that the broad view of public use was not as universally accepted as many experts had come to believe.

Between 1981 and the early 2000s, rising skepticism about government control of the economy and the emergence of pro-property rights political movements helped lead to additional state court decisions limiting the use of eminent domain.[44] By far the most famous was the Michigan Supreme Court's reversal of *Poletown* in 2004.[45] Still, most experts believed that the broad view of public use continued to be a largely unchallenged orthodoxy. As late as 2002, a treatise by two leading takings scholars concluded that "nearly all courts have settled on a broader understanding [of public use] that requires only that the taking yield some public benefit or advantage."[46]

Kelo and the Renewed Debate over Public Use

Although skepticism had been building for a long time, the perceived consensus in favor of the broad view of public use was only definitively broken by the Supreme Court's controversial 2005 decision in *Kelo v. City of New London*.[47] The *Kelo* case arose from the condemnation of 15 residential properties in the small city of New London, Connecticut, for the purpose of transfer to private developers in order to facilitate "economic development." The takings were part of a building project promoted by the state and local governments and Pfizer, Inc., a major pharmaceutical firm that had recently opened a headquarters nearby and hoped to benefit from the project.[48]

Most of the 90 property owners in the area chose to sell their land (sometimes because of pressure tactics) rather than try to challenge condemnation in court.[49] But seven owners, who between them owned 15 properties, were able to resist the condemnations thanks to the pro

[43] *Poletown*, 304 N.W.2d at 459. [44] See Somin, *Grasping Hand*, 61–62.

[45] By *County of Wayne v. Hathcock*, 684 N.W.2d 765 (Mich. 2004).

[46] Thomas W. Merrill and David A. Dana, *Property: Takings* (New York: Foundation Press, 2002), 196.

[47] 545 U.S. 469 (2005).

[48] For detailed accounts of the history of the *Kelo* case, see Somin, *Grasping Hand*, ch. 1 and Jeff Benedict, *Little Pink House: A True Story of Defiance and Courage* (New York: Grand Central Publishing, 2009).

[49] Somin, *Grasping Hand*, 19–22.

bono assistance of the Institute for Justice, a pro-property rights public interest law firm that had long sought to revive public use constraints on takings.[50]

Eleven of the fifteen condemnations were initially invalidated by Connecticut state trial court.[51] But this partial victory for the property owners was overruled in a closely divided 4:3 decision by the state supreme court, which ruled that such "economic development" takings are permissible under both the federal Public Use Clause and the Connecticut state constitution, and that the government was not required to provide evidence that the promised economic development would actually occur.[52]

To the surprise of most experts, the federal Supreme Court agreed to review the case.[53] In a 5:4 ruling issued in June 2005, the justices affirmed the state supreme court decision.[54] The majority largely reiterated the broad view of public use adopted in previous decisions such as *Berman* and *Midkiff*, holding that the government could take property for virtually any "public purpose" and emphasizing the supposed need to continue the Court's "policy of deference to legislative judgment in this field."[55] It also ruled that the "economic development" rationale for takings was a permissible justification for transferring property to private owners, and that the government was not required to prove that the takings would actually achieve the development that supposedly justified the use of eminent domain in the first place. The Court refused to "second-guess [New London officials'] considered judgments about the efficacy of the development plan."[56] In some minor ways, the *Kelo* decision was slightly less deferential than previous precedent.[57] But overall, it largely applied its previous endorsement of the broad view of public use to the specific case of economic development takings.

But unlike *Berman* and *Midkiff*, *Kelo* was a closely divided 5:4 decision. Justices Sandra Day O'Connor and Clarence Thomas each wrote powerful dissents that not only rejected the majority's arguments, but

[50] Ibid., 24–26.

[51] *Kelo v. City of New London*, 2002 Conn. Super. Lexis 789 (Conn. Super. Ct. 2002).

[52] *Kelo v. City of New London*, 843 A.2d 500 (Conn. 2004), *affirmed* 545 U.S. 469 (2005). For discussion of the state court decisions and their reasoning, see Somin, *Grasping Hand*, 24–31.

[53] In the United States, nearly all of the cases heard by the federal Supreme Court are considered only if at least four of the nine justices wish to take them. The Court generally accepts only a tiny fraction of the cases for which litigants seek review.

[54] *Kelo*, 545, U.S. at 470–83. [55] Ibid., 480. [56] Ibid., 488.

[57] See Somin, *Grasping Hand*, 113–14.

concluded that economic development condemnations that transfer property to private parties should be categorically banned as inconsistent with the Public Use Clause.[58] In a dissent joined by three other justices, O'Connor worried that "[u]nder the banner of economic development, all private property is now vulnerable to being taken and transferred to another private owner, so long as it might be upgraded—*i.e.*, given to an owner who will use it in a way that the legislature deems more beneficial to the public—in the process."[59]

Justice O'Connor argued that the Public Use Clause forbids economic development takings, while continuing to allow "blight" condemnations of the sort at issue in *Berman v. Parker*.[60] In his solo dissent, Justice Thomas urged the Court to go further than this, and consider overruling *Berman* and other similar precedents completely. He "would revisit our Public Use Clause cases and consider returning to the original meaning of the Public Use Clause: that the government may take property only if it actually uses or gives the public a legal right to use the property."[61] Justice Anthony Kennedy, who gave the majority its decisive fifth vote, wrote a difficult-to-interpret concurring opinion that holds out the possibility that he might be willing to support more rigorous judicial scrutiny of public use issues in some future cases.[62]

Although *Kelo* largely reiterated previous precedent, it had the effect of undermining the previous supposed consensus in favor of the broad definition of public use. The close division in the Supreme Court and the forceful dissents by Justices O'Connor and Thomas demonstrated that there was no longer a consensus on the issue among jurists. O'Connor's view was particularly notable, given her longstanding status as a relative moderate and key swing voter on the Court.

Perhaps even more importantly, *Kelo* generated an enormous political backlash, broader than almost any other modern US Supreme Court decision. Polls showed that over 80 per cent of the public disapproved of the ruling, a hostility that cut across partisan, ideological, and racial divisions.[63] The decision was denounced by politicians, commentators,

[58] *Kelo*, 545 U.S. at 499–506 (O'Conner, J., dissenting); ibid., 518–23 (Thomas, J., dissenting).

[59] *Kelo*, 545 U.S. at 494 (O'Connor, J., dissenting). [60] Ibid., 499–501.

[61] Ibid., 521 (Thomas, J., dissenting).

[62] Ibid., 492–94 (Kennedy, J., concurring). Perhaps somewhat inconsistently, Kennedy also joined the majority opinion, which held out fewer caveats of this kind. For an analysis of Kennedy's opinion, see Somin, *Grasping Hand*, 114–16.

[63] For an overviews of the public reaction to *Kelo*, see Somin, *Grasping Hand*, ch. 5; Ilya Somin, "The limits of backlash: assessing the political response to Kelo," 93 (2009)

and activist groups across the political spectrum.[64] Outrage was also heightened by the fact that New London's poorly conceived development plan ultimately failed, just as critics had predicted it would from early on. Over a decade after the Supreme Court ruling, nothing has been built on any of the condemned properties. The land is used only by a colony of feral cats.[65]

In the aftermath of *Kelo*, 45 of the 50 states adopted reform laws intended to restrict the power of eminent domain – more than have enacted laws in response to any other Supreme Court decision in all of American history.[66] While a substantial number of states enacted strong laws that impose tight constraints on blight and economic development takings, a majority adopted only very weak reforms that provide little new protection for property owners.[67] Several factors account for this shortfall. But a crucial one is the ignorance of most voters about the details of state reform laws, which enabled political leaders to pass off largely cosmetic reforms as genuine protections for property rights.[68] Survey data shows that only 13 per cent of the public knew both whether their state had enacted a post-*Kelo* reform law, and whether it was likely to be effective; and even this figure may overestimate the true level of

Minnesota Law Review 2100, 2108–14; and Janice Nadler and Shari Seidman Diamond, "Government takings of private property," in Nathaniel Persily, Jack Citrin, and Patrick Egan (eds.), *Public Opinion and Constitutional Controversy* (New York: Oxford University Press, 2008).

64 For examples, see Somin, *Grasping Hand*, 137–38.

65 Ibid., 234–37; see also Kathleen Edgecomb, "'It still hurts': fight to save home scars one Fort Trumbull family" (June 23, 2013) *The Day*; Charlotte Allen, "'*Kelo*' Revisited," (February 10, 2014) *Weekly Standard*, available at www.weeklystandard.com/articles/kelo-revisited_776021.html.

66 For overviews of post-*Kelo* reform legislation, see ibid.; Somin, "Limits of backlash"; Marc Mihaly and Turner Smith, "Kelo's trail: a survey of state and federal legislative and judicial activity five years later," 38 (2011) *Ecology Law Quarterly* 703; Edward J. López, Todd Jewell, and Noel Campbell., "Pass a law, any law: state legislative responses to the Kelo backlash," 5 (2009) *Review of Law and Economics* 101; Andrew Morriss, "Symbol or substance? An empirical assessment of state responses to Kelo," 17 (2009) *Supreme Court Economic* Review 237; James W. Ely, Jr., "Post-Kelo reform: is the glass half-full or half-empty?," 17 (2009) *Supreme Court Economic Review* 127; Elaine B. Sharp and Donald Haider-Markel, "At the invitation of the court: eminent domain reform in state legislatures in the wake of the Kelo decision," 38 (2008) *Publius: Journal of Federalism* 556; Timothy Sandefur, "The 'backlash' so far: will Americans get meaningful eminent domain reform?," (2006) *Michigan State Law Review* 709; Lynn Blais, "Urban revitalization in the post-Kelo era," 34 (2007) *Fordham Urban Law Journal* 657.

67 Somin, *Grasping Hand*, ch. 5.

68 On the role of political ignorance in limiting the effectiveness of the *Kelo* backlash, see ibid., ch. 6.

public knowledge.[69] Nonetheless, the political backlash generated by *Kelo* did lead to significant new constraints on eminent domain in many parts of the country. It also focused public attention on the issue in a way that had not happened previously for many decades, if ever.

In the years since *Kelo*, eminent domain abuse has continued to attract greater public attention than in the past, though not as much as in the immediate aftermath of the case. Most recently, it entered the political spotlight as a result of controversial real estate developer Donald Trump's surprisingly successful presidential campaign in the 2016 election. Trump is a vocal defender of the *Kelo* decision and the use of eminent domain for private development projects – including some dubious ones of his own. As Trump emerged as the front-runner for the Republican Party nomination, his record on eminent domain got considerable negative attention from the media and from rival candidates.[70]

In addition to the massive political reaction against it, *Kelo* also generated a mostly negative reaction from state judges. Several state supreme courts repudiated it as a guide to the interpretation of their state constitutions' public use clauses by ruling that those constitutions forbid *Kelo*-like "economic development" takings that transfer property to private parties.[71] Other state court rulings deviated from *Kelo's* ultra-deferential stance on public use in less sweeping ways.[72] This skeptical judicial reaction was in sharp contrast to most state courts' acceptance of

[69] Ibid, 167–79.

[70] For my analysis of Trump's record on eminent domain and a critique of his defense of economic development takings, see Ilya Somin, "Donald Trump's lightweight defense of taking property for private development," Volokh Conspiracy blog (February 6, 2016), *Washington Post*, available at www.washingtonpost.com/news/volokh-conspiracy/wp/2016/02/06/donald-trumps-lightweight-defense-of-taking-property-for-private-projects/; and Ilya Somin, "Donald Trump's history of eminent domain abuse," Volokh Conspiracy blog (August 19, 2015), *Washington Post*, available at www.washingtonpost.com/news/volokh-conspiracy/wp/2015/08/19/donald-trumps-abuse-of-eminent-domain/?tid=a_inl.

[71] See, e.g., *City of Norwood v. Horney*, 853 N.E.2d 1115, 1136 (Ohio 2006) (holding that "economic development" alone does not justify condemnation); *Board of County Commissioners of Muskogee County v. Lowery*, 136 P.3d 639, 650–51 (Okla. 2006) (holding that "economic development" is not a "public purpose" under the Oklahoma state constitution, and rejecting *Kelo* as a guide to interpretation of Oklahoma's state constitution); *Benson v. State*, 710 N.W.2d 131, 146 (S.D. 2006) (concluding that the South Dakota constitution gives property owners broader protection than *Kelo*). For analysis of these cases and other judicial reactions to *Kelo*, see Somin, *Grasping Hand*, ch. 7; Ilya Somin, "The judicial reaction to Kelo" 4 (2011) *Albany Government Law Review* 1 (introduction to the Symposium on Eminent Domain in the United States).

[72] See Somin, *Grasping Hand*, ch. 7.

Berman several decades earlier. It is yet another indication of the collapse of consensus over public use issues.

Today, more than a decade after *Kelo*, the debate over public use continues, and there is no indication that a new consensus will emerge any time soon. Many state and local governments continue to engage in dubious *Kelo*-style takings, even as others have cut back.[73] Numerous states also continue to condemn property under definitions of blight broad enough to apply to virtually any area, although some have limited or even banned blight condemnations under their post-*Kelo* reform laws.[74]

The *Kelo* decision itself remains controversial, as well. Most academic experts approve of the result, as do urban planners and others. They contend that broad eminent domain power is needed to promote economic development, and prevent valuable projects from being blocked by holdouts.[75] But the decision also has many critics who hope it will be overruled,[76] and argue that there are better ways to address holdout problems.[77] This disagreement is in itself a major change from the era immediately following *Berman v. Parker*, when relatively few questioned the idea that government should be able to condemn private property for almost any reason.

73 For discussions of two particularly egregious cases in New York City, see Ilya Somin, "Let there be blight: blight condemnations in New York after Goldstein and Kaur," 38 *Fordham Urban Law Journal* 1193 (2011) (symposium on eminent domain in New York); and Amy Lavine and Norman Oder, "Urban redevelopment policy, judicial deference to unaccountable agencies, and reality in Brooklyn's Atlantic Yards project," 42 (2010) *The Urban Lawyer* 287.

74 Somin, *Grasping Hand*, ch. 5.

75 For an overview of the holdout problem and associated literature, see Daniel B. Kelly, "Acquiring land through eminent domain: justifications, limitations, and alternatives," in Kenneth Ayotte and Henry E. Smith (eds.), *Research Handbook on the Economics of Property Law* (Northampton, MA: Edward Elgar, 2011), 344, 345–48. For arguments that the holdout problem justifies broad eminent domain authority, see, e.g., Michael Heller, *The Gridlock Economy: How Too Much Ownership Wrecks Markets, Stops Innovation, and Costs Lives* (New York: Basic Books, 2008), 108–17; and Robert Dreher and John Echeverria, "Kelo's unanswered questions: the policy debate over the use of eminent domain for economic development," (2006) *Georgetown Environmental Law and Policy Institute*, 28–32.

76 For an assessment of the prospects for overruling *Kelo*, see Somin, *Grasping Hand*, 238–41.

77 See, e.g., ibid. ch. 4; and Daniel B. Kelly, "The 'public use' requirement in eminent domain law: a rationale based on secret purchases and private influence," 92 (2006) *Cornell Law Review* 1.

For a long time, a nation known for its emphasis on private property rights often failed to live up to its own supposed principles. It deviated from them to the extent of forcibly displacing millions of people from their homes and businesses. In recent years – especially in the aftermath of the *Kelo* decision – many Americans have begun to question the economic, legal, and moral justifications for such policies. The ultimate result of that questioning still remains to be seen.

II Just Compensation

In contrast to their shifting positions on the meaning of public use, American courts have been much more consistent in their interpretations of the Fifth Amendment's requirement that owners of condemned property are entitled to "just compensation."[78] The Supreme Court has long interpreted this provision as requiring the payment of "fair market value," usually defined as the price the property would bring if sold on the open market.[79] "Deviation from this measure of just compensation has been required only 'when market value has been too difficult to find, or when its application would result in manifest injustice to owner or public.'"[80] Some state governments, as well as the federal government, provide additional compensation for relocation costs,[81] though this is not required under the Supreme Court's interpretation of the federal Constitution. The problem of just compensation also has never caused as much political controversy as the debate over public use. For the most part, it has remained the province of lawyers, judges, academics, and other experts.

Nonetheless, critics have long argued that the fair market value approach leads to undercompensation. Many scholars on both the right and the left have advocated increasing compensation because the fair market value formula fails to account for "subjective" value: the value many owners attach to their property over and above what it might bring on the market.[82]

78 U.S. Const., Amend. V.

79 See, e.g., *Kirby Forest Industries Inc. v. United States*, 467 U.S. 1, 10 (1984); *United States v. 50 Acres of Land*, 469 U.S. 24, 29 (1984); *United States v. Miller*, 317 U.S. 369, 374 (1943); *Olson v. United States*, 292 U.S. 246, 255 (1934).

80 *50 Acres of Land*, 469 U.S. at 29 (quoting *United States v. Commodities Trading Corp.*, 339 U.S. 121, 123 (1950)).

81 See Nicole Stelle Garnett, "The neglected political economy of eminent domain," 105 (2006) *Michigan Law Review* 101.

82 See, e.g., Yun-chien Chang, *Private Property and Takings Compensation: Theoretical Framework and Empirical Analysis* (Northampton: Edward Elgar, 2013), 167–72;

For example, homeowners who have lived in the same location for many years often develop social ties to their neighborhoods that they value far beyond the market price of the property. Wilhelmina Dery, one of the New London residents threatened with displacement by the *Kelo* takings, had been born in that house in 1918, had never lived elsewhere, and fervently wished to remain in the house to the end of her life.[83] Mrs. Dery almost certainly attached subjective value to the house far beyond its market price.

Small business properties also often have significant subjective value to their owners, since these enterprises may lose customer good will and other valuable economic advantages if forced to move.[84] Other high subjective value properties include houses of worship and charitable institutions, some of which are often targeted for condemnation because they produce less tax revenue and economic development for local governments than commercial properties might.[85] A number of academic commentators also argue that owners of condemned property should receive a share of the premium created by new development.[86]

During oral argument in the *Kelo* case, several justices echoed these criticisms of the fair market value formula. They include Justices Stephen Breyer, Anthony Kennedy, and David Souter – all of whom ultimately voted to uphold the *Kelo* takings.[87] Justice Breyer asked whether "there is

Margaret Jane Radin, "The liberal conception of property: cross currents in the jurisprudence of takings," 88 (1988) *Columbia Law Review* 1667, 1689–96; Gideon Parchomovsky and Peter Siegelman, "Selling Mayberry: communities and individuals in law and economics," 92 (2004) *California Law Review* 75, 139–42. Aaron N. Green, "Takings, just compensation, and efficient use of land, urban, and environmental resources," 33 (2001) *The Urban Lawyer* 517; Richard A. Epstein, "Property, speech and the politics of distrust," 59 (1992) *University of Chicago Law Review* 41, 62 n. 60, 62–63; Gideon Kanner, "Condemnation blight: just how just is just compensation?," 48 (1973) *Notre Dame Law Review* 765.

83 Interview with Matthew Dery, July 31, 2013. See also Benedict, *Little Pink House*, 88. Mrs. Dery ultimately passed away not long before her home was taken by the city in the aftermath of the Supreme Court decision upholding its condemnation. See Somin, *Grasping Hand*, 233.

84 See Somin, *Grasping Hand*, 213; Garnett, "Neglected political economy of eminent domain," 106.

85 See Brief for Becket Fund for Religious Liberty as Amicus Curiae in support of Petitioners, *Kelo v. City of New London*, 545 U.S. 469 (2005) 2004 WL 2787141, at *8–11 & n.20.

86 See, e.g., Richard A. Epstein, *Takings: Private Property and the Power of Eminent Domain* (Cambridge: Harvard University Press, 1985), 115–17; see also James Krier and Christopher Serkin, "Public ruses," (2004) *Michigan State Law Review* 859, 869–72.

87 U.S. Supreme Court Oral Argument Transcript, *Kelo v. City of New London*, No 04–108, (argued February 22, 2005) (available on Westlaw at 2005 WL 529436), at *15, 30, 32–34.

some way of assuring that the just compensation actually puts the [owner of a condemned home] in the position he would be in if he didn't have to sell his house."[88] Justice Kennedy wondered whether owners of property condemned for economic development should "receive some sort of a premium for the development."[89]

Some leading property scholars, such as James Krier and Christopher Serkin, and Thomas Merrill, have also argued for increasing compensation as a tool for alleviating eminent domain abuse.[90] If the government has to pay compensation closer to the full value of displaced owners' losses, it might be deterred from undertaking condemnations that destroy more value than they create. This theory, however, is vulnerable to the objection that government decision-makers rarely, if ever, pay for the compensation themselves. And generally ignorant voters rarely keep track of the payments and punish officials who approve excessive takings by refusing to re-elect them.[91]

On the other hand, some economists argue that compensation levels should be lowered rather than increased. They contend that paying any compensation at all incentivizes overinvestment in property likely to be condemned by the state.[92]

The most obvious difficulty with increasing compensation to account for the full amount of the loss suffered by the owner is the challenge of ascertaining the true extent of subjective value. Scholars have proposed a variety of schemes for incentivizing owners to reveal their true valuations. But all have substantial conceptual problems, are unlikely to be feasible with real-world governments, or both.[93]

There are also two other, less well-known, flaws in most proposals to increase takings compensation. First, increasing compensation can exacerbate the harm inflicted by dubious takings on taxpayers, who are

[88] Ibid., *32–33. [89] Ibid., *15.

[90] See, e.g., Krier and Serkin, "Public ruses," 865–75; United States Senate Committee on the Judiciary, *The* Kelo *Decision: Investigating Takings of Homes and Other Private Property* (September 20, 2005), p. 6, (testimony of Professor Thomas W Merrill) (hereinafter Merrill Testimony).

[91] I discuss these points in greater detail in Somin, *Grasping Hand*, 208–09.

[92] See Lawrence Blume, Daniel Rubinfeld, and Perry Shapiro, "The taking of land: when should compensation be paid?" 99 (1984) *Quarterly Journal of Economics* 71. For a recent evaluation and critique of this type of argument, see Thomas J. Miceli, *The Economic Theory of Eminent Domain: Private Property, Public Use* (Cambridge University Press, 2011), 85–112.

[93] For overviews and critiques of the relevant literature, see Chang, *Private Property and Takings Compensation*, chs. 4, 8; Miceli, *Economic Theory of Eminent Domain*, 62–66; Somin, *Grasping Hand*, 205–09.

forced to pay for the compensation payments. In the extreme case, excessive compensation might even incentivize politically influential property owners to lobby for the condemnation of their land, since the compensation payments would actually be higher than the value they attach to the property.[94]

Second, even if the state and federal governments increase compensation levels, it may be very difficult to ensure that poor and politically weak owners actually receive as much compensation as they are legally entitled to. The appraisal processes used by local and state governments are often biased against poor and legally unsophisticated owners, many of whom are short-changed as a result.[95] Empirical studies find that relatively poor owners often get compensation awards that fall far short of even the currently mandated fair market value standard, though wealthy owners often get more than the standard requires.[96] Such systematic bias may prove hard to correct.

In sum, there is widespread, though certainly not universal,[97] agreement that American condemning authorities often undercompensate property owners whose land is taken by eminent domain. There is much less agreement on how best to solve the problem.

Both estimating the amount of subjective value that should be compensated and ensuring that owners actually receive the full amount they

[94] I discuss these dangers in greater detail in Somin, *Grasping Hand*, 205–08.

[95] For a summary of several such biases by an experienced appraiser, see Wallace Kaufman, "How fair is market value? An appraiser's report of temptations, deficiencies, and distortions in the condemnation process," in Bruce Benson (ed.), *Property Rights: Eminent Domain and Regulatory Takings Re-Examined* (New York: Palgrave Macmillan, 2010), 79–86.

[96] See Chang, *Private Property and Takings Compensation*, chs. 5–8. In New York City, undercompensation is prevalent in cases that are settled (ibid., ch. 7), while overcompensation occurs far more often in cases that go to court, which are usually cases involving larger and wealthier landowners (ibid., ch. 8), perhaps because these types of owners can more readily afford a prolonged legal battle. For an early study reaching similar conclusions, see Patricia Munch, "An economic analysis of eminent domain," 84 (1976) *Journal of Political Economy* 473.

[97] For a recent claim that fair market value compensation does in fact capture most types of subjective value, see Brian Angelo Lee, "Just undercompensation: the idiosyncratic premium in eminent domain," 113 (2013) *Columbia Law Review* 593. However, even Lee recognizes that the fair market value formula undercompensates for the loss owner's "autonomy" (ibid.). Moreover, Lee's argument has been subjected to strong criticism by Lee Ann Fennell, "Just enough," 113 (2013) *Columbia Law Review Side Bar* 109, which points out some important aspects of subjective value that Lee's analysis underestimates or overlooks. It also ignores the reality that many owners fail to receive even fair market value.

are due, turn out to be extremely difficult challenges. These problems and others like them weaken claims that increasing compensation is by itself a sufficient solution for the problem of eminent domain abuse in the United States.

III Procedural Constraints on Takings

Like compensation, eminent domain procedure is a complex issue that has attracted more attention from experts than the general public. Some procedural constraints on takings are very widely accepted and implemented, including the requirement that owners receive advance notice of the government's intention to condemn, that they have the opportunity to challenge the taking in court on public use grounds, and that they can go to court to contest the state's appraisal of the value of their property in order to try to get an increased compensation payment.[98]

Some states permit streamlined "quick take" condemnations that bypass some of the usual procedures in order to ensure that the government can acquire the property quickly, for supposedly urgent projects. In recent years, however, state supreme courts have construed these laws narrowly, forcing officials to use standard procedures as much as possible.[99]

In the aftermath of *Kelo*, new attention has focused on the extent to which condemning authorities engage in a detailed planning process before resorting to the use of eminent domain. The *Kelo* majority opinion emphasized that it was deferring to the political process in part because the New London takings were part of an "integrated development plan," which allegedly makes it less likely that the takings were the result of favoritism towards influential private parties.[100] Some scholars and lower court decisions since *Kelo* have emphasized extensive planning as an important safeguard against abusive takings.[101]

[98] These procedures are summarized in detail in Julius L. Sackman, et al., *Nichols on Eminent Domain*, 3rd edn. Vol. 6 (Lexis, 2008). For a discussion of compensation procedures, see Kaufman, "How fair is fair market value?".

[99] See e.g., *Mayor of Baltimore v. Valsamaki*, 916 A.2d 324, 356 (Md. 2007); *Sapero v. Mayor of Baltimore*, 920 A.2d 1061, 1079–80 (Md. 2007); *Rhode Island Economic Development Corp. v. The Parking Co.*, 892 A.2d 87, 102 (R.I. 2006).

[100] *Kelo*, 545 U.S. at 472–74. On the role of confidence in the planning process in Justice Stevens' opinion, see Nicole Stelle Garnett, "Planning as public use?," 34 (2007) *Ecology Law Quarterly* 443.

[101] See discussion of this issue in Somin, *Grasping Hand*, 192–93, 195.

Some reformers argue that increasing procedural safeguards is a promising strategy for protecting property owners against abusive takings without restricting the substantive scope of condemning authorities' power to use eminent domain.[102] Possible additional protections include requiring extra advance notice of condemnation proceedings, mandating a detailed report laying out the purpose for which eminent domain is to be used, extensive public hearings to justify the planned taking, and an opportunity for opponents of the project to "voice their objections to being uprooted."[103] If the theory is sound, "strict enforcement of these procedural protections makes eminent domain largely self-regulating" because "[r]equiring the condemning authority to jump through enough procedural hoops will cause the costs of eminent domain to rise relative to the costs of voluntary exchange," thereby ensuring that "[e]minent domain will be used only when the transaction costs of voluntary exchange are truly prohibitive."[104]

Almost all expert observers agree that procedural restrictions on eminent domain have at least some merit. Few if any deny that it would be dangerous to allow the government to take property without notice or without giving owners any opportunity to contest the takings before an impartial tribunal. What is less clear is whether increasing the extent and complexity of procedural rules beyond the widely accepted minimum really provides meaningful protection for property owners.

Unfortunately, elaborate procedural rules are a double-edged sword. While they increase the time and effort it takes to push through a condemnation, they also increase the costs of the condemnation process for those owners who actually try to use the procedures to their fullest extent. Less affluent owners often lack the resources necessary to pay for prolonged procedural battles, or live with extended uncertainty about the future of their property.

In the *Kelo* case, for example, the resisting property owners would almost certainly have had to give in to the government's demands early on, were it not for the high-quality pro bono legal assistance provided by

[102] United States Senate Committee on the Judiciary, *The* Kelo *Decision*; Thomas W. Merrill, "The misplaced flight to substance," 19 (2005) *Probate and Property* 16, 18; Gerald E. Frug and David J. Barron. "Making planning matter: a new approach to eminent domain," 71 (2005) *Harvard Design Magazine*; David J. Barron and Gerald E. Frug, "Make eminent domain fair for all" (August 12, 2005) *Boston Globe*.

[103] Merrill, Testimony, p. 6.

[104] Merrill, "The misplaced flight to substance," p. 18. For an early version of the same argument, see Merrill, "The economics of public use," 80–81.

the Institute for Justice.[105] Even with the Institute's help, the lengthy legal and political battle took a major toll. As Susette Kelo described her experience, "[a]ll we did for eight years, was eat and drink eminent domain . . . that's what we thought about all day long."[106]

By contrast, the government can more easily bear the expense of prolonged procedural wrangling, since it has access to taxpayer resources. The same is often true of influential private interests who hope to benefit from the takings, many of which are "repeat players" with extensive resources, who can afford to wait out resisters. This imbalance of power at least partially explains why most owners of property targeted for condemnation do not in fact try to avail themselves of the full range of procedural options open to them, but instead quickly reach a "voluntary" settlement with the state, as happened with the vast majority of those targeted in the *Kelo* case. They realize that prolonged resistance is likely to end up costing them a lot more time, effort, and money, than giving in will.[107] Such factors may also help explain why many relatively poor owners fail to get the fair market value compensation required by law.[108]

Relying on the planning process to ferret out abuse raises similar issues. Although Justice John Paul Stevens, author of the *Kelo* majority opinion, may have been unaware of this fact, the overwhelming majority of significant condemnations in modern American history have in fact been the result of planning processes.[109] Even *99 Cents Only Stores v. Lancaster Redevelopment Agency*, a lower court decision cited by Stevens as an example of a pure "one-to-one transfer,"[110] actually struck down a taking that the government justified as necessary to implement a redevelopment plan.[111]

But the drafting of a plan provides little protection against "capture" of the process by private interest group, or abusive treatment of resisting owners.[112] Indeed, the more complex and elaborate the planning process becomes, the more likely it will be that insiders and organized interests

105 Somin, *Grasping Hand*, 24–26. 106 Interview with Susette Kelo, September 4, 2013.

107 For a more detailed discussion of these issues, see Somin, *Grasping Hand*, 209–12.

108 See discussion earlier in this chapter. 109 Somin, *Grasping Hand*, 120–21.

110 *Kelo*, 545 U.S. at 487 n.17.

111 *99 Cents Only Store v. Lancaster Redevelopment Agency*, 237 F. Supp. 2d 1123, 1125–26 (C.D. Cal. 2001) (noting that the case involves condemnation powers established pursuant to the "Amargosa Redevelopment Plan").

112 For a more detailed discussion see Somin, *Grasping Hand*, 120–21.

will be able to exercise influence over it more easily than either ordinary citizens or targeted property owners.[113]

While planning for the use of eminent domain is largely under the control of executive and legislative bodies of state and local governments, public use challenges to takings and claims that the government is offering insufficient compensation are generally adjudicated by courts (usually state rather than federal). It is not clear, however, whether increasing the role of courts at the expense of the other branches of government (or vice versa) will improve either the efficiency or the fairness of the condemnation process.

The difficulty of making procedural constraints effective tools for preventing abusive takings have led some scholars to propose that property owners be given more direct influence over the decision to condemn. For example, Michael Heller and Roderick Hills propose the establishment of "land assembly districts" in which condemnations would only be permitted if a majority of property owners in the area vote in favor.[114] Others advocate the creation of government agencies tasked with helping owners to protect their interests. In a recent book on eminent domain, sociologist Debbie Becher suggests that the government should appoint state-funded "community organizers" to help residents of areas targeted for condemnation mobilize to defend themselves.[115]

Proposals like these deserve greater consideration and might potentially be improvements over the status quo. But they also have notable weaknesses. Among other things, it is difficult to figure out how to properly organize the citizen groups, and what their territorial boundaries should be.[116] Most fundamentally, it is hard to see what incentives the political process would have to adopt these plans, even (or perhaps, especially) if they would prove effective.[117] Becher acknowledges that her proposed reform would be extremely difficult to implement because "[p]oliticians will be reluctant to provide such a resource, and will be very tempted to cut the lifeline to any professionals explicitly organizing against official plans."[118]

113 Ibid.

114 Michael Heller and Roderick Hills, "Land assembly districts," 121 (2008) *Harvard Law Review* 1465; For criticism of this proposal see Daniel B. Kelly, "The limitations of majoritarian land assembly," 122 (2009) *Harvard Law Review Forum* 7; and Somin, *Grasping Hand*, 219–21.

115 Debbie Becher, *Private Property and Public Power: Eminent Domain in Philadelphia* (New York: Oxford University Press, 2014), pp. 234–35.

116 For discussion, see Somin, *Grasping Hand*, 220.

117 Ibid.

118 Becher, *Private Property and Public Power*, 235.

The direct delegation of eminent domain authority to private entities is another procedural issue that deserves attention. Today, most blight condemnations, economic development takings, and takings for public infrastructure (such as airports, military facilities, or railroads) are generally conducted by public agencies, even if the property is later transferred to a new private owner.[119] In the nineteenth century (and to a lesser extent today), the delegation of condemnation authority to private railroads, owners of private roads, and various common carriers was frequently practiced. So long as such enterprises had a legal duty to serve the entire public, this was permissible even under the narrow interpretation of public use.[120]

In more recent decades, the delegation of eminent domain authority to private parties is more often undertaken in the case of privately owned pipelines, utilities, and power lines.[121] As legal scholar Alexandra Klass has shown in a series of articles, many states – especially in the central and western parts of the country – have very loose standards for such takings, thereby opening the door to a variety of abuses.[122]

As with railroad takings in the nineteenth century, pipeline and utility condemnations are permissible under the narrow definition of public use, so long as the resulting facilities are legally open to the general public – required to serve all potential customers who are willing to pay. But such requirements are not always effectively supervised and enforced; even when they are, it is likely that some condemnations occur in situations where they destroy more economic value than they create.

A variety of reforms could potentially alleviate such abuses,[123] including stricter enforcement of public use requirements. In 2011, for

[119] The *Kelo* case was an unusual exception: the takings at issue there were conducted by the New London Development Corporation – a non-profit organization created by the City of New London and authorized by it to use eminent domain after the city council approved its development plan. Somin, *Grasping Hand*, ch. 1.

[120] As the Delaware Supreme Court ruled in 1839, takings by private railroads were permitted if the railway is "designed for use by the public," which is given a right to use the railway "by all upon the same terms." *Whiteman v. Wilmington & S.R. Co.*, 2 Harr. 514, 519 (Del. 1839).

[121] For extensive discussion of such takings, see Alexandra Klass, "Takings and transmission," 91 (2013) *North Carolina Law Review* 1079; Alexandra Klass, "The frontier of eminent domain," 79 (2008) *University of Colorado Law Review* 651. For a condensed version of the latter article, see Alexandra Klass, "The frontier of eminent domain," (Fall 2008) *Regulation*.

[122] See works cited in the previous note.

[123] For some possible reforms, see Klass, "Takings and transmission," pp. 1134–53, and Klass, "Frontier of eminent domain," pp. 691–700. In recent years, a political backlash

example, the Texas Supreme Court ruled that a private firm cannot use eminent domain to build a pipeline due to its status as a "common carrier" if the pipeline, although theoretically open to the general public, in reality only connects two facilities owned by the firm itself.[124] Obviously, here as elsewhere, the implementation of reforms is made more complicated by the combination of the political influence of private beneficiaries of takings and the general public's ignorance about the details of eminent domain policy.[125]

Overall, procedural constraints on takings in the United States provide important, but modest protections for property owners. Whether and to what extent they can be reformed in ways that provide stronger guarantees against eminent domain abuse is far more debatable.

IV Eminent Domain and American Federalism

The purpose of this chapter is to provide an overview of eminent domain policy in the United States. But on many issues, there is no single policy. Instead, we have more than 50 different ones; one for each state, the federal government (in the relatively rare cases where it condemns property), and the District of Columbia.[126] The federal Supreme Court imposes some minimum constraints on eminent domain under the Fifth Amendment of the federal Constitution. But with the important exception of requiring fair market value compensation, these constraints – as currently interpreted by the Court – are generally weak.

This in turn leads to a wide variation in state policies. Even two seemingly similar neighboring states, such as New York and New Jersey, have major divergences in their policies on blight condemnations. New York courts allow virtually any property to be declared blighted,

has developed against pipeline takings. See Ilya Somin, "The growing battle over the use of eminent domain to take property for pipelines," *Washington Post*, June 7, 2016, available at www.washingtonpost.com/news/volokh-conspiracy/wp/2016/06/07/the-growing-battle-over-the-use-of-eminent-domain-to-take-property-for-pipelines/?utm_term=.ea1be69cc3c2.

124 *Texas Rice Land Partners, Ltd. v. Denbury-Green Pipeline*, 381 S.W.3d 465 (Tex. 2011).

125 Klass recognizes that interest group power may be an obstacle to effective reform in this area because "natural resource companies still wield significant political power in the region." Klass, "Frontier of eminent domain," p. 694.

126 The District of Columbia, which includes the capital city of Washington, is under the direct control of the federal government. But Congress has chosen to delegate much of its authority over the District – including the power of eminent domain – to an elected city government.

while New Jersey's standards are considerably more restrictive.[127] In the aftermath of the *Kelo* decision and the resulting political backlash, the extent of such divergence has become even greater. Some states have enacted very strong reform laws, while others have enacted extremely weak ones or none at all.[128] It is therefore often wrong to make strong generalizations about "American" eminent domain policy, as opposed to that of individual states, and sometimes even individual local governments.

Some judges and scholars view this diversity as a justification for avoiding federal judicial supervision of state condemnations. Given the enormous variations in culture, geography, and economic needs across such a large nation, it is possible that no one eminent domain policy is the right approach for the entire country.

The Supreme Court's majority opinion in *Kelo* uses diversity as a rationale for refusing to enforce anything more than the most minimal possible public use restrictions on takings. As Justice John Paul Stevens put it, "the needs of society have varied between different parts of the Nation," thereby justifying "a strong theme of federalism, emphasizing the 'great respect' that we owe to state legislatures and state courts in discerning local public needs."[129] Some academic defenders of *Kelo* and other highly deferential eminent domain decisions have adopted similar arguments.[130] Federal courts, they contend, simply lack the knowledge necessary to assess takings in far-flung jurisdictions with widely varying local conditions.

Such claims must be taken seriously. But there is also a sense in which America's diversity justifies stronger rather than weaker federal judicial enforcement of limits on eminent domain. Although conditions in the different states are indeed highly diverse, there is also great diversity within states, and even within localities – especially large cities such as New York, Los Angeles or Chicago that include tens of thousands of different properties.

127 See Ronald K. Chen, "*Gallenthin v. Kaur*: a comparative analysis of how the New Jersey and New York Courts approach judicial review of the exercise of eminent domain for redevelopment," 38 (2010) *Fordham Urban Law Journal* 987.

128 See Somin, *Grasping Hand*, ch. 5.

129 *Kelo*, 545 U.S. at 482 (quoting *Hairston v. Danville & Western Railway Co.*, 208 U.S. 598, 606–07 (1908)).

130 See, e.g Roderick Hills, Jr., "How federalism inevitably trumps taking doctrine – and a good thing too," (June 18, 2010), *Prawfsblawg*, available at http://prawfsblawg.blogs.com/prawfs blawg/2010/06/how-federalism-inevitably-trumps-takings-doctrine-1.html; Roderick Hills, Jr., "The individual right to federalism in the Rehnquist court," 74 (2006) *George Washington Law Review* 888, 891–92; Merrill, "The misplaced flight to substance."

If federal courts impose tighter restrictions on eminent domain, the ultimate decision about the use of particular properties will not be made by the judges themselves, but by private owners. Though state and local officials probably have greater knowledge about local conditions than federal judges do, it is likely that landowners usually have greater knowledge than either federal judges *or* state and local officials. They also often have stronger incentives to use that knowledge efficiently than government officials, since owners themselves usually bear the cost of mistakes they make. For this reason, America's diversity might potentially justify not weaker, but stronger federal court enforcement of limitations on takings.[131]

Moreover, if regional diversity justifies weakening federal enforcement of constitutional property rights, the same argument can just as easily justify abjuring federal court enforcement of many other constitutional rights, including freedom of speech and religion, and restrictions on the powers of law enforcement agencies.[132] As with property rights, the economic and social impact of these other rights also varies greatly by region. In some cases, it even varies enormously as between different neighborhoods in the same city.[133] If federal courts are nonetheless justified in aggressively enforcing these other constitutional rights, perhaps the same is true in the case of property rights threatened by eminent domain. As with other individual rights, allowing state and local governments to do as they please can – and often does – lead to the unjust victimization of poor and politically weak groups.

However we perceive the debate over federalism and takings, it is at least clear that federalism is a vital element of efforts to understand the use of eminent domain in the United States.

Conclusion

If there is one thing that can be said about eminent domain in the United States, it is that Americans themselves disagree widely over the issue. Fierce debates over the legality, justice, and economic necessity of various

131 For an elaboration of these points, see Ilya Somin, "Federalism and property rights," (2011) *University of Chicago Legal Forum* 53.

132 Ibid., 80–87.

133 This is true, for example, in the case of the Fourth Amendment's ban on "unreasonable" searches and seizures by the police. The optimal strategy for searching for criminals is likely to vary widely between different neighborhoods, perhaps even between different houses on the same street. See ibid., 80–81.

types of takings date back almost to the founding of the nation. These debates have extended to all six of the "pillars" considered in this volume, though they are most evident on the question of "public interest criteria," which American lawyers usually refer to as "public use."

In recent years, the American debate over eminent domain has been reinvigorated by the *Kelo* decision and the negative reaction it generated. In my view, many state and local governments have resorted to eminent domain far too often over the last 60 to 70 years, in the process violating our Constitution, destroying valuable economic resources, and victimizing the poor and politically weak.[134] But I readily acknowledge that many respected experts – both scholars and judges – hold the exact opposite view, believing that we may be imposing too many constraints on eminent domain rather than too few. This debate is unlikely to be definitively resolved any time soon.

Whether foreign observers can learn any lessons from the American experience with eminent domain is a complex issue. Obviously, just as there are wide variations between the different American states, there are also important differences between the United States and other nations which have experienced major debates over takings in recent years, such as China, India and Korea.

At the same time, there are also striking parallels between the American debate and those currently raging in at least some other countries.[135] As in the United States, Chinese, Indian, and other proponents of broad eminent domain authority argue that it is needed to promote economic development, alleviate social problems, and enable expert government planners to apply their specialized knowledge effectively. Like their American counterparts, critics of eminent domain in these nations argue that it destroys more economic value than it creates, and that it tends to victimize the poor and those lacking in political power – often for the benefit of influential interest groups.

When I first started writing about public use issues in the United States more than a decade ago, I did not expect that my work would be of interest to foreigners, except perhaps academic experts on American constitutional law and property law. But since that time, the American debate over *Kelo* has attracted widespread attention in other nations dealing with similar issues. A very small indication of that resonance is

[134] I defend this perspective in Somin, *Grasping Hand*, chs. 2–4, and 8.

[135] For a brief discussion of these parallels, see Somin, *Grasping Hand*, 244–45. See also the Introduction and Conclusion of the present volume.

that my work on the subject resulted in unexpected invitations to lecture on these issues in China, Korea, and elsewhere.

The US experience with eminent domain is a complex story that Americans themselves disagree about. Its possible relevance for debates in other countries is perhaps an even more complex question that observers in those nations must ultimately decide for themselves. But I would tentatively suggest that the modern history of eminent domain in America is a cautionary tale. Even a nation with a strong tradition of judicial review and respect for property rights for a long time managed to lose its way on these issues, allowing government officials to engage in takings that inflicted enormous economic and social harm.

3

Direct Expropriation: Multi-Layered Legal Protection in Europe

ANNE VAN AAKEN

I Introduction

Direct expropriation was a highly pressing issue in Europe after World War II when many Eastern European states nationalized large parts of their land and industries. It was not confined to the East – there were waves of expropriation of certain industries *inter alia* in the United Kingdom in the late 1940s and in France in 1982. Expropriation in single cases, e.g. for infrastructure projects, has always happened and continues to happen. Both types of direct expropriation were adjudicated in national as well as in international judicial fora. Currently, indirect or regulatory expropriations have gained higher prevalence and pose the much bigger legal problem.

First and foremost, national constitutions in European countries guarantee property rights and protect against direct expropriation without compensation. Of course, the wording and the level of protection may vary, depending on legal culture, history of the country and context of the constitution's drafting. But next to the national guarantee, there is a multi-layered system of protection. If the country is a member state of the Council of Europe (CoE), its residents will be protected by the European Convention on Human Rights (ECHR).[1] If the respective European country is a member state of the European Union (EU), property rights will also be protected by the EU. If a country is a member of both, property will be protected by both. Additionally, not specific to Europe, property rights of foreign investors are protected against direct expropriation without compensation by public international law, namely International Investment Agreements (IIAs) or Bilateral Investment

[1] European Convention for the Protection of Human Rights and Fundamental Freedoms, 213 UNTS 222, entered into force 3 September 1953.

Agreements (BITs). In Europe, the foreign investor can be a national of another European state or a national of a non-European state. Those different layers can at times represent conflicting and difficult questions of jurisdiction, applicable law and conflicts. Thus, I will describe the different layers of rights protection in Europe first (II), before turning to the more specific question of direct expropriation in the CoE and the EU (III). The last part concludes (IV).

II Multi-Layered Property Rights Protection in Europe

I will first deal with the ECHR (1), turn then to rights protection in the EU (2) and then discuss the international law level of IIAs (3). The multi-layered system of human rights protection in Europe poses difficult question of jurisdiction and applicable law (4).

1 European Convention on Human Rights

The ECHR is an international treaty to protect human rights and fundamental freedoms in Europe. It was drafted in 1950 by the then newly formed CoE, drawing on the inspiration of the Universal Declaration of Human Rights[2] and was a first attempt to bring together the war-torn European states by international law. The Convention entered into force on 3 September 1953. All 47 CoE member states are party to the Convention. With the exception of Belorussia, all European states are state parties of the CoE.

The ECHR established the European Court of Human Rights (ECtHR) in Strasbourg. Any person who feels his or her rights have been violated under the Convention by a state party can take a case to the court[3] but

[2] A right to property is recognized in Art. 17 of the Universal Declaration of Human Rights but is not recognized in the International Covenant on Civil and Political Rights or the International Covenant on Economic, Social and Cultural Rights.

[3] The system is overseen and enforced by the ECtHR and the CoE. The Committee of Ministers of the CoE monitors the execution of judgments, particularly to ensure payment of the amounts awarded by the Court to the applicants in compensation for the damage they have sustained. Until procedural reforms in the late 1990s, the Convention was also overseen by a European Commission on Human Rights. Applicants had to go through the Commission first. Since 1998 (Protocol 11), an applicant has direct access to the ECtHR, leading to a heavy backlog of cases. New reforms are trying to solve the problem. It should not be forgotten that the ECtHR acts as human rights reviewer of last resort for more than 820 million inhabitants. If a country does not have constitutional review, as e.g. Switzerland, it functionally works as a constitutional court too. In 2013, 65,900 applications were allocated to a judicial

needs to exhaust local remedies first. This requirement, a customary rule of international law,[4] makes the ECHR subsidiary to national systems safeguarding human rights. National courts initially have the opportunity to determine questions regarding the compatibility of domestic law with the ECHR.[5] The rationale for the exhaustion rule is to afford the national authorities, primarily the courts, the opportunity to prevent or put right the alleged violations of the Convention. It is based on the assumption, reflected in Art. 13 ECHR (right to an effective remedy), that the domestic legal order will provide an effective remedy for violations of Convention rights. If an application is nonetheless subsequently brought to Strasbourg, the ECtHR has the benefit of the views of the national courts, thus being in direct and continuous contact with the law and legal reasoning of the member states.[6] This system allows for an intermingling of legal systems and the adhesion of the Convention to the national legal orders. The ECtHR, via its scope of review and deference to national authorities (margin of appreciation), allows flexibility for states and respects the national diversity of the many CoE states. Thus, property rights protection is not uniform across the CoE. The ECHR sets a minimum level of property rights protection, thereby limiting the takings power of the member states. States are free to choose a higher protection standard.

Judgments finding violations are binding on the states concerned and they are obliged to execute them.[7] The ECHR is still the only international human rights agreement providing such a high degree of individual protection; all other regional systems have a two-tier system as the ECHR had before its reform in 1998. State parties can also take cases against other state parties to the court but this power is very rarely used.

formation, an overall increase of 2 per cent compared with 2012 (64,900); 45,750 of these were identified as single-judge cases likely to be declared inadmissible (a decrease of 7 per cent in relation to 2012); and 20,150 were identified as probable Chamber or Committee 1 cases (an increase of 27 per cent). See ECHR, Analysis of statistics 2013, at p. 4, available at: www.echr.coe.int/Documents/Stats_analysis_2013_ENG.pdf.

4 See Art. 35(I) ECHR and the International Court of Justice Case *Interhandel (Switzerland v. the United States)*, Judgment of 21 March 1959.

5 ECtHR Case *A, B and C v. Ireland* [GC], Application no. 25579/05, Judgment of 16 December 2010, para. 142.

6 ECtHR Case *Burden v. The United Kingdom* [GC], Application no. 13378/05, Judgment of 29 April 2008, para. 42.

7 They also mostly do so, especially the liberal democracies, see Andreas von Staden, *Shaping Human Rights Policy in Liberal Democracies: Assessing and Explaining Compliance with the Judgments of the European Court of Human Rights* (Princeton University/ProQuest, UMI Dissertations Publishing, 2009).

The ECHR has several protocols, which amend the framework and add new rights. As of January 2015, 16 protocols to the Convention have been opened for signature. These can be divided into two main groups: those amending the framework of the Convention system, and those expanding the rights that are protected.[8] The former require unanimous ratification by member states before coming into force, while the latter require a certain number of states to sign before coming into force. The right to property was only introduced in Protocol 1 in 1952.[9] This Protocol contains three different rights[10] on which the signatories could not agree to place in the Convention itself. Monaco and Switzerland have signed but never ratified Protocol 1.[11] All EU states have, but some have declared reservations.[12]

2 *Protection in the EU: Charter of Fundamental Rights and Common Traditions of EU Member States*

In the EU, fundamental rights are now guaranteed by multi-level protections.[13] We find these rights in the Charter of Fundamental Rights

8 The original ECHR sets forth a number of fundamental rights and freedoms (right to life, prohibition of torture, prohibition of slavery and forced labor, right to liberty and security, right to a fair trial, no punishment without law, right to respect for private and family life, freedom of thought, conscience and religion, freedom of expression, freedom of assembly and association, right to marry, right to an effective remedy, prohibition of discrimination). More rights are granted by additional protocols to the Convention (Protocols 1 (ETS No. 009), 4 (ETS No. 046), 6 (ETS No. 114), 7 (ETS No. 117), 12 (ETS No. 177) and 13 (ETS No. 187)).

9 Of 20 March 1952 (in force: 18 May 1954). It reads: "Article 1 – Protection of property: Every natural or legal person is entitled to the peaceful enjoyment of his possessions. *No one shall be deprived of his possessions except in the public interest and subject to the conditions provided for by law and by the general principles of international law.* The preceding provisions shall not, however, in any way impair the right of a State to enforce such laws as it deems necessary to control the use of property in accordance with the general interest or to secure the payment of taxes or other contributions or penalties." (my emphasis)

10 As well as the right to property, there are also the right to education and the right to free elections.

11 As of 6 February 2015: http://conventions.coe.int/Treaty/Commun/ChercheSig.asp?NT=009&CM=7&DF=06/02/2015&CL=ENG.

12 For a list, see http://conventions.coe.int/treaty/.

13 For a short description, see Giacomo Di Frederico, "Fundamental rights in the EU: legal pluralism and multi-level protection after the Lisbon Treaty," in Giacomo Di Frederico (ed.), *The EU Charter of Fundamental Rights. from Declaration to Binding Instrument* (Dordrecht et al.: Springer 2011), p. 15.

(CFR),[14] the ECHR and the general principles common to the constitutional traditions of the member states.[15] The CFR is a creature of the EU. The CFR enshrines certain political, social, and economic rights for EU citizens and residents into EU law. It was proclaimed on 7 December 2000 by the European Parliament, the Council of Ministers and the European Commission.[16] However, its then legal status was uncertain and it did not have full legal effect until the entry into force of the latest primary law changes in the EU with the Treaty of Lisbon on 1 December 2009.[17] Before that, residents of the EU were protected against infringements of property rights by the general principles common to the constitutional traditions of the member states as developed by the European Court of Justice (ECJ) and the ECHR but there was no written instrument for the EU specifically. The common traditions are important for the interpretation of the CFR pursuant to Art. 6(3) TEU and Art. 52(4) CFR which mandates that it shall be "interpreted in harmony with those traditions." They can surpass the scope of protection of the ECHR, thereby taking into account the higher level of integration and uniformity between EU member states[18] in comparison with the 47 CoE states.

Due to the different ages of the ECHR and the CFR, the jurisprudence of the ECtHR is much more elaborated on property rights than the

[14] Due to the status of the CFR as primary EU law in Art. 6 para 1 Treaty of the European Union (TEU).

[15] As Art. 6 para 3 TEU states: "Fundamental rights, as guaranteed by the European Convention for the Protection of Human Rights and Fundamental Freedoms and as they result from the constitutional traditions common to the Member States, shall constitute general principles of the Union's law." Before that: Case 11/70 *Internationale Handelsgesellschaft mbH v. Einfuhr- und Vorratsstelle für Getreide und Futtermittel* [1970] ECR 1125 and Case 4/73 J. *Nold, Kohlen- und Baustoffgroßhandlung of the European Communities* [1974] ECR 491.

[16] Before that the Parliament, the Council and the Commission of the European Communities have stressed in a joint declaration of 5 April 1977 that they attach prime importance to the protection of fundamental rights, as derived in particular from the Constitution of the member states and the ECHR. They pledged that, in the exercise of their powers and in pursuance of the aims of the European Communities, they would respect and continue to respect these human rights (Official Journal of the European Communities, XX, 1977, Information and Notices, No. C 103/I). The ECJ has followed this line.

[17] Treaty on European Union (TEU) and the Treaty on the Functioning of the European Union (TFEU) [2010] OJ C83/1 (consolidated version). On the history and details of drafting, see www.europarl.europa.eu/charter/default_en.htm.

[18] Dagmar Richter, 'Lücken der EMRK und lückenloser Grunsrechtsschutz,' in Oliver Dörr, Rainer Grote and Thilo Marhauhn (eds.), *EMRK/GG, Konkordanzkommentar* Vol. I (Tübingen: Mohr/Siebeck, 2013), para. 20.

jurisprudence of the ECJ and more authoritative for the interpretation of the CFR. The ECHR, as a Convention ratified by all EU members and protecting human rights long before the European Communities (later the EU) did, nevertheless inform the interpretation of the CFR to a great extent.[19]

Under the CFR, the EU must act and legislate consistently with the CFR; the EU courts strike down any legislation adopted by the EU institutions that contravenes it. The CFR binds the institutions of the EU and its member states when implementing EU law. Purely national measures are adjudicated in national courts and then the ECtHR.

3 *International Investment Treaties*

International investment treaties are public international law treaties between states. They can be bilateral or multilateral,[20] standing alone or being part of a more encompassing trade treaty.[21] They protect foreign investors against several types of state measures, *inter alia* direct and indirect expropriation[22] and lack of due process via the "fair and equitable" treatment provision. Although the texts (and the interpretation) of the treaties differ, they have a considerable level of conformity. And nowadays, full, effective and prompt compensation in a convertible currency is state of the art of IIAs.[23] Due process in expropriation cases is

[19] Art. 52(3) CFR. See also Dirk Ehlers, "§14 General Principles," in Dirk Ehlers (eds.), *European Fundamental Rights and Freedoms* (Berlin: De Gruyter, 2007), p. 371, para. 13.

[20] For Europe, the Energy Charter Treaty (ECT; signed in December 1994 and in force since April 1998) is very important. It comprises many CoE countries and also the EU. The ECT establishes a multilateral legal framework for cross-border energy cooperation. This treaty contains an investment chapter and has seen plenty of cases in the energy sector, often with high stakes such as the recent *Yukos* case with a damage award of US$50 billion (*Yukos Universal Limited (Isle of Man) v. The Russian Federation* (PCA Case No. AA 227), 2014.

[21] For a history on those, see Kenneth J. Vandevelde, 'A brief history of international investment agreements,' 12 (2005) *U.C. Davis Journal of International Law and Policy* 157; on the content, see Rudolf Dolzer and Christoph Schreuer, *Principles of International Investment Law*, 2nd edn. (Oxford University Press, 2012) and Peter Muchlinski, Federico Ortino and Christoph Schreuer (eds.), *The Oxford Handbook of International Investment Law* (Oxford University Press, 2008).

[22] August Reinisch, "Expropriation," in Peter Muchlinski, Federico Ortino and Christoph Schreuer (eds.), *The Oxford Handbook of International Investment Law* (Oxford University Press, 2008), p. 407.

[23] The Western position has mostly been that there is an international law obligation of full compensation; that is expressed in terms such as "prompt, adequate and effective" (the Hull formula), as "market" or "genuine value". For details, see Thomas Wälde and

also guaranteed. If a state violates those provisions, sometimes high damage payments are the result.

EU countries have a whole range of BITs, either within themselves (as legacies of treaty-making with formerly non-EU-countries which then acceded to the EU, so-called intra-EU BITs[24]), or with third countries (so called extra-EU BITs). Both are still valid although, after the entry into force of the Treaty of Lisbon in 2009, the EU now has the exclusive external competence for the conclusion of investment treaties concerning foreign direct investment.[25] The important point here is that some foreign investors in the EU have the additional protection of a BIT which might grant them stronger rights against expropriation than the ECHR. This implies that, within the EU, there can be differential treatment for expropriation between foreign investors protected by a BIT on the one hand and nationals of that expropriating host state or investors of countries which have no BITs with the host state on the other hand. Although this is much debated, there are several arguments of why investment protection is stronger from a property rights perspective than national law or the ECHR. First, there is usually no exhaustion of local remedies rules in IIAs which means that there is no need for a foreign investor to go to national courts before going to international arbitration.[26] Second, international arbitral awards are executed in all member states of either the ICSID Convention[27] or the New York

Borzu Sabahi, "Compensation, damages and valuation in international investment law," in Peter Muchlinski, Federico Ortino and Christoph Schreuer (eds.), *The Oxford Handbook of International Investment Law* (Oxford University Press, 2008), p. 1049. See for a discussion of the "Hull doctrine", now codified, Hans-Bernd Schäfer, chapter 1, this volume.

24 Although the European Commission has long pledged countries that it will terminate intra-EU BITs, arguing that there is no need for international protection outside of the EU system and assuming that all EU countries are rule of law states which handle expropriation appropriately, states still keep their approximately 190 intra-EU BITs. For the position of the European Commission, see *Eastern Sugar v. Czech Republic* arbitration, SCC Case No. 088/2004 (Partial Award, 27 March 2007), para. 115 *et seq.*

25 Since portfolio investments are usually also covered by IIAs, but arguable not by Art. 207 TFEU, the EU is currently negotiating its treaties as mixed agreements. See for a prospectus of how the EU will likely design its IIAs: August Reinisch, 'Putting the pieces together . . . an EU model bit?,' 15 (2014) *Journal of World Investment and Trade* 679.

26 For a debate on remedies and a comparison with national laws, see Anne van Aaken, "Primary and secondary remedies in international investment law and national state liability: a functional and comparative view," in Stephan Schill (ed.), *International Investment Law and Comparative Public Law* (Oxford University Press, 2010), p. 721.

27 Convention on the Settlement of Investment Disputes between States and Nationals of Other States (Washington Convention), 575 UNTS 159; 4 ILM 524 (1965). It has 150 member states. All ICSID contracting member states, whether or not they are parties to

Convention[28] and mostly complied with. Third, investment tribunals are said not to be home-biased. Fourth, they follow the stricter rules of the IIAs on direct expropriation and, in particular, effective and prompt compensation (not necessarily the case under the ECHR). Fifth, there is no room for balancing in the view of investment tribunals in cases of direct expropriation (in contrast to the ECtHR).

Although the effects of interaction and the possible better treatment of foreign investors cover a broad field and are currently hotly debated in the context of the Transatlantic Trade and Investment Partnership (TTIP) between the EU and the United States, for reasons of place restraint, this short description must suffice.

4 *Multi-Layered Protections*

As can be seen from the above, the protection against expropriation is multi-layered and multifaceted in Europe. Indeed, it is foremost the nation-state which is responsible for expropriatory measures, especially eminent domain. But depending on who is expropriated, there might already be a differentiation in the venue for redress and the applicable law.

If there is an IIA between the host country and the home country of the expropriated person (or firm), that person may immediately seek redress in international arbitration under the respective IIA. This supposedly puts them at an advantage with nationals. Still unsolved is the relationship between future EU investment treaties, like the Comprehensive Economic and Trade Agreement (CETA: Canada–EU) and the TTIP as well as EU law and EU courts; different political and academic opinions abound.[29]

Nationals of the CoE but not of the EU, e.g. Turkey or Russia, may, after they have exhausted local remedies, seek redress in Strasbourg. They thus have an additional layer of control of deprivation of property (with the exception of Switzerland and Monaco which have not ratified

a given dispute, are required by the ICSID Convention to recognize and enforce ICSID arbitral awards.

[28] Convention on the Recognition and Enforcement of Foreign Arbitral Awards (New York Convention), 330 UNTS 38 (1968). It has 149 member states. It is not as self-contained as the ICSID Convention; national courts may review the arbitral award in narrow circumstances.

[29] Further discussion and references can be found here: http://epthinktank.eu/2015/02/10/ttip-isds/.

Protocol 1 and are not EU member states; their nationals are thus confined to national review of property rights violations only).

EU nationals can do the same, i.e. complain to the ECHR, but with delimitations: only if the measure in question was a genuine national measure can redress be sought in Strasbourg. If the measure is solely based on EU law, the nation-state is not held liable[30] – and nor is the EU because it is not a member of the ECHR. This has led to criticism of gaps in human rights protection within the EU:[31] if the national measure is wholly or partially based on an EU measure (the EU, with few exceptions, relies on national administrations to execute its laws) or just executing an EU measure without discretion, it is more difficult for it to be challenged in Strasbourg. Thus, depending on who is the originator of the potential violation, different jurisdictional venues and different legal standard are applied and purely EU measures are not subject to the control of the ECtHR but only the ECJ.[32]

Since 1990, the ECtHR (in that case the former European Commission of Human Rights) has though indirectly reviewed EU acts.[33] Although "it is in fact not competent ratione personae to examine proceedings before or decisions of organs of the European Communities, the latter not being a Party to the European Convention on Human Rights", it held that "the transfer of powers does not necessarily exclude a State's responsibility under the Convention with regard to the exercise of transferred powers."[34] EU member states as parties to the ECHR could, under this reasoning, not escape their obligations under the ECHR by setting up supranational bodies and ceding their powers to an international organization, like the EU. But with the *Bosphorus* judgment of 2005,[35] the ECtHR confirmed its former case law that it has no competence to review Community acts as such although it recognized a competence to review these acts indirectly through examining specific implementation measures at national level. Both, primary and secondary EU law can now be subject to (indirect) review by the ECtHR and EU member states

[30] See *Bosphorus Hava Yolllars Turizm ve Ticaret Anonim Sirketi v. Ireland* 2005-VI; 42 EHRR 1 GC, paras 155 *et seq.*, privileging the EU legal order.

[31] For a discussion, see Tobias Lock, "EU accession to the ECHR: implications for the judicial review in Strasbourg," 35 (2010) *European Law Review* 777.

[32] For details of the problems and the interaction of EU law and ECHR, see Kathrin Kuhnert, "*Bosphorus* – Double standards in European human rights protection?," 2 (2006) *Utrecht Law Review* 177.

[33] The landmark case on the ECtHR's competence to judicially review EC law is considered to be the *M. & Co. v. Germany* [1990] ECHR (Ser. A), p. 138.

[34] Ibid., p. 145. [35] Supra note 30.

can be held responsible for (nearly) all EU acts with the exception of EU acts which do not require any implementation by the member states i.e. whose effect is purely internal to the EU.[36] This gap is thus solely filled by the CFR adjudicated by the EU courts. EU acts and national measures within the EU sphere, scope, field or area may be subject to review by the ECJ, which has always used the ECHR as a yardstick, even before the explicit reference to it in the CFR.[37] The same applies to national measures implementing EU acts.[38] In short: purely EU measures or measures executed without discretion by EU states are not subject to review by the ECtHR, implementing measures by EU states are subject to review of the ECtHR, thereby subjecting EU measures indirectly to review by the Strasbourg court.

Due to the above-mentioned gap, the accession of the EU (previously the European Communities) has been discussed for over 30 years[39] but was not effectuated due to the missing competence of the EU.[40] With the entry into force of the Lisbon Treaty and Protocol 14 to the ECHR,[41] these main obstacles to accession were supposedly removed. Article 6(2) TEU not only gives the EU the competence to conclude an accession treaty, but also puts it under an obligation to effectuate it ("Union shall accede"). Nevertheless, all is open again. The ECJ rendered an opinion on 18 December 2014 pursuant to Art. 218(11) of TFEU, following a request from the European Commission. The purpose of the request was to determine whether the draft agreement[42] providing for the accession of the EU to the ECHR is compatible with the EU treaties. Whereas the view delivered by Advocate General Kokott on 13 June 2014 was

[36] For details of the development of the case law, see Kuhnert, supra note 32, and for the conflicts arising, see Lock, supra note 31.

[37] Case C-260/89, *ERT* [1991] ECR I-2925; Case C-159/90, *SPUC v. Grogan* [1991] ECR I-4685; Joined Cases C-46/87 and C-227/88, *Hoechst AG v. Commission* [1989] ECR 2859.

[38] Case 5/88, *Wachauf* [1989] ECR 2609.

[39] European Commission, Memorandum on the Accession of the European Communities to the European Convention for the Protection of Human Rights and Fundamental Freedoms, *Bulletin of the European Communities*, Supplement 2/79.

[40] Accession of the Community to the European Human Rights Convention, Re (Opinion 2/94) ECR [1996] I-1759; [1996] 2 CMLR. 265.

[41] That Protocol introduced a new Art. 59(2) ECHR, which reads: "The European Union may accede to this Convention."

[42] Fifth Negotiation Meeting between the CDDH ad hoc Negotiation Group and the European Commission on the Accession of the European Union to the European Convention on Human Rights. Final report to the CDDH, 47+1(2013)008rev2, available at: www.coe.int/t/dghl/standardsetting/hrpolicy/Accession/Meeting_reports/47_1(2013)008rev2_EN.pdf.

positive,[43] the ECJ delivered an opinion which rocked Europe because the court concluded that the agreement is not compatible with Art. 6(2) TEU, according to which the EU shall accede to the ECHR, but the accession "shall not affect the Union's competences as defined in the Treaties," or with Protocol 8 to the TEU and the TFEU.[44] Thus, for the foreseeable future, if an expropriatory act is an act of the EU or is solely based on and executing an EU act, the ECJ will be the correct and only court to address this issue, and apply the common traditions of the member states as well as the CFR in the light of the interpretation of the ECtHR. The ECtHR will not be able to review the act.

III Direct Expropriation in Europe

The ECHR remains the most important instrument for judging expropriation beyond the nation-state in Europe. It not only informs the limits of property rights violations and the minimum standard within the member states of the CoE, it also is highly informative for the interpretation of the CFR in the EU. I will therefore deal extensively with the ECHR (1) and describe the jurisprudence of the ECJ only insofar as it differs (2)

1 Direct Expropriation under the ECHR

As mentioned before, it was difficult to reach an agreement on the protection of property rights within the ECHR as such, but finding an acceptable formulation for Protocol 1 also demonstrated considerable differences between states.[45] Eventually, the right was qualified, allowing states a wide power to interfere with property rights. The drafting history is still frequently referenced by the ECtHR, confirming the wide latitude of interference with property rights that states have.[46]

[43] Available at: http://curia.europa.eu/juris/document/document.jsf?docid=160929&mode=lst&pageIndex=1&dir=&occ=first&part=1&text=&doclang=EN&cid=199782.

[44] ECJ Opinion 2/13 of 18 December 2014, available at: http://curia.europa.eu/juris/document/document.jsf?docid=160882&mode=lst&pageIndex=1&dir=&occ=first&part=1&text=&doclang=EN&cid=199782.

[45] David Harris, Michael O'Boyle, Edward Bates and Carla Buckley, *Law of the European Convention on Human Rights*, 3rd edn (Oxford University Press, 2014), p. 862. This concerned especially the possibility of nationalizations for political and social purposes, as proposed by Sweden and the United Kingdom at that time.

[46] On the drafting history and preparatory work, see 3 TP 92–96, 106–08 (Consultative Assembly) and 134–36 (Secretary General's memorandum).

Jurisprudence has identified three kinds of interference with property rights.[47] It is, first, the right to "peaceful enjoyment" of possessions, that is, the right to use, repair, dispose of, pledge, lend or destroy one's possessions. This enjoyment is basically protected against interference by the state. Second, property rights are protected against deprivation (direct expropriation, eminent domain). Third, the state can control the use of property (possibly indirect expropriation). The distinction between control of use and deprivation *in praxis* is not always watertight[48] and the court follows the same scheme of judging violations.[49] It reserves its right to "look behind the appearances and investigate the realities of the situation complained of …."[50] Since the Convention is intended to guarantee rights that are "practical and effective," the court may always ascertain whether a certain measure amounts to a *de facto* expropriation,[51] possibly requiring compensation.

In particular, it determines whether a fair balance has been struck between the demands of the general interest of the community and the requirements of the protection of the individual's fundamental rights. The search for this balance is, according to the court, inherent in the whole Convention and is also reflected in the structure of Art. 1.[52] For direct expropriation, it may influence the level of compensation.

[47] *Sporrong and Lännroth v. Sweden*, A 52 (1982); 5 EHRR 35 para. 61 PC: "Article (P1-1) comprises three distinct rules. The first rule, which is of a general nature, enounces the principle of peaceful enjoyment of property; it is set out in the first sentence of the first paragraph. The second rule covers deprivation of possessions and subjects it to certain conditions; it appears in the second sentence of the same paragraph. The third rule recognises that the States are entitled, amongst other things, to control the use of property in accordance with the general interest, by enforcing such laws as they deem necessary for the purpose; it is contained in the second paragraph."

[48] For a discussion, see Harris, O'Boyle, Bates and Buckley, supra note 45, p. 876.

[49] On the relationship between those protections, see *James and Others v. UK* A98 (1986); 8 EHRR 123 para 37 PC. "The Court further observed that, before inquiring whether the first general rule has been complied with, it must determine whether the last two are applicable … The three rules are not, however, 'distinct' in the sense of being unconnected. The second and third rules are concerned with particular instances of interference with the right to peaceful enjoyment of property and should therefore be construed in the light of the general principle enunciated in the first rule."

[50] *Sporrong and Lännroth*, supra note 47, para. 63.

[51] For *de facto* expropriation cases, see *Papamichalopoulos v. Greece*, A260-B (1993) and *Köktepe v. Turkey* hudoc (2008), para. 84 *et seq.* For a discussion, see Harris, O'Boyle, Bates and Buckley, supra note 45, p. 886 *et seq.* and Christoph Grabenwarter, *European Convention on Human Rights. Commentary* (München: C.H. Beck, 2014), p. 372.

[52] See *Sporrong and Lännroth*, supra note 47, para. 69.

Direct expropriation is seen as the transfer of the formal title linked with the loss of property for the benefit of the state or in the public interest. Direct expropriation means that there was a deprivation of property, i.e. the applicant must show (in principle) that he or she had a title to it. Deprivation of property is defined as the taking of all the legal rights of the owner via extinguishing the rights by operation of law[53] or by the exercise of legal power to the same effect.[54]

In the following, the several pillars of direct expropriation will be described as they are adjudicated under the ECHR. Not all questions raised in the pillars elaborated by the Korea Development Institute are of relevance under the jurisprudence of the ECtHR. The problem of who are subjects who can exercise the power of eminent domain has, to my knowledge, not been explicitly dealt with and surely not problematized by the ECtHR, as long as the taking was based on laws, administrative acts or civil law contracts if it was based on acts attributable to the state (usually via a law).[55] Thus, at this stage, it is unclear whether the same very extensive scope as in Korea, ranging from the central government and state-owned enterprises to local governments and their numerous enterprises, and to private entities such as construction companies and development firms, would be accepted by the ECtHR or whether it would demand the stricter German approach.[56] But given the wide margin of appreciation and whether this kind of delegation is itself based on law, as well as due process being guaranteed, I would argue that the ECtHR would permit a similarly wide scope of subjects.

a Scope of Protection

The scope of protection of the property right protection under the ECHR is broad.[57] In spite of the wording "possession," there is broad consensus that a wide range of proprietorial interests are covered, confirmed by the French word "*biens*."[58] The essential characteristic of a possession is the

53 E.g. *Pressos Compania Naviera A and Others v. Belgium* A 332 (1995); 21 EHRR 301 and *Althoff and Others v. Germany* hudoc (2011).

54 Harris, O'Boyle, Bates and Buckley, supra note 45, p. 886 with further references.

55 Grabenwarter, supra note 51, p. 371, although the latter is academic opinion and not case law.

56 See for details, Schäfer, supra note 23.

57 For an overview, see Grabenwarter, supra note 51, pp. 367–70.

58 In *Marckx v. Belgium* (App. No. 6833/74) of 13 June 1979, the court described as follows the object of this Article (P1-1): "By recognising that everyone has the right to the peaceful enjoyment of his possessions, Article 1 (P1-1) is in substance guaranteeing the right of property. This is the clear impression left by the words 'possessions' and 'use of property'

acquired economic value of the individual interest, including intellectual property rights, permission to build on land, even tolerating illegal dwellings.[59] It also comprises legitimate expectations, that is, possession "in the meaning of Art. 1 Protocol 1 can either be existing possessions or assets in including claims, in respect of which an applicant can argue that he has a least a legitimate expectation that they will be realized."[60] Whether the expectations are legitimate is determined by the respective national laws.[61] Nevertheless, the definition of possessions is autonomous to the Convention,[62] thus the mere fact that a national law does not recognize a possession as a property right cannot exclusively determine the scope of protection. Rather, as the court has held in *Anheuser Busch Inc v. Portugal*, it would examine "whether the circumstances of the case, considered as a whole, conferred on the applicant title to a substantive interest protected by Art. 1."[63] After 1990, the court had to deal with many cases where restitution was asked for by former owners of land which were expropriated under communist rule after 1945. The court held that property rights constituting possessions may cease to be protected rights if they have "long been impossible to exercise effectively."[64] It thereby saved many Eastern European countries from economy-distorting re-ordering of property rights, 45 years after land reforms.

b Public Interest Criteria

Art. 1 contains two different wordings, namely "public interest" in sentence 1 and "general interest" in sentence 2. Is this of further significance when interpreting the public interest requirement of Art. 1 sentence 1 dealing with direct expropriation? The court held this is not the case.[65]

(in French: 'biens,' 'propriété,' 'usage des biens'); the 'travaux préparatoires,' for their part, confirm this unequivocally: the drafters continually spoke of 'right of property' or 'right to property' to describe the subject-matter of the successive drafts which were the forerunners of the present Article 1 (P1-1)." (Series A no. 31, p. 27, para. 63)

59 ECtHR *Oneryildiz v. Turkey*, 2004-XII; 41 EHRR 325 GC.

60 ECtHR *Gratzinger and Gratzinger v. Czech Republic*, App. No. 39794/2002-VII; EHRR CD 202, para. 69, GC.

61 Harris, O'Boyle, Bates and Buckley, supra note 45, p. 864 with further references.

62 E.g. ECtHR *Gasus Dosier und Fördertechnik GmbH v. Netherlands* A 306 B (1995); 20 EHRR 403; *Broniowski v. Poland* 2004-V; 40 EHRR 495 GC.

63 2007-I; 45 EHRR 830, para. 75 GC.

64 See *von Maltzan and Others v. Germany* 2005-V; 42 EHRR SE 93, para. 74 GC.

65 *James and Others*, supra note 49, para. 43. For a discussion and further references, see Harris, O'Boyle, Bates and Buckley, supra note 45, p. 876 *et seq.*

The leading case on the interpretation of the "public interest" is *James and Others v. UK*.[66] The claimants, trustees acting under the will of the Second Duke of Westminster, challenged the 1967 Leasehold Reform Act, saying that it deprived them of their property rights when long-time lessees were given the power to purchase the freehold reversion (the Duke of Westminster owned large parts of Belgravia in London). The applicants first contended that the "public interest" test in the deprivation rule "is satisfied only if the property is taken for a public purpose of benefit to the community generally and that, as a corollary, the transfer of property from one person to another for the latter's private benefit alone can never be 'in the public interest'" whereas the government of the United Kingdom held that "a compulsory transfer of property from one individual to another may in principle be considered to be 'in the public interest' if the taking is effected in pursuance of legitimate social policies."[67] The court agreed that "a deprivation of property effected for no reason other than to confer a private benefit on a private party cannot be 'in the public interest.'" Nonetheless, it held that "the compulsory transfer of property from one individual to another may, depending upon the circumstances, constitute a legitimate means for promoting the public interest. In this connection, even where the texts in force employ expressions like 'for the public use,' no common principle can be identified in the constitutions, legislation and case-law of the Contracting States that would warrant understanding the notion of public interest as outlawing compulsory transfer between private parties."[68] The court further elaborated on the public interest criterion by stating that it could be read "into the English expression 'in the public interest' that the transferred property should be put into use for the general public or that the community generally, or even a substantial proportion of it, should directly benefit from the taking."[69] But this was deemed too narrow a reading since the "taking of property in pursuance of a policy calculated to enhance social justice within the community can properly be described as being "in the public interest". In particular, the fairness of a system of law governing the contractual or property rights of private parties is a matter of public concern and therefore legislative measures intended to bring about such fairness are capable of being "in the public interest," even if they

[66] See also, following, *The Holy Monasteries v. Greece*, A 301-A (1994); 20 EHRR 1, paras. 67–69.

[67] *James and Others*, supra note 49, para. 39. [68] Ibid., para. 40. [69] Ibid., para. 41.

involve the compulsory transfer of property from one individual to another."[70]

As with the definition of "possessions," the court gives an autonomous meaning to the public interest (or 'utilité publique').[71] In order to explore this, the court relies not only on the language versions but also on the object and purpose of Art. 1 "which is primarily to guard against the arbitrary confiscation of property."[72] Thus, a "taking of property effected in pursuance of legitimate social, economic or other policies may be 'in the public interest,' even if the community at large has no direct use or enjoyment of the property taken."[73] It is confirmed by the Court that measures designed to ensure equitable distribution of economic advantages, for example by way of taxation, are licensed by Art. 1.[74]

This kind of interpretation already gives much leeway to states. And this is enhanced by the margin of appreciation which the Court grants under all rights. As it held: "because of their direct knowledge of their society and its needs, the national authorities are in principle better placed than the international judge to appreciate what is 'in the public interest'. Under the system of protection established by the Convention, it is thus for the national authorities to make the initial assessment both of the existence of a problem of public concern warranting measures of deprivation of property and of the remedial action to be taken."[75] Furthermore, the Court considered that a decision to enact laws expropriating property will commonly involve consideration of political, economic and social issues on which opinions within a democratic society may reasonably differ widely: so unless that judgment be manifestly without reasonable foundation, the Court would accept the interpretation of public interest and will not substitute its own assessment for that of the national authorities.[76]

In sum: it is clear that under the ECHR, public interest has to be understood broadly and can include development, economic and social goals. Only manifestly arbitrary goals or the absence of a legitimate aim

[70] Ibid.

[71] Ibid., para. 42: In "the domestic law of some, but not all, of the Contracting States . . . the expression or its equivalent (public interest) is found in the context of expropriation of property. That, however, is not decisive, as many Convention concepts have been recognised in the Court's case-law as having an 'autonomous' meaning. Moreover, the words 'utilité publique' are also capable of bearing a wider meaning, covering expropriation measures taken in implementation of policies calculated to enhance social justice."

[72] Ibid., para. 42. [73] Ibid., para. 45. [74] Ibid., para. 44. [75] Ibid., para. 46. [76] Ibid.

would not pass the court's scrutiny.[77] The burden rests with the applicant to show that the state's judgment is "manifestly without reasonable foundation."[78] A measure taken to comply with EU law is deemed to pursue a legitimate aim.[79]

There is no further elaboration on the notion of "public interest," e.g. there is nothing said about requirements of allocative efficiency of the expropriation or the publicness of it apart from the very broad limits stated above. Nor does the ECtHR explicitly require that all three branches of government review the public interest criterion. But, since the expropriation has to be based on law and the exhaustion of local remedies is required under the ECHR, usually all three branches of government are involved before a case is adjudicated in Strasbourg. Some countries may follow stricter rules for the public interest criterion: as mentioned before, the ECHR only sets a minimum standard.

c Just Compensation

The reference in Art. 1 sentence 2 that deprivation of property is "subject to the conditions provided for by law and by the general principles of international law" created confusion on the issue of what the role of the general principles of international law would mean in this context. In principle, international law is applicable only between states or between states and aliens, but not for the relationship between a state and its own citizens. The general principles of international law protect alien property against arbitrary expropriation without compensation as the so-called minimum standard of treatment of aliens, being part of customary international law and having special relevance at the time of the drafting of Protocol 1 due to expropriation and nationalization waves in times of decolonialization.[80] Two divergent standards of alien

77 Harris, O'Boyle, Bates and Buckley, supra note 45, p. 876.

78 *Broniowski*, supra note 62, para. 149. But the standard of proof is low, see, e.g. *Ambruosi v. Italy* hudoc (2000); 35 EHRR 125, para. 28.

79 *SA Dangeville v. France* 2002-III; 38 EHRR 699 and *Bosphorus*, supra note 30.

80 For details, see Hollin Dickerson, "Minimum standards," in Rüdiger Wolfrum (ed.), *Max Planck Encyclopedia of Public International Law* (Oxford University Press, online edn., www.mpepil.com, 2010), para. 14 *et seq.* International law protects, next to other rights, the rights of aliens who enjoy property ownership in foreign states. Within the context of expropriation, the minimum standard is believed to include one or more of the following three requirements: (a) the expropriation must be made for a public purpose; (b) it must not discriminate against foreigners; and (c) it must be accompanied by compensation. The United Nations General Assembly's Resolution on Permanent Sovereignty over Natural Resources (UNGA UN Doc. A/RES/1803(XVII), GAOR 17th Session Supp. 17, 15) requires all three of the above factors to be present for an expropriation to be lawful.

treatment developed during the nineteenth and early twentieth centuries. Latin American states supported the Calvo doctrine,[81] also known as the national treatment standard, which treated foreign investors the same as nationals. Under this doctrine, if a national received no compensation for an expropriation, then neither would an alien or foreign investor. This was discarded, *inter alia*, via the above-described treaty practice of IIAs containing absolute standards of treatment concerning fair and equitable treatment and expropriation, including full compensation in most of them.[82] However, both compensation standards and methods of evaluation are still very much disputed; the latter also in international law.

The wording of Art. 1 sentence 2 leaves two options of interpretation.[83] The first is that the reference benefits only alien property holders, since they are the beneficiaries under international law (albeit indirectly via diplomatic protection).[84] The effect is to give aliens the possibility of bringing a case without the diplomatic protection of their governments to the ECtHR and receive international law treatment (instead of the potentially lower standard of the ECHR on compensation). Alternatively, the ECHR incorporates international law standards for the benefit of all persons covered by the Convention, i.e. including the state's own nationals. Compensation would then be payable according to the standards of international law to everybody. In *James and Others v. UK*,[85] the court decided for the former option. This leaves more leeway to states on how to compensate their own nationals and also allows for a variety of practices within the CoE states, including different historical and political circumstances.

Nevertheless, the ECHR does not leave nationals bereft of protection and compensation. As has been said, the court always stresses the need for a "fair balance" between the public and the private interest and the amount of compensation is one important factor in that balance: this also

[81] Patrick Juillard, "Calvo doctrine/Calvo clause," in Rüdiger Wolfrum (ed.), *Max Planck Encyclopedia of Public International Law* (Oxford University Press, 2007).

[82] Cf. supra note 23.

[83] See also J. G. Merrills and Arthur H. Roberston, *Human Rights in Europe. A Study of the European Convention on Human Rights*, 4th edn (Manchester University Press, 2001), p. 237.

[84] See *Case Concerning Elettronica Sicula S.p.A.* (ELSI) (*United States of America v. Italy*) [1989] ICJ Rep 15.

[85] *James and Others*, supra note 49, paras. 58–66, and *Lithgow and Others v. UK* 102 (1986); 8 EHRR 239, paras. 111–19; relying on the wording and *the travaux préparatoires* of Art. 1. *Lithgow and Others* is a case on nationalization of the ship-building industry in the United Kingdom and is a leading case on evaluation methods.

implies that, in all but exceptional cases, some compensation is due;[86] an entitlement to compensation is thus in principle necessary.[87] If a state has no right to any compensation in national law, it will likely be in violation of the ECHR.[88] The same holds true if compensation is not paid in a reasonable amount of time.[89] Thus, also under the ECHR, compensation needs to be prompt, a period of five years is clearly in breach; even more so in states with high inflation rates.[90]

Different from the international law rule on full compensation, under the ECHR, the level of compensation must be "reasonably related" to the "value" of property taken.[91] This has several implications. The Court has stated that the standard of compensation may vary depending on the nature of the property and the circumstances of the taking. In cases of large economic or political transitions, different standards and less than full compensation may be accepted.[92] The standard of compensation required in a nationalization case may be different from that required in regard to other takings of property, e.g. the compulsory acquisition of land for public purposes in individual instances.[93] Although there is no

86 *Lithgow and Others*, supra note 85, para. 120: "[T]he Court observes that under the legal systems of the Contracting States, the taking of property in the public interest without payment of compensation is treated as justifiable only in exceptional circumstances ... As far as Article 1 (P1-1) is concerned, the protection of the right of property it affords would be largely illusory and ineffective in the absence of any equivalent principle." *James and Others*, supra note 49, para. 54: "Clearly, compensation terms are material to the assessment whether the contested legislation respects a fair balance between the various interests at stake and, notably, whether it does not impose a disproportionate burden on the applicant ... "

87 Cf. *The Holy Monasteries*, supra note 66, where the court then approved a friendly settlement.

88 *Papastravrou and Others v. Greece*, 2003-IV; 40 EHRR 361.

89 *Guillemin v. France* 1997-I; 25 EHRR 435 and *Jucys v Lithuania* hudoc (2008).

90 Grabenwarter, supra note 51, p. 380 with further references.

91 Instead of many, see *Draon v. France* hudoc (2005); 42 EHRR 807 GC.

92 E.g. *The Former King of Greece and Others v. Greece* hudoc (2002); 36 EHRR CD 43, para. 78 GC (just satisfaction).

93 *Lithgow and Others*, supra note 85, para. 121: "the taking of property without payment of an amount reasonably related to its value would normally constitute a disproportionate interference which could not be considered justifiable under Article 1 (P1-1). Article 1 (P1-1) does not, however, guarantee a right to full compensation in all circumstances, since legitimate objectives of 'public interest,' such as pursued in measures of economic reform or measures designed to achieve greater social justice, may call for less than reimbursement of the full market value .... Both the nature of the property taken and the circumstances of the taking in these two categories of cases give rise to different considerations which may legitimately be taken into account in determining a fair balance between the public interest and the private interests concerned. The valuation of major industrial enterprises for the purpose of nationalising

clear percentage of market value to be compensated, in compensation cases for land property lost following the redrawing of boundaries after World War II, the Polish promise of compensation of 15 per cent of market value was deemed insufficient[94] and compensation at around 40 per cent of market value was also deemed a violation.[95] Furthermore, it was held to be a violation of the Convention if the compensation for a company's nationalization was less than its cash holdings.[96] There have been other cases where the Court has had no qualms about awarding rather high damages when it has found that a state has exceeded its powers under Art. 1. The highest amount awarded so far, was in the *Yukos* case[97] where the court awarded almost €1.9 billion.

The court may take into account moral values of the applicant, e.g. attachment to his family home,[98] but not doing so, is not necessarily a violation. Furthermore, compensation not taking into account the architectural and historical value of an expropriated building could violate the Convention.[99]

The court has always held that the margin of appreciation applies not only to the act of expropriation itself but also to the standard and level of compensation.[100] It also extends to the valuation methods; although owners of land must have the opportunity to make representations in the valuation proceedings.[101] This mixing of the substantive part with the procedural part is typical of the court´s reasoning. The language of the court is not of "'pressing social need or 'strict necessity,' but whether the applicant has shown that the state measures impose an 'individual

a whole industry is in itself a far more complex operation than, for instance, the valuation of land compulsorily acquired and normally calls for specific legislation which can be applied across the board to all the undertakings involved. Accordingly, provided always that the aforesaid fair balance is preserved, the standard of compensation required in a nationalisation case may be different from that required in regard to other takings of property."

94 *Broniowski*, supra note 62, para 186.

95 *Scordino v. Italy* hudoc (2006) App Nr 36813/97, adopted 29 March 2006, paras. 82 *et seq.* See also for a discussion Grabenwarter, supra note 51, p. 380.

96 *Lithgow and Others*, supra note 85, para. 173.

97 *Oao Neftyanaya Kompaniya Yukos v. Russia* hudoc (App. No. 14902/04), adopted on 24 June 2014. Not only a violation of Art. 1 Protocol 1, but also of Art. 6(1) and 3 ECHR was found. Cf. also the much higher *Yukos* arbitral award, supra note 20.

98 *Lallement v. France* hudoc 46044/99, [2002] ECHR 413.

99 *Kozacioglu v. Turkey* hudoc (2009) GC. This case also contains a comparative survey of compensation in member states at para 34.

100 *Lithgow and Others*, supra note 85, para. 122.

101 *Efstathiou and Michailidis and Co Motel Amerika v. Greece* 2003-IX; 43 EHRR 490.

and excessive burden' or are 'disproportionate.'"[102] This leads us to the next point.

d Overall Due Process and Dispute Resolution System

Art. 1 also demands "lawfulness" of an expropriation ("subject to the conditions provided for by law"). This has been understood to mean that the state measure must ultimately have a basis in national law.[103] The deprivation of property must be based on an instrument of general application, except in special circumstances where a specific law may lay down the specific circumstances.[104] Furthermore, the law must be accessible, precise and foreseeable.[105] It must be compatible with the rule of law and must protect against arbitrariness.[106]

The court has always taken into account procedural possibilities for the applicants to challenge the expropriating act, i.e. the control of the court is at the same time substantive and procedural by taking into account the "fair balance" requirement. In the *Sporrong and Lännroth* case,[107] the applicants won because there was no procedure by which they could challenge the long continued application of the expropriation permits of over 15 years (even if for city planning purposes) since those were greatly impacting upon their property right. Also, in the *Hentrich* case, the applicant was not given the opportunity in domestic proceedings to make submissions (concerning tax matters). The court stated clearly its principle: "A pre-emption decision cannot be legitimate in the absence of adversarial proceedings that comply with the principle of equality of arms, enabling argument to be presented on the issue of the underestimation of the price and, consequently, on the Revenue's position – all elements which were lacking in the present case."[108]

102 Harris, O'Boyle, Bates and Buckley, supra note 45, p. 904.

103 Law means both statutory and case law, see *Spacek sro v. Czech Republic* hudoc (1999); 30 EHRR 1010. For measures taken on the basis of EU law, this would provide a sufficient basis, see *Bosphorus*, supra note 30.

104 Grabenwarter, supra note 51, p. 375. See e.g. *The Former King of Greece and Others*, supra note 92, paras. 80 *et seq.*

105 *Carbonara and Ventura v. Italy* 2000-VI, paras. 91, 107 and *Beyerler v. Italy* 2000-I; 33 EHRR 1225, para. 88 GC. In the former case, the local authorities took possession of the applicants' land and built a school on it without following the procedures for expropriation set down in legislation.

106 Grabenwarter, supra note 51, p. 375.

107 *Sporrong and Lännroth*, supra note 47.

108 *Hentrich v. France* A 296A (1994); 18 EHRR 440, para. 42.

The court would additionally consider a violation of Art. 6(1) of the ECHR[109] which protects, in civil matters (including administrative matters), when a fair and public hearing within a reasonable time was not granted. An applicant alleging expropriation must have the "right to a court," one aspect of which is the right to access, that is the right to institute proceedings before a court having competence in civil matters.[110]

In sum: while there are factors a state must take into account when expropriating and determining the amount of compensation, states overall are granted a large margin of appreciation by the ECtHR. Factors to be taken into account include timeliness, predictability and certainty in the exercise of state power, the impact of the interference on the individual, procedural safeguards, the payment of compensation and alternative avenues of securing the legitimate aim. The exact justiciability of those factors is problematic due to the deference of the Court to national bodies. The Court would find violations of the fair balance test if there were evidence of a systemic breach of the right to property by states or where the law is manifestly without reasonable foundation.[111]

2 *Direct Expropriation under the CFR and the Common Traditions of the EU Member States*

The CFR contains a property rights protection in Art. 17.[112] Unlike Art. 1 of Protocol 1 ECHR, Art. 17 CFR is more detailed, as it specifies all the essential aspects of the right to property: to enjoy possessions, to use the property, to dispose of it and to bequeath it. Moreover, Art. 17 makes it

[109] Art. 6(1) reads as follows: "1. In the determination of his civil rights and obligations or of any criminal charge against him, everyone is entitled to a fair and public hearing within a reasonable time by an independent and impartial tribunal established by law. Judgment shall be pronounced publicly but the press and public may be excluded from all or part of the trial in the interest of morals, public order or national security in a democratic society, where the interests of juveniles or the protection of the private life of the parties so require, or the extent strictly necessary in the opinion of the court in special circumstances where publicity would prejudice the interests of justice."

[110] *Sporrong and Lännroth*, supra note 47, para. 84.

[111] Harris, O'Boyle, Bates and Buckley, supra note 45, p. 904.

[112] "Article 17: Right to property. 1. Everyone has the right to own, use, dispose of and bequeath his or her lawfully acquired possessions. *No one may be deprived of his or her possessions, except in the public interest and in the cases and under the conditions provided for by law, subject to fair compensation being paid in good time for their loss.* The use of property may be regulated by law in so far as is necessary for the general interest. 2. Intellectual property shall be protected." (my emphasis)

clear that this protection concerns only legally acquired property which seems to outlaw any form of, e.g., money laundering.[113]

Art. 52 (3) CFR requires interpreting the meaning and scope of Art. 17 CFR in line with Art. 1 Protocol 1 ECHR; nevertheless, the CFR may provide a more extensive protection. The right to property also forms part of the common traditions of the member states which also have to be taken into account pursuant to Art. 52 (4) CFR.[114] Nevertheless, Art. 345 TFEU prescribes that the "(t)reaties shall in no ways prejudice the rules in member states governing the system of property ownership." In so far that property-related decisions of the states are considered protected by this (controversial, but historically explicable) provision, the EU must not interfere; thus this limitation also needs to be considered when interpreting Art. 17 CFR.[115]

Art. 17 CFR follows the same structure, elements and distinctions as Art. 1 Protocol 1 ECHR, namely: (1) the entitlement to peaceful enjoyment of possessions; (2) the prohibition of deprivation of possessions, subject to specified conditions; and (3) the right of the state to control the use of property, subject to specified conditions.[116] According to the ECJ, a deprivation of possessions requires not only that the person is deprived of the property but also that it is transferred to another person. Thus, e.g. the duty to destroy property or slaughter animals due to diseases without compensation does not constitute an expropriation.[117] Nevertheless, those situations can give rise to a compensable *de facto* expropriation, as has also been held by the ECtHR.[118]

113 Ferdinand Wollenschläger, "Art. 17 (1)," in Steve Peers, Tamara Hervey, Jeff Kenner and Angela Ward (eds.), *The EU Charter of Fundamental Rights. A Commentary* (Oxford: Hart, 2014), p. 465, p. 473.

114 For further references on the (controversial) discussion of what exactly is the content of those common traditions, see ibid., p. 469, footnote 21.

115 Ibid., p. 470.

116 For this delineation, see ibid., p. 476 *et seq.* and especially *Hauer v. Land Rheinland-Pfalz*, Case C-44/79, 1979 ECR 3727.

117 Joined Cases C-20/00 and C-64/00 *Booker Aquaculture and Hydor Seafood* [2003] ECR I7411, para. 58 *et seq.* and Advocate General Mischo, ibid., para. 93: "We are, in such a case, poles apart from the appropriation of a private person's property by the public authority, such as the compulsory purchase of a building. There is *no transfer of ownership* in property of definite economic value to satisfy a need in the general interest. There is only property which, even if it may possibly still hold some economic value, must be eliminated and which therefore no longer has any prospect of being sold for profit." See also para. 90: "no State has, to date, at least to my knowledge, *laid down in principle* that losses caused by the outbreak of a disease must always give rise to the payment of compensation from public funds." (original emphasis)

118 See supra note 51.

The second paragraph of Art. 17 CFR is *prima facie* the main new element in comparison to Art. 1 of Protocol 1 ECHR. The protection of intellectual property is an aspect of the right to property since the notion of possessions in the first paragraph includes in principle also intellectual property. However, taking into consideration an increasing importance of the protection of intellectual property in general, and in EU law in particular, it has been mentioned expressly in Art. 17, para. 2 CFR which is now *lex specialis* to para. 1.

Art. 17 CFR, as the rest of the rights in the CFR, was characterized as a "creative distillation of the rights contained in the various European and international agreements and national constitutions on which the ECJ had for some years already been drawing."[119] Already, before the existence of the CFR, the ECJ had delineated the notion of property,[120] but now the CFR also contains, next to the right to property, the right to engage in work (Art. 15) and the freedom to conduct a business (Art. 16). Thus, an extensive interpretation of property is less necessary for closing protection gaps in comparison with Art. 1 Protocol 1 ECHR.

For our purpose, Art. 17 para. 1, sentence 2 CFR is important.[121] It sets up three requirements for an expropriation to be lawful. The ECJ has always taken Art. 1 Prot. 1 ECHR as a starting point. First, it must be based on a sufficiently precise and accessible legal basis, regulating the conditions and modalities. Expropriation by legislation and administrative act is permitted.[122] Second, the deprivation must be in the public interest. The court follows the extensive interpretation of "public interest" of the ECtHR[123] and also allows the expropriation in favour of a private person if this is motivated by considerations of public interest. Member states mostly also have the notion of "public interest" or an

119 Paul Craig and Gráinne de Búrca, *EU Law. Text, Cases and Materials* (Oxford University Press, 2003), p. 359.

120 See *Nold v. Commission*, Case 4/73, 1974 ECT 491 and *Hauer v. Land Rheinland-Pfalz*, Case C-44/79, 1979 ECR 3727. Since then, property rights protection is well-established case law.

121 Cf. also supra note 112: "No one may be deprived of his or her possessions, except in the public interest and in the cases and under the conditions provided for by law, subject to fair compensation being paid in good time for their loss."

122 With further references, see Wollenschläger, supra note 113, p. 479.

123 Cf. Alberto Lucarelli, "Article 17 – Right to Property," in William B. T. Mock, Gianmario Demuro, Raffaele Bifulco, Marta Cartabia and Alfonso Celotto (eds.), *Human Rights in Europe. Commentary on the Charter of Fundamental Rights of the European Union* (Durham, NC: Carolina Academic Press, 2010), p. 106, p. 110 with a critique.

equivalent notion in their constitutions,[124] relevant for the common traditions.

Third, a fair compensation for the loss must be paid in good time. The "fair compensation in good time" requirement leaves room for not full compensation as an exception (full market value would be the principle). Fair compensation allows for a balancing of private interests versus public interests and would not always demand full compensation.[125] In this, the CFR follows the ECHR. "In good time" forbids undue delay of payment which again resonates already in the jurisprudence of the ECtHR.[126] Both can stand in contrast to international investment treaties which mostly demand full and prompt compensation without exceptions even for general nationalizations.

National and EU measures interfering with the right to property may be challenged according to the general rules of the EU and national procedural law. It is well accepted that Art. 17 para. 1 CFR requires effective legal remedies in order to establish appropriate protection for private property.[127] The CFR refers for all procedural aspects to the laws of the single member state – as member states would in principle execute an expropriation, even if it is based on an EU measure.[128]

IV Conclusion

In Europe, a multi-layered protection of property rights against direct expropriation exists. Although there is double scrutiny, the ECtHR and the ECJ, while setting minimum standards concerning substantive law and procedures, largely defer to the nation states. One reason for this is

124 E.g. Art. 16 Belgian Constitution; section 15(2) Finnish Constitution; Art. 17(2) Greek Constitution; Art. 16 Luxembourg Constitution; Art. 6(2) Portuguese Constitution; Art. 33(3) Spanish Constitution. More broadly in their wording: Art. 14(3) Dutch Constitution; Art. 14(3) German Constitution (Basic Law; "public good").

125 See only Advocate General Mischo, supra note 117, para. 80: "[T]he Court's case-law concerning the right of property has never stated that any restriction of this right must necessarily be accompanied by compensation. Even *Wachauf* [supra note 38, AvA] in which the Court recognised that, in the situation before it, respect for fundamental rights could not be reconciled with the absence of any compensation, falls short of laying down such a rule."

126 Lucarelli, supra note 123, p. 112.

127 Joined Cases C-402/05 P and C-415/05 P *Kadi v. Council and Commission* [2008] ECR I-6351, para. 368 *et seq.*

128 Lucarelli, supra note 123, p. 111, footnote 13.

the diversity of legal cultures, economic policies and history of the different states, even more so in the many CoE states.

From an economic perspective, it is difficult to judge this right or wrong.[129] Law and Economics have produced widely differing arguments and theories on how far protection against expropriation should go, how incentives are set for states and for private individuals respectively and what kind of compensation should be paid.[130] Insecure property rights may lead to underinvestment, moral hazard may lead to overinvestment,[131] and public use may lead to economic growth. All those arguments can produce different outcomes depending on context and the weight given to them. Ultimately, at least if economic efficiency is the normative goal to be pursued, the economic correctness of legal rules, including expropriation rules, is an empirical question[132] which depends on many legal, political and economic details. Encompassing empirical research on that question is, to my knowledge, still missing.

129 For a discussion, see Schäfer, supra note 23.

130 Richard Epstein, *Takings, Private Property and the Power of Eminent Domain* (Cambridge MA: Harvard University Press, 1985) and Louis Kaplow, "An economic analysis of legal transition," 99 (1986) *Harvard Law Review* 509, the latter being more attentive to the problem of overinvestment.

131 For the hold-up problem which may inhibit public investment, see James M. Buchanan and Yong J. Yoon, "Symmetric tragedies: commons and anticommons," 43 (2000) *Journal of Law and Economics* 1.

132 See for one study Daniel L. Chen and Susan Yeh, "The impact of government power to expropriate on economic growth and racial inequality," (2013) Working Paper, available at: www.law.umich.edu/centersandprograms/lawandeconomics/workshops/Documents/Paper%204.Chen.The%20Impact%20of%20Government%20Power%20to%20Expropriate%20on%20Economic%20Growth%20and%20Racial%20Inequality.pdf.

4

Eminent Domain Law in Taiwan: New Law, Old Practice?

YUN-CHIEN CHANG*

I Introduction

The Constitution of Taiwan fails to include a "just compensation" clause or a "public use" clause. Article 143, Section 1 of the Constitution of Taiwan *does* prescribe that "[a]ll land within the territory of the Republic of China shall belong to the whole body of citizens. Private ownership of land, acquired by the people in accordance with law, shall be protected and restricted by law. Privately-owned land shall be liable to taxation according to its value, and the Government may buy such land according to its value." As the final clause (buy . . . land) is interpreted as different from expropriation, the constitution provides little guidance in determining the scope and limit of eminent domain. However, the Constitutional Court is not entirely absent from this scene. In fact, in a number of constitutional interpretations,[1] the Constitutional Court constructed the constitutional mandate regarding the governmental use of the eminent domain power. Not all of the interpretations are equally influential. It would be fair to say that those on due process have shaped the evolution of takings law by prompting the revision of the relevant statutes had been declared unconstitutional. By contrast, the interpretations regarding just compensation and public interest are more expressive than substantive, as the Constitutional Court has yet to advance concrete tests that the government or the administrative courts can apply in future cases.

* I thank the Korea Development Institute for inviting me to present at its conference and publish this work. Yifat Holzman-Gazit, Sungkyu Park, Hans-Bernd Schäfer, and Ilya Somin provide helpful comments. Ming-chung Lin and Hilary Tsai provide helpful research assistance.

1 Interpretation Nos. 110, 215, 236, 336, 400, 409, 425, 440, 508, 513, 516, 534, 579, and 652.

As a result, eminent domain law in Taiwan is mainly statutory and regulatory. The legislature and the administration have a wide discretion in shaping the takings law. In introducing the "Six Pillars" of the taking laws in Taiwan, this chapter draws heavily on statutes and administrative regulations, while also keeping an eye on decisions made by the administrative courts. Since the year 2000, the Land Expropriation Act (hereinafter LEA) has been the major source of law for takings of land and fixtures. Before then, expropriation stipulations were scattered in many different statutes. Now, pursuant to Article 1, Paragraphs 1–2 of the LEA, "Land expropriation shall be governed by this Act. Matters not provided in this Act shall be governed by other applicable laws. Where other laws are inconsistent with this Act with regard to expropriation procedures and expropriation compensation standards, this Act shall prevail."[2] Hence, this chapter frequently turns to the LEA and the regulations stipulated to complement the LEA.

In the LEA,[3] there are three types of expropriation: land expropriation, zone expropriation, and incidental expropriation. This chapter focuses on land expropriation, which is used in a broad swathe of undertakings to condemn one or multiple land parcels. Zone expropriation is the condemnation of all land parcels in one specific area. The fundamentals of zone expropriations and land expropriation are the same, but zone expropriation can only be used in more limited circumstances (such as urban revitalization) and is subject to stricter procedural requirements. Due to limited space, zone expropriation will be covered only in Part VI, where the unique compensation options are summarized. Incidental expropriation refers to the condemnation of fixtures on the land. Its procedure is combined with that of land expropriation and zone expropriation. As such, incidental expropriation will be covered in the discussions of the Six Pillars below. Official statistics regarding the practice of land expropriation and zone expropriation in Taiwan from 2001 to 2013 are shown in Table 4.1 and Table 4.2, respectively.

This chapter is divided into seven parts, the first six of which introduce the Six Pillars of eminent domain: public interest criteria, subjects of the eminent domain power, just compensation, due process, distribution of development surpluses, and the dispute resolution system. Before

[2] In this chapter, I will rely on the official translations of the Constitution, statutes, and regulations, available at the official website of the Ministry of Justice, Taiwan, http://law.moj.gov.tw/Eng/.

[3] The Land Act also considers a "moratorium on development" as one type of takings. Land subject to the moratorium will usually be condemned at a later date.

Table 4.1. *Land Expropriation in Taiwan by Type of Public Use, 2001–2013*

Year	Grand total	National defense	Transportation	Public utilities	Water conservation	Public health and environmental protection	Education and culture	Public building	State-own enterprise	Social welfare	Others
2001	1340.9	15.0	843.4	4.2	267.7	14.4	13.8	1.3	22.7	0.2	158.2
2002	1075.2	41.2	455.7	43.7	292.6	1.9	9.7	12.8	10.5	0.6	206.5
2003	967.0	64.6	554.1	7.9	185.6	41.0	3.5	43.2	11.8	0.1	55.1
2004	970.7	62.2	379.4	4.0	194.2	11.0	5.8	0.4	20.3	0.0	293.3
2005	1085.6	17.5	503.0	20.5	178.5	9.5	10.2	8.8	2.7	0.0	334.7
2006	704.8	100.5	193.7	18.2	133.6	0.3	2.3	0.5	4.6	0.0	251.0
2007	672.1	6.1	286.8	0.7	211.4	9.0	1.0	0.8	3.5	—	152.8
2008	572.9	3.9	188.6	27.6	221.4	17.2	4.7	2.7	7.7	0.2	98.8
2009	1658.4	0.6	438.6	16.9	259.8	3.6	1.0	0.5	4.6	0.1	932.6
2010	1169.7	30.6	219.6	3.5	840.6	6.6	1.1	0.8	2.5	0.0	64.5
2011	669.4	0.0	135.0	0.1	488.9	0.0	0.4	1.5	1.6	0.0	41.9
2012	320.2	12.6	73.0	0.2	232.3	0.0	0.0	0.9	0.1	0.0	1.2
2013	565.6	13.2	112.2	48.1	111.5	3.2	7.6	0.0	0.0	0.0	269.7
Total	11772.4	368.2	4383.2	195.6	3618.1	117.9	61.2	74.3	92.7	1.2	2860.0

Unit: Hectare. *Source:* Ministry of the Interior, available at http://sowf.moi.gov.tw/stat/year/y05-08.xls.

Table 4.2. *Zone Expropriation in Taiwan, 2001–2013*

		Expropriated area			Usage of land		
Year	Zone number	Total	Public	Private	Construction land	Public facility land	Special agricultural zone
2001	40	2686.4	713.4	1973.0	1413.5	1272.8	0.0
2002	42	2895.8	722.1	2173.7	1521.6	1374.2	0.0
2003	50	3414.1	813.4	2600.7	1852.2	1561.8	0.0
2004	59	4584.7	873.1	3711.6	2621.7	1962.9	0.0
2005	64	5320.0	911.6	4408.4	2982.0	2337.9	0.0
2006	75	6652.8	1159.2	5493.5	3644.1	3008.7	0.0
2007	77	6711.4	1163.0	5548.4	3678.9	3032.5	0.0
2008	79	7020.5	1284.3	5736.3	3782.4	3238.2	0.0
2009	84	7137.2	1307.1	5830.1	3839.2	3298.1	0.0
2010	91	7448.8	1344.7	6104.0	4004.0	3444.8	0.0
2011	93	7650.2	1375.0	6275.1	4111.6	3538.5	0.0
2012	95	7672.2	1377.5	6294.7	4122.3	3549.9	0.0
2013	100	8002.2	1409.3	6592.9	4310.8	3691.3	0.1
Total	**949**	**77196.1**	**14453.7**	**62742.4**	**41884.3**	**35311.7**	**0.1**

Unit: Hectare. *Source:* Ministry of the Interior, available at http://sowf.moi.gov.tw/stat/year/y05-15.xls.

concluding, Part VII provides the author's own reform proposal of eminent domain law in Taiwan.

II Public Interest Criteria

Public interest and necessity are the two key criteria to meet before the state exercises its eminent domain power. Article 15 of the Taiwan Constitution protects private property rights, and Article 23 and a long list of constitutional interpretations have established that private property rights and other human rights can be limited, if commensurate with the "proportionality principle."[4] Article 3 of the LEA further spells out that takings must be "for public interest purposes" and "to the extent strictly required." These two criteria are abstract. Unfortunately, neither the Constitutional Court nor the Supreme Administrative Court has developed clearer tests to implement these two statutory requirements. Administrative courts, in particular, have been extremely deferential to the government in these two matters, essentially giving the latter a blank check (Chang 2010).

Takings of real properties are further limited to certain undertakings. Article 3 of the LEA first lists nine concrete undertakings: national defense; communication or transportation; public utility enterprises; water conservancy; public health and environmental protection; government office buildings, office buildings of local self-governing bodies and other public buildings; educational, academic and cultural undertakings; social welfare; and state-owned enterprises. Then Article 3 of the LEA is willing to accommodate "other undertakings for which land may be expropriated according to law." The devil is in the detail. The Ministry of the Interior, the central competent agency in charge of the LEA, has identified 29 other statutes that authorize expropriation of real estates. In short, the state can also condemn properties for the following undertakings: building subways, railroads, highways, city roads, science parks, export zones, national parks, public housing, public cemeteries, airports, fishery ports and international business ports, wild animal protection zones, water aqueducts, and high schools and elementary schools; preserving landmarks; consolidating oddly-shaped land; urban renewal; flood prevention; establishing produce markets; among others (Ministry of the Interior 2013a: 7–10). Due to the open-ended nature of the list, the legislature can at any time expand the scope of takings without amending the high-profile LEA.

4 For application of the proportionality principle in Taiwan and other East Asian countries, see Huang and Law (2015).

The hands-off attitude of the court led to several controversial, large-scale takings around 2011. Mass protests, scholarly critiques, and the presidential election in March 2012 led to a major revision of the LEA in December 2011. The newly enacted Article 3–1 of the LEA, for the first time in decades, tied the hands of the state from wielding eminent domain power. More specifically, a "land use applicant" (more on this in Part III) should "whenever possible, avoid choosing farmland and give priority consideration to public land or land owned by state-owned enterprises without existing land use plan." In response to the controversy of condemning premium farmland to build science parks, Article 3–1 stipulates that for agricultural land, "the competent authority in charge of the relevant industry should give consideration to the public interest purpose and necessity of expropriation at the time of designation or rezoning . . . If the agricultural land located within the land selected by a land use applicant is exempted from the approval of the regional plan preparing authority with regard to its rezoning, the approval of the agriculture authority under the municipal or county (city) government shall first be obtained before the land is changed to non-agricultural use." Premium agricultural land, according to the last paragraph of Article 3–1, in principle cannot be condemned, unless odd pieces of such land are interspersed and it is difficult to circumvent condemning it.[5]

Moreover, the also newly enacted Article 3–2 of the LEA requires a comprehensive assessment of the public interest and necessity of the takings project. The legislature even lays out the variables to be considered:

"1. Social factors: Including the size of population affected by the expropriation, the age structure of the affected population, and the extent of effects of the expropriation plan on the current status of the surrounding communities, the life style of and health risk to disadvantaged groups.
2. Economic factors: Including the effects of the expropriation plan on tax revenue, food security, increase/decrease in jobs or population that might be forced to change jobs, the costs of expropriation, public facilities required of governments at all levels, the fiscal expenditure and burden of governments, the agriculture, forestry, fishery, or animal husbandry industry chain and the integrity of land use.

[5] Article 3–1 of the LEA also details that the exceptions to this no-taking principle are takings for "national defense, communication or transportation, or water conservancy undertaking; a public utility enterprise for erecting power transmission lines; or for use in an infrastructure project already approved by the Executive Yuan."

3. Cultural and ecological factors: Including changes in natural urban/rural sceneries, cultural relics, living conditions or life style caused by the expropriation plan, and its impacts on the ecological environment of the area, surrounding residents or the society as a whole.
4. Sustainable development factors: Including national sustainable development policies, sustainability indicators, and national land use planning.
5. Others: Other relevant factors or factors that should be evaluated based on the individual expropriation plan."

The Ministry of the Interior reviews the assessment of public interest and necessity. Articles 2, 14, and 15 of the LEA prescribe that the Ministry of the Interior establish a "Takings Review Task Force."[6] Articles 13 and 13–1 authorize the Ministry of the Interior, through the Takings Review Task Force, to review the assessment of public interest and necessity, among others. The Ministry of the Interior, in two administrative rules announced in 2011 and 2012 (the Ministry of the Interior 2013a: 1044), requires an additional review of public interest and necessity for certain takings projects in an earlier stage of the whole process (see Part V and Figure 4.1). More specifically, these takings projects (1) are implemented as zone expropriation (see also Article 4 of Regulations on Implementing Zone Expropriation); (2) involve certain undertakings (for example, building or establishing export zones, science parks, produce markets, airports); (3) expand urban planning; or (4) develop more than 30 hectares. The two-time reviews have to be substantive and *de novo* each time (Chen 2013: 283–84).

Administrative courts since 2012 also have to review the public interest and necessity of the takings project. In the several cases so far, courts appear to spill more ink on necessity than on public interest. Nonetheless, in every case the court concludes that the government has passed the tests. Thus, the more stringent requirements by the legislature may not have nudged the administrative courts to adopt a stricter review standard of the takings projects by the administrative branch.

III Subjects of the Eminent Domain Power

Only the state can exercise the eminent domain power. The Ministry of the Interior has the power to approve or disapprove a takings

[6] The Task Force consists of 17 members. Eight members are officials from several relevant government agencies. Nine members are scholars, experts, and representatives of private organizations.

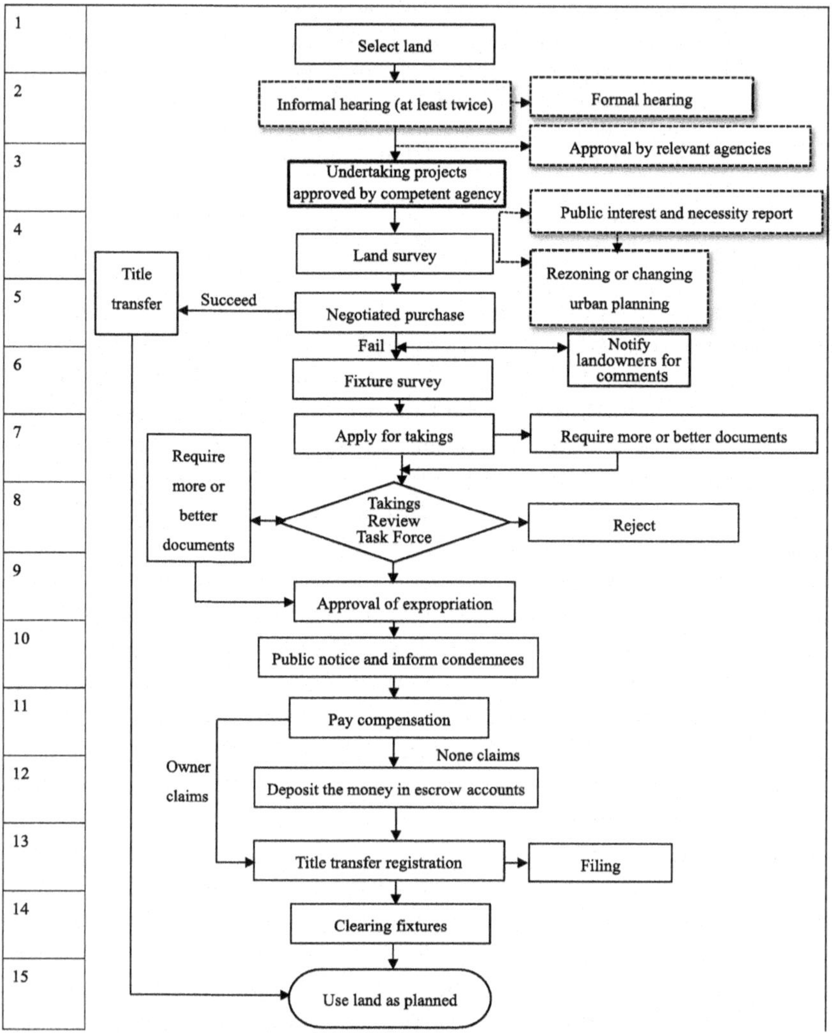

Figure 4.1. Flow Chart of the Eminent Domain Procedure
Source: The Ministry of the Interior (2013a: 24). Note: dotted arrows and boxes are procedures not always required.

project as the designated organ of the state (Article 14 of the LEA). The more important question under Taiwan law is who can apply as a "land use applicant" to the Ministry of the Interior for condemning real properties? In theory, private (legal) persons can be land use applicants (Wen 2013: 528), but in practice, no statute has authorized any private parties to become a land use applicant (Ministry of the Interior 2013a: 11). According to Article 15 of the Enforcement Rules for the LEA, central government agencies, city governments, county governments, town governments, and irrigation associations[7] are land use applicants.

Private takings, however, are not an empty set. As Bell (2009) points out, private takings are often disguised. Article 787 of the Taiwan Civil Code, for instance, recognizes "statutory easement" (Chang 2016). Statutory easement, often called legal servitude of passage in civil law jurisdictions such as Louisiana (Wilmore 1986; Sentell 1994; Yiannopoulos 1996; Merwe 1999; Huffstetler 2002), deals with the problem of accessing public roads for landlocked land. In general, a statutory easement is granted to landlocked owners to pass through neighboring land. The passage has to be necessary, and landlocked owners are required to compensate owners of neighboring parcels. In the United States, the takings nature of statutory easement is clearer because administrative agencies are often involved in the process of establishing a statutory easement (Merrill and Smith 2010: 204; Bruce and Ely 2011: 4:14). The US Supreme Court, in *Leo Sheep Co. v. United States*, 440 U.S. 668, 679–80 (1979), has explicitly pointed out that easements of necessity (the doctrinal brother of statutory easement) and eminent domain are alternative ways to reach the same results for the state. Civil law, including Taiwan law, however, has rarely drawn analogy of private condemnation to statutory easement. Hence, this chapter will not foray further into statutory easement, but it is worth pointing out that statutes regarding administrative law are not the exclusive sources for stipulations of takings (in the functional sense).

IV Just Compensation

In Chang (2009, 2012, 2013), I provide theoretical analysis and empirical examinations of takings compensation law in Taiwan in 1954–1977 and 1977–2012. One of the major changes in the 2012 revision of the LEA reformed the compensation law. Before the reform, land value was assessed by combining a pre-determined and under-assessed official land value with a pre-determined extra bonus. After the reform, market value of land should be used to compensate condemnees. While land

[7] Irrigation associations are *public* legal persons in Taiwan law.

value is a major component of the compensation package, it is not the only one. Section A describes all the elements of takings compensation. Section B then focuses on how market value of land has been appraised since 2012. Section C surveys the judicial review of takings compensation cases.

A The Elements of Takings Compensation

Total takings compensation includes that for land; constructional improvements (such as a house); agricultural improvements (such as trees); incurred expenses for land improvements; business losses; and relocation expenses. Takings compensation "shall be paid within fifteen days after the expiration of the public announcement period" (Article 20 of the LEA), and the public announcement period is 30 days after the city/county government, upon receiving the notice of approval from the Ministry of the Interior, makes a public announcement and notifies condemnees (Article 18 of the LEA). Except for land value compensation (which is discussed in Section B), I introduce the appraisal methods for these compensations in turn.[8]

Compensation for constructional improvements equals "replacement cost at the time of expropriation" (Article 31 of the LEA). The Ministry of the Interior has stipulated a few regulations that detail the proper assessment method. The city/county governments (the first-level local governments in Taiwan) are responsible for calculating the replacement costs themselves or commissioning real estate appraisers to do the work (Ministry of the Interior 2013a: 288). Only legal buildings are eligible for compensation.[9]

Compensation for agricultural improvements "shall be determined based on the value of the ripened crops thereof, provided the crops are due to ripen in less than one year from the date of expropriation, or based on the cost incurred in their planting and cultivation with reference to their current value, provided the crops are due to ripen in more than one year from the date of expropriation" (Article 31 of the LEA). The Ministry of the Interior has enacted incredibly detailed tables for determining the compensable value of various types of trees and flowers. As the tables are public information and some plants are more valuable than others, condemnees have incentives to rush to grow certain highly

[8] I omit the discussion of compensation for contiguous land (not condemned but affected).

[9] For a study on illegal buildings in Taiwan, see Chang and Smith (2015).

compensable plants before the date of expropriation. The Ministry of the Interior, in response, stipulates in its regulation that only "normal planting" is compensable.[10] Many litigants in the administrative courts dispute whether their planting process is normal. Satellite photos of the land in question are often used to solve these cases (Chang 2012b).

According to the relevant laws and regulations, landowners who have incurred expenses for improving land (such as constructing a conduit or a dam and paving a road) and stopped the improvement work can receive reimbursement for the expenses (Article 32 of the LEA).

Article 33 of the LEA stipulates that "[i]f the expropriated land or land improvement was originally provided for legal business operations, the loss sustained due to the cessation of business or shrinkage of business scale as a result of land or land improvement expropriation shall be compensated." Note that, again, only legal businesses will be compensated. The Ministry of the Interior designed a formula to compute positive business losses (Ministry of the Interior 2013a: 291). Firms that are losing money will of course not receive compensation.

Relocation expenses are a combination of different fees related to moving. In short, the following items are compensable: moving fees for graves, memorials, and other constructions that owners prefer relocating; moving fees for residents whose household registration records show that they are in residence six months before the takings notice is posted; moving fees for large machinery, livestock, etc. There are assessment standards for each category (the Ministry of the Interior 2013a: 292–93).

B *Appraisal of Land Value*

Assessment of land value is the most complicated and controversial part of determining the amount of takings compensation, as appraisal of land value now is *not* formulaic and land value takes up the lion's share of the total takings compensation. Before 2012, determining the compensable land value was mechanical. Chang (2009; 2013) has shown that a majority of condemnees were under-compensated under the old regime, which relied on official land value for tax purposes in the critical calculation.

[10] This practice is authorized by Article 23 of the LEA: " . . . Nor shall the landowners or users . . . plant more agricultural improvements on the land [since the public announcement of expropriation]. In case any of the aforementioned works is ongoing when the public announcement is made, it shall be immediately stopped."

This section introduces and evaluates the new regime. My reform proposal will appear in Part VIII.

Condemnees shall receive "current market value" as compensation for expropriation of their land (Article 30 of the LEA). The Land Value Evaluation Committee in each city/county government determines the current market value.[11] The Committee is not itself an agency; rather, it makes decisions in the name of the local city/county government. The compensation is paid from the budget of the land use applicant. Below is a summary of how current market value is assessed and adjusted.

The current market value is appraised by either local governments themselves or real estate appraisers commissioned by local governments. Both have to follow the Regulations on Appraising Current Market Value for Takings Compensation Purposes in assessing the value of condemned land.[12] In short, the Regulation prescribes that the comparable sale approach (also known as the market data approach) is the principle, and the income capitalization approach is the exception.

More specifically, in principle, appraising current market value for takings compensation purposes can be broken down into several steps (Articles 4–21 of the Regulations on Appraising Current Market Value for Takings Compensation Purposes):

(1) collecting or revising all kinds of maps (such as urban planning and zoning maps);
(2) collecting information on real estate sales between March 2 and September 1 of the "baseline year" (Y_1);
(3) demarcating the jurisdictions into "land value zones" by land value, zoning, infrastructure, among others;
(4) estimating the "normal"[13] adjusted-to-September-1 unit price (Taiwan dollars per square meter) of the collected sales;

[11] This committee has 17–19 members, and comprises the (deputy) mayor, a local legislator, five local government officials, and several representatives from relevant associations.

[12] Scholars have heavily criticized this stipulation, contending that (1) the Regulations on Appraising Current Market Value for Takings Compensation Purposes are not as sophisticated and accurate as the Regulations on Real Estate Appraisals; (2) real estate appraisers have to follow the Regulations on Real Estate Appraisals in their other works. Why is an idiosyncratic approach necessary for assessing compensable land value (Kang 2014: 21–22; Lin 2012: 84; Chen 2012: 102)?

[13] The Regulations on Appraising Current Market Value for Takings Compensation Purposes specify rules for appraisers to adjust the abnormality of the sale prices.

(5) among the collected sales, choosing three comparable land parcels within the land value zones where the takings project in question takes place;
(6) comparing with the comparable land parcels and estimating the unit price of the condemned land;
(7) submitting the estimations to Land Value Evaluation Committee for approval or adjustment. The approved unit land will then be used for condemnations taking place in the next, "current year" (Y2=Y1+1).[14]

Market value of land fluctuates on a daily basis, so an up-to-date land value has to be estimated for land expropriations that take place after July 1 of the current year. An adjustment ratio should be computed based on the relative estimated price on September 1 of the baseline year and March 1 of the current year.[15] Since August 2012, the actual sale prices of all real estate transactions have to be reported to the government (Chang 2015). Thus, the government now has a firm grasp of the market value of land. Since 2014 (the Ministry of the Interior 2013b: 14), the actual sale price data were used to compute the adjustment ratio. More specifically, local governments compare the average sale prices of comparable properties whose unit prices are between the 25 percentile and the 75 percentile in both the baseline period (March 2 to September 1 of the baseline year) and the current period (September 2 of the baseline year to March 1 of the current year) to estimate the percentage changes in land value (the Ministry of the Interior 2013b: 14–16; Articles 26 and 29 of the Regulations on Appraising Current Market Value for Takings Compensation Purposes).[16] Finally, the estimations of adjustment ratios should be sent to the Land Value Evaluation Committee for approval or adjustment.

In principle, condemnees receive the up-to-date current market value as compensation. Takings projects finalized between January 1 and June 30 of the current year should use the current market value estimated on the basis of market value on September 1 of the baseline year. Those closed in the second half of the current year should use the aforementioned market value adjusted by the adjustment ratio, to

[14] There are exceptions, but I omit the details here.

[15] March 1 of the current year is six months after September 1 of the baseline year. September 1, as described in the text, is the baseline date for adjusting sale prices of comparable land. Article 30 of the LEA prescribes that local governments have to investigate market conditions every six months.

[16] That is, the 25 per cent highest and 25 per cent lowest unit prices are excluded. The average prices of the rest of the unit prices in both periods are calculated separately and then compared. Adjustment ratio=average price in the current period/average price in the baseline period.

update the current market value to March 1 of the current year. An exception: if the current market value of the baseline year has been publicly announced and notified to the condemnees, and the adjusted current market value of the current year is lower than the former value, the higher market value of the baseline year shall still be used to compensate the condemnees (Article 30 of the Enforcement Rules for the LEA).

C *Judicial Review*

Administrative courts defer to the local governments' assessment of current market value. In the pre-2012 regime, takings compensation was determined by the pre-announced official land value. Administrative courts' hesitation in giving the official values a hard look is understandable, but not justified. In the post-2012 regime, however, the legislature prescribes compensation of current market value. As current market value is an objective, verifiable fact that anyone with the right training can estimate, administrative courts should substantively review the estimates of current market value by the governments, rather than deferring to them. So far (until October 10, 2014), I have found six administrative court cases which apply the new Article 30 of the LEA. In all six cases, however, the courts defer to the local governments. In Chang (2013c), I found that administrative courts in Taiwan before 2012 only conducted a "procedural review" of takings compensation determination, rather than a "substantive review." That is, administrative courts only examined whether all the procedures stipulated in the regulations and statutes were followed. If they were, administrative courts assumed that the estimates were correct, or at least worthy of their deference. It appears that this mindset has not changed.

V Overall Due Process

The due process for takings and its preceding procedures stipulated by the LEA are shown in a flow chart (Figure 4.1). Stages 1–5 are the preceding procedures, and stages 6–15 are the takings procedures. Due to limited space, I will only focus on the negotiated purchase procedure (stage 5), a mandatory process before a land use applicant can apply for expropriation.

In principle, land use applicants have to negotiate in good faith and in their best efforts with the owners of the land needed for the undertakings, before applying to the Ministry of the Interior for expropriation (Article 11 of the LEA). Land use applicants should bargain with the owners based on "market value" (Article 11 of the LEA). In both the negotiated purchase here and the takings setting, the legislature uses market value as the standard for compensation. Nonetheless, Article 30 of the LEA stipulates that the market value in the takings procedure has to be approved by the Land Value Evaluation Committee, while Article 11 of the LEA defines market value to "mean normal transaction price in the market" without designating any agency or committee to approve the estimated market value. The Ministry of the Interior has advised land use applicants that the market value used in the negotiated purchase procedure need not equate the market value approved by the Land Value Evaluation Committee; in fact, a hard, non-negotiable bottom line is the antithesis of the spirit of negotiated purchase (the Ministry of the Interior 2013a: 50–51, 1071–73).

The current practice of negotiated purchase is still in flux. Taoyuan County still relied on the pre-2012 regime, using Publicly Announced Land Value (an official land value for property tax purposes) plus a 40 per cent bonus, claiming that this would give condemnees more than the government-assessed market value – which, I should note, probably is below the real market value. By contrast, the New Taipei City commissioned independent real estate appraisers to assess the market value to be offered to condemnees. I cannot find any data on how often land use applicants "successfully" persuade the landowners to sell the land in question to them. My conjecture is that if the offered price in the negotiation is not much different from the current market value to be used in the takings stage (as it is often alleged to be the case), landowners would not have incentives to sell their properties to the land use applicants, as they receive tax benefits and condemnee status in takings procedures, among other reasons. Finally, I have found a Supreme Administrative Court case rendered in 2013 that took a hard look at the negotiated purchase procedure, revoking and remanding the case to the lower court to review again as to whether the land use applicant had made a good-faith negotiated purchase (Supreme Administrative Court No. 371 Decision in 2013).

VI Distribution of Development Surpluses

In Taiwan, landowners are excluded from appropriating any part of the development surplus. Sharing surpluses implies that condemnees will receive more than the market value of their properties as compensation. For Taiwanese condemnees in the past few decades who did not receive even market-value compensation, getting a dip of the surplus is unrealistic. The Constitutional Court of Taiwan, in Interpretation No. 579, has ruled that the takings compensation must be commensurate with the losses of the condemnees.[17] Losses refer to the property value taken away from the condemnees, not the lost opportunities to gain from the takings project. Hence, for ordinary takings, all development surpluses go to the state.

The compensation mechanism for zone expropriation, however, might enable condemnees to share some of the development surpluses. In zone expropriation procedures, condemnees have the option to choose between compensation in cash (as in land expropriation procedure) and compensation in kind – namely, condemnees can request to receive post-development land in lieu of cash compensation (Articles 39–40 of the LEA). The size of the post-development land parcel shall, in principle, be no larger than 50 per cent, but be larger than 40 per cent of the area of the condemned land parcel, unless "otherwise approved by the superior competent authority under special circumstances" (Article 39). In general, the floor-area ratios of the post-development land increase, market unit value often more than doubles, and condemnees who choose the in-kind option also receive tax benefits (Chen 2013: 272). As a result, the market value of the smaller post-development plot received by the condemnees as in-kind compensation is higher than the cash compensation the condemnees would have received. As the cash compensation is assessed based on pre-development land value, condemnees in zone expropriation who opt for in-kind compensation receive some of the development surplus. The government, however, still keeps most of the development surplus.

VII The Dispute Resolution System

The dispute resolution system regarding takings contains several levels of scrutiny. Any person with a property interest in the expropriated land or land improvement (often, but not limited to, condemnees of land ownership) can object to the contents of the public announcements of takings

[17] An English translation of this Interpretation is available at the official website of the Constitutional Court. See: www.judicial.gov.tw/constitutionalcourt/en/p03_01.asp?expno=579.

within the announcement period. The amount of compensation is included in the announcement, but other matters (such as the scope of the expropriation) are contained in it, too. Local governments have to investigate the matter and notify the objecting person in writing of the findings and actions taken. If the objecting person is still discontent, and they have contested the amount of the compensation, the local government has the discretion to refer the matter to the Land Value Evaluation Committee for reconsideration. If the objecting person still disagrees with the result of reconsideration, they can initiate an "administrative appeal." Provided that the interested people were challenging matters other than compensation, the reconsideration stage would be skipped.

"Review committees" in the administrative appeal are expected to conduct a "merits review"; that is, modifying improper yet legal administrative decisions. In other words, they should consider every aspect of an administrative act, examine whether it fits government policies, and explore whether a different decision would better realize the legislative intent. When an agency uses its discretion and makes a bad judgment (but not to the extent of abuse of discretion), or an agency interprets a statute in an allowable (but not ideal) way, the administrative court cannot vacate it. Instead, the law requires the review committees to redress the harms by revoking the original administrative act and directing the administrative agencies to come up with a better decision. Therefore, although administrative agencies have discretion in interpreting statutes, review committees' discretion trumps the agencies,' and the law does not expect review committees to defer to administrative agencies' discretion in fact-finding or statutory interpretation. Review committees, however, do not appear to be very active. The revocation rate in all the administrative appeal procedures at central government level was 10 per cent between 2005 and 2009 (Chang 2014). In a prior empirical study, I found that takings compensation cases took up about 14 per cent of all administrative appeal cases handled by the Review Committee of the Ministry of the Interior in 2006–2009, and the revocation rate of these takings compensation cases was 10.3 per cent; more importantly, review committees rarely conducted merits reviews, limiting themselves to merely legality reviews (Chang 2012b). My comprehensive survey of all administrative reviews rendered in the first nine months of 2014 revealed that, in applying the new law, the Review Committee of the Ministry of the Interior has taken a more active role in certain cases, revoking the assessment of takings compensation by the administrative agency; nevertheless, deference to such decisions still appears to be the norm.

The last stop in the dispute resolution mechanism is the administrative court – unless the condemnees lose and bring their cases to the Constitutional Court, and the cases are taken. As the condemned land or fixtures are most likely worth more than $US13,000, the court of the first instance is the High Administrative Court (Articles 104–1 and 229 of the Administrative Litigation Act). In principle, the condemnees can appeal to the Supreme Administrative Court if the high court decisions are in contravention of the law (Articles 238, 242–43 of the Administrative Litigation Act). The administrative courts in Taiwan generally are not big believers in judicial activism. Chen (2013: 165), however, has identified several administrative court cases that chastised the administrative agencies that treat negotiated purchases as a mere formality, instead of bargaining in good faith. That said, as noted above, administrative courts are highly deferential to the administrative agencies in terms of assessment of takings compensation.

VIII Evaluating the Takings Regime in Taiwan

The 2012 reform of the LEA marked the third major change of takings compensation since 1949 (Chang 2013). Generally speaking, this latest reform may be optimal in terms of law in books. Of course, it is the law in action that matters for the condemnees and the general public. As the new LEA is still young, it is unclear whether the amended regime can guarantee condemnees with the basic respect they deserve in a democracy. This chapter has offered evidence for worries, as the administrative agencies have not shown significant changes in their course of business and the administrative courts appear to be deferential as usual. One should not rely too heavily on the inactive administrative court to raise the standard of review of the public interest in takings cases. If land value appraisals are still considered highly technical matters that only the governments or the real estate appraisers they hire can understand, administrative courts will still pass on reviewing these critical decisions. This part advances a new approach, under which estimation of market value of condemned land through hedonic regression models with block-level sale data is mandatory. By making the estimation more transparent, I hope that courts will become more willing to review the decision. Provided that condemnees can really receive market value as compensation, it leaves much less room for governments to condemn unnecessary land. This is the law of demand.

Real estate appraisers in Taiwan, like their colleagues elsewhere, still largely rely on the conventional method to estimate market value. Appraisals are handiwork, based on experience, and their subjectivity makes them unlikely to be contested.

The era of big data has come to Taiwan, and hedonic regression models that utilize big data to assess market value of land have become too powerful to ignore. Actual market sale prices of real estates had been kept secret for decades. None other than the transacting parties themselves (and perhaps their agents) knew the actual prices. Transaction taxes were levied based on official land value, not actual sale prices. As a result, no one had large enough data to utilize regression models.

Things changed, however, in 2012. As part of his presidential re-election campaign, President MA Ying-jeou advocated "residential justice." The legislature passed or revised five statutes, three of which mandate that the *actual* sale prices of immovable properties be reported to the government. The "actual price report" regime came into effect on August 1, 2012. The raw data are available for download, and the competent agency, the Ministry of the Interior, has set up a website that enables users to check sale prices in any region in Taiwan through a graphic interface.[18] Users can also acquire information on that website regarding the transacting month, total area, zoning, layout of the apartment (such as how many rooms), etc. (Chang 2015).

New and larger data sets are churned out every day. From August 2012 to February 2013 alone, there were 188,900 reported sales of land and/or buildings. The data regarding the sales of land are summarized in Table 4.3. From August 2012 to November 2014, the reported number of sales of land and/or building increased to 840,165.

With these (ever-increasing) sets of data and a properly specified hedonic regression model, market value of any land parcel in Taiwan since August 2012 can be estimated with pretty high accuracy. My co-authors and I have developed a hedonic regression model elsewhere (Chang, Chen, and Lin 2014). The model, introduced in detail below on page 113, is an ordinary least square (OLS) model with robust standard errors. The dependent variable is the actual sale price. The independent variables control for the land size, zoning, transaction month, and the number of plots involved. The models take the following form (see page 113):

[18] http://lvr.land.moi.gov.tw/N11/homePage.action#.

Table 4.3. *Summary Statistics of Variables Used in the Hedonic Regression Models*

Panel A: Continuous Variables

Variables	N	Mean	Median	St. Dev.	Min.	Max.
Sale price	60,530	110,258,700	2,900,000	524,863,400	54	5,682,620,000
Land area	60,530	1,471	358	4,598	0.01	411,300
Number of plot	60,530	1.9	1	2.8	1	88

Note: Price in New Taiwan Dollars and area in square meters.

Panel B: Categorical Variables (N=60,530.)

Variable types and names	%
Zoning	100
non-urban (agricultural – not prime)	9.6
non-urban (preserved)	12.5
non-urban (industrial)	0.8
non-urban (agricultural – prime)	19.5
non-urban (residential)	4.4
urban (industrial)	1.7
urban (residential)	21.0
urban (business)	2.2
urban (agricultural)	9.5
urban (other)	18.8
Strata	**100**
1	7.3
2	15.3
3	32.1
4	17.8
5	19.5
6	6.5
7	1.6
Months	**100**
Before 2012/8	8.6
2012/8	15.5
2012/9	15.1
2012/10	14.4
2012/11	15.0
2012/12	17.9
2013/1	11.5
2013/2	2.0

Source: Chang, Chen, and Lin (2014).

$$P_i = \alpha + \beta A_i + \theta N_i + \delta Z_i + \eta M_i + \gamma S_i + v_i$$

where P is natural log of sale prices; A is natural log of land area; N is natural log of the number of land plots involved; Z are nine zoning dummies that capture ten types of zonings: non-urban (agricultural – not prime), non-urban (agricultural – prime), non-urban (industrial), non-urban (preserved), non-urban (residential), urban (industrial), urban (residential), urban (business), urban (agricultural), and urban (other); M are dummy variables indicating the month of the transaction. S are a series of dummies indicating the strata of the town/city in which the land in question is located. Strata 1 to 7 represent central business districts, industrial and business districts, growing towns, towns with traditional industries, lowly developed towns, aging towns, and least developed towns, respectively.[19] v is the error term. The coefficients to be estimated are α, β, δ, θ, η, γ. The regression result is shown in Table 4.4. A high R-square of 0.73 means that this simple model can capture 73 per cent of the deviations of the actual market prices from the average market prices. I am positive that most social scientists who do quantitative work will agree that an R-square of 0.73 is very satisfactory. With more data and more information to improve the model, using hedonic regression models to estimate market value will become more and more accurate in Taiwan.

I am not proposing the banishment of real estate appraisers from the takings procedure. Not at all. There is a confidence interval in any statistical estimates, and hedonic regression models are vulnerable to idiosyncrasies of land characteristics. Instead of entirely relying on statistical methods or subjective appraisals, why not get the best of both worlds? Governments can (and, I think, should) use the estimates (with, say, a 95 per cent or 90 per cent confidence interval) by the hedonic regression model as the benchmark, and require real estate appraisers to adjust the benchmark, if necessary. The appraisal reports should detail the reasons for the adjustments. Both the regression estimates and the appraisal reports should be provided to the landowners no later than the negotiated purchase stage. The informed landowners can then decide to accept the offer or challenge the amount of takings compensation later. Market value appraisal is objective, and local governments and real estate appraisers should thus be held more accountable than before by administrative courts. In other words, administrative courts should no longer defer on appraisal matters. Rather, experts hired by the condemnees should be allowed to debate the merits of

[19] The stratum classification is based on Hou et al. (2008).

Table 4.4. *Regression Results for Estimating Market Price and Market Rent*

Dependent Variable: ln of Total sale price	
=1 if stratum 1	2.746***
	(0.025)
=1 if stratum 2	2.024***
	(0.021)
=1 if stratum 3	1.549***
	(0.018)
=1 if stratum 4	1.394***
	(0.018)
=1 if stratum 5	0.424***
	(0.018)
Ln of land area	0.857***
	(0.003)
Ln of number of plot	0.053***
	(0.007)
Zoning dummies	Yes
Month dummies	Yes
Constant	7.779***
	(0.088)
Observations	60,530
R-squared	0.730

Robust standard errors in parentheses
*** $p<0.001$, ** $p<0.01$, * $p<0.05$, + $p<0.1$
Source: Chang, Chen, and Lin (2014).

the land value assessed by local governments. Administrative courts should commission independent appraisers to evaluate the quality of the appraisal reports by both sides. In the long run, only a more active court can bring equity to the condemnees.

IX Conclusion

A pessimistic story emerges from my survey of the Six Pillars of eminent domain law in Taiwan. In four pillars – public interest criteria, just compensation, due process, and the dispute resolution system – the 2012 legislative reform improved the takings law in books.

Nevertheless, the new law did not appear to bring along new practices, at least not yet. The administrative agencies and the administrative courts, as current evidence suggests, followed the letter but not the spirit of the new legislative mandate. The subjects of the eminent domain power remain unchanged, as also did their attitude toward wielding the eminent domain power. The new law promises market value compensation for landowners, who still have no share of the development surpluses.

The lesson for other jurisdictions is that a quantitative method should be used in the eminent domain procedure. In my prior work and this chapter, I have demonstrated the power of hedonic regression models in accurately estimating land value. Also, I have shown that various assessment methods, based on owners' self-assessment or on real estate appraisers' assessments for condemnors, have failed to reach the goal of giving condemnees market value compensation. It is not that a human being's evaluation is always inaccurate (though it is sometimes). Rather, the problem has often been that the evaluation is biased by various other concerns, such as paying less taxes or gaining more business. Statistical methods have a cold appearance. Human right advocates hardly characterize statistics as protectors of property or other human rights. The counter-intuitive lesson from the takings law is that cold method can yield warm results.

References in Chinese

Chang, Yun-chien. 2010. Takings Compensation Standard Pursuant to Article 30 of Land Condemnation Act: With an Overview of Relevant Supreme Administrative Court Cases Since 2000. *Academia Sinica Law Journal* 6: 167–06.

2012. Takings Compensation Cases in Administrative Appeal Procedures: Empirical Observations and Reform Suggestions. *Journal of New Perspectives on Law* 36: 75–96.

2013. *Eminent Domain Compensation in Taiwan: Theory and Practice.* Taipei, Taiwan: Angle Publishing.

Chen, Kan. 2012. Can Regulations on Appraising Current Market Value for Takings Compensation Purposes Satisfy the Public?. *Environmental and Land Law Journal* 1(3): 101–05.

Chen, Ming-Tsann. 2013. *Introduction to Land Expropriation.* Taipei: New Sharing.

Hou, Pei-chun, Su-Hao Tu, Pei-shan Laio, Yung-Tai Hung, and Ying-Hwa Chang. 2008. The Typology of Townships in Taiwan: The Analysis of Sampling

Stratification of the 2005–2006 "Taiwan Social Change Survey." *Survey Research—Method and Application* 23: 7–32.

Kang, Chiu-kui. 2014. On Appraising Current Market Value for Takings Compensation Purposes and Assessing Announced Current Land Value. *Land Issues Research Quarterly* 13(2): 20–31.

Lin, Chiou-Mien. 2012. Market Value in Takings Compensation Assessment. *Taiwan Environmental and Land Law Journal* 1(3): 79–85.

Ministry of the Interior. 2013a. *Handbook on Land Expropriation*. Taipei: Ministry of the Interior. Available at www.land.moi.gov.tw/chhtml/filedown.asp?cid=115.

2013b. *Handbook on Appraisal of Land Value for Takings Purposes*. Taipei: Ministry of the Interior. Available at www.land.moi.gov.tw/content/4793-U.pdf.

Wen, Feng-Wen. 2013. *Land Law*. Taipei: Author.

References in English

Bell, Abraham. 2009. Private Takings. *University of Chicago Law Review* 76: 517–85.

Bruce, Jon W., and James W. Ely, Jr. 2011. *The Law of Easements and Licenses in Land*. New York, NY: West.

Chang, Yun-chien. 2009. Empire Building and Fiscal Illusion? An Empirical Study of Government Official Behaviors in Takings. *Journal of Empirical Legal Studies* 6: 541–84.

2012. Self-Assessment of Takings Compensation: An Empirical Study. *Journal of Law, Economics and Organization* 28: 265–85.

2013. *Private Property and Takings Compensation: Theoretical Framework and Empirical Analysis*. Northampton, MA: Edward Elgar.

2014. An Empirical Study of Administrative Appeal in Taiwan: A Cautionary Tale. *Transnational Law and Contemporary Problems* 23(2): 261–304.

2015. Condominium Law in Taiwan: Doctrinal Overview under the Lens of Information-Cost Theory. *Asia Pacific Law Review* 23(2): 89–120.

2016. Hybrid Rule: Hidden Entitlement Protection Rule in Access to Landlocked Land Doctrine. *Tulane Law Review* 91(2): 217–57.

Chang, Yun-chien, Kong-Pin Chen, and Chang-ching Lin. 2014. *Anchoring Effect in Real Litigations* ssrn.com/abstract=2726903.

Chang, Yun-chien, and Henry E. Smith. 2015. The Numerus Clausus Principle, Property Custom, and the Emergence of New Property Forms. *Iowa Law Review* 100: 2275–308.

Huang, Chengyi, and David Law. 2015. Proportionality Review of Administrative Action in Japan, Korea, Taiwan, and China. In *Research Handbook in*

Comparative Law and Regulation, edited by Francesca Bignami and David Zaring. Northampton, MA: Edward Elgar.

Huffstetler, Scott D. 2002. Don't Fence Me In: Louisiana's Fourth Circuit Expands "Voluntariness" Under Louisiana Civil Code Article 693. *Louisiana Law Review* 63: 111–26.

Merrill, Thomas W., and Henry E. Smith. 2010. *The Oxford Introductions to U.S. Law: Property*. New York NY: Oxford University Press.

Merwe, C. G. Van der. 1999. The Louisiana Right to Forced Passage Compared to the South African Way of Necessity. *Tulane Law Review* 73: 1363–1413.

Sentell, C. Sherburne, III. 1994. Fixing the Right of Passage from an Enclosed Estate: Deciding Where to Break out Using Louisiana Civil Code Article 692. *Louisiana Law Review* 54: 1659–84.

Wilmore, Randall L. 1986. Right of Passage for the Benefit of an Enclosed Estate. *Louisiana Law Review* 47: 199–216.

Yiannopoulos, A. N. 1996. The Legal Servitude of Passage. *Tulane Law Review* 71: 1–44.

5

Compulsory Land Acquisition in Developing Countries: Shifting Paradigm or Entrenched Legacy?

JONATHAN LINDSAY, KLAUS DEININGER, THEA HILHORST[1]

1 Introduction

While compulsory acquisition[2] (or taking) of land has been the subject of an active intellectual debate in many developed countries, actual acquisition of land has proceeded very rapidly in many developing ones. By many definitions, the process of development itself is associated with large-scale change in land use from agriculture to non-agriculture, urbanization, expansion of infrastructure, and urban redevelopment, all processes for which land needs to be made available and for which use of compulsory acquisition is now commonplace. Given its importance for development, it is surprising that the conceptual and empirical literature on compulsory acquisition is focused mainly on developed countries.

With access to land one of the frequently mentioned constraints to private investment in developing countries, there has been considerable government interest in making land available more quickly to attract investors, including through devices such as special economic zones and industrial parks. The relative ease of land acquisition in China has indeed been suggested not only as a major contributor to its rapid growth but also as one of the factors underlying differences in growth performance between China and India. On the other hand, as World Bank and other

[1] The World Bank. The views expressed in this chapter are those of the authors and do not represent the position of the World Bank, its member countries, or its Executive Directors.

[2] This power is known by a variety of names depending on a country's legal traditions, including eminent domain, takings, expropriation, condemnation, compulsory purchase, etc., to list only those appellations used in English.

research over the last several decades has confirmed, development-induced displacement can frequently lead to the greater impoverishment of those affected, with often far-reaching negative consequences for communities and local economies (Cernea and Mathur 2007).

The conceptual literature illustrates that, for an impartial government that aims to maximize social welfare, compulsory acquisition of land allows for the provision of a non-rival public good and for addressing possible holdout problems (Miceli and Segerson 2014). The latter issue arises from the fact that – due to the need to acquire contiguous land – sellers whose land is necessary to realize the gain from a large-scale project may have an incentive to strategically misrepresent the true valuation of land in order to gain a higher price (Miceli and Segerson 2012). The need to pay compensation at full market value even if land is expropriated will, in principle, address this (Nosal 2001). Thus, while the government could either buy the land in question or acquire it using eminent domain with compensation at market prices, the latter option is more appealing if the number of landowners is large (Shavell 2010).

However, the principal aim of a government may not be to maximize social welfare, but instead to acquire land for other purposes or to enhance its own revenue. This has been well documented for cases such as China (Du and Peiser 2014; Liu and Li 2015) and Vietnam (Vo 2011). There, local governments' ability to acquire land with levels of compensation that reflect agricultural values and then to transfer it to higher value uses has played a huge role in filling government treasuries, but at the same time has affected financial and social stability. Although most land is now transferred via auction, there is evidence that this has not helped to eliminate corruption (Cai et al. 2013). Creation of special purpose vehicles to borrow against future land acquisition has resulted in a significant amount of bad debt, and local landholders' inability to share in land value appreciation has given rise to social conflict (Zheng et al. 2014). An ability to acquire land from farmers at low cost can also lead to over-acquisition and inefficient land use, rent-seeking, and social conflict. In fact, the potential for a similar "unholy alliance between local governments and property developers" has also been identified as a challenge in the United States (Miceli 2014).

Avoiding undesirable outcomes without unduly limiting the scope for land acquisition that will truly enhance social welfare is a key concern for developing countries. It is complicated by the fact that, although the demands for land they face are intense, the legal and institutional frameworks governing land taking are often poorly adapted to the social and economic milieu in which they operate. Indeed, as the experience of the World Bank and other international agencies confirms, and as the global consensus represented by the Voluntary Guidelines for Governance of Tenure (VGGTs) underscores, this is an area where pronounced gaps exist between national frameworks and international "best practice."

To improve land governance, a number of developing countries have, in recent decades, introduced far-reaching legal innovations such as the recognition of diverse tenure regimes including customary ones, stronger local rights to natural resources, decentralized forms of administering land rights, low-cost and simplified recording, and strong provisions to mandate gender equality. By contrast, legal reforms related to compulsory acquisition have tended to lag, especially in countries where by law all land is owned by the state. There are interesting recent attempts to innovate at the level of national and sub-national law (for example, India, South Africa and Brazil), although these also illustrate just how hard it is to design and implement a law that establishes a balanced approach in very complex land rights environments.

Compulsory acquisition in developing countries has to contend with a number of practical challenges. First, non-existent or outdated land records often make it difficult to determine those affected and thus eligible for compensation. This is frequently compounded by the coexistence of different types of customary and statutory land rights that may or may not be legally recognized and that are rarely recorded or, even if recorded, not mapped on the ground. Second, large numbers of land holders hold only informal possessory rights, with a single piece of land often subject to a complex layering of such rights. Finally, ill-functioning, informal, or distorted land markets make it difficult to determine a fair "market value." As a consequence, even if national laws were sufficiently focused on ensuring that people affected by a taking are restored to a situation equivalent to their pre-taking status, lack of necessary information will make doing so difficult in practice, especially in situations where demand for land acquisition is rising rapidly.

In the pages that follow we explore different dimensions of these problems. We aim to illustrate that key design features of conventional compulsory acquisition laws and processes – which continue to characterize many developing-country legal frameworks – are often at odds with the complex land governance and social challenges such countries may face.

2 Defining Limits on the Exercise of Compulsory Acquisition

In developing-country legal frameworks, as in most developed countries, national constitutions and laws typically define the limits of the compulsory acquisition power by reference to concepts such as "public use," "public purpose," "public benefit," "public interest," "utilité publique," etc. Frequently, these terms are used interchangeably, and for practical purposes treated as if they mean more or less the same thing. Yet, in the English-speaking world at least, the distinction between "public use" and "public purpose" (for example) is not without potential significance, and the fact that this distinction has become blurred over time is emblematic of the trajectory of jurisprudence on the subject in a number of countries.

In the United States, for example, the Supreme Court in *Berman v. Parker* (US Supreme Court 1954) stretched the "public use" concept beyond a focus on standard examples of public goods – infrastructure, parks, schools, etc. – to encompass activities that serve a "public purpose," such as the promotion of economic development. Eminent domain has consequently been available to local governments engaged in assembling land for urban renewal, even when the ultimate end use is private low-cost housing or a commercial building intended to stimulate economic revival in a blighted area.

In this sense, the controversial Supreme Court decision in *Kelo v. City of New London* (US Supreme Court 2005) is part of a continuum rather than a radical departure. The Court in *Kelo* held that the city's use of eminent domain in order to enable the construction of an urban redevelopment plan featuring a mix of private uses met the public purpose test because the construction would increase the city's tax base and would bring general economic benefits to the community. In her famous dissent, Justice Sandra Day O'Connor argued that the majority decision would allow the rich to benefit at the expense of the poor, asserting that: "Any property may now be taken for the benefit of another private party, but the fallout from this decision will not be random. The beneficiaries are likely to be those citizens with disproportionate influence and power in the political process, including large corporations and development firms." She argued that the decision eliminates "any distinction between private and public use of property – and thereby effectively delete[s] the words 'for public use' from the Takings Clause of the Fifth Amendment"(US Supreme Court 2005; Mangioni 2009).

A large literature explores the nuances and aftermath of *Kelo*, which are beyond the scope of this chapter to examine.[3] For our purposes, what is notable is that the tension at the heart of the *Kelo* debate finds its parallel in many developing-country contexts, as do the concerns expressed by Justice O'Connor about the potential capture of eminent domain processes by those with "disproportionate influence and power" (Downing 2013). It is safe to say that, in most legal systems, an overarching principle is that a government's taking powers are *extraordinary* powers – it is not typical for laws to allow governments to use compulsory acquisition as the normal means of assembling land for purposes that are clearly for commercial, industrial or other profitable private uses alone. At the same time, in many countries around the world (though not all) the fact that a beneficiary is a private entity does not in itself disqualify it from benefiting from the exercise of government takings power, provided there is a significant public benefit involved.

Defining credible limits on the use of public takings power in support of private users can be difficult, particularly in countries with no clear process for making such decisions, and where there is little transparency in the decision-making process, weak accountability and virtually no judicial oversight. This has consequently been the focus of considerable controversy in many parts of the developing world, where governments increasingly seek to use the public purpose/use concept to support private activities or public–private partnerships on the basis that they will contribute to national economic growth – as opposed to the more tangible public benefits usually associated with compulsory acquisition (Lindsay 2012).

There is a wide spectrum of approaches to this issue in national laws and policies. At the restrictive end of this spectrum, some countries have at least formally resisted the temptation to expand the takings power into direct support for private investment. Their laws typically retain a standard list of uses that fall within the definition of public purpose – infrastructure, utilities, schools, parks and the like – with little scope for discretion. In Peru, for example, constitutional rules tightly circumscribe cases where expropriation can be used. Article 70 of the Constitution stipulates that expropriations can only be carried out for reasons of national security or "public need," e.g. to build a road or bridge. The expropriation law provides that expropriations are void unless the

[3] See, for example, Saginor and McDonald (2009), Turnbull and Salvino (2009), Kerekes and Williamson (2010), and Lanza et al. (2013).

state is the direct beneficiary. Public scrutiny and debate of individual expropriations is ensured by the requirement that any case of expropriation must be authorized by Congress in a law explicitly spelling out the future use of expropriated goods.

In Uganda, the Constitution, the Land Act of 1998 and the Land Acquisition Act of 1965 all limit the use of compulsory acquisition for promotion of private investment. The government attempted to include the authority to use compulsory acquisition for investment promotion in the Draft National Land Policy, but these efforts were successfully turned back during the policy consultation process, with the result that the final National Land Policy (2013) leaves the prohibition on compulsory acquisition for private investment intact (Stickler 2012), although not always observed in practice.

Toward the other end of the spectrum are legal frameworks that are more permissive when it comes to takings on behalf of private uses. A topical illustration can be found in the case of investment by foreign firms in large-scale agricultural holdings in developing countries. This phenomenon has attracted a lot of international attention, promoted by some as key to unleashing the agricultural potential of regions such as sub-Saharan Africa, while others characterize it as "land grabbing" bringing few benefits to host communities and putting local livelihoods at risk. Whatever the merits of these viewpoints, it is noteworthy that a number of countries – Ethiopia, Tanzania and Senegal to mention a few – have included "commercial agriculture" or "agricultural development" amongst the public purposes justifying the exercise of compulsory acquisition, and have at times used that power as a tool for assembling land for large-scale investments. From the perspective of the large-scale investor, this approach has evident attractions – compulsory acquisition in essence "wipes the slate clean" as far as existing rights are concerned, which in many cases are widely scattered among different rights holders, are obscurely defined by law and may not be transactable (see below). At the same time, however, this legal "cleanness" can come at a high price for investors, who may discover that governance problems surrounding government taking procedures, as well as deep-rooted local distrust of such procedures, have poisoned relationships with local communities.

China provides an illustrative case of compulsory acquisition used for channeling land into ultimately non-public uses in the context of urban expansion. Although the law stipulates that the state can acquire collectively owned rural land only in the public interest, this term is not defined. Under law, rural land can *only* be converted to urban uses if it has first been acquired by the state – although there is now an active market for urban land use rights in China, the options for rural users to sell to urban users are extremely limited. Therefore, the exercise of compulsory acquisition is widespread on the edges of China's exploding cities as local governments struggle to find land for urban expansion. The public interest in such situations is implicitly defined to include actions deemed to be required for rational urban growth. As part of China's ongoing efforts to address a wide range of problems associated with compulsory acquisition, however, ways of limiting the concept of public interest are being considered (Lindsay 2012).

The debate over the use of government taking powers in support of private business was also prominent in the lead up to the passage of the new Land Law in Vietnam in 2013. As in China, the extensive use of compulsory acquisition on behalf of private end-users in Vietnam has sparked significant unrest among affected communities, who are particularly aggrieved by the low compensation received for land that typically skyrockets in value when converted to a commercial or industrial use (Kim 2011). Estimates compiled as part of the 2014 Land Governance Assessment Framework process suggest that over half of all recent takings in Vietnam have been on behalf of private businesses and investors, facilitated by provisions in the 2003 Land Law that authorized the state to "recover land" whenever it needs "to use the land for purposes of national defense and security, national interests, public interests or *economic development*"(World Bank 2013b, emphasis added). There was considerable pressure from civil society and the international community during the drafting of the new land law to remove broad reference to "economic development" and revert to a more standard and restricted list of permissible public uses. Ultimately, the Land Law was adopted with allowance for recovery of land for "socio-economic development in the national or public interest," which as compared to the 2003 law was circumscribed by a number of limitations – an extensive list of activities that can be considered "socio-economic development"; requirements that any such recovery be approved by the Prime Minister or the People's Councils, depending on the intended use; and requirements that any end use be contemplated by an approved land use plan (Government of Vietnam 2013).

There are a number of other legislative techniques designed to "raise the bar" on a determination of public purpose that can be found in recent legislation, though their implementation and effectiveness is hard to verify. In some countries (Kenya, India and Croatia, to name three examples), proponents are required to show that the benefit to the public of the acquisition will outweigh the hardships to those affected. While theoretically appealing, the methodological difficulties of credibly estimating the public benefits of a proposed development can be daunting; nevertheless, to the extent proponents are actually required to undertake such exercises, this may at least shed light on situations where there is a clear imbalance between public benefits and private impacts.

With an eye towards ensuring that a public purpose justification is genuine, and not simply a disguise for facilitating future commercial transfers, a number of laws target subsequent transfers and land use changes, or failures of government to use the land that it has taken. Thus, some laws require governments to offer the land back to the original owners if not used for the intended purpose, or provide some remedies to original owners if land is transferred to an unanticipated private use. Both of these respond to situations commonly found in the developing world. In Ghana, for example, there are extensive areas of land acquired by the government in the 1980s that were either never used or only partially used. A land diagnostic of part of the Accra Plains, undertaken as part of the World Bank-supported Ghana Commercial Agriculture Project revealed large areas of land where takings were completed but virtually none of the planned development implemented, or where takings were initiated but never completed, leaving the legal status of the land in limbo (Kasanga and Mahama 2011). The Government of Ghana has found itself in recent years subject to increasingly strong calls for the return of land to communities who were expropriated for a public purpose that never materialized either because the land was not developed or because it was transferred to a private use. Efforts to respond systematically to these calls are constrained by the fact that records of state-acquired land themselves are often incomplete or inaccurate. Evidence of unused or partially used land after government acquisition abound. Records in Kwara State in Nigeria, for example, reveal that of the total land (25,267.41 Ha) acquired between 2007 and 2011, only 17 hectares (0.0673 per cent) is fully utilized, some 7,547.85 hectares (29.87 per cent) is under partial utilization – more than 70.06 per cent has not been utilized at all (Adeniyi 2011).

The most elaborate recent legislative effort to address problems associated with the application of a public purpose standard – both generally and with specific reference to its use in support of private enterprises – can be found in India's Right to Fair Compensation and Transparency in Land Acquisition, Rehabilitation and Resettlement Act, 2013 (LARR). The LARR was adopted after many years of debate, against a backdrop of increasingly vociferous public protest about large land acquisitions on behalf of private industries such as Tata Motors in Singur, West Bengal. Such takings were facilitated in part by expansive legal interpretations of the public use/purpose doctrine in the 1894 Land Acquisition Act (the Act which LARR finally replaced). In the last decades of the twentieth century, the Indian Supreme Court delivered a number of rulings in favor of the transfer of land by eminent domain from farmers to industry on the grounds that the broad economic development benefits of the private industries constituted a public benefit. In one case, the court read "public purpose" to include "any purpose wherein even a fraction of the community may be interested or by which it may be benefitted," which prompted one observer to comment that "there does not seem to be any conceivable limit to what purposes will be deemed to be in the best interest of the public by the acquiring governments"(Downing 2013).

The new Indian law attacks this problem from a number of angles.

- It requires the preparation of a social impact assessment, that would, among other things (a) assess the extent to which the proposed acquisition meets a public purpose; (b) confirm that the area being taken is the minimum area required for the purpose and that all alternatives have been considered and found unviable; (c) demonstrate that the social impacts have been weighed against the public benefits of the project; (d) be publicly consulted and published; and (e) be evaluated by an expert group.
- It requires a specific finding by Government, based on the social assessment, an environmental impact assessment and, in some cases, a food security assessment, that (a) there is a clear and *bona fide* public interest; (b) the benefits outweigh the costs; (c) the minimum necessary land is being acquired; (d) there is no other previously acquired but unused land in the area; and (e) if such previously acquired but unused land is present, it is used for the proposed purpose of the current acquisition.
- The Act stipulates that if land remains unutilized for five years, it will be returned to the original owners.

- If the land is sold before being utilized for an amount larger than the acquisition price, the LARR requires that 40 per cent of the appreciated value will be paid to the people from whom the land was acquired.
- If land is being acquired for a private company or for a public–private partnership, the acquisition must be consented to by 80 per cent or 70 per cent, respectively, of the impacted people.

These are extraordinary provisions, together representing one of the most comprehensive legislative attempts in either the developing or developed world to ensure meaningful application of the public purpose requirements. Yet there has been considerable pushback against the LARR from the private sector, and growing concern even among some proponents about its implementation challenges. One of the early actions of the Modi government in December 2014 was to pass an emergency ordinance exempting certain types of projects from the social impact assessment and consent provisions of the Act, ostensibly to unblock billions of dollars of investment that has been stalled in the pipeline for months (Government of India 2014). This ordinance provoked an outcry among civil society groups who questioned the credibility of its rationale. But the controversy highlighted a persistent dilemma – where extensive safeguards are unaccompanied by the institutional capacity and political will to implement them, the process may simply freeze, inspiring efforts to dismantle those safeguards or to find informal ways to work around them.

3 Just Compensation

Issues surrounding compensation for losses suffered – "who gets what" when government acquires a piece of land – are typically the most complex and controversial aspects of compulsory acquisition. A long-standing principle in many jurisdictions is that compensation should be guided by the objectives of "equity" and "equivalence" – that is, the adequacy of compensation should be measured against the goal of ensuring that people are neither impoverished nor enriched (Keith et al. 2009).

In developed-country contexts, legislation typically approaches these objectives by positing the existence of a well-defined property interest held by an easily identified owner or interest holder. While never free of controversy, the property interest is assumed to have a value that can be more or less scientifically determined. The payment of this value, along (in many jurisdictions) with additional payments intended to address incidental costs associated with disturbance and relocation, is judged sufficient to achieve the goals of equity and equivalence.

Experience increasingly confirms that legal approaches developed in the context of Europe or North America – where land rights are generally standardized and well-defined, land markets function, and land records are reliable – are ill-equipped for contexts where such attributes are less common. In many developing-country contexts, application of standard compulsory acquisition models means that there is a frequent mismatch between compensation offered and losses actually suffered.

There are a number of factors that contribute to this overarching problem:

- *Weak or unrecognized land tenure rights.* In many developing countries, a wide-range of rights to the possession and use of land are unrecognized or poorly protected by formal law. Indeed, as one observer has pointed out, the inequities often associated with a government taking are not necessarily "the result of the expropriation itself, but of the operation of an ill-conceived tenure system" (Azuela 2009). As a consequence, many interests considered valuable in a particular social context may not be considered legitimate objects of compensation.
- *Difficulties in determining value.* The underlying legal weakness of rights, along with the absence of functioning formal markets in those rights can make the determination of value a highly artificial exercise, often linked to badly outdated government schedules, understated tax appraisals or simply left up to unguided discretion.
- *Insufficiency of monetary compensation to address impacts.* Experts have long asserted that economic compensation linked to the value of lost land or assets can often not adequately address the disruption to livelihoods and social cohesion that often accompanies large-scale takings in developing countries (Cernea and Mathur 2007). Hence, international standards such as the World Bank's Policy on Involuntary Resettlement focus not only on the technical calculation of compensation but on the broader (and more elusive) standard of restoring or enhancing people's livelihoods. When viewed from this perspective, it could be said that most developing country expropriation laws are only "half the story"; while focusing on calculating and

compensating lost economic value, they usually leave out resettlement and rehabilitation issues altogether.

- *Weak rule of law.* Compounding flaws in their design is the fact that expropriation laws and procedures – whether well or poorly conceived are often flaunted in practice. In a sector widely recognized for its poor governance (studies routinely rank land administration as among the most corrupt government institutions in developing countries (Transparency International 2011)), compulsory land acquisition holds a prominent place. Tales abound throughout the developing world of compensation being underpaid or not paid at all, non-transparent decision-making, unresponsive grievance mechanisms and resort to harsh, sometimes violent, eviction techniques. While important efforts are underway in many countries to remedy these deficiencies, expropriation remains an issue characterized by opacity, distrust and abuse.

Compensation issues can be grouped according to two overlapping sets of questions: *who should receive compensation for what kind of loss;* and *how should the quantum and type of compensation be determined?*

3.1 Who Are the Interest Holders and What Are Their Interests?

As noted, standard models presume a clearly identifiable interest in land owned by an easily identifiable person. In many developing country contexts, this presumption encounters a wide range of exceptions and complications, often poorly or incompletely addressed in national legislation.

Unregistered or inaccurately documented rights. It is not unusual for compulsory acquisition laws to presume a level of documentation of rights that may in fact not exist. Some laws, for example, tie eligibility for compensation to whether a right is registered in accordance with the country's land registration legislation. This can be problematic where, as is frequently the case, only a fraction of a country's land has actually been registered, notwithstanding the presence for many decades of land registration laws. In sub-Saharan Africa, for example, it is estimated that more than 90 per cent of all rural land rights are unrecorded in a manner that is recognized by law. If strictly applied, a "registered-interests-only" rule to compensation would result in many interests going uncompensated or under-compensated.

There are several variations on this theme that appear in laws or in the way they are applied. Some progressive land laws, for example, in Mozambique, stipulate that valid rights to land exist, whether registered or not; in practice, however, it is often only those with documented rights that are taken into account when land rights are withdrawn and compensation paid. Ghanaian practice similarly focuses on registered or documented rights. In the complex architecture of land rights in Ghana's customary sector, this can lead to situations in which "outsiders" with formal, written leases from traditional authorities are eligible for compensation, while "customary freeholders" – i.e., community members with perpetual but undocumented rights to land by virtue of membership in the community – are ineligible (Larbi 2004). Under customary law, which in Ghana is enshrined in the constitution, "customary freeholds" are stronger and more durable rights than leaseholds, yet efforts to promote the documentation and registration of these rights has run into resistance from the Ghanaian House of Chiefs, whose members are concerned that this could erode customary land management arrangements and the prerogative of chiefs. The result is an anomalous situation where, at least in theory, leaseholders are compensated directly, while customary freeholders must derive any compensation for their land from the traditional authority, which is treated as the appropriate recipient of government compensation.

World Bank analysis of the expropriation process in Albania illustrates another dimension of this problem, namely the cost to both government and the property owner of trying to ensure a just outcome where the law requires strict adherence to a "registered-property-only" principle. Albania's Immovable Property Rights Office (IPRO) estimated at the time of the World Bank study (World Bank 2011) that it had records for about 60 per cent to 70 per cent of the parcels in the country. Thus, as properties were unregistered in approximately one-third of all cases, it was not uncommon for properties subject to expropriation to have no record at IPRO. This is a problem because Law No. 8561 on Expropriation requires the property to be registered in IPRO before it can be expropriated. For rural land this process requires "special registration" which is essentially a sporadic First Registration process with required public display, resulting in the issuance of an Ownership Certificate (*Certifikat i Pronesise*). For urban property the "sporadic registration" process is used whereby the IPRO researches its archive, opens a *Kartela* (legal register) for the property and attempts to determine who the legal owner is. However, only an "Ownership Verification" document

(*Vertetim i Pronesise*) is issued and the property will still have go through the systematic registration and public display process before the final Ownership Certificate is issued. As a result of the incomplete registration records, a great deal of work has been undertaken by government officials and property owners to identify the properties, their boundaries and ownership so that the properties can be registered, *with the only purpose being to expropriate the property almost immediately afterwards.* (The chief of the Directorate of Roads noted that he has two jobs – his own expropriation job and that of fixing the registration system.) There are no figures for the amount of time and the cost to the government of undertaking this work, but the costs are significant.

The Albania situation also entails high costs for owners, for locating and certifying documents, obtaining a survey of the property, registration fees, and other costs in terms of lost time, stress, transport, etc. For example, the survey could cost between US$50 and US$100, and the IPRO fee for "special registration" of a rural property is approximately US$250, both of which the owner would be obliged to pay. In fact, officials report that, if the area of land to be expropriated is only small, and thus the amount of compensation is small, then owners do not bother with registering their property, and simply abandon the compensation altogether. However, if a building is being expropriated, then a larger amount is involved, and owners will go to the cost and effort to register their property. The person being expropriated carries the burden of the time and costs for registration, which therefore lessens the total compensation package that he or she receives. This is not the case in all countries that follow something similar to the Albanian approach. In some countries, while expropriation may still require prior registration of a property in the equivalent of IPRO, the duty to register lies with the expropriating authority, which also takes responsibility for the work and costs (World Bank 2011).

The issue of documentary evidence of rights touches upon the broader problem of official records that are inaccurate or out-of-date, again a common feature in many countries. Even where countries (or portions of countries) have gone through a rigorous and substantially complete systematic first registration process, experience shows that many countries have not been able to tackle the challenge of keeping information up-to-date. This can be an artifact of a number of weaknesses in land administration – for example, the tendency to under-estimate the urgency of institution-building in order to maintain and update systems once they have been populated with first registration data; or a lack of incentives on the part of property owners to utilize the system for subsequent transactions. The result is often geographic data that may wrongly define the size or location of the parcel being acquired, and legal data that lists the wrong person as the holder of the land right.

In some countries, rules linking eligibility to registration are not as stringent, or may be flexibly applied. In practice, governments may in fact rely on alternate forms of evidence such as tax records or utility receipts, relaxing the formal rule to accommodate facts on the ground. In Rwanda, for example, the 2007 Law on Expropriation (Rwanda 2007) is explicitly receptive to alternative proof of ownership: the person being expropriated can demonstrate ownership of the expropriated right by (a) written evidence indicating that he or she purchased the land, received it as a donation, as a legacy or through succession; (b) a document or a statement of local administrative entities indicating rights of the expropriated person on the land; (c) a document or testimony of the neighbors confirming the ownership of the land; or (d) a court certificate. But even in countries with a relaxed approach to questions of evidence, the frequent reality is that those who do not have easy access to strong, formally recognized documentation are disadvantaged or overlooked in the allocation of compensation.

Multiple and customary rights. In virtually all systems, land may be subject to multiple layers of rights held by any number of rights holders. A privately owned parcel may be subject to leaseholds, mortgages, rights of way for utilities or transportation, concessions, rights to water, hunting or forest products, grazing rights, etc. Ownership of land, trees, buildings and other improvements may all be separately held, and various rights of access and use may be held by multiple individuals, groups or classes of people. Each of these separate interests may represent a significant loss to its holder(s) if the land parcel is acquired by government and the right is terminated.

In most developed country systems, these subsidiary rights are registered (by notation on the owner's title, for example), otherwise documented, or ascertainable through certain established legal processes. In many developing countries, the situation is less clear for a number of reasons. First and foremost is the weakness in the documentation of land rights in general – the deficiencies mentioned above in the documentation of primary rights are compounded many times over in the case of secondary rights, which are frequently recorded only orally or in the collective memory of a community (Keith et al. 2009). Second is the fact that many such rights are not accorded any official status under law, given only ambiguous recognition or treated as "privileges" that can be terminated without consent or compensation. Third is simply the proliferation and complexity of such rights, particularly in rural areas, where rights over land owned by others, held in common, or vested in the government are key to livelihood strategies and ingrained in local agricultural systems.

These complexities are especially pronounced in countries where formal tenure regimes co-exist with customary systems. In many parts of Africa, Latin America, Asia and the Pacific and elsewhere, a significant amount of land is held under customary tenure, with traditional authorities being responsible for the administration of land according to customary practices. Land within a customary tenure regime may be held according to various rights configurations, with the group collectively holding some rights alongside an array of individual or household rights to individual parcels or resources. Recent decades have witnessed a growing willingness on the part of a number of national governments to accord some formal recognition to customary rights. A clear example of this is Ghana, where up to 80 per cent of all land is recognized in accordance with the Constitution as owned by traditional communities. In a range of other countries, including Mozambique, Tanzania, Uganda, Burkina Faso, Philippines, Cambodia, Peru and elsewhere in Latin America, land laws have been adopted that provide for the recognition of customary or indigenous tenure regimes to varying degrees. In short, the distinction between customary and statutory tenure is in a number of places less significant than it used to be. On the one hand, this trend is encouraging because it promises more robust and equitable treatment under law for land rights that governments have historically tended to ignore or only to acknowledge weakly. On the other hand, in many countries, while the principle of recognition of customary rights is proclaimed, the legal framework for such recognition is vaguely articulated and moves towards operationalizing it have been ambivalent. As a result, the situation on the ground is often one where rights remain unclear and vulnerable. (Lindsay 2012)

Once again, standard compulsory acquisition laws and practices are frequently not well adapted to "catching" all relevant interests in a land parcel. Some laws may target landowners and a number of legally established commercial or financial rights without contemplating the array of other potential rights and practices that come into play. And even where the legal framework clearly recognizes customary, subsidiary or secondary rights, the *processes* put in place for identifying, notifying and compensating interest holders are often not well-designed to discover the existence of such rights, or to bring the holders of those rights into the discussion of compensation. The information deficit described above makes it difficult for outsiders, including government and investors, to ascertain the true tenurial situation on the ground, sometimes leading to facile assumptions that land is "empty." Genuine stakeholders are liable to being disadvantaged or left out of negotiations and excluded from compensation or other benefits. Investors in turn may be exposed to possible future conflict with persons whose claims – legitimate or not – may have been previously overlooked. Conflicting claims to the same land by neighboring groups may also be present, fueled in part by the absence of clearly defined boundaries between traditional areas, as most such areas have never been mapped or documented.

Group rights. Land held by groups or under some sort of collective arrangement represent a variation on the above themes, and can pose special challenges to the application of the principles of compensation if rights are not registered.[4] In such instances, the law may treat the traditional authority or the collective entity as the holder of the compensable interest in land, and implicitly rely on them to ensure that land rights compensation is appropriately shared within the group.

An example from a customary law setting is Ghana, where traditional authorities (referred to in some parts of the country as "stools" or "skins") hold "allodial" (full) ownership to the land on behalf of their communities. As described above, under Ghanaian compulsory acquisition practice, this means that the legal focus of compensation when stool or skin land is taken is the traditional authority itself, despite the co-existence of strong individual rights over parts of the land held by community members. At customary law, chiefs have traditionally acted as trustees of the land, yet increasingly, especially in peri-urban areas and

[4] Countries such as Mexico, Tanzania, and Mozambique suggest registration is possible if (i) mechanisms for community management of basic land administration processes (such as allocation of individual rights, updating of registries, and other internal affairs, according to given bylaws) are well defined; (ii) boundaries are recorded and a clear internal governance structure (with internal control structures) is established to allow interaction with outsiders; (iii) records are integrated with those used in the regular land administration system to prevent double-allocation of land, to allow land users to enter into joint ventures with investors, or to allow groups to gradually individualize land rights if desired; and (iv) relevant secondary rights, including use rights, such as those held by pastoralists or migrants, and forest dwellers, are recorded and protected, rather than eliminated or ignored, e.g. by documenting them in land use plans that identify cattle tracks, seasonal grazing areas, and watering sources.

areas of high investment potential, there are signs that chiefs have begun to conceive of their role as that of landowners in their own right, with subjects in essence reduced to lessees. There are reports of chiefs striking deals with government or outside investors, in essence engaging in the sale of areas that by custom were considered common forest, water or grazing resources, or alienating land that was fallow or reserved for future generations (Kasanga and Mahama 2011).

A non-customary law example is the ownership of rural agricultural land in China, where law recognizes the collective as owner. Here, the issue of compensation and its adequacy is complicated by the fact that there are three levels involved: government, collective and individual farming households, and there are important concerns about whether those funds reach the farmers. The practice has been for much of this compensation to be taken by the collective and invested in ways that might ultimately provide alternative employment for those who have lost their farmland. But farmers have often complained that they rarely get the jobs or see the other benefits projected. Responding to the difficulties stemming from current practice, the central government of China has issued successive policy documents urging local governments to focus efforts on improving compensation, and calling for the distribution of land compensation within the rural collective economic organizations on the basis of the principle of "land compensation being primarily used for the farmer households whose land is taken over." Interestingly, a survey conducted by China's Development Research Centre in collaboration with the World Bank revealed that, at least in the selected survey areas, there was not widespread explicit concern that compensation was being unfairly siphoned off by collectives before reaching the farmers. However, a significant percentage of respondents did indicate that they were *unclear* as to how the distribution of funds has been handled – the process by which proceeds are shared and allocated is simply not known by many participants (World Bank and Development Research Center 2007).

Compensation for informal or illegal occupation. The problem of informal or "squatter" settlements is a sub-species of the wider problem of unrecognized or under-recognized rights, more likely to arise in urban settings where links to long-standing customary practices may not be available to lend a measure of "legitimacy" to what governments refer to as "illegal" or sometimes "criminal" occupation. The policies of international organizations for the most part include "squatters" and other informal occupants as among those entitled to received resettlement assistance,[5] but this is a frequent area in which international norms and national law diverge. Many governments object to the idea that even those who are clearly occupying land illegally are entitled to some level of compensation. This, it is argued, creates perverse incentives for people to ignore rules when they occupy land, and rewards illegal behavior to the detriment of the rule of law. These objections are compounded when the illegal occupiers in question are not poor and vulnerable but are relatively well-off and well-connected investors. On the other hand, it needs to be recognized that a resettlement approach that focuses only on those with formal legal rights could have detrimental development consequences. Informal occupation of land in many settings is not a matter of choice but of necessity, induced by poverty, exacerbated by inaccessible land markets and poorly functioning planning regimes, and in some cases condoned and encouraged by the very authorities who are now interested in acquiring the land. Hence, while a full legislative embrace of the notion that squatters should be compensated is unlikely to occur in most countries, there is a growing trend on the part of governments to adjust law and practice to deal with individual and societal consequences associated with displacement of informal occupants that have been occupying land for a long period of time. Brazil's Ministry of Cities Ordinance 317 is a case in point, focusing on addressing the housing needs of all those affected by displacement, whether formal or informal (World Bank 2015). The Indian LARR Act refers to "affected families" rather than defining eligibility in terms of whether or not a property right exists and is recognized by law. In the same vein, Article 40(4) of the new Kenyan Constitution stipulates that "provisions may be made for compensation to be paid to occupants in good faith of land . . . who may not hold title to the land."

3.2 What Is the Appropriate Quantum and Type of Compensation?

Assessing the fair market value of lost assets. Although market value is the benchmark found in most compulsory acquisition laws when it comes to the calculation of compensation for an acquired asset, determining it in practice is not easy. Laws and constitutions may also refer more broadly to principles such as "just" or "fair" compensation, and in

[5] The Voluntary Guidelines for the Responsible Governance of Tenure use the term "legitimate" rights to include informal rights broadly recognized by a society as legitimate, whether or not enshrined in law.

many cases contemplate compensation for losses associated with disturbance, costs related to moving and transition, harm to business, etc. International norms such as those promoted by the World Bank, International Finance Corporation and others refer to "replacement cost" as the appropriate benchmark for valuation of assets. This is also a term found in a minority of national laws (for example, Rwanda). Where land markets are robust, replacement cost and fair market value should be roughly equivalent. When it comes to non-land assets such as housing and other improvements, a replacement cost approach also ensures that the depreciation of lost assets is not taken into account in the calculation of compensation, and that transaction costs associated with the purchase of new assets are covered.

A common legislative approach is to define market value as the amount a willing buyer would pay a willing seller on the open market where some choice exists (Keith et al. 2009). There are several reasons this calculation might be difficult to make in a given setting (particularly when it comes to land values as opposed to other non-land assets). In some places, formal land markets may be non-existent or extremely thin, especially in rural areas. Some legal systems disallow the sale of particular categories of land or place severe limits on such sales. Underlying rights, as we have seen, may be poorly defined in terms of content or duration. In some cases, active informal markets may exist that if studied could in theory reveal what land is selling for in the area, but governments are generally reluctant to acknowledge officially the existence of such markets. And even where formal land markets may exist, the absence of an established, independent valuation profession and the tendency of buyers and sellers to understate prices in order to minimize taxation can conspire to make the ascertainment of market value very difficult.

In the face of these constraints, laws may rely on a variety of proxies for land value.

- In China, the value of agricultural land is determined by applying a multiplier (which varies from place to place) to the average productivity of the land over a three-year period (World Bank and Development Research Center 2007).
- In Albania, values are assigned to different categories of land on the basis of schedules and maps prepared periodically by government, often seriously out of date (World Bank 2011).

- Mexico, El Salvador and Guatemala use tax valuation as a guide for compensation – the landowner is entitled to the (often low) value of the property he or she has declared the property to be worth for tax purposes.
- Philippine practice, at least with respect to certain classes of projects, is to rely on the self-declaration of owners as found in conveyancing documents, or on tax appraisals records of local governments that are almost always seriously outdated. The result in some cases is that values are set at levels that are up to 1000 per cent below the actual price required to purchase equivalent property on the market (World Bank 2013a).
- In Madagascar, case studies conducted between 2005 and 2010 reveal that compensation was frequently paid at a level between 30 per cent to 65 per cent of the actual value of the land and assets being taken (Burnod 2012).
- In India's LARR Act, market value is defined as the highest of (a) the market value as stipulated in accordance with the Indian Stamp Act, (b) the average sale price of similar land in nearby villages, or (c) in the case of takings in support of a private entity or public–private partnership, the amount agreed to through the consent provisions (described above). In rural areas, this amount may then be further adjusted by application of a multiple of up to 2, although how this multiple is to be determined in a particular case is not described (Government of India 2013). While the LARR takes laudable pains to describe the process of determining market value, it has disappointed some critics who argue that the process is disconnected from actual values, and that in many rural contexts, it would indeed be possible for on-the-ground valuation processes to arrive at a genuine estimate of what land is worth.

Land-for-land v. cash compensation. The complexities associated with assigning realistic monetary values to lost assets and displaced rights is symptomatic of the difficulties of applying a "standard" compulsory acquisition legal framework to social situations in which land is valued differently than it is in functioning market economies. In developed countries, modern takings law is predicated on the assumption that land is a fungible commodity. While this assumption does not always hold true even in such countries, it encounters numerous exceptions in the developing world, particularly in rural areas. Some land rights that are critical to rural livelihoods, such as rights of pasture or access to forest resources, may simply not be susceptible to monetization – their loss may only be genuinely addressed by providing alternatives.

More generally, where markets for land are weak or severely distorted, cash compensation based on fair market value may be insufficient to compensate for the disruption to livelihoods and social cohesion caused by a taking. Affected persons may be unable to use financial compensation to purchase similar land elsewhere or to find new ways to earn a living. In such settings, owners and occupants may prefer to receive land as compensation rather than money. The offer of alternative land as compensation may also avoid problems that can arise when financial compensation is paid to people who are unused to handling large amounts of money and who may, soon after receiving compensation, find themselves with no land to farm, no income stream to support themselves, and no job skills to compete in a non-agricultural economy. Hence, the World Bank Operational Policy on Involuntary Resettlement stresses the provision of alternative and equivalent land as a preferred solution where livelihoods are land-based. A number of countries have also explicitly included such a concept in their laws. In other cases legal frameworks are flexible enough to accommodate the provision of "in kind" compensation where appropriate. There are, of course, constraints that limit the application of such an approach, particularly in rapidly changing areas where suitable alternative land may be difficult to find in light of population pressures.

Livelihood restoration or enhancement. As mentioned, these elements, so central to the underlying philosophy of internationally accepted norms, are absent or virtually absent from expropriation legislation. This is again in part an artifact of the legacy of most such legislation – resettlement and rehabilitation are rarely part of the discussion when land is expropriated in Europe or North America, because cash compensation in functioning market economies is seen as meeting the need. This does not necessarily mean that countries with such circumscribed legislation are not committed to addressing the livelihood impacts of displacement. This may instead simply reflect a philosophy of legislative design that posits that expropriation and resettlement are appropriately dealt with by different legislative or administrative instruments, rather than rolled into a single law. Governments may, for example, point to a corpus of social protection legislation and practice that they claim addresses the livelihood side of the equation.

Be that as it may, resettlement and rehabilitation receive relatively little attention in compulsory acquisition statutes. As a World Bank assessment of the Land Acquisition Act (LAA) of Nepal notes:

> The LAA is the overarching policy governing land acquisition and involuntary resettlement in Nepal. It mandates cash compensation as the only mitigation measure for acquisition for private land and properties. It does not require or prescribe any mitigation or livelihood restoration measures if required. The institutional mandate and responsibilities are clearly set out in the LAA as far as land compensation payment is concerned, but it does not describe any mandate or responsibilities for planning and implementing livelihood restoration and physical relocation. (World Bank 2012)

This assessment could be considered representative of laws and processes in many developing countries.

There are, however, notable recent counter-examples. Brazil's Ministry of Cities Ordinance 317, for instance, makes explicit reference to and recognizes rights that go beyond replacement of lost assets. It affirms the right to housing, requires measures to restore the social and livelihood conditions of affected families and individuals and the preparation of resettlement plans. As a condition for works to be considered complete, there must be full implementation of the resettlement plans. And as noted earlier, the Ordinance aims at providing housing and public services to people whether or not they currently have legally recognized tenure to land or housing (World Bank 2015).

India's LARR Act once again can be said to establish new ground. The Act's preamble states as one of its objectives that "the cumulative outcome of compulsory acquisition should be that affected persons become partners in development leading to an improvement in their post-acquisition social and economic status." The Act requires preparation of a "Resettlement and Rehabilitation Scheme," taking into account the livelihood impacts of the acquisition on people whose livelihoods are dependent on the land. Chapter V and Schedule 3 are devoted to the subject of "Rehabilitation and Resettlement," envisaging a wide range of steps from the provision of alternative land and housing to mandatory employment and annuities. Here again, the aspirations of the Indian Act are applauded by many, but there is genuine concern among proponents that there is insufficient human and financial capacity to put them into effect, and alarm in private-sector quarters that such elaborate provisions will significantly constrain access to land.

4 Distribution of Development Surplus

Given the difficulties and hardships often associated with compulsory acquisition, there has been increasing attention in recent years to identifying possible alternatives to the standard compulsory acquisition approach. In addition to the considerations outlined above, a number of other factors have underscored the desirability of exploring different approaches. In peri-urban areas, for example, at the interface of urban and agricultural land, the taking and compensating of land is frequently fraught with tension because of the steep appreciation in value that occurs when land is converted to higher-value urban uses. Local populations compensated at agricultural land rates may watch with considerable resentment as the value of their former land skyrockets. To some extent, this might be addressed by including a compensatory increment designed to represent a share in the presumed future value increase, but generally this is disfavored by national law and valuation standards.

A basic requirement is to ensure that there are indeed expected benefits before any land acquisition is undertaken and to subsequently monitor that these materialize and are distributed as planned. While a number of countries have time-bound provisions requiring unused acquired land to revert back to the original land users, such provisions lack bite for three reasons. First, the public sector's capacity to monitor is severely limited. Second, criteria to be monitored (e.g. amounts of investment or job generation) are rarely laid down unambiguously or publicized. Finally, the processes that are envisaged to be used, for example, to transfer land back to original holders are often not well laid out or understood by those affected, implying that even if evidence were available, it would be difficult to act upon it quickly.

In some cases, affected land holders are offered equity shares in acquiring enterprises. This approach, while promising in theory, can be risky in practice, depending on the economic soundness of the enterprise, and on whether governance mechanisms are in place to ensure that unsophisticated participants are not victimized by corruption or asymmetries in knowledge or access to information. Often, such schemes are viewed skeptically by affected people and their advocates, who worry that "land bonds" and the like are simply efforts to obscure the fact that a government is not able, or not willing, to provide cash up front, and that these substitutes will in fact prove to have little real value.

Finally, attention is given to the potential of "benefit sharing" as a way of both financing and enhancing resettlement assistance. This principle is given prominence in the World Bank's Policy on Involuntary Resettlement, which states as one of its objectives that "resettlement activities should be conceived and executed as sustainable development programs, providing sufficient investment resources to enable the persons displaced by the project to share in project benefits." Cernea (Cernea and Mathur 2007) identifies several mechanisms for sharing and reinvesting benefits from development that requires resettling populations, including:

- *direct transfers* of a share of royalties from hydropower to finance post-relocation development – experiments with this approach have been tried in Colombia, China and Brazil;
- *revolving development funds*, where the interest from principal is used for stimulating development after relocation, again with examples from China and Brazil;
- *equity sharing* in the new, project-created enterprise through various forms of co-ownership;
- *allocations of electrical power* on a legally mandated basis, or provision of subsidized utilities and lower water rates.

Arrangements like these are not routine features of national legislation, but there are scattered examples. Perhaps one of the most striking examples is from Brazil, where the 1988 Constitution includes the principle of reinvesting a percentage of royalties from hydropower in resettlement areas (Cernea and Mathur 2007). It may also be argued that in many situations involving the taking of land, the type of development involved and the nature of the resettlement impacts do not lend themselves to a benefit-sharing approach. Hence, including benefit sharing as a strict requirement in compulsory acquisition legislation may not be appropriate, though creating the legal "space" for such arrangements to be put in place where suitable would be a desirable advance.

In urban settings, especially in the context of redevelopment, one way of minimizing compulsory acquisition that is often believed to deserve wider use in the developing world is land pooling or land readjustment. In these arrangements, land targeted for investment is first pooled, and individual holdings are consolidated within a portion of the area and offered to existing residents. Though often downsized, the values of the plots or housing that existing residents receive are expected to increase, often many-fold, by virtue of the adjacent development (Lindsay 2012).

Although it may still require invoking eminent domain powers, this process is not only more participatory than compulsory acquisition but, more importantly, also provides increased opportunities for landowners to share in the increment of land values created by investment. Reviews suggest that it is most easily implemented if land markets are fluid, particularly when they are grounded in strong institutions that (i) assign and protect property rights, (ii) enable independent valuation and public dissemination of land values across uses, and (iii) enable the judicial system to handle disputes that may arise in the process (Lozano-Gracia et al. 2013).

There have also been interesting proposals put forward regarding the use of auctions covering not only a project site but also the surrounding agricultural land. This could in principle allow those affected to choose compensation in land or cash, determine their own price instead of leaving it to the government's discretion, and also reallocate the remaining farmland in the most efficient manner (Ghatak and Ghosh 2011).

5 Due Process

Following the *Kelo* decision, a number of US states reformed their eminent domain laws in an effort to ensure that the takings power is not abused, providing examples of the different aspects to be considered in this context and the likely impact following due process in this domain (Hudson 2010). Adopting either moderate or major eminent domain restrictions does not seem to have affected economic performance (Carpenter and Ross 2010), while the importance of procedural aspects has increasingly come to the fore. These aspects are likely to be even more important in developing countries as they play a significant part in the cost to government and its private sector partners on the one hand, and to impacts on displaced people and the communities of which they are a part on the other.

In discussions of process, the desire for efficiency and speed on the one hand (prized especially by the acquiring entity and the private sector), and, on the other, the objective of safeguarding the interests of affected people are sometimes seen as co-existing in a state of tension – the latter "bogging down" the former, while speed is assumed to work to the detriment of social justice. It is clear, however, that the two can work in complementary ways. Endlessly drawn out processes disadvantage those who are being displaced, not only those who are waiting to use the land. At the same time, cutting corners on procedures designed to address the needs and aspirations of affected people can have severe debilitating effects on the success of the eventual investment, by creating long-standing local resentments and other negative legacies.

Generally speaking there is significant room for improvement in process, both in terms of how it is spelled out in national legislation and in how it is administered in practice. Key areas that are likely to need attention are:

Participation and consultation. Most national laws pay little explicit attention to the need for consultation with and participation of those affected by a taking. In standard expropriation models, affected people are essentially passive objects of a government action, and hence participation is typically reduced to matters such as the publication of the government's intent to acquire land and the manner in which people are supposed to file claims for compensation. However, a model which takes into account the livelihood restoration and resettlement dimensions described earlier, requires a fundamentally different approach to engagement, and serious involvement of affected people at various critical junctures, such as:

- *Designing development activities in a way that minimizes the need for displacement.* Social assessment, participatory land use planning and other consultative methods are key to illuminating options for project design that may not be obvious to planners from outside the community.
- *Identifying rights and the holders of those rights.* As discussed at length earlier in this chapter, many land rights and land use practices are essentially invisible to outside observers, in part because they are undocumented and unmapped, and in part because some of them do not take the form of settled activities that are observable through standard methods. Only through consultation and participatory techniques will these come to light. Often notification of an impending expropriation is done through general announcements and direct notification is required only to registered owners. This is a problem if an owner or third-party right holder is not registered or the registration data is incorrect or not current.
- *Understanding land values and livelihood impacts.* Once again, the social value of land may often exceed what can be deduced from records or standard valuation techniques. Close engagement is required to design resettlement and livelihood packages that are well

tailored to the needs of the affected population and hence have some prospect of being sustainable.

- *Understanding rights and process.* Attention should be given to devising proactive ways for ensuring that people are genuinely informed of a process that may affect their interest, and that they understand the rights they have both to compensation and to seek redress if something goes wrong.

Rwanda provides an illustration of a new and growing breed of expropriation laws that begins to take into account the need for effective consultation. The 2007 Expropriation Law provides for public sensitization on the importance of the project to be established and the need for expropriation. In addition to sensitization, the Expropriation Law requires prior consultative meetings and examination of the project proposal involving expropriation, with a view to avoiding unintended consequences. Normally, a consultative meeting is held within 30 days of receipt of the application for expropriation, based on which the relevant Land Commission or Committee takes a decision whether or not to approve the project within a period of 15 days. Recent laws in Brazil, Indonesia, India and South Africa all incorporate significant improvements along similar lines.

Independent grievance mechanisms. Although perhaps not necessary where only a few landowners are affected, where projects involve large-scale resettlement, international practice and some national laws encourage the creation and use of local, targeted and accessible bodies to deal with grievances, at least as a first step. This reduces the problem of complaints being immediately funneled into court systems, which often have a reputation for being slow, backlogged and expensive. Properly constituted, a grievance mechanism would involve representation from amongst the affected community, some government representation from institutions not directly involved in the acquisition and other independent experts. This needs to be accompanied by clear communication channels and proactive measures to improve the legal literacy of affected people (Keith et al. 2009).

All too often, however, avenues for seeking redress are constrained. Under Nigerian law, the only avenue available is the Land Use and Allocation Committee which is meant to treat matters of dispute regarding the amount of compensation payable. This institution is, however, under the control of the government, and hence not seen as independent of the body that made the initial decision regarding the contested compensation. The Land Use Act also stipulates that no court shall have jurisdiction to inquire into any question concerning or pertaining to the amount or adequacy of any compensation (Adeniyi 2011). Concerns about the absence of independent channels of appeal have also been raised in Ethiopia, where members of the executive who decide on compensation amounts may also sit with the Clearance Orders Appeals Committee, which hears appeals in expropriation cases (Deininger et al. 2011). Studies of Malawi and Mexico, while reporting on vastly different contexts, both highlight situations in which grievance mechanisms are expensive and generally inaccessible for the poor.

Timing of compensation. International standards strive to ensure that compensation and other resettlement-related assistance is paid or is in place prior to people being displaced. This principle is also reflected in many laws around the world (for example, Albania). And yet the failure of governments to pay compensation on time – or sometimes, ever – is a frequently recurring theme in assessments of compulsory acquisition practice in developing countries.

Promises to pay after displacement can leave dispossessed people in limbo, without the leverage that comes from still occupying the property that was the subject of the expropriation. This outcome is perhaps often a symptom of poor governance that does not respect the legislation in force, and hence improved legislation alone is unlikely to serve as a cure. In other instances, however, it is facilitated by national laws that in essence leave compensation as a post-taking obligation of government. For example:

- In Ghana, issuance of an Executive Instrument (EI) for the acquisition of land vests ownership of land in the government from the moment the EI is issued. In practice, the government aims to pay before actual displacement occurs, but legally, entitlement to the land has already been relinquished (Larbi 2004).
- Malawi provides another variation on this theme. There, the declaration of a customary area as a planning area results in its immediate reclassification as "public land." This represents a form of expropriation of land for which tenure holders are entitled to in-kind or cash compensation. However, in many instances tenure holders are not immediately compensated after such declaration. Usually large parts of planning areas are premature for development and remain rural in character for a long period of time. As such, there is no urgency to compensate and resettle the tenure holders. The experts participating

in Malawi's Land Governance Assessment Framework project estimated that less than 50 per cent of expropriated landowners receive compensation within one year (Jere 2013).

- In the Philippines, in certain situations the government is empowered to take possession of and dispose of property having paid only 10 per cent to 15 per cent of the compensation up front (World Bank 2013a).
- In Turkey, compensation can be paid out over six installments, most of which are paid after the government has taken the land (Turkey 1983).

Failure to make timely payment is sometimes a function of money not being available in the acquiring agency's coffers when it is needed. This can be the result of an agency making commitments that it is unable to meet because it has failed to secure adequate funding through the budget process. Some laws attempt to grapple with this phenomenon, requiring a showing by the acquiring entity that the funds for compensation have been budgeted and set aside before the taking is approved by government decision makers (e.g., Albania). Yet even this does not ensure that a compensation fund will be immune to the vagaries of subsequent budgetary action – the phenomenon of funds appropriately set aside being reallocated after displacement has occurred is one that occurs from time to time, as agencies in cash-poor governments compete for scarce resources.

While payment before displacement is the internationally recognized principle, there are occasions where its rigid application would result in distorted outcomes. To prevent the possibility of development being stalled indefinitely by affected people challenging the compensation in court, a number of laws (as well as the World Bank's Involuntary Resettlement Policy) provide for the possibility of establishing an escrow account for the payment of compensation when disputes have been finally adjudicated. An escrow approach may also be used in some countries for situations where it has been difficult to identify all potential recipients of compensation, due to unclear land records or disputes between different claimants to the property. This approach, while sensible in some contexts, poses risks that governments may not aggressively pursue a solution and leave matters unresolved for years, with displaced people receiving little if any help in the meantime.

Delegation, monitoring and transparency issues. In developed countries, compulsory acquisition powers may be delegated not only to local governments but also often to private firms or regulated utilities that provide key infrastructure. One study found this to be consistent with rules that would be applied by an efficiency-oriented government (Turnbull 2012). In developing countries, a key issue is that local governments or investment promotion agencies often have powers to acquire land below a certain threshold and transfer it to investors even if they lack the capacity to properly access and interpret land records or to implement necessary social or environmental safeguards.

In Ethiopia, Mozambique, and Zambia, local governments have the authority to transfer "unoccupied" land (which by law is owned by the state) below a certain size to investors. Not surprisingly, this has led to a large amount of land transfers just below the threshold before recognition of the associated dangers led to a tightening of controls by central government. In India, the difficulty of acquiring land through proper process is reported to have led Industrial Area Development Boards to acquire or transfer land to private industrial use in improper ways (Task Force for Recovery and Protection of Government Lands 2011), something that led to passage of legislation aimed not only to prevent such behavior but also to establish greater transparency and oversight. A closely related issue is that in many instances land is transferred to private interests subject to certain development conditions without the capacity to monitor or enforce such conditions. In fact, there is evidence that a large share of the land which African or Asian countries acquired and transferred to investors is not used in line with original provisions. Unless the veil of secrecy that often surrounds such information is lifted, it will be difficult to effectively address this issue.

Can the process by avoided altogether? This is indeed a threshold question when speaking about expropriation procedures. As already discussed, in few countries expropriation is not the only way that governments can acquire land, nor, in situations where private end users may legitimately benefit from a government taking, is it the only way that private actors may approach land acquisition. The incentive is often strong to seek alternatives in the form of voluntary transactions or negotiated settlements that do not require full deployment of the expropriation process. Governments may see negotiated outcomes as a way of avoiding the adversarial nature of expropriation proceedings, thus lowering temperatures all around and avoiding the potential for discontent from delays. Less optimally, they may also see it as a way of bypassing the safeguards built into the process.

In international development practice, voluntary donation of land often comes into play in community-driven development (CDD) projects, where community members may donate a small portion of land towards a community development project from which they will directly benefit. Governments claim in such situations that the donations, being voluntary, are by definition outside the application of either national compulsory acquisition laws or World Bank policy. Yet care needs to be taken to ensure that such practices are truly voluntary, that they are not the result of indirect coercion and that benefits received do in fact compensate for the relinquishment of the land. There is considerable evidence that the process can be abused, particularly outside the CDD context where governments purport to be relying on voluntary donations for the building of large infrastructure projects or civil works.

Similar, though often more serious, concerns may arise in situations where a government is trying to purchase large areas of land directly through a market transaction (thus avoiding the compulsory acquisition process) or facilitating such a purchase by a private investor. In the context of large-scale land acquisitions for commercial agriculture, for example, there may be significant reasons for being skeptical that a transaction is truly voluntary. Concerns in Ghana, for example, revolve around the increasingly frequent phenomenon of chiefs or other community leaders selling land out from under the community without observing traditional consensual processes (Kasanga and Mahama 2011). There have also been repeated claims that investors and governments take advantage of information asymmetries and negotiating weakness on the part of local communities in acquiring land.

All this suggests that a case could be made that even ostensibly voluntary transactions of a certain size need some of the same scrutiny, substantive safeguards and procedural transparency that one would optimally find in an a well-crafted compulsory acquisition law. Few expropriation laws go this far. The Indian LARR Act is a recent exception, requiring application of many of its provisions regarding consultation, consent, compensation and resettlement planning to certain types of private voluntary transactions as well.

6 Conclusion

A secular increase in demand for land to provide infrastructure and support economic development through urbanization, mining, and commercial agriculture is likely to result in more and more calls for governments to use land acquisition. This note has illustrated the complexity of the underlying issues.

The analysis points towards a multi-pronged agenda. First, there remains an enormous need for a legislative paradigm shift in many parts of the world. The legacy of models from countries with developed land markets and vastly different cultural and economic conditions has resulted in legal frameworks that are poorly aligned with the actual contours of land relations in many developing countries, and poorly equipped to address the livelihood impacts and governance challenges associated with land taking and displacement. Experience increasingly confirms that approaches developed in the context of Europe or North America – where land rights are generally standardized and well-defined, land markets function, and land records are reliable – are ill-equipped for contexts where such attributes are less common. Recent years have seen the emergence of important efforts to break free of this legacy at national level, and an international convergence towards common standards as represented by instruments such as the VGGTs. Together these bode well for a possible acceleration of reform across the developing world.

Beyond the need for such reforms, the examples presented in this chapter also illustrate that, without good and up-to-date land information, even the most progressive legislation will be difficult to implement. In the short term, there is an urgent need for greater transparency to allow scrutiny of cases of land acquisition, including independent assessment of the extent to which the desired objectives are realistic, have been attained and what remedies are available if this is not the case. In the longer term, improved land governance will be critical to improve the informational basis on which to base decisions about whether or not to pursue any given land acquisition, how to best ensure that desired benefits materialize and whether those whose land rights are affected will be able to share such benefits. Two steps are particularly important in this regard:

- *Increase availability of up-to-date information on existing rights.* Without up-to-date information on actual holders of different types of rights, any transfer of land, whether through markets or compulsory acquisition, will be difficult. In fact, it has been suggested that lack of updated land records, which made it difficult to properly assess the amount of compensation due to each individual land holder, may have been at the root of a well-publicized failure to acquire land for industrial development in West Bengal that subsequently led to the fall of the state government (Ghatak et al. 2013).[6] Ascertaining existing rights is

[6] Interestingly, a recent study of the United States in the 1930s found incentives to hold out only for individuals who received initially low settlement proposals (Kitchens 2014).

even more important in situations where, despite land having been occupied for a long time by communities, it may be considered "state land" in purely legal terms. Establishing an inventory of state land and adjudication of individual or community rights to all lands – whether legally state or non-state – can help identify who has rights to land as a precondition for either direct negotiation or the eventual payment of compensation. This should be combined with measures to avoid land speculation, such as land taxes that have desirable properties of their own (Kelly 2013), allow the public to benefit from increased land values as a result of, for example, infrastructure investment, and can help compensate those negatively affected (Grossman et al. 2010).

- *Make genuinely voluntary market-based land transfers easier and disseminate the price information they generate.* Compulsory acquisition should be a last resort rather than a means for private parties to clear the record or avoid due diligence in title investigation (Lopez and Clark 2013). Unnecessary obstacles to truly voluntary transactions between private parties, bearing in mind the need for safeguards to ensure genuine voluntariness, can help ensure that takings are indeed a last resort. Prices at which land is transacted are an important signal of the opportunity cost of land and the amount of compensation in case of acquisition. In cases where land acquisition is for economic purposes, this may be complemented with a requirement to demonstrate local consent through various means, including the fact that a large share of the land in question has been acquired via market-based transactions as in the Indian LARR Act.

While these systemic improvements will of necessity take some time to be implemented, it is important that they be complemented by more immediate measures to increase transparency of compulsory acquisition and establish a basis for accountability and redress where needed. This will also help to fill the gap of evidence-based research on this issue in developing countries so as to document how, in practice, land acquisition can be dealt with even in situations where the challenges to doing so are vast.

- *Documentation and transparency.* At the most basic level, consultation and publicity of information on land acquisitions can help constrain rent seeking and increase incentives for compulsory acquisition to be used only if resulting social benefits exceed the private value of the land. It will also help to document the potential benefits and to develop a body of good practice that can then be shared across countries.

Finally, it can provide a basis for much-needed evidence-driven research in this area. Advances in technology that make it easier to access administrative data and compare them with remotely sensed images that can be used to monitor actual land use, can greatly facilitate this if the legal basis for doing so is in place. This is particularly important in decentralized settings. For example, the 2013 Vietnam land law mandates regular monitoring of outcomes across provinces, including the amount of land that is acquired by different levels of government and the use to which it is put, and the government is currently developing a system to put this into practice through a "provincial land governance index" that could provide interested parties, including investors, with the means to identify potential risks in advance. Similarly, in Ethiopia, evidence on the extent to which land transferred is actually put to its destined use and generates the desired benefits is important to ascertain the extent to which such transfers produce desired benefits and improve coordination among different government institutions (Deininger et al. 2015).

- *Possibilities for redress.* Information on the extent and conditions of compulsory land acquisition, in particular for economic use, will be useful only if an agile and impartial mechanism to seek redress by those aggrieved is available. If capacity is lacking, ways to assist affected people to more effectively represent their interests may be needed. Having independent ombudsman-like institutions to provide independent vigilance and oversight proved to be critical in some contexts, e.g. that of Mexico's *Procuraduria Agraria.*

Our review suggests that, in many developing countries, compulsory acquisition poses enormous challenges. A number of countries have taken remarkably bold and innovative approaches to deal with these. Empirical research to quantitatively document the impact of such innovations and link it back to theory will be important to minimize the risks associated with land acquisition and implement policies that contribute to enhanced social welfare in the long term.

References

Adeniyi, P. 2011. *Improving Land Sector Governance in Nigeria: Implementation of the Land Governance Assessment Framework [Draft].* World Bank, Washington DC.

Azuela, A. 2009. "Taking Land around the World: International Trends in the Expropriation for Urban and Infrastructure Projects." In S. Lall, M. Freire, B. Yuen, R. Rajack and J. Helluin (eds), *Urban Land Markets: Improving Land Management for Successful Urbanization.* Springer.

Balasubramanian, V., 2011. *Chairman's Report: Greed and Connivance.* Task Force for Recovery and Protection of Government Lands, Bangalore.

Burnod, P. 2012. *Between the Legal and the Legitimate: Status of Land Governance in Madagascar. Key Findings of the Land Governance Assessment Framework.* World Bank.

Cai, H., J. V. Henderson and Q. Zhang. 2013. "China's Land Market Auctions: Evidence of Corruption?" *RAND Journal of Economics*, 44(3), 488–521.

Carpenter, D. M., and J. K. Ross. 2010. "Do Restrictions on Eminent Domain Harm Economic Development?" *Economic Development Quarterly*, 24(4), 337–51.

Cernea, M. and H. M. Mathur 2007. *Can Compensation Prevent Impoverishment? Reforming Resettlement through Investments and Benefit-Sharing.* Oxford University Press.

Deininger, K., et. al. 2011. *The Land Governance Assessment Framework: Identifying and Monitoring Good Practice in the Land Sector* World Bank, Washington DC.

Downing, C. 2013. "Eminent Domain in 21st Century India: What New Delhi Can Learn from New London." *New York University International Law and Politics*, 46, 207–89.

Du, J. and R. B. Peiser. 2014. "Land Supply, Pricing and Local Governments' Land Hoarding in China." *Regional Science and Urban Economics*, 48, 180–89.

Ghatak, M. and P. Ghosh. 2011. "The Land Acquisition Bill: A Critique and a Proposal." *Economic and Political Weekly*, 46(41), 65–72.

Ghatak, M., S. Mitra, D. Mookherjee and A. Nath. 2013. *Land Acquisition and Compensation in Singur: What Really Happened?* London School of Economics, mimio.

Government of India. 2013. *Right to Fair Compensation and Transparency in Land Acquisition, Rehabilitation and Resettlement Act, 2013.* Government Printer, New Delhi.

Government of India. 2014. *Right to Fair Compensation and Transparency in Land Acquisition, Rehabilitation and Resettlement (Amendment) Ordinance, 2014.* Government Printer, New Delhi.

Government of Rwanda. 2007. *Law on Expropriation.* Kigali.

Government of Turkey. 1983. *Expropriation Law.* Government of Turkey, Ankara

Government of Vietnam. 2013. *Land Law.* Government of Vietnam, Hanoi.

Grossman, Z., J. Pincus and P. Shapiro. 2010. *A Second-Best Mechanism for Land Assembly.* Economics Working Paper Series. Department of Economics, University of California, Santa Barbara.

Hudson, D. Z. 2010. "Eminent Domain Due Process." *Yale Law Journal*, 119(6), 1280–1327.

Jere, P. 2013. "Issues and Options for Improved Land Sector Governance in Malawi: Results of the Application of the Land Governance Assessment Framework." World Bank, Washington DC.

Kasanga, K. and Mahama, S. 2011. *Diagnostic Review of Land Ownership and Land Rights in the Accra Plains*. Ghana Commercial Agriculture Project, Accra, Ghana.

Keith, S. et. al. 2009. *Compulsory Acquisition of Land and Compensation*. FAO, Rome.

Kelly, R. 2013. *Making the Property Tax Work*. International Center for Public Policy Working Paper Series. International Center for Public Policy, Andrew Young School of Policy Studies, Georgia State University, Atlanta.

Kerekes, C. B. and C. R. Williamson. 2010. "Propertyless in Peru, Even with a Government Land Title." *American Journal of Economics and Sociology*, 69(3), 1011–33.

Kim, A. 2011. "Land Takings in the Private Interest: Comparisons of Urban Land Development Controversies in the United States, China, and Vietnam." *Cityscape*, 11(1).

Kitchens, C. 2014. "The Use of Eminent Domain in Land Assembly: The Case of the Tennessee Valley Authority." *Public Choice*, 160(3–4), 455–66.

Lanza, S. P., T. J. Miceli, C. F. Sirmans and M. Diop. 2013. "The Use of Eminent Domain for Economic Development in the Era of Kelo." *Economic Development Quarterly*, 27(4), 352–62.

Larbi, W. O., Adarkwah Antwi and Paul Olomolaiye. 2004. "Compulsory Land Acquisition in Ghana – Policy and Praxis." *Land Use Policy*, 21(2), 115–27.

Lindsay, J. M. 2012. "Compulsory Acquisition of Land and Compensation in Infrastructure Projects." *PPP Insights*, 1(3) World Bank, Washington DC.

Liu, S. and Y. Li. 2015. "*Land Institutional Change and China's Economic Miracle: An Economic Interpretation*." Unpublished Paper, Harvard University, Cambridge MA.

Lopez, E. J. and J. R. Clark. 2013. "The Problem with the Holdout Problem." *Review of Law and Economics*, 9(2), 151–67.

Lozano-Gracia, N., C. Young, S. V. Lall and T. Vishwanath. 2013. *Leveraging Land to Enable Urban Transformation: Lessons from Global Experience*. Policy Research Working Paper Series: 6312, World Bank, Washington DC.

Mangioni, V. 2009. "The Evolution of the Public Purpose Rule in Compulsory Acquisition." Pacific Rim Real Estate Society Conference, Sydney, Australia.

Miceli, T. J. 2014. *The Cost of* Kelo*: Are Property Taxes a Form of Public Use?* University of Connecticut, Storrs CT.

Miceli, T. J. and K. Segerson. 2012. "Land Assembly and the Holdout Problem under Sequential Bargaining." *American Law and Economics Review*, 14(2), 372–90.

Miceli, T. J. and K. Segerson. 2014. *Takings*. Department of Economics Working Papers: 2014–17, University of Connecticut, Storrs CT.

Nosal, E. 2001. "The Taking of Land: Market Value Compensation Should Be Paid." *Journal of Public Economics*, 82(3), 431–43.

Saginor, J. and J. F. McDonald. 2009. "Eminent Domain: A Review of the Issues." *Journal of Real Estate Literature*, 17(1), 3–43.

Shavell, S. 2010. "Eminent Domain Versus Government Purchase of Land Given Imperfect Information About Owners' Valuations." *Journal of Law and Economics*, 53(1), 1–27.

Stickler, M. M. 2012. "Governance of Large-Scale Land Acquisitions in Uganda: The Role of the Uganda Investment Authority." International Conference on Global Land Grabbing II, Cornell University, New York.

Transparency International. 2011. *Corruption in the Land Sector*. Working Paper, Transparency International, Berlin.

Turnbull, G. K. 2012. "Delegating Eminent Domain Powers to Private Firms: Land Use and Efficiency Implications." *Journal of Real Estate Finance and Economics*, 45(2), 305–25.

Turnbull, G. K. and R. F. Salvino. 2009. "Do Broader Eminent Domain Powers Increase Government Size?" *Review of Law and Economics*, 5(1), 785–806.

US Supreme Court. 1954. *Berman v. Parker*. 348 US 26 (1954).

US Supreme Court. 2005. *Kelo v. City of New London*. 545 US 469 (2005).

Vo, D. H. 2011. *Compulsory Land Acquisition and Voluntary Land Conversion in Vietnam: The Conceptual Approach, Land Valuation and Grievance Redress Mechanisms*. World Bank, Hanoi.

World Bank. 2011. *The Law and Practice of Expropriation in Albania: An Issues and Options Paper*. World Bank, Washington, DC.

World Bank. 2012. *Nepal Bridge Development Program: Environment and Social Systems Assessment (ESSA)*. World Bank, Washington, DC.

World Bank. 2013a. *Improving Land Sector Governance in Philippines: Implementation of the Land Governance Assessment Framework*. World Bank, Washington, DC.

World Bank. 2013b. *Improving Land Sector Governance in Vietnam: Draft Report*. World Bank, Washington, DC.

World Bank. 2015. *Urban Land Acquisition and Involuntary Resettlement: Linking Innovation and Local Benefits*. World Bank, Washington, DC.

World Bank and Development Research Center. 2007. *China: Integrating Land Policy Reforms Ii: Strengthening Land Rights for Equitable Growth and Social Harmony*. World Bank, Beijing.

Zheng, H., X. Wang and S. Cao. 2014. "The Land Finance Model Jeopardizes China's Sustainable Development." *Habitat International*, 44(0), 130–36.

6

Public Interest Criteria and Korea's Scrutiny System

HOJUN LEE

I Introduction

Article 23 of the Constitution of the Republic of Korea contains a clause on eminent domain, "Taking, use, or limitation of private property for the sake of public necessity and the related compensation shall be governed by acts, and just compensation should be paid," which is similar to the clauses of many countries, stating that eminent domain should be exercised only for fulfilling public necessity according to the law and that just compensation should be paid. Thus, the Constitution declares that public necessity and just compensation are the two key factors to justify the use of eminent domain power.

In order to comply with the Constitution, it is important to determine whether a specific project that involves eminent domain satisfies the basic requirements. Therefore, we need to clarify the meanings of the basic requirements: public necessity and just compensation. In this chapter, I review the concepts of public interest and try to set out the detailed requirements for a specific project to meet the public interest criteria of eminent domain.

Moreover, I consider the overall procedure and the main criteria of public interest scrutiny for a public project in Korea. As eminent domain, by nature, results in the infringement of the right to private property, scrutiny should be very thorough to prevent the abuse of taking power and the excessive encroachment on property rights. The rising property-right consciousness of the Korean people, poor scrutiny and lack of justification for a development plan, along with eminent domain, may cause major disputes and harm sustainable development in Korea. I examine the pros and cons of the current process and the criteria of scrutiny in Korea, and consider how to improve them.

II Public Interest Criteria in Eminent Domain

1 Public Interest in Literature

According to Merrill (1986) and Lueck and Miceli (2007), public use requirements can be distinguished by two different approaches: "means" and "ends." The "means" approach implies that the use of eminent domain power is justifiable when market-based transaction costs are excessively high due to the holdout problem. According to the means approach, power should be granted to condemners – even to private developers – when they face a holdout problem regardless of their characteristics, be it in terms of public or private ownership, motive, or otherwise. This approach mainly focuses on whether the economic efficiency of transactions can be improved by takings.

The "ends" approach implies that takings power is justifiable only when the use of the property is for providing public goods. According to the ends approach, the power should be given only to public agents; and it is justifiable only when the project benefits the public. If the use of private property by takings is for supplying a private good that is only beneficial to private parties, then the use of eminent domain power is not justifiable. So, the approach mainly focuses on the "publicness" of the condemners and the projects.

While Merrill (1986) weighs more on the former, we should not take a singular approach to judge the justification of the use of taking power. If we only care about the efficiency of takings, the power can be abused by private parties, which may cause unfair results in that one private party's property is unwillingly taken for another private party's benefit. Also, if we only consider the publicness of takings, inefficient transactions can easily occur, as the takings are justified even when the holdout problems are not severe. Thus, the power can be abused when unwanted transactions with unreasonably low compensation are forced on the condemnees even though the market-based transaction prices are reasonable. For these reasons courts have applied both approaches, while the means approach is more consistent with the plain meaning of public use (Lueck and Miceli, 2007, p. 239).

Weisbrod, Handler, and Komesar (1978), in a general law and economics context, analyze the public interest by the concepts of (allocative) "efficiency" and "equity." In Weisbrod, Handler, and Komesar (1978, p. 8), the term "equity" is used instead of "publicness," which is achieved by "an equitable division of society's income and other rewards." By the ends approach and the publicness concept, the benefit from a development project should be shared by the public to justify use of the power. In this sense, the concept of equity in Weisbrod, Handler, and Komesar (1978) is quite closely related to the concept of publicness, while the exact definitions of the terms are slightly different.

In much of the economics literature, the issue of how to define the social welfare criterion has been an important topic, as it gives a backbone based on which the economic welfare under various economic circumstances can be compared, which helps to analyze the impact or usefulness of economic policies. Therefore, there have been many attempts to define social welfare and the public interest. Among others, for considering public interest in the eminent domain, we apply two typical concepts of social welfare criteria: "Pareto efficiency", firstly invented by Pareto (1906), and "Kaldor-Hicks efficiency", based on Hicks (1939) and Kaldor (1939).

A Pareto efficient allocation is defined as "one for which there is no way to make all agents better off" (Varian 1992, p. 235). If some agents can be better off given other agents' utilities by a change of an initial resource allocation, then we call the change a "Pareto improvement." If a resource reallocation results in a Pareto improvement because of a particular economic policy, it is considered as a desirable policy from the perspectives of the Pareto efficiency concept. The two key points are improving efficiency and not worsening any agents' welfare in an economy.

Referring to the above, improving the efficiency of an economy, the Pareto efficiency concept naturally includes efficiency. It also includes fairness, which is achieved by balancing the net benefits of each agent. If an agent loses more than he gets resulting from a resource reallocation while other agents get much more than they lose, we cannot call the reallocation fair. In an eminent domain context, a project with takings is a Pareto improvement if the project results in improving some agent's economic status (efficiency) and not worsening other agents' economic status (fairness).

Under Kaldor-Hicks efficiency, an economic allocation becomes more efficient if the sum of all agents' benefit is greater than before. In Kaldor-Hicks efficiency concept, efficiency is the most important criterion. However, we cannot say that efficiency is the only criterion in the Kaldor-Hicks efficiency. Under Kaldor-Hicks efficiency, we can focus on efficiency assuming that, as long as the sum of benefits under a new economic allocation increases, in theory, agents who are better off can compensate other agents who are worse off, and thus we can achieve a Pareto improvement. Considering this basic assumption, Kaldor-Hicks efficiency also includes the fairness concept, as well as the efficiency concept. So, we often call Kaldor-Hicks efficiency the "potential Pareto efficiency."

2 *A Theoretical Economic Approach to Public Interest Criteria in Eminent Domain*

In this section, I consider an economic model to study the characteristics of eminent domain and the public interest criteria. A simple model that describes the situation where a holdout problem arises creating obstacles in the implementation stage of a development project in market transactions can help understand the mechanism underlying the concepts of eminent domain and the interest of related agents. Then we try to set up the public interest criteria based on the mechanism and the motivation of introducing the eminent domain system.

Let me start with the assumptions of the theoretical model. Each person attaches a different value on a certain piece of land, and usually the person whose value is the highest owns the land, if we do not have a certain amount of transaction cost in the land market. Thus, the owner of the land usually has a higher value than the price that she pays to buy it. We assume that we can split a person's value on a piece of land in two parts, an objective value and a subjective value. An objective value in the model means the value that can be determined by objective criteria and does not vary depending on an individual's preference. In the model, we consider the objective value as the price that is used in a fair market transaction. A subjective value is considered as the difference between the price in a fair market transaction and the individual value. Thus, someone's subjective value can be negative if his value is lower than the market price and so he would not be willing to buy the land.

Consider a model where there are two landowners (A and B) and each owns a unit of land, L_A and L_B respectively. Also there is a developer (G) who is a public entity or a private developer whose eminent domain power was given (approved) by the government. Each landowner has his own value ($v_i, i = A \text{ or } B$) on his land and each value consists of two parts, an objective value ($x_i, i = A \text{ or } B$) and a subjective value ($y_i, i = A \text{ or } B$). As A and B own the pieces of land, it is reasonable to assume that $y_i > 0$.

Suppose G plans to build a bridge connecting the two pieces of land, L_A and L_B. When the project is implemented, the socio-economic cost of using the lands is $\sum v_i$ as we can assume that the opportunity cost of using the land is the same as the sum of the values as perceived by the two owners, whose values are the highest in the market without the project. Assume the socio-economic benefit of the project is $\sum v_i + \mathrm{b}$: the socio-economic cost including the cost of DBFO (design, build, finance, and operation) as well as the cost of using lands, which is $\sum v_i + \mathrm{c}$. I assume that the project is socio-economically feasible, that is, $\sum v_i + \mathrm{b} > \sum v_i + c$.

Assumption 1 The project is socio-economically feasible, that is, b > c.

Let us assume that, when the project is successfully implemented after paying the price ($\mathrm{p_i}, \mathrm{i} = \mathrm{A}$ or B) for L_A and L_B the developer G enjoys the net socio-economic benefit, $\sum v_i + \mathrm{b} - \sum p_i - \mathrm{c}$. If the project is not implemented due to not having purchased any land, G gets 0. If the project is not implemented due to having purchased only one of the pieces of land, L_{i}, then G's value perception of L_{i} is equal to the objective value, x_i, as G cannot develop the project with only one of the pieces of land and should sell L_{i} to a third party at the price of the fair market transaction. Therefore, the maximization of G is as follows.

$$\text{Max}\left[\sum v_i + \mathrm{b} - \mathrm{c} - \sum p_i\right]\cdot \mathrm{I} + (\mathrm{x_k} - \mathrm{p_k})\cdot(1 - \mathrm{I})$$

$$\text{where } \mathrm{I} = \begin{cases} 1, \text{if G succeeds in buying both lands} \\ 0, \text{otherwise} \end{cases},$$

$\mathrm{x_k}$ is the objective value of the land that G purchased.
$\mathrm{p_k}$ is the price that G pays for purchasing the land.

Consider a two-period game where G bargains with landowners one by one, one for each period. There is no discounting over the periods and all values including subjective values are assumed to be common knowledge for simplicity.

Without loss of generality, suppose G bargains with A during the first period. During the first period, we suppose that A offers $\mathrm{p_A}$ and G makes a decision on whether to accept it or not. After the decision, G determines whether to move on to the second period for bargaining with B. If the bargain goes on, at the second period, B offers $\mathrm{p_B}$ and G decides whether to accept it or not. After the second period, if G succeeds in purchasing both pieces of land, L_A and L_B, G will be able to start the project and get the net benefit, $\sum v_i + \mathrm{b} - \mathrm{c} - \sum p_i$. If G could get one of the lands, L_{i}, then G sells the land with the objective value and stops the project, thus

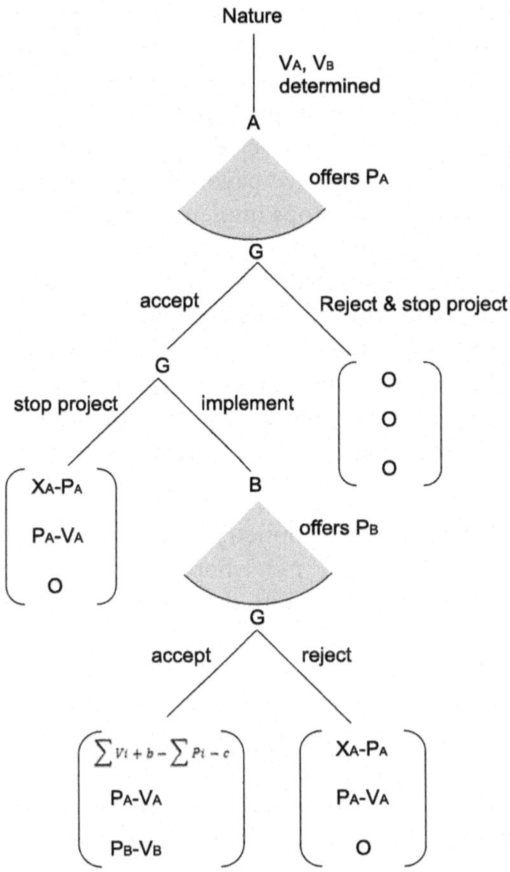

Figure 6.1. Structure of the Game

getting $x_i - p_i$. When G gets neither of the lands, G just stops the project and gets 0. Figure 6.1 shows the structure of the game.

The first best outcome of the game is that the ownership is transferred to an agent who can use the resource most efficiently. In this sense, if G could purchase the lands and develop the project with the price $p_i = v_i$, a Pareto improvement as well as the first best outcome could be achieved. However, the first best outcome cannot be achieved by voluntary transactions as in Proposition 1.

Proposition 1 The project is impossible to be implemented by market transactions.

<Proof> See the Appendix.

At the second period, B has all the bargaining power, thus, if B refuses to sell the land, G, who had already bought L_A should resell the land in the market at a lower price than the paid price. So, as long as G has already bought L_A, G desperately needs to buy L_B and implement the project, and that is why B has strong bargaining power to extract all the net benefit of the project. Therefore, G always gets a negative payoff when trying to implement the project, and thus eventually stops implementing it.

This case shows the traditional example of the holdout problem and market failure. Due to the existence of the holdout problem and market failure, eminent domain has been introduced. If a government enforces a transaction with predetermined prices, the project can be implemented without the holdout problem. The key is whether the enforced transaction improves social/individual welfare. The following proposition shows how the market failure can be corrected and Pareto improvement can be achieved.

Proposition 2 Under the "No Information Asymmetry Assumption" and Assumption 1, there exists a price set (p_A, p_B) where a compulsory purchase achieves a Pareto improvement from the initial resource allocation.

<Proof> See the Appendix.

Propositions 1 and 2 show why the eminent domain system is necessary and has been introduced in most countries. Without the system, many of the large-scale public investment projects, such as bridge construction projects, would not have been implemented although the net benefit of the project is sufficient. This is a justification of the eminent domain system and the compulsory purchase.

In other words, the compulsory purchase can be justifiable only when the circumstance around the project is similar to the model. We need to consider the key characteristics of the circumstances where the compulsory purchase is justifiable as in the model for examining the public interest criteria of eminent domain.

Firstly, we need to consider the efficiency of a project. As indicated in Assumption 1, the socio-economic net benefit should be of a positive value (or be sufficiently large). However, it is hard to measure the socio-economic benefit in the real world. Some values, such as balanced development or political benefit, cannot be easily quantified. If we suppose all the values to be quantified, the efficiency concept seems to be an ideal and theoretical criterion. Nonetheless, the efficiency concept suggests the direction towards which the real world criteria should be heading.

Secondly, the landowners should be compensated for more than their perceived value of the land. This criterion is strongly related to just compensation and the fairness concept. If the project implementation is based on a lopsided sacrifice of landowners as the compensation is much less than their perceived value, we cannot regard the transaction to be justifiable. Also, the fairness sustained by just compensation helps to maintain the efficiency criteria. If a compensation p_i is less than v_i, G has an incentive to implement the project when $\mathrm{b} - \mathrm{c}$ is negative but $\sum v_i + \mathrm{b} - \mathrm{c} - \sum p_i$ is positive. In this sense, the criterion that the landowner should be compensated more than her perceived value of the land is about both fairness and efficiency. Therefore, we have derived the two public interest criteria of eminent domain, *efficiency* and *fairness* so far.

In the basic model, we have assumed that the information about the subjective value perception of each landowner is public knowledge. However, in the real world, the existence of the subjective value, which is private information, makes the problem harder to solve. With the asymmetric information of the subjective value it is almost impossible to satisfy the previous criteria, especially the fairness concept. As only the landowner knows the subjective value of the land, G or other third parties cannot determine the amount of compensation that is greater than or equal to the landowner's value, which includes the subjective value. Meanwhile, if the landowner knows that G is willing to pay the price, which is greater than or equal to his perceived value, he has an incentive to exaggerate his subjective value and to try to increase the amount of compensation as long as G has the positive net benefit after paying for it, which makes G suspicious about the landowner's claim on his perceived value. Due to the *hidden information problem*, G should pick a set price for compulsory purchase in the real world. Then there is always a possibility that the purchase cannot satisfy the fairness criterion in the sense that it is possible for the landowner's perceived value of his land to be greater than the price chosen. The following proposition shows that under the information asymmetry assumption, there is always a possibility for the fairness concept to be unsatisfied by compulsory purchase.

Proposition 3 Suppose that each subjective value y_i is the private information of landowner i and only the distribution functions of the values are common knowledge. If each distribution function is an increasing function over the domain $(0, \infty)$, then any price set (p_A, p_B)

for compulsory purchase will have a possibility of being unable to achieve a Pareto improvement from the initial resource allocation.

<**Proof**> See the Appendix.

Since eminent domain includes a compulsory transaction even when the landowner does not want to sell and that there is always a possibility for the fairness concept to be unsatisfied, we need another criterion of public interest. Although there is always a possibility that fairness is not satisfied in the real world, we cannot stop every project to be implemented because of that possibility. Instead, we can consider adding another criterion to make up for the limitation of fairness and the just compensation concept. In the next section, we suggest *publicness* as the third criterion of public interest. A compulsory purchase for the public benefit is relatively more justifiable than that for a specific private benefit, even when the transaction is involuntary and there is a possibility that the compensation is less than the landowner's perceived value.

3 Necessary Conditions for Justifiable Use of Eminent Domain

After reviewing the concepts of public interest and the economic theory model, we have noticed that efficiency is the common concept used to discuss the public interest requirement. As long as a public policy or a project results in a positive economic effect in the sense that it increases the economic "pie" that can be distributed in an economy, it can satisfy one of the necessary conditions for fulfilling the public interest requirements. The economic efficiency does not always imply financial profit from the project. It could include intangible value as well as monetary value. From the perspective of eminent domain, only if the inefficiency arises due to high transaction costs, such as the holdout problem, should use of eminent domain be considered.

However, efficiency cannot be the only criterion of public interest when we regard efficiency as the Kaldor-Hicks efficiency, which focuses on the increase of the economic pie to be distributed. Even if the pie increases because of a policy or a project, it is not always justifiable when it is achieved at the expense of some people's lopsided sacrifice or economic loss. When we consider the liability rules that are commonly used in courts, the economic loss by the policy (or project) should be fully compensated. Otherwise, we lose the value of fairness. The efficiency of a policy can be aligned with the public interest when we keep the fairness by compensating for the economic loss of the sacrificing agents, which was also the intrinsic assumption when the Kaldor-Hicks efficiency concept became widely adopted in public economics. From the eminent domain perspective, the landowner whose property is taken by the condemner should be fully compensated to satisfy the fairness criterion.

For a development plan with eminent domain to satisfy the efficiency and fairness concepts, we should be able to mimic a market transaction without holdout problems by compensating the fair value of the condemned property to satisfy the just compensation of Article 23 of the Constitution of Korea. However, in the real world, it is quite difficult to measure the fair value of a condemned property and to satisfy the just compensation concept due to information asymmetry and the subjective property value perceived by condemnees.

Even if it is fair to compensate the condemnee for the private value of the condemned property (the fair value when there are no holdout problems), it is almost impossible to determine the exact private value. So, we need to use reference prices to calculate the fair value. Each person values each object differently, and owning something means that the owner's private value may be higher than the market price if there is no transaction cost. With the assumption of having low enough transaction costs, the private value of the property is greater than the market price, which is the most important reference when calculating the amount of compensation.

The amount of compensation is close to the (estimated) market price of the property in Korea. However, we can say that the market price is the amount one is willing to pay for BUYING the property, not what one is willing to receive for SELLING the property even without the holdout problems. In most economic transactions, the value to a buyer is higher than that of a seller, and the price is set between these values. For a successful transaction, a buyer should be willing (subjectively) to pay more than the price for buying a product and a seller should be willing (subjectively) to get less than the price for selling a product. Therefore, under the no-transaction cost assumption, the owner's willingness to receive for selling the property is higher than the market price or the (potential) buyer's willingness to pay. Otherwise, a transaction occurs. In this sense, some countries or states, such as Australia, Canada,[1] India, and the United States[2] have adopted a rule that requires the amount of

[1] "The Canadian provinces of Manitoba and Ontario require payment of a 5 per cent bonus above fair market value when the taken property is a residence. The Australian states of Victoria and Western Australia provide bonus payments capped at 10 per cent above market value. India provides for a 30 per cent bonus. Pakistan provides a bonus of 15 per cent to 25 per cent, depending on the nature of the acquirer." (Lee, 2013, p. 635)

[2] States of Michigan, Indiana and Kansas.

compensation for takings to be greater than the market price, i.e. 1.x times the market price. This is how they get closer to a fair value and it can be said that it is fairer than the purely market-based method of calculating the compensation amount, which is used in Korea.

Even if the amount of compensation is higher than the market price, we cannot be sure that the public interest criteria are always well satisfied as there is still some possibility that the standardized method of compensation is below a fair amount.[3] Fundamentally, the takings are compulsory transactions and there is always a possibility that the condemnees are not willing to sell according to a standardized set of compensation. For justifying the possibility of not fulfilling the fairness criterion of the specific use of eminent domain, we need another criterion of public interest, which is publicness.

The publicness concept is on the belief that the benefits from a project under eminent domain should be shared by the public. If the benefit from the involuntary transaction only goes to a specific group or private companies, it is hardly justifiable, especially when there is a possibility that the compensation amount for the involuntary transaction is not the fair amount. When the benefit can be shared by the public, including the condemnee, the use of eminent domain becomes more persuasive. Therefore, the publicness criterion is related to the subjects of takings. If the takings occur only for a private developer's profit, they are less justifiable than public projects developed by public agents.

In sum, we propose three necessary conditions of eminent domain for fulfilling the public interest criterion: *efficiency*, *fairness*, and *publicness*. A compulsory purchase should increase the total net benefit of an economy (efficiency), it should not be based on the lopsided sacrifice of some agents (fairness), and it should be aiming to serve the interest of the public, not just specific agents (publicness).

III Public Interest Scrutiny of Korea

In this section, we review two typical forms of scrutiny on a public project that involve the use of eminent domain: scrutiny in the

[3] According to the compensation data of a development project implemented in Seoul in 2007 where the project runner had to acquire two-thirds of the project site by voluntary transaction ("bargain purchase") for the eminent domain power to be granted, the average amount of compensation for the land acquired by bargain purchase is 10 per cent to 30 per cent greater than the average amount of compensation for the land acquired through "compulsory purchase."

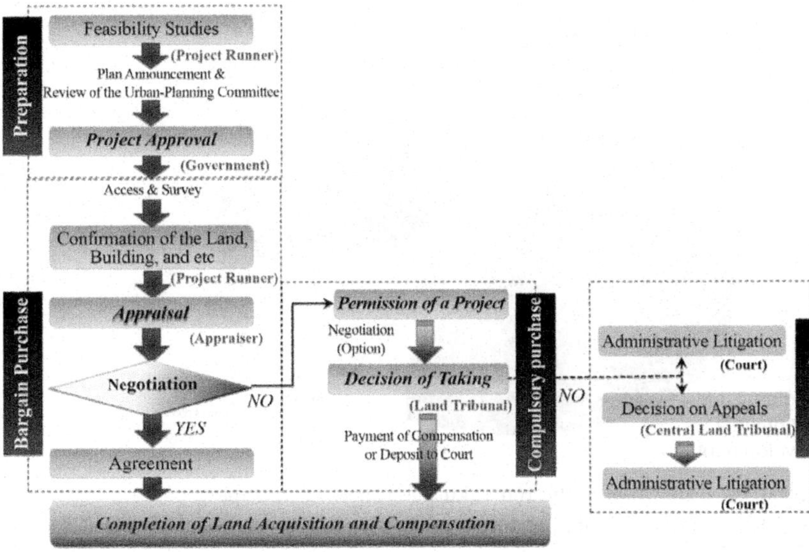

Figure 6.2. Takings Procedures in Korea: The Most Basic Sequence
Note: the names of the agencies in charge for each stage are written in parentheses.
Source: The KLTC (Kim et al., 2013)

"Permission of a Public Project" stage and the "Preliminary Feasibility Study." Also, the characteristics of those two forms from the perspectives of the public interest criteria mentioned previously will be considered.

1 *Scrutiny in the Permission of a Public Project Stage*

In Korea, the Korea Land Takings and Compensation Act (hereafter, the KLTC) is the basic law pertaining to eminent domain, and it describes the procedure of public projects including eminent domain, the general ways of determining compensation, allowed types of public projects, and so on. The general procedure of compulsory purchase under the KLTC, including voluntary transactions by bargaining, is as described in Figure 6.2.

According to Articles 20, 21 and 22 of the KLTC, a condemner, who failed to make a bargain purchase and wants to make a compulsory purchase, should receive a "Permission of Project" from the Minister of Land, Infrastructure, and Transport as prescribed in the enforcement decree, and the Minister should heed to the opinions of relevant authorities, local governments, and interested parties.

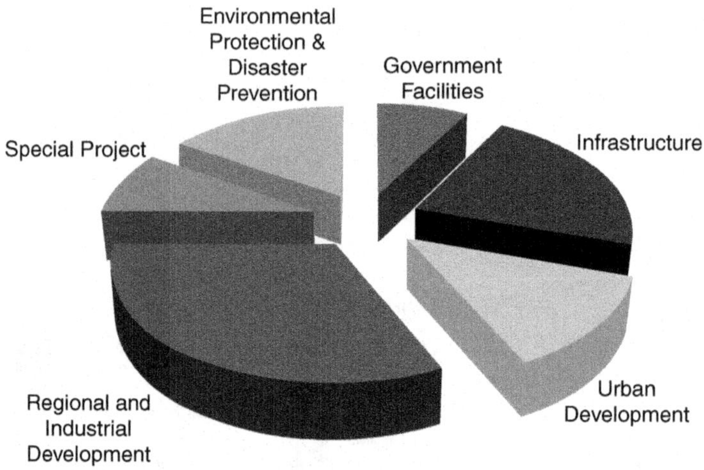

Figure 6.3. Proportion of the 100 Taking Acts by Project Type
Source: Statutes of the Republic of Korea (http://elaw.klri.re.kr/) and Kim et al. (2013)

However, as there are no explicit criteria for making a decision on granting a Permission of Project in the KLTC and the relevant enforcement decrees, approval strongly depends on the discretion of the Ministry of Land, Infrastructure, and Transport (hereafter, MOLIT). Moreover, for MOLIT, which is in charge of building infrastructure and planning nationwide development projects, thus being a project runner itself, the discretionary decision is possibly biased in favor of the condemner of the project.

Furthermore, according to Article 4.8 of the KLTC, individual acts can designate lands to be taken in addition to the KLTC. This provides flexibility for developing large-scale projects with a special Act that includes a compulsory purchase clause. There are 100 individual Acts that allow eminent domain power to condemners in addition to the KLTC.

When a project is implemented by an individual act, it can sometimes bypass the regular process of eminent domain governed by the KLTC, particularly the "Permission of a Public Project" stage. Many individual acts allow skipping the formal Permission of a Public Project stage. However, we regard the project as receiving Permission if the detailed design and plan is approved by the government in the "Approval Announcement" stage (Quasi-Permission of a Public Project). As the detailed and technical design and plan are mainly reviewed at the

Table 6.1. *Number of Decisions of Taking and Number of Permissions of a Public Project*
(Unit: Case)

Year	2005	2006	2007	2008	2009	2010
Number of decisions of taking (A)	2,705	2,772	2,197	2,464	3,690	2,858
Number of permissions of a public project (B)	17	8	18	9	29	23
B/A	0.6%	0.3%	0.8%	0.3%	0.7%	0.8%

Source: Kim et al. (2013)

"Approval Announcement" stage, the requirements of the public interest criteria are hardly considered so that the "Quasi-Permission of a Public Project" allows the project runner to almost completely skip public interest scrutiny.

Government agencies that are project runners and have an incentive to implement the project successfully, therefore, prefer to create a special Act by persuading legislators who also care about political interests related to the project implementation. When the incentives are aligned between administration and legislature, or legislation is not specialized enough, an individual Act can be legislated, and there are now 110 Acts to bypass the KLTC. The development-oriented legislation helps a project to be implemented effectively and fast. However, effective and fast implementation can weaken scrutiny so that the requirements for meeting the public interest criteria are not reviewed adequately. Most of the individual Acts have a clause that shortens or bypasses the Permission of a Public Project stage.

According to the Acts, the decision on the Quasi-Permission of a Public Project is not always made by the Minister of MOLIT, but sometimes by the head of local government or ministers of other ministries. As the decisions of takings are made by different agents, it is possible to lose the consistency of the criteria, which will be worsened when we rely on the discretionary criteria of the agent. Some of the Acts allow the project runner to be the decision maker of the scrutiny process, which makes the scrutiny process more development-friendly.

As in Table 6.1, most projects with takings are not achieved through formal Permission of a Public Project, which covers less than 1 per cent of all projects involving compulsory purchase. This means that the requirement for meeting the public interest criteria is not thoroughly reviewed and this may raise social disputes involving compulsory purchases in the future.

2 *Budgetary Decision Making and Scrutiny*

Immediately after the Asian Economic Crisis in 1997 and 1998, in pursuit of budget efficiency, the Preliminary Feasibility Study (hereafter the PFS) was introduced in Korea to improve fiscal efficiency by assessing large-scale public investment projects based on objective ex-ante project evaluations. According to Article 38 of the National Financial Act (hereafter KNFA), all new large-scale projects are subject to a PFS if the total project cost is greater than KRW 50 billion (about US$50 million) and the subsidy from the central government budget into the project is greater than KRW 30 billion (about US$ 30 million), and the PFS procedure comes under the early part of the Preparation stage in Figure 6.2. Since 1999 when the PFS was introduced, the Public and Private Infrastructure Investment Management Center (hereafter, PIMAC) at the Korea Development Institute (hereafter KDI), the country's first think-tank for public policy, has been conducting the PFS for more than 600 public investment projects. The study has become a key point of scrutiny in the budgetary decision process.

While the PFS has been introduced to help budgetary decision making, it is worth reviewing it when we consider that scrutiny in the eminent domain procedure of most large-scale pubic projects, which includes eminent domain, are under the domain of the PFS. Also, during the whole cycle of project implementation, the PFS is the rare point of scrutiny that considers public interest criteria.

The main criteria of the PFS consist of three parts: Economic Analysis, Policy Analysis, and Balanced Regional Development Analysis. Each part seems to correspond to the three components of the public interest criteria that we reviewed in Chapter 1. Cost–benefit analysis, which is based on the philosophy of the Kaldor-Hicks efficiency, is conducted in the Economic Analysis of the PFS. Therefore, a project is considered to be an efficient project if the expected socio-economic benefit of the project is greater than the expected socio-economic cost.

Under the Policy Analysis, the research team checks the consistency of the project with government plans of a higher level, opinions of relevant authorities and interested groups relevant to the project, along with other risks and issues. As the team checks whether the project is consistent with

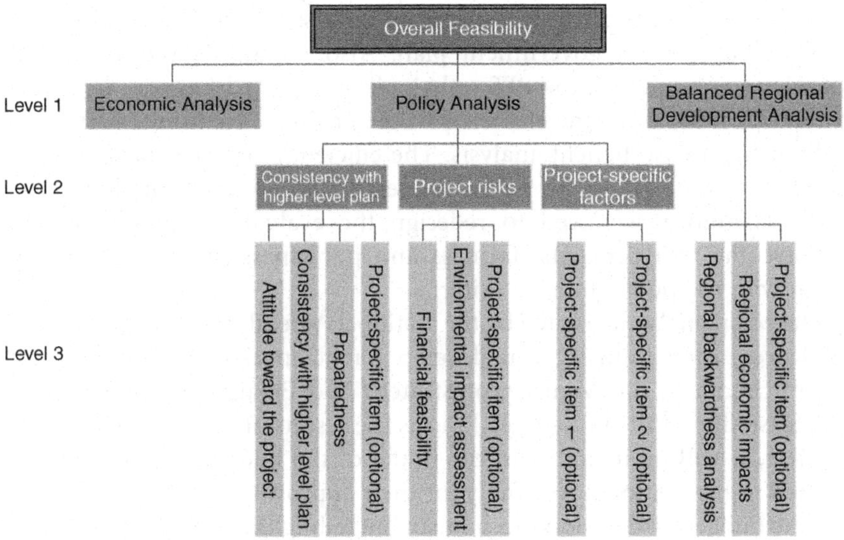

Figure 6.4. Analysis Structure of PFS
Source: KDI (2008)

the government's role and public opinion, the analysis fine-tunes to the publicness condition of the public interest criterion.

Under the Balanced Regional Development Analysis, the effect on balanced development among the regions is considered. If the project is expected to contribute to the improvement of balanced development, it receives additional points in the evaluation. As the projects subject to the PFS require a large amount of central government subsidy, the benefit from the projects should be distributed preferentially to less-developed areas, which have received relatively little support from government previously. In this sense, the analysis is concerned with fairness among the regions in Korea.

The above three analyses are put together using the Analytic Hierarchy Process methodology, which was originally developed in business management for comprehensive decision making. The structure of the analysis is described in Figure 6.4.

The three components of PFS can be seen as corresponding to the three conceptual requirements of public interest criteria. However, the weight falls somewhat more on the efficiency side than the publicness and fairness sides. As the PFS only covers nationally funded projects, it is assumed that the project satisfies the publicness criteria if it is consistent with a higher-level government plan. Also, in the balanced regional development analysis, the PFS only looks at regional fairness, not individual fairness, while the efficiency of the project is examined very carefully using a cost–benefit analysis. The efficiency criterion having more weight than the other two public interest criteria is the limitation of the PFS. Therefore, we need to redesign the evaluation components to involve the two concepts, fairness and publicness, making the study align with the public interest criteria.

Based on an Act legislated by the National Assembly, or the parliament of Korea, each ministry can develop public investment projects and submit them to the Ministry of Strategy and Finance which evaluates the feasibility of the project. As long as the results of the PFS support the project, it will be included in the drafts of the budget, which are submitted to the National Assembly for their approval.

The budgetary decision mechanism, including the PFS scrutiny, is not enough to meet the public interest criteria. One of the problems is that the budgetary decision is strongly influenced by political interests during the budget approval process. Politicians in the National Assembly try to directly include the project in the budget without the appraisal process. This occurs when a politician strongly insists on the necessity and urgency of a project. In such cases, conflict between the National Assembly and the Ministry of Strategy and Finance sometimes arises.

Figure 6.5 shows one of the main results of Kim and Lee (2013) on the relationship between the re-election rate of a politician and the amount of budget expenditure on transport projects in his constituency that passed the PFS during his last term. This shows that pork barrel politics is useful in Korea and that politicians have strong incentives to manipulate central government budget expenditure to ensure that national projects are implemented in their constituencies.

In response to the political behavior to skip the appraisal, the Ministry of Strategy and Finance has introduced the Reassessment Study of Feasibility (RSF), which is based on the same methodologies as the PFS and which is conducted when the appraisal has been skipped before being included in the approved budget. According to the enforcement decree under the National Financial Act, which is enacted by a Cabinet meeting, not by parliament, projects are subject to an RSF if their budget is allocated by parliament without a PFS even though they are subject to a PFS. If the result of the RSF for the project is negative, which is directly

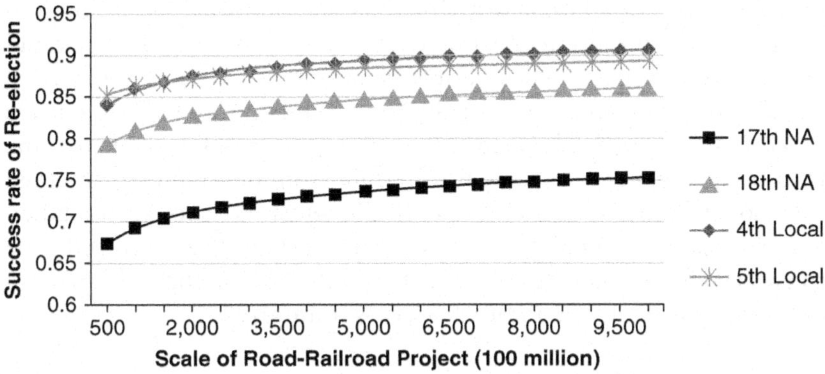

Figure 6.5. Success Rate of Re-election and Scale of Transport Project that Passed the PFS in Constituencies During the Term
17th NA: Data from the 17th election of the members of the National Assembly of Korea
18th NA: Data from the 18th election of the members of the National Assembly of Korea
4th Local: Data from the 4th election of heads of local governments
5th Local: Data from the 5th election of heads of local governments
Source: Kim and Lee (2013)

included in budgets that do not have the PFS, then the ministry excludes the project from the draft of the following year's budget. The enforcement decree includes the possibility of usurping the budget authority of parliament in the sense that the budgetary decision of the legislature is overturned by the administration, which may possibly cause political and legal disputes in the future. Therefore, we need to consider strengthening the legal base of the RSF.

V Conclusion

In this chapter we considered the necessary conditions for compulsory purchase to meet the public interest criteria and derived three conceptual conditions of public interest: efficiency, publicness, and fairness. A compulsory purchase should increase the total net benefit of an economy (efficiency), should not be based on the lopsided sacrifice of some agents (fairness), and should aim to serve the interests of the public, not just the interests of specific agents (publicness).

We also reviewed the typical scrutiny on public projects in Korea and the criteria involved, along with the discussions on the pros and cons of the Korean system and recent issues regarding the scrutiny stage and the criteria. The development-oriented legislation, which is common in Korea, helps a project to be implemented effectively and in a rapid manner, but effective and fast implementation can weaken scrutiny so that the requirements for meeting the public interest criteria are not always reviewed adequately. Therefore, we need to consider the institutional/legal rearrangement to refrain from development-oriented legislation, which is subverted by political interest. We should strengthen the Permission of a Public Project stage and extend the coverage to the projects implemented by laws other than the KLTC so that the coverage of Quasi-Permission of a Public Project is minimized.

	Legislature	Administration	Judiciary
Legislation	Permissive Attitudes towards Development-oriented Bills	Submission of Development-oriented Bills including Omission or Shortening of 'Permission' stage)	
Permission of a Public Project		- 'Permission' by Condemner - Shortening of 'Permission' stage	Passive Judgment (Recognition of Administration's Permission)
Budgetary Decision Making	Budgetary Decision Making Flawed by Political Interests	Efficiency-oriented Scrutiny	

Figure 6.6. Cons of Public Interest Scrutiny in Korea
Source: Kim et al. (2013)

The PFS, the key scrutinizer of budgetary decision making, was also reviewed from the perspective of the public interest criteria. The analysis criteria of the PFS consist of three components: Economic Analysis, Policy Analysis, and Balanced Regional Development Analysis. These components can be seen as corresponding to the three conceptual requirements of the public interest criteria. However, the PFS weighs somewhat more on efficiency than publicness and fairness. From the perspective of the public interest criteria, we need to improve the scrutiny components regarding fairness and publicness concepts in the PFS. We also need to strengthen the legal base of RFS so that we can effectively minimize politically subverted budgetary decision making. To conclude, the cons of public interest scrutiny in Korea can be described as in Figure 6.6.

Appendix

<Proof of Proposition 1>

After the bargain with A, if G fails to purchase L_A, G will stop the project and not move on to bargaining with B. Without L_A, by accepting B's offer, G gets $y_B - p_B$, which is negative as B's offer p_B will be at least v_B. Let us consider the case when G succeeds to purchase L_A with the price p_A. G's payoff is $v_A + v_B + b - c - p_A - p_B$ when G can buy L_B with the price p_B, and $y_A - p_A$ when G cannot buy L_B. Then p_B will be equal to the value which makes the two payoffs indifferent, thus, $p_B = v_B + x_A + b - c$. Therefore, when G succeeds to purchase L_A with the price p_A and moves on to the second stage, G's payoff is $y_A - p_A$. At the first period, A's offer will be always greater than or equal to v_A. Thus G's payoff when she accepts the offer $y_A - p_A$ is negative. Therefore, G will not accept A's offer at the first period, and will stop the project and not move on to the second stage. ■

<Proof of Proposition 2>

Let us pick any pair from the set $\{(\alpha, \beta)|\alpha \geq 0, \beta \geq 0, \alpha + \beta \leq b - c\}$ and set the prices as follows, $p_A = v_A + \alpha$, $p_A = v_B + \beta$. If G compulsorily purchases L_A and L_B with the prices p_A and p_B respectively, G's payoff after implementing the project is $b - c - (\alpha + \beta)$, which is nonnegative. A(or B)'s marginal payoff is $\alpha(or\ \beta)$, which is non-negative. Therefore, the marginal gain from the compulsory purchase is non-negative, which satisfies the Pareto improvement condition. ■

<Proof of Proposition 3>

For any given price p_i for compulsory purchase, there is a positive possibility that $v_i > p_i$. Therefore there is a positive possibility that Pareto improvement cannot be achieved by any compulsory purchase. ■

References

Hicks, John, 1939, "The Foundations of Welfare Economics." *Economic Journal*, Vol. 49, pp. 696–712.

Kaldor, Nicholas, 1939, "Welfare Propositions in Economics and Interpersonal Comparisons of Utility." *Economic Journal*, Vol. 49, pp. 549–52.

KDI, 2008, *A Study on General Guidelines for Pre-feasiblity Study* (5th edn), PIMAC, KDI (in Korean)

Kim, Iljoong, ByungKoo Cho, Duol Kim, Sungkyu Park, Hojun Lee, and Kisang Jung, 2013, *A Law-and-Economics Study on Takings Law in Korea*, KDI (in Korean).

Kim, Jaehoon, and Hojun Lee, 2013, *Political Economy of Public Investment Management in Korea*, KDI (in Korean).

Lee, A. Brian, 2013, *Just Under-compensation: The Idiosyncratic Premium in Eminent Domain*, Legal Studies Research Papers, Brooklyn Law School.

Lueck, Dean, and Thomas J. Miceli, 2007, "Property Law," Chapter 3, *Handbook of Law and Economics*, Vol. 1, (edited by Mitchell Polinsky and Steven Shavell), Elsevier.

Merrill, Thomas W., 1986, "The Economics of Public Use," *Cornell Law Review* 72, 61–116.

Pareto, Vilfredo, 1906, *Manual of Political Economy*.

Shepsle, Kenneth A., and Barry R. Weingast, 1981, "Political Preferences for the Pork Barrel: A Generalization," *American Journal of Political Science*, Vol. 26 (February), 86–111.

Varian, Hal R., 1992, *Microeconomic Analysis*, Norton.

Weisbrod, Burton A., Joel F. Handler, and Neil K. Komesar, 1978, *Public Interest Law*, University of California Press.

7

Who Exercises the Eminent Domain Power in Korea? A Focus on Private Takings

ILJOONG KIM*

I Introduction

The scope of subjects who can exercise the power of eminent domain varies across countries. In Korea, the scope is very extensive, ranging from the central government and state-owned corporations to local governments and their numerous public corporations, and to private entities such as construction companies and development firms.[1] In particular, private takings are generously allowed in many individual substantive laws, and the objects of private taking are widely distributed.

Eminent domain power can, in principle, be exercised by private entities in other jurisdictions, too. The two most representative ways for this to happen are as follows: First, private entities can "directly" take lands as long as they fulfill the conditions stipulated in relevant laws. Second, the private sector can ultimately go through government; state or local governments take lands for private developers.[2]

* I greatly appreciate encouragement and constructive comments from Soon-il Kwon, Hans-Bernd Schaefer, and Jinsu Yune, as well as from many attentive participants in various conferences and seminars.

[1] A similar situation applies, for example, to the US Fifth Amendment. The Supreme Court in the controversial case, *Kelo v. City of London* [545 US 469, 2005], made it clear that the public use requirement therein allows the government to take private property for transferring it to other private parties. This ruling also suggested that almost all claims of public benefits satisfy the criterion. As is well known, however, the case generated an enormous backlash over "public use" among jurists and scholars (Somin, 2015, p. 3).

[2] In the United States, for instance, these government-mediated takings are also often called "public–private takings" (e.g., Kulick, 2000; Scott, 2003; Cohen, 2006; Bell, 2009), and include famous cases such as *Poletown Neighborhood Council v. City of Detroit* [304 NW2d 455, Mich 1981] and *Kelo v. City of New London* [545 US 469, 2005]. Thus, according to Bouckaert and De Geests' (1995, p. 463) broad definition, these two types in the text belong to "private takings" in that private lands are ultimately transferred to private by coercion.

In this chapter I mainly focus on the first "direct private takings," but hereafter I shall just call them "private takings."[3] According to the first-time survey (Kim et al., 2013), private takings are permitted by 49 individual laws. This is possible because §4.8 of the Korea Land Takings and Compensation Act (KLTC), which is the baseline law governing takings in Korea, stipulates simply that "other laws also can designate lands to be taken." Private takings, thus, are allowed in a great deal of public constructions ranging from government offices, roads, railroads, industrial complexes, apartments, business cities and universities to various sporting facilities including golf courses. In fact, private takings have been so frequent and commonplace in Korea that some of the takings drew wide public attention in the 2000s. Some landowners challenged the constitutionality of private takings. However, the Constitutional Court of Korea upheld eminent domain power by private entities in itself.[4] Although a few decisions in later cases required stricter conditions to be met, there have consistently been strong dissenting opinions among justices at the Constitutional Court who are concerned about the abuse of taking power.

The purposes of this chapter are two-fold. First, I explain the current legal framework concerning private takings in Korea with related court decisions and subsequent controversies. International comparison that is of direct relevance will be made. Second, I probe the efficiency of private takings from the law and economics perspective. I suggest that private takings may be more inefficient when the profit-maximization motive is intermingled with the lack of proper *public oversight* against private entities' unscrupulous incentives. To reinforce this argument I also summarize the recent work by Kim and Park (2015), which utilized a dataset of 259 large-scale taking projects for industrial complexes in Korea. Considering that empirical investigations concerning this topic have been almost nil, the summary is believed to shed important insights.

The order of the remaining discussion is as follows. Section II explains the related legal aspects of Korea. Section III outlines the legal provisions

[3] In other words, "private takings" as the term is used in the current chapter are a most extreme form of takings where eminent domain power is exercised by private entities. Nonetheless, as shown below, if there is any merit in public–private takings, the merit tends to be reinforced in direct private takings. Also, the literature opposing public–private takings can be readily applied to direct private takings.

[4] "§23.3 [the eminent power clause] of the Constitution . . . does not specify the subject of taking. Thus, we should not confine it to a public entity such as the state" (2007_C.C_BA114).

for private takings for a few representative countries, and verifies the fact that private takings are allowed very generously in Korea. It also highlights that the scrutiny on the public-interest criterion is drastically weakened in private takings as compared with public takings. In addition, competing opinions on private takings by the justices at the Constitutional Court are explained. In Section IV, as a major part of this chapter, I present the economic discussions concerning the characteristics of private takings. I first briefly summarize the literature. Then, conjectures are made based on reasonable assumptions about the economic incentives of private entities that intend to execute the eminent domain power. In particular, the main hypothesis is drawn: private takings can be more inefficient than public takings and cause irregularities after taking, such as more cancellations and changes in project runners. Section V summarizes an empirical investigation by Kim and Park (2015).[5] Section VI concludes with policy implications and assesses a rather different decision recently made by the Constitutional Court of Korea.

II Private Takings in Korea and Related Legal Controversies

1 *Availability of Takings and Private Takings in Korea*

In Korea, condemners must obtain an administrative disposition called the "permission of a public project" according to §2.7 of the KLTC. The disposition is equivalent to finalizing the scrutiny on the public-interest criterion, and so it is followed by the process of compensation to landowners. This is, in principle, equivalent to the public-interest scrutiny embedded in the legal procedure of eminent domain of other countries although the precise form and/or the subject of this scrutiny may vary across countries.

However, this filtering process, which, by law, should be conducted by the Minister of Land, Infrastructure, and Transport, can be effectively circumvented by the so-called "quasi-permission of a public project" based on §4.8 of KLTC. §4.8 of KLTC stipulates that a project be regarded to have received the "permission of a public project" if public entities such as heads of local governments, who are delegated with the power from the

[5] To be more precise, in this Section V I will summarize section IV of Kim and Park's work. Also, although Sections II and III of this chapter draw upon a very comprehensive unpublished report (written in Korean) by Kim et al. (2013) to an extent, much of it has been updated significantly. The part mainly referred to in this chapter was, of course, originally written by me.

aforementioned Minister, simply endorse the actual plan of designating the area for different public projects. In other words, the quasi-permission of a public project is an extremely simplified administrative disposition that helps to bypass a stricter process.[6]

According to the first-time examination of all substantive laws provided by the website of the Korean Law Information Center (www.law.go.kr) of the Ministry of Government legislation, takings were being allowed in as many as 100 Acts[7] as of June 2013 (Kim et al., 2013). The scope of public projects stipulated in these acts was indeed widely distributed from typical textbook-type taking constructions to projects that would befuddle most people as to "why" and "how". Taking clauses were even found in a few laws that are mainly concerned with the organization and operation of public firms. In such cases, what the public firms routinely do, with some additional requirements, automatically grants the firms eminent domain power.

Most striking is that many projects specified in these separate laws overlap precisely with those already stipulated in detail by KLTC. I suspect that a major motivation behind this phenomenon lies in the incentive of project runners or local governments to do away with the stricter process of permitting a public project (§2.7 of KLTC) mentioned above. That is, the phenomenon has been the outcome of accumulated efforts on the part of the various condemners and the legislators who favorably responded to their efforts. It is publicly known that the overwhelming majority of takings in Korea are now conducted through this quasi-permission, and, consequently, I strongly argue that the scrutiny on the public-interest criterion has been rendered ineffectual. In fact, it was found from the survey that the quasi-permission of a public project was being allowed by as many as 81 individual Acts. I firmly believe that this is a truly unique "legal trickery" worldwide in eminent domain jurisprudence.

As a finding of more relevance to this chapter, it was discovered that, out of these 100 separate Acts, private takings were possible in as many as 49 Acts (see the Appendix). Therefore, in Korea, private entities are able to take other private owners' lands for a variety of reasons: schooling facilities, water supply plants, marinas, warehouses, and golf courses, just to name a few.

[6] Although this clause (i.e., §4.8 of KLTC) was challenged, the Constitutional Court generally upheld it as it allegedly speeds up the completion of public projects. Nevertheless, there are still many commentators who are critical of the decision.

[7] Acts here indicate the laws enacted by the National Assembly, the legislative branch in Korea. Thus, these Acts can be regarded as relatively high-level legal bodies in Korea.

At least five Acts out of these 49 allow private takings for generally developing specific "regions", regardless of their physical size, such as Saemangeum and Incheon, or for specific "events" such as international boat races or military athletic meets, not to mention *Universiades* and the Olympics. However, the predominant types of projects were associated with developing areas for industrial, commercial, residential, or even cultural purposes.

The representative example of such Acts is the Industrial Location and Development Act.[8] Further, although a certain qualification (e.g. possession of a relevant license) is often required to be eligible for becoming a private condemner, there is no single requirement in as many as 22 Acts. Notice also that the quasi-permission process is available in *all* 49 Acts. There are no official statistics, but I am fairly confident that *every* private taking in Korea has been conducted through these individual Acts.

2 *Related Legal Controversies*

Taking into account all of the results so far from the survey concerning the legal structure of private eminent domain, I can strongly infer that stringency on the public-interest criterion must have been even further undermined in private takings. Moreover, I can also easily speculate that such legal structure has frustrated actual and potential condemnees as well as legal commentators.

It was natural that, given these backgrounds, debates intensified from the 1980s regarding whether private takings can be justified on the ground of public necessity or public interest. Later, landowners also challenged the constitutionality of private takings themselves. However, the Constitutional Court of Korea firmly upheld eminent domain power by private entities in the 2007_C.C_BA114 case which involved §11 of the aforementioned Industrial Location and Development Act. This decision was solidified in the 2008_C.C_BA166 case which involved §2 and §6 of the National Land Planning and Utilization Act.

Apart from the quote mentioned in the Introduction in favor of the constitutionality of private takings themselves, the main arguments in favor of private takings are twofold. First of all, the majority believed that their legislative purposes conform to the public necessity condition stipulated in the Constitution as follows.

[8] Private taking power provided by this Act appears to be so extensive that Kim and Park (2015) analyzed the case of developing industrial complexes.

> This clause in question contributes to a healthy growth of the national economy by harmoniously supplying industrial locations and reasonably allocating industries ... and to proper promotion of diversifying industrial complexes throughout the nation ... The clause is thus *consistent with the public necessity condition* stipulated in the Constitution (2007_C.C_BA114) (emphasis added).
>
> Projects for city planning, in themselves, fulfill *the public necessity requirement* ... The taking clause is therefore constitutional because of *just legislative purpose* (2008_C.C_BA166) (emphases added).

The second argument of the majority opinion hinged on a due process that can be sufficient enough to protect private properties as private takings should, in principle, also be subject to the same due procedural requirements for public takings. The justices appeared to believe that the "appropriate means" would be able to guarantee to protect the interests of the condemned, indeed, an opinion on which I hardly agree as I elaborated slightly above.

> [Just as in public takings] all phases *are subject to due process*, condemners must pay just compensation, and our legal system *provides effective remedies* such as administrative litigation to the condemned if there is any specific defect embedded in the administrative disposition of permitting the takings. (2008_C.C_BA166) (emphases added).

Although there already were exchanges of debates, these two decisions triggered huge controversy among legal scholars in Korea. On the one hand, a group of scholars provided rationales for private takings. The rationales were almost identical to the arguments made by the majority of the Constitutional Court justices above. In addition, some emphasized the positive aspect of private takings such as providing a "wide variety of benefits to the region."[9]

The opposing group provided various counter-arguments. Although there are several scholars, lawyers, and judges in this opposing group, let us briefly focus on the threefold dissenting reasoning of Justice J. Kim in both decisions, which encapsulate the opposition's arguments fairly well. First, he emphasized the risk of compulsory redistribution that can take place casually from one private party to another.

> When the range of public necessity is defined *too broadly*, a land may often be *transferred forcibly from its owner to a third private party* whenever it is shown that the latter can make better use of it ... which causes

[9] This rationale, along with other favorable arguments made in the literature, will be reviewed in more detail in Section IV.

> *a risk of contradicting our constitutional basis of the protection of property rights.* (J. Kim dissenting in 2008_C.C_BA166) (emphases added).

Second, as illustrated below, he expressed his concern about the contingency in which private condemners show post-taking unaccountability for the public necessity condition, which I believe is almost identical to the criticism argued by Justice Ryan dissenting in *Poletown Neighborhood Council.*[10] Third, as quoted below, Justice Kim was critical of the exclusive enjoyment of surplus only by private developers as he believed that the harvest is the outcome created from eminent domain to begin with. This concern appears to share exactly the principle represented in the famous tale of two pies in Epstein (1985, pp. 3–5).[11]

> Private takings can be constitutionally justified *only with institutional arrangements that consistently protect the public necessity condition* . . . (J. Kim dissenting in 2008_C.C_BA166) (emphasis added).
>
> There should be guarantees that the surplus from the project can be shared by the relevant community such as . . . Through a solid institutional device, a splendid harvest *should be shared by the entire community rather than exclusively by the private condemner.* (J. Kim dissenting in 2007_C.C_BA114) (emphasis added).

Note that these counter-arguments above generally are in very similar spirit to the "reverse Robin Hood fashion" argument made by Justice O'Connor:[12] "Any property may now be taken for the benefit of another private party, but the fallout from this decision will not be random. The beneficiaries are likely to be those citizens with disproportionate influence and power in the political process, including large corporations and development firms." I can infer from his entire dissenting opinions and personal conversation that Justice J. Kim overall intended to admonish against the danger of people taking others' property with impunity. Economic discussions in Section IV of this chapter will lend support to his concerns.

[10] In fact, the *Poletown* court's failure to impose any binding obligations on the new private owners of property has not been idiosyncratic in the United States (Somin, 2015, p. 77).

[11] "Finally, the public use requirement condition the use of the coercive power by demanding that any surplus generated by the action, here the outer ring, is divided among individuals in accordance with the size of their original contributions. Each gain from public action therefore is uniquely assigned to some individual, so that none is left to the state, transcending its citizens." (p. 5)

[12] In particular, the first counter-argument bears most direct relevance.

III Comparative Survey and Legal Aspects of Private Takings

1 *Legal Provisions for Private Takings: Direct Private Taking*

I intend to investigate the serious shortcomings of the legal system for private takings in Korea by a cross-country comparison. This international comparison will help maintain a balanced perspective in assessing the Korean system. Nonetheless, due to data constraints, in this section, I briefly look at legal systems for private takings across only six countries (Australia, Germany, Japan, the United Kingdom, the United States, and Korea). First, I examine "direct private taking" (DPT) which is the main topic in this chapter.

DPT is allowed in Korea, Germany, the United Kingdom, and the United States. In the last three countries, however, the scope of DPT is significantly limited to standard social infrastructures such as railroads, roads, electric power plants, and harbors. Private takings appear to have been allowed because government was not able to meet the increasing demand for infrastructure in the process of rapid industrialization, or partly because these countries undertook privatization of public corporations.

The Mill Acts in the nineteenth century in the United States are a representative example of the takings for infrastructures (Scheiber, 1973; Epstein, 1985), that is, DPT due to the limited ability of government. Currently, DPT is legal in only 11 states (Turnbull, 2012, p. 311). Also, the full-scale privatization of public corporations (e.g., petroleum, rail, and gas in the United Kingdom and electronic power, railroad, and telecommunication in Germany) over the 1980s to 1990s became another basis for DPT (Office of the Deputy Prime Minister, 2004, p. 7; Voss, 2010, p. 8).[13] Nevertheless, public projects delegated to the private sector are strictly subject to specific legal constraints such as the Transport and Works Act in the United Kingdom and the Energy Industry Act in Germany.

In contrast, private takings are hardly allowed in Japan, and, even in the case of public takings, the Land Takings Law, which lists public projects very narrowly, encourages negotiations rather than takings (Azuela, 2007, p. 16; Lum, 2007, p. 462). Australia, by §6 of the Lands

[13] In Germany, takings clauses are included in different laws such as Baugesetzbuch (BauGB), Bundesfernstraßengesetz (FStrG), or Energiewirtschaftsgesetz (EnWG). For example, §87.3 of BauGB (Federal Building Code), which is the main takings law in Germany, allows, in principle, eminent domain power to "private agencies in charge with public infrastructure provision."

Acquisition Act, confines the acquiring authority as the Commonwealth authority. It also makes clear that an eligible authority excludes an incorporated association or society, an incorporated company, and a body of trustees. Therefore, these two countries take completely opposite stands, in terms of private takings, to that of Korea. DPT is allowed in 49 individual Acts, and the scope of private takings in Korea is very wide, extending even to small sporting facilities, golf resorts, and housing, to name a few.

2 *Legal Provisions for Private Takings: Public–Private Taking*

The government-mediated "public–private taking" (PPT) is usually regarded as public takings in Korea. This is probably because the availability of DPT is overwhelmingly abundant. However, I detect a general sense from the literature that PPT has been treated rather as a private taking in many other jurisdictions.

PPT is, in principle, allowed in all six countries. It has much to do with promptly supporting regional development projects particularly associated with urban regeneration. In this regard, PPT is often regarded as a subsidy to developers in the form of supplying lands for cheaper prices (Fischel, 1995, pp. 80–84; Miceli, 2011, pp. 68–71), and the primary mediators of PPT are local government or (public) development corporations (Schill, 1997; Johnson, 2007).

Historically, PPT has drawn huge public attention when it is often recognized as giving privilege to a private entity in many countries. Examples include *Kelo v. City of New London* [545 US 469, 2005], *Boxberg* [BVerG, 1 BvR 1046, Germany, 1985], and *Alliance Spring Co. Ltd. and Others v. The First Secretary of State* [EWHC 18 UK, 2005]. In fact, according to Cypher and Forgey (2003, pp. 259–61) who studied takings by American municipalities, 49 per cent of the lands taken were transferred to private real estate developers and, in 94 per cent of the samples, the transfer prices were lower than the compensation amounts to land owners.

But the requisite conditions differ across countries. In the United States, PPT is allowed in most states, but more restrictions have been imposed since *Kelo*.[14] PPT is allowed in Japan and Australia, but only as an exception, i.e., when public and private entities are co-participants in a project.[15]

[14] Refer to www.ncsl.org/research/environment-and-natural-resources/eminent-domain-overview.aspx for various responses to the *Kelo* case.

[15] Refer to Kotaka and Callies (2002) and Lum (2007) for Japan, and to Mangioni (2009) and Finlay (2010) for Australia.

Further, the taking decision with a strict scrutiny on the public necessity requirement is made at the level of the central government, i.e., by the Minister of Land, Infrastructure, Transport and Tourism in Japan and by the Minister for Finance and Deregulation in Australia.

The two countries in Europe are also cautious in making use of PPT. In the United Kingdom, the taking decision in the form of a compulsory purchase order (CPO) can be made by local authorities, the highway agency, and regional development agencies. Yet, in the presence of objections to CPOs, the decisions are subject to the final approval by the Secretary of State upon finishing public inquiry (Office of the Deputy Prime Minister, 2004, pp. 13–14). In Germany, PPT can be exercised based on the "land-use plan" which is determined only after sufficient scrutiny, as stipulated in the planning law, on specific scopes and methods for efficient land use in the future (Voss, 2010, p. 8).

By contrast, PPT is virtually recognized as public takings in Korea as mentioned above. A great number of PPTs are undertaken by the state or its numerous affiliated public corporations, and this is one of the reasons I claimed in the Introduction that I would term DPT as "private takings" in this chapter unless otherwise indicated. In any case, the international surveys on DPT and PPT lead me to conclude certainly that in Korea private takings are allowed to the greatest extent both in the scope of projects and the type of condemnation. Further, in other countries there exist various *ex-ante* and *ex-post* mechanisms to make them comply with the public-interest criterion.

Also, the survey, although not of an exhaustive nature, reveals that the filtering process concerning the public-interest criterion in other countries tends to be stricter in the case of private takings than in public takings. As discussed earlier, stringent control is exercised to evaluate the public-interest criterion in the United States, Germany, and the United Kingdom as well as in Japan and Australia where DPT is prohibited. In the United States, for example, the public use test has been strengthened, especially since *Kelo*.[16] This hardly applies in Korea. As explained in Section II.1, in Korea, condemners only have to obtain the quasi-permission of a public project based on §4.8 of KLTC and can circumvent a stricter filtering process. Of course, this quasi-permission process has been incorporated into all 49 Acts listed in the Appendix.

[16] See Epstein (http://chicagounbound.uchicago.edu/journal_articles/2908/) or Institute of Justice (www.ij.org/five-years-after-kelo-the-sleping-backlash-against-one-of-the-supreme-courts-most-despised-decisions).

IV Private Takings from the Law and Economics Perspective[17]

1 Claims Regarding the Comparative Merits of Private Takings

In this subsection, I provide survey results on the arguments in the literature suggesting the *bright sides* of private takings. Although I first emphasize that virtually all arguments have been conjectural without empirical substantiation, those various rationales may be summarized as in the following fourfold fashion.

First of all, as most commonly claimed by local governments and courts, private development activities contribute to creating a "wide variety of benefits to the region" in question. A representative example is the majority opinion in *Kelo*: "[T]he City has carefully formulated an economic development plan that it believes will provide *appreciable benefits to the community, including ... new jobs and increased tax revenues* ..." (Justice Stevens in *Kelo*, emphasis added).[18] Note that this conceivably benefiting-the-public rationale has frequently been used in many court decisions in Korea, too. (Such decisions were often reinforced by the so-called judicial deference to legislative judgment.)

The remaining three arguments hinge on distinct characteristics of private condemners. First, the private sector's superior efficiency in production is merited, based on the compatibility with its profit-maximizing incentive, because it can reap the surplus from completed development projects (Bell, 2009, p. 521). Also, private entrepreneurs are perceived to be less burdened by the corruption of politics, distortions of the political process, and rent seeking (Bell, 2009, p. 575). Second, the superior advantage in the private entities' funding ability is also lauded *vis-à-vis* the public sector that has to undergo inefficiency-causing taxation (Shavell, 2010, p. 18). Finally, the granting of eminent domain power to private developers is justified on the ground that holdouts can threaten private projects as well (Miceli, 2011, p. 46; Brooks and Lutz, 2011).

The four arguments above might be generally correct in describing the nature of the private sector and the outcome of private development plans. In the context of takings, these arguments can hold true when core requirements for takings are assumed to have been met: that is, *public*

[17] This section draws upon section III of Kim and Park (2015).

[18] It is well known that the so-called "conceivable public purpose" argument was upheld repeatedly in the US Supreme Court decisions including *Berman v. Parker* [348 U.S. 26, 1954] and *Hawaii Housing Authority v. Midkiff* [467 U.S. 229, 1984].

interest, high transaction costs, and *just compensation.* However, critics have questioned whether such requirements are indeed actually in place. In particular, they express doubt about the assumptions of public interest and high transaction costs, and subsequently suggest that, under such incomplete circumstances, the private takings may result in more inefficiency.

First, as Bell (2009, p. 522) correctly observed, the requirement of public interest (or necessity) has been expanded from strict "public ownership or use" to "public purpose or interest". However, critics argue that there is a risk of the occurrence of private takings that not only fail to meet the relaxed public requirement but also cause a multitude of rent-seeking activities.[19] The primary reason is that the ambiguous definition of "public interest" allows for a broad interpretation to include boosting regional development, increasing employment, or raising tax revenues. This ambiguity allows condemners to hide private interests and distort the taking procedure (Kelly, 2006, p. 34). This argument is reinforced considering incomplete information on the part of the condemned and sometimes public agencies in charge of approving the takings.

The second criticism is concerned with the common assumption of high transaction costs. Researchers such as Bell (2009, p. 530) and Miceli (2011, p. 46) presuppose that the holdout obstacle in private takings is as serious as in public takings. Regardless, private condemners possess varying ways to overcome holdout. Representative examples include transactions through secret agents (Merrill, 1986, p. 81; Cohen, 1991, p. 352; Kelly, 2006, p. 1; Somin 2007, pp. 205–08), land assembly districts, or auction mechanism (Lehavi and Licht, 2007, p. 1735; Heller and Hills, 2008, p. 1473; Kelly, 2011, pp. 364–68). In fact, as claimed by Benson and Brown (2010, p. 152), actual market participants have discovered many ways to induce people to reveal their relative preferences in situations similar to those that would characterize purchases of contiguous parcels of land from multiple owners by private firms. Thus, the bottom-line is that holdout, particularly in private takings, is not as severe as some academic writings tend to suggest.[20]

I re-emphasize that it is unfortunate that the existing empirical work on this issue is almost nil. Despite our extensive surveying efforts,

[19] Refer to Merrill (1986), Kelly (2006; 2009), Somin (2007), Kim and Park (2010), Eagle (2011) among others for rent seeking in the process of takings.

[20] Moreover, a landowner's holdout incentives for sellers might be weaker, particularly in the case of selling only part of his or her land, as the value of the remaining land can be increased with the development (Engel et al., 2005).

Kerekes (2011) and Lanza et al. (2013) appear to be the only empirical analyses that bear some relevance. They attempted to explain differences in the frequency of private takings across the states of the United States from 1998 to 2002, both utilizing the identical data provided by the Castle Coalition. There are some interesting findings, for example, the relationship between corruption and the dependent variable. Nevertheless, the relevance still appears to be very limited to the major tenet of this chapter (i.e., relative efficiency or inefficiency of private takings).

2 *Private Takings in the Non-Coasian World: Plausible Inefficiency*

Assume, with complete government, that the core requirements for takings such as public interest and high transaction costs are fulfilled. The literature suggests that causes for the potential inefficiency of private takings are at least threefold. The first is a *socially inefficient* choice of land. Suppose that the condemner can freely choose the location of land to take. While a benevolent government supposedly chooses land to maximize social welfare, private condemners would choose land to maximize the profit (Turnbull, 2012, p. 3). While they prefer underpriced lands that would mainly lead to greater profits, they are hardly concerned with other factors such as the subjective value of landowners (Merrill, 1986, p. 107).

The possibility of an inefficient choice of land is higher in private takings than in public takings even if I suspend our assumption of complete government. Public servants may have an incentive to choose locations with a lower subjective value of landowners *ceteris paribus*, partly because they cannot directly appropriate profits, and partly because strong dissent from landowners and constituents can have adverse impacts on their political careers. On the contrary, private condemners, being able to appropriate profits from land price increase (Kelly, 2006; 2011), persistently endeavor to obtain underpriced lands sometimes even with irregular activities including bribes, rebates, and illegal campaign support (Kelly, 2009, p. 178). To be sure, illegal activities can take place in public takings as well, but the process of private takings tends to be more opaque, which decreases the detection probability of illegal activities. Even if an appeal is made by landowners to a public agency in charge, the agency as a third party now can be less cooperative.[21]

[21] Local governments or politicians of the jurisdiction in question often build partnerships with private condemners because of the expected outcomes of a private taking such as increases in regional development, employment, or tax revenues (Kanner, 2007; Mihaly,

The second source of inefficiency is the risk of excessive taking. It is well known that one of the major rationales underlying *just* compensation for taking is to discourage excessive taking due to fiscal illusion. Nonetheless, it is also established that even compensation based on market value can cause under-compensation bias (e.g., Ellickson, 1973; Epstein, 1985; Burrows, 1991; Cho and Kim, 2002; Wyman, 2007). Also, Turnbull (2012) argues that, based on the Averch-Johnson effect, condemners have incentives to invest overly in physical assets such as lands under rate regulations.

In this regard, I submit that the possibility of excessive taking can be higher in private takings. Given the same magnitude of under-compensation bias, private condemners have stronger incentives to take as they can enjoy profits, for example, by selling the land. This phenomenon has been termed "speculative takings" by Cooney (1996, p. 752). Especially in Korea, as long as the original purpose of the taking is maintained, landowners are not eligible for the so-called "repurchase right" at all (Kim and Park, 2010). Thus, profits from land transactions are solely expropriated by the private condemners. In contrast, public takings are generally subject to much stricter guidelines against selling the lands condemned, and potential profits cannot be easily enjoyed by public servants either.[22] Overall, private takings are associated with a higher likelihood of mere arbitrage.

The third source of inefficiency, which has been highlighted in Kim and Park (2015), stems from private condemners' various forms of *opportunism*. Scrutiny of the public-interest requirement, at the initial stage of taking procedures, tends to hinge overwhelmingly on the official purpose of the taking *as it is announced*. However, I observe that, in reality, there often exists a huge information gap concerning *other* critical components of the public-interest requirement such as the precise value of the proposed project and the likelihood of actual completion (e.g., condemners' technical expertise or financial capacity).

This observation is clearly consistent with Somin's (2015, pp. 81–82) claim that the complexity of calculating benefits and costs and the time-lag

2007). Further, in a similar context, they may even endorse a private taking which does not fulfill the public interest requirement.

22 Even if public entities profitably sell the lands to a third party, they tend to be immediately faced with media coverage very critical of such transactions. In fact, this has been the case in Korea where a headline of the coverage reads as "Government Earning a Huge Windfall from Land Brokerages." Knowing this, public servants are relatively more cautious about speculative takings. Refer to Kim and Park (2015) for more detail.

tends to make scrutiny on these components not thorough at all. Knowing this, condemners inherently have incentives to undertake opportunism, a representative example of which is "adverse selection." Note also that private developers, compared with public servants, are inherently less accountable for the outcome of taking; they are only responsible for their own pecuniary losses even under the worst circumstance. Therefore, the (severe) informational gap in combination with less accountability suggests that the problem of adverse selection is more serious in private takings.[23]

Furthermore, local governments, which usually expect more jobs and tax revenues to result from private takings, provide subsidies in various forms. They range from tax privileges to loan guarantees, basic infra-facilities, lifting of extant regulations, and Minimum Revenue Guarantee. However, these supports can prompt private developers to exercise less precautionary efforts as the support may be perceived as unconditional insurance. That is because the marginal benefit of precaution, i.e., reduction in the expected losses, will decline. Thus, given the same cost function of precautionary effort, the privately optimal level of precaution may fall short of the social optimum. This increased possibility of project failure is a typical example of moral hazard.

Both types of the condemners' opportunism - adverse selection and moral hazard - increase the occurrence of irregularities in the progress of public projects *via* taking. The two most tangible examples of the post-taking irregularities are "cancellation" and "change in the project runner" by selling-off or disposition through public seizure and auction. Both incur social costs: the former sinks all pre-investments by developers and local governments, while the latter, particularly in the case of public seizure and auction, frequently causes massive delays in project launching and completion.[24]

[23] Moreover, Somin (2015, p. 83) argues that the overall non-transparent nature of developers in undertaking public projects render property owners unlikely to be able to determine which development condemnations serve their interests and which do not.

[24] In most countries, right upon the announcement or permission of a taking, landowners are subject to severe restraints in the use of their lands until they finally leave. In Korea, there is no compensation for such regulatory takings and their durations are often longer than a multitude of years. Types of regulatory takings are really wide-ranging; for instance, they include complete bans on road and bridge construction and repairs, discontinuation of financial support for projects to improve agricultural villages, restraints on changing businesses, prohibitions against using lands for new purposes and against the growing of perennial plants and trees, limitations on new construction and enlargements of housing, and effective interruption of secured loans, to name a few. The obvious under-utilization of lands for longer durations certainly indicates higher social costs.

Table 7.1. *Estimation Results: Inefficiency of Private Takings*

	TIME	NH^{METRO}	*LFR*	$AREA^{SMALL}$	*Dmd*	RGN^{SEOUL}	*PRI*	PUB^{LOC}	PRI^{BIG}	PRI^{MEDIAN}	PRI^{SMALL}	*SUPPORT*	*SUP ∗ PRI*	*Cons.*	*McFadden* R^2
M1	2.585***	−0.599**												−1.250***	45.9%
	(0.280)	(0.274)												(0.141)	
M2	2.597***	−0.520*	−0.011											−1.133***	46.2%
	(0.280)	(0.288)	(0.013)											(0.193)	
M3	2.635***	−0.451	−0.013	−0.339										−1.032***	46.9%
	(0.285)	(0.292)	(0.013)	(0.258)										>(0.206)	
M4	2.648***	−0.426	−0.011	−0.315	−0.304									−1.018***	47.2%
	(0.287)	(0.293)	(0.013)	(0.260)	(0.342)									(0.208)	
M5	2.642***	−0.517*	−0.010	−0.273	−0.362	−0.777*								−0.918***	48.8%
	(0.288)	(0.299)	(0.013)	(0.268)	(0.351)	(0.405)								(0.214)	
M6	2.553***	−0.647**	−0.010	−0.460	−0.737**	−0.721	0.770***							−1.144***	51.6%
	(0.298)	(0.309)	(0.013)	(0.287)	(0.369)	(0.444)	(0.286)							(0.238)	
M7	2.556***	−0.618**	−0.007	−0.500*	−0.709*	−0.649		1.130**	1.154*	1.707***	1.536***			−1.976***	54.7%
	(0.307)	(0.328)	(0.015)	(0.296)	(0.380)	(0.454)		(0.481)	(0.659)	(0.529)	(0.503)			(0.473)	
M8	2.546***	−0.566*	−0.003	−0.464	−0.697*	−0.668		1.116**	1.157*	1.700***	1.497***	0.100		−2.082***	54.8%
	(0.307)	(0.337)	(0.016)	(0.301)	(0.381)	(0.463)		(0.480)	(0.697)	(0.528)	(0.504)	(0.157)		(0.503)	
M9	2.665***	−0.434	−0.004	−0.448	−0.656*	−0.583		1.239**	0.979	1.460***	1.191***	−0.281	1.007*	−2.047***	55.9%
	(0.326)	(0.343)	(0.016)	(0.306)	(0.386)	(0.475)		(0.500)	(0.727)	(0.557)	(0.525)	(0.435)	(0.603)	(0.516)	

Note: · ***, **, and * represent statistical significance at 1%, 5%, and 10%, respectively. Standard errors in parentheses.

Yet, it is by no means easy for a public agency in charge to curb such opportunism, whether due to incomplete screening/oversight or due to the difficulty in designing a contract that deters them from exercising insufficient precaution. Moreover, this opportunism appears to be reinforced through partnership with private condemners cultivated particularly by politicians in local governments, as emphasized by Kanner (2007). Therefore, I conclude that private takings can incur higher inefficiency in terms of more cancellations and changes in project runners as compared with public takings in the *Non-Coasian World*. Of course, the third conjecture in association with the higher likelihood of private condemners' opportunism should be subject to empirical investigation. In the next section, I summarize a recent empirical investigation that bears direct relevance to this claim.

V Summary of an Empirical Investigation by Kim and Park

1 *The Data and the Model*

The 2015 empirical work by Kim and Park (hereafter KP) tested, with the data of 259 large-scale taking projects for general industrial complexes, the aforementioned hypothesis in Section IV.2 that private takings can be more inefficient. In reality, post-taking "irregularities" can take place often right after an official taking decision. Representative examples are "cancellation" or "changes in the project runner."[25] KP called these two contingencies "*CoC*", regarded them as indications of inefficiency, and inquired about factors that affect the occurrence of *CoC*.

The sample period is from 2003 to 2010. The final year was fixed as 2010 because KP intended to reserve a follow-up period to observe *CoC* for three years to the end of 2013 in order to minimize the right-censoring problem. Out of 259 cases, private takings account for 48.6 per cent, and the number of *CoC* was 55 (21.2 per cent). In particular, it is noteworthy that the *CoC* rate of private takings (30.2 per cent) more than doubled that of public takings (12.8 per cent).

KP estimates the probit equation (1). The dependent variable, *CoC*, takes a value of 1 if *CoC* has occurred, 0 otherwise. Vector X contains

[25] Cancellation makes sunk all pre-investments by the condemner and local government, while change in project runners often causes massive delays in project launching and completion. Both irregularities also incur more social harm in terms of regulatory takings (i.e., all sorts of restrictions on land use) strictly imposed upon landowners.

various control variables,[26] and Z includes the main variables related to the entity of takings that will hopefully reflect inefficiency implications stemming from adverse selection or moral hazard.

$$\Pr(CoC_i = 1|X_i, Z_i) = \alpha + X_i'\beta + Z_i'\gamma + \varepsilon_i, \ where \ i = 1, \ldots, 259. \quad (1)$$

As to vector Z, KP first distinguished the types of condemners in a dichotomous way, public (*PUB*) or private (*PRI*). To capture differentiating effects of each entity, KP then subcategorized each. For public entities, KP distinguish metropolitan (including central and provincial) governments and their affiliated public corporations (PUB^{MET}) from smaller local governments (PUB^{LOC}). For private entities, following the current legal standards, PRI^{BIG} first represents a big private company. $PRI^{MEDIAN}$and PRI^{SMALL} indicate medium and small-sized companies, respectively. Furthermore, Z includes *SUPPORT*, which is a dummy variable taking a value of 1 if the taking decision was made in 2008 when the number of takings soared to 63. This was the first year of President M. Lee's administration, an exceedingly generous package of supports and promises was literally poured out to these condemners by the central government. KP suspected that *SUPPORT* would reflect not only adverse selection to an extent but also significantly reflect the 63 project runners' moral hazard.[27]

26 I follow the classification regarding the size of private corporations by annual sales as legally stipulated in the Medium and Small Companies Law. As for explanatory variables, a time dummy, *TIME*, takes a value of 1 if *CoC* occurred from 2011 to 2013. This is simply to reflect KP's observation that more than 70 per cent of *CoC* took place over these three years. NH^{METRO}, a dummy taking a value of 1 if the construction site is located in metropolitan areas, would reflect better conditions for industrial complexes in terms of transportations, securing labors, and other social infrastructures. Thus, other things being constant, NH^{METRO} would lower the probability of *CoC*. KP also included land price changes (*LFR*) to take into account the condemner's higher incentives not to cancel the project as the value of the complex would increase with increases in land price. (However, land price increases might induce the initial condemners to sell off the land to a third party.) $AREA^{SMALL}$ is a size-related dummy taking the value of 1 if the size of the complex is less than the legal standard (300,000m2). A smaller area indicates less difficulty in raising the required fund, lowering the probability of *CoC*. *Dmd* is a dummy indicating that the complex in question is to be used exclusively for the condemner's own ongoing business, i.e., the demand by the end user. *Dmd* is expected to have a negative coefficient. Finally, RGN^{SEOUL} is a dummy indicating a complex located within the Seoul metropolitan area. Obtaining a taking permission in the area is usually considered a privilege, which would make a negative effect on the occurrence of *CoC*.

27 Refer to KP for more detailed rationales on this expectation as well as descriptive statistics.

2 Estimation Results

Estimation results by KP are reported in Table 7.1 (Table 3 in KP). In *M*1, the coefficient estimates of the two basic variables, *TIME* and NH^{METRO}, showed the expected positive and negative signs at the 1 per cent and 5 per cent significance levels, respectively. However, *LFR*, $AREA^{SMALL}$, and *Dmd* did not show significant coefficient estimates in models *M*2 to *M*4. RGN^{SEOUL} showed an expected negative estimate in *M*5. KP regarded *M*5 as the baseline specification of (1) with the R^2 of 48.8 per cent

KP then turned to additional analyses that can provide efficiency implications conceivably related to the taking entities. KP noted that the private takings dummy, *PRI*, in *M*6, provided a positive coefficient estimate at the 1 per cent significance level in *M*6. Its inclusion increased the R^2 by 1.8 per cent points. KP interpreted this to indicate that private takings may cause cancellations or changes in project runners more frequently. According to the marginal impact analysis on the average (MIA), private takings raised the probability of *CoC* by 5.3 per cent points *ceteris paribus.*

Next, KP broke down the entities of private takings into PRI^{BIG}, PRI^{MEDIAN}, and PRI^{SMALL}, while KP separated the entities of public takings by PUB^{LOC} from PUB^{MET}. The R^2 was raised by 3.1 per cent points. Inclusion of the first four variables into *M*6, with PUB^{MET} used as the default situation, revealed surprising results in *M*7. All four coefficient estimates were positive as expected if KP's hypothesis holds with respect to adverse selection. In particular, PRI^{MEDIAN} and PRI^{SMALL} had the biggest coefficient estimates in absolute terms with the highest significance levels.

Finally, in the last two models, *M*8 and *M*9, KP attempted to discover what effects *SUPPORT* made on the likelihood of post-taking opportunism. In other words, KP intended to test the relative efficiency of private takings using the abrupt increases in the central government's subsidies as a source of *exogenous variations. SUPPORT* in *M*8 had a positive coefficient estimate, but it was insignificant. Nonetheless, KP obtained a very meaningful result from *M*9 where *SUPPORT* was interacted with *PRI*.[28] The interaction variable had a positive coefficient estimate which was also statistically significant. This suggests that only the private takings out of the 63 takings that took place in 2008 tended to increase

[28] KP initially intended to make *SUPPORT* interact with the three broken-down dummies of private takings. However, it caused a multicollinearity problem, thus KP used the entire private entity dummy.

the probability of *CoC*. Therefore, KP cautiously submitted that a generous package of privileges can make private takings more inefficient in terms of adverse selection and/or moral hazard.

3 On the Interpretation of the Estimation Results by KP

In their last subsection, Kim and Park examine the twofold suspicion that can arise surrounding the above empirical claim. First, the industrial complexes through private takings in the current sample could be by nature more difficult to complete than those by public takings. KP postulated that, in spite of the question's potential validity, regrettably they cannot provide further testing results in that regard due to data constraints. Nonetheless, KP submitted that this issue was already recognized. They explained that, for example, although three other types of industrial complexes were available for which eminent domain power can be exercised, they included *only* general industrial complexes in order to maintain a higher level of *homogeneity* in project characteristics. They further claimed that at least part of this issue has been dealt with, in their estimation, by the explanatory variables that may reflect such project characteristics to a certain degree.[29]

Secondly and more fundamentally, the authors focused on a question that can be raised with regard to the development projects that tend to be engaged in by private firms *vis-à-vis* by the public sector.[30] For example, if private firms usually engage in projects with higher failure rates, the above empirical results may be subject to the controversy of two competing arguments: "abuse of private takings" vs. inherent "difficulty in performing private projects." Certainly, KP intended to deliver the former. Yet, KP acknowledged that this controversy is legitimate because the latter, if it is ever the case, will represent a source of selection bias in their estimation. Therefore, KP further admitted that, in order to capture the impact of taking *per se*, the dataset would be ideal if it also included industrial complexes that were privately constructed *without* the assistance of takings.

[29] They noted that no extremely large disparities were observed in the means of the two groups for such variables as LFR, NH^{METRO}, RGN^{SEOUL}, and $AREA^{SMALL}$. However, they emphasized that even these differences have already been controlled in the estimation.

[30] KP explained that this suspicion would need to rely on assumptions such as that private firms participate in taking projects with both higher risks and higher returns, or that, given the expected return, they are systematically less risk-averse than public agencies. While these assumptions certainly are very strong, KP suggested that they are not in a position to assess the assumptions.

However, such an ideal dataset was impossible to construct because, in Korea, again, all industrial complexes were developed *via* takings. To examine the critical controversy, therefore, KP explained the empirical investigation undertaken by Kim and Park (2012, pp. 88–96) because KP found their empirical work to be fairly illuminating in this second question of abuse of private takings vs. difficulty in performing private projects. In Korea, the absolute majority of golf courses are private. Nonetheless, land for constructing golf courses is acquired either through market transactions or through private takings. Kim and Park (2012) collected a total of 215 cases, of which private takings were used in 42.8 per cent, and analyzed the relative efficiency of the two different land acquisitions. They discovered that the mode of market transactions was superior.[31]

Therefore, KP concluded that the results obtained by Kim and Park (2012) support the argument of "abuse of private takings" rather than that of "difficulty in performing the private projects," considering both the *higher homogeneity* in project type (i.e., constructing golf courses) and the *relatively shorter time* needed to finish the construction (i.e., about two years on average). KP also suggested that this in turn would most probably reinforce their empirical design and subsequent findings discussed earlier. Nonetheless, in spite of all these endeavors, KP still acknowledged that they were not providing an uncontested identification strategy for *CoC* as *an inefficiency index* (rather than *post-taking performance*), and strongly urged more rigorous studies on this issue in the future.

VI Conclusion and a Recent Decision by the Constitutional Court

In Korea, the scope of subjects that exercise the eminent domain power is very extensive. In particular, private takings are most generously allowed in terms of forms of takings, types of projects, procedural ease, etc. Conjectures on the efficiency of private takings abound, but in this chapter I focused on their operations in the Non-Coasian World,

[31] The authors first used the "delay in construction" (τ_d) compared to the normal progress as a proxy for inefficiency, because the contingency of *CoC* hardly took place in their sample for some legitimate reasons. Second, they numerically showed that a longer τ_d for an 18-hole golf course increases social costs at least by US$7 million per year, due to fixed costs such as paying interest to banks, underuse of lands, including loss of sales, and sometimes even legal expenses of seizing and public auction. Finally, the authors discovered, using various measures of τ_d, that delays in the cases involving the eminent domain were significantly more serious than in those through market transactions, by 1.72 to 2.08 times depending on the measures used.

following heavily the main work of Kim and Park (2015) and Kim et al. (2013). I subsequently suggested a hypothesis that eminent domain power can be abused more grievously in private takings when the profit-maximization motive is coupled with *incomplete public oversight* against private entities' opportunism. All of this suggests that private takings especially for economic development should be approached with substantial caution and supplementary devices, as Eagle (2010) stressed.

A very scarce empirical investigation of this issue by Kim and Park (2015) does support the above theoretical conjecture concerning the high likelihood of relative inefficiency in private takings. The argument in this chapter may be summarized as: smart students *ceteris paribus* can cheat better in tests when teachers are absent. It is thus necessary to be alert against the common claim that private economic development is indeed of public benefit because it can yield higher tax revenue and stimulate job growth. If such a misconception becomes prevalent, the distinction between public and private use will simply erode, causing many unintended ill consequences. Therefore, the law and economics analyses in this chapter are expected to shed beneficial insights, especially for countries that intend to use private takings as an effective instrument in achieving rapid economic development.

Several solutions can be explored to curb problems arising from private takings. One prevalent argument is to adopt stricter criteria for public use; Staley (2010) or Somin (2011) offered a checklist for determining whether a taking project in question actually would generate public benefits.[32] Particularly for Korea, I assess that measures should be implemented immediately in order to minimize the abuse of the "quasi-permission of a public project" based on §4.8 of KLTC. The quasi-permission process renders private condemners to circumvent routinely the regular public-interest scrutiny. In fact, such circumventions are currently being used in the majority of private takings.

[32] For the same goal, Eagle (2010) argues for other alternative devices. In particular, he suggests that the abuse can be curbed as landowners become involved from the planning stage and are also given a legal opportunity to join the development project with a more equitable status. I agree with this suggestion. Even in the taking case through KLTC, landowners cannot be officially involved at the planning stage. Also, the landowner's involvement in the "permission of a public project", which is an almost final stage, is usually nil although §21 of KLTC, in principle, stipulates such involvement. Yet worse, landowners can access the relevant information from the *Administrate Gazette* "only for 14 days" after the permission is finalized (§21 of KLTC). Under these circumstances, it is actually impossible for landowners to become involved in a taking project in any meaningful way.

Also, legislating more generous compensation to landowners including partial sharing of development surplus might be another beneficial policy for Korea in the short run. In the same vein of the logic that creating a wide variety of benefits to the region hinges on a private condemner's incentive in search of profitability, a generous compensation rule for landowners can effectively overcome at least the informational asymmetry which has been the major source of adverse selection and inequitable redistribution. Of course, rigorous policy simulations regarding how generous compensation should be are required before its actual implementation.[33]

Finally, in October 2014, the Constitutional Court of Korea made a rather progressive decision after a three-year-long scrutiny for the 2011_C.C_BA129 case, which involved §16.1.4 of the Act on Balanced Regional Development and Support for Local Small and Medium Enterprises (i.e., the 37th Act listed in the Appendix). This specific clause explicitly stipulates that non-public entities can be in charge of development projects for which eminent domain power is needed. The case was initially brought by a landowner whose land was taken to be used in building a prestigious private golf course. Six Justices out of the nine held that the clause is not constitutional.

The majority opinion did not, for the sake of legal stability, nullify the clause immediately, but requested the legislature to revise it (i.e., the decision officially called "suspended unconstitutionality"). However, this decision is still significantly meaningful. First, it is the first decision against private takings, in Korea, for the *substantive* reason. Second, the opinion emphasized explicitly the limited nature of *publicness* (or *public access*), in its expression of the "luxurious" golf course in question. Third, the decision, in scrutinizing the *necessity* part of the taking in question, made it clear that the existence of benefits to the community *does not always* justify eminent domain.[34]

[33] Although it does not appear so at first glance, this policy of generous compensation is indeed consistent with the inherent nature of the private sector's profit-maximizing incentive. Refer to Kim, Park, and Lee (2016) for further details.

[34] "The public interests intended to bring forth through a taking for projects such as *luxurious golf courses must be compared with* the private interests associated with an infringement on the property rights of landowners. In the current, based on the characteristics of public projects such as luxurious golf courses, the public interests of increased tax revenues and boosting the local economy are *only ancillary* from their operations so that we do *not* consider them *superior* enough to justify the infringement of the basic rights of landowners" (2011_C.C_BA129) (emphases added). In fact, the last sentence in this quote alone even reminded me of Justice Kim's warning against "a risk of contradicting our constitutional basis of the

I assess that the last two judgments above are much more faithful to the public interest requirement concept that has been customarily interpreted by scholars in the field of law and economics. Certainly, this decision is only a beginning of the changes in the Constitutional Court's stand toward private takings. While the decision also left several questions unresolved,[35] it will hopefully affect several future decisions in a more positive way.

Appendix: The Acts that Allow Private Takings and the Type of Public Projects

No	Act	Type of Public Project
1	Act on the Agricultural Utilization and Management of Reclaimed Land†	Utilization for reclaimed land
2	Special Act on Designation and Management of Free Economic Zones†	Designation of free economic zones
3	Tourism Promotion Act†	Development for tourist sites
4	Prevention of Mining Damage and Restoration Act	Prevention of mining damage
5	Mining Industry Act	Establishment of mining area entrances and piling-up yards
6	National Transport System Efficiency Act	Multi-transfer complex and intelligence transportation system
7	International Contest Support Act	Installation and utilization, etc. of contesting facilities, etc.

protection of property rights" in his dissenting opinion in the 2008_C.C_BA166 case as explained earlier in Section II.2.

35 For example, the definition of "being luxurious" appears to be arbitrary or abstract, and this decision makes no discussions or guidelines regarding whether other types of public projects, which are under §16.1.4 of the Act in question, are luxurious or not. The decision is also silent on a multitude of other issues, not only of private takings for luxurious golf courses that are allowed in different Acts, but also of other types of public projects falling short of the *publicness* or *necessity* requirement that are again allowed in different Acts as listed in the Appendix. I believe that these issues must be resolved in the near future although a tremendous amount of effort will certainly be needed, as similar cases will be continuously brought to the Constitutional Court.

(cont.)

No	Act	Type of Public Project
8	National Land Planning and Utilization Act†	Urban planning facilities
9	Special Act on Relocation of Military Airbase and Supporting	Supporting
10	Special Act on Development of Enterprise Cities†	Construction of enterprise cities
11	Act on Maintenance and Improvement of Road Networks in Agricultural and Fishing Villages	Building roads
12	Rearrangement of Agricultural and Fishing Villages Act†	Rearranging agricultural and fishing villages
13	Urban Development Act†	Urban development
14	Act on Maintenance and Improvement of Urban Areas and Dwelling Conditions for Residents†	Maintenance and improvement
15	Urban Railroad Act	Maintenance
16	Special Act on Development of the Eastern, Western, and Southern Coastal and Inland Areas†	Development
17	Act on Development and Management, etc. of Marinas†	Development
18	Act on Development and Management of Logistics Facilities†	Construction of logistics facilities
19	Special Act on Construction of Bogeumjari Housing, etc.†	Housing construction
20	Act on Public–Private Partnerships in Infrastructure†	Private investment in infrastructure
21	Industrial Location and Development Act	Construction of industrial complexes
22	Special Act on Promotion of the Saemangeum Project	Undertaking the Saemangeum project
23	Act on Promoting Construction of a New Airport for the Seoul Metropolitan Area†	Construction of a new airport
24	Water Supply and Waterworks Installation Act	Undertaking waterworks
25	Water Quality and Aquatic Ecosystem Conservation Act†	Installation of sewage treatment plants

(cont.)

No	Act	Type of Public Project
26	Special Act on Promotion of Development Investments in Underdeveloped Areas†	Development
27	New Harbors Construction Promotion Act	Construction of new harbors
28	Special Act on Supporting Specialization and Development for Fishing Villages	Specialization for fishing villages
29	Act on Development and Utilization of Station Influence Areas†	Development of station influence areas
30	Special Act on Promotion of Research and Development Zones†	Development
31	Coast Management Act	Coast maintenance
32	Special Act on Improvement of Disaster Risk and Relocating Plans	Improvement of disaster risk
33	Border Area Support Act†	Supporting
34	Special Act on Establishment of the Jeju Special Self-Governing Province and Development of the Free International City	Development
35	Special Act on Support for Areas, etc. Adjacent to the Districts Granted to the United States Armed Forces in Korea†	Supporting
36	Act on Assisting Development of Small Local Towns†	Development
37	Act on Balanced Regional Development and Support for Local Small and Medium Enterprises	Regional development
38	Act on Special Cases Concerning Regulation of the Special Economic Zones for Specialized Regional Development	Research and development
39	Integrated Energy Supply Act	Installation of facilities
40	Juvenile Activity Promotion Act†	Building training facilities
41	Act on Promotion of Taekwondo and Creation of the Taekwondo Park†	Landscape design
42	Act on Promotion of Housing Site Development	Housing site development

(*cont.*)

No	Act	Type of Public Project
43	Act on Promotion of School Facility Projects	Construction of schools
44	Aviation Act	Development of airports
45	Harbor Act†	Development of hinterlands
46	Act on Development of Submarine Mineral Resources	Development of submarine mineral resources
47	Act on Assistance to the 2011 IAAF World Championships in Daegu, the 2013 World Rowing Championships in Chungju, the 2014 Incheon Asian Games, the 2014 Incheon Asian Para Games, and the 2015 Gwangju Summer Universiade	Supporting
48	Act on Assistance to the 2015 Mungyeong Military World Games	Supporting
49	Special Act on Support, etc. for the 2018 Pyeongchang Olympic and Para-Olympic Winter Games	Supporting

Note: † indicates that the relevant act does not stipulate any eligibility condition for a private entity to exercise eminent domain power for the designated projects.

References

Azuela, Antonio, 2007, *Taking Land around the World: International Trends in the Expropriation for Urban and Infrastructure Projects*, Working Paper, Lincoln Institute of Land Policy.

Bell, Abraham, 2009, "Private Takings," *University of Chicago Law Review*, vol. 76, no. 2, pp. 517–85.

Benson, Bruce and Matthew Brown, 2010, "Eminent Domain for Private Use: Is It Justified Market Failure or an Example of Government Failure," Bruce Benson (ed.), *Property Rights: Eminent Domain and Regulatory Takings Re-Examined*, New York: Palgrave Macmillan, pp. 149–72.

Bouckaert, Boudewijn and Gerrit De Geest, 1995, "Private Takings, Private Taxes, Private Compulsory Services: The Economic Doctrine of Quasi Contracts," *International Review of Law and Economics*, vol. 15, no. 4, pp. 463–87.

Brooks, Leah and Byron Lutz, 2011, *Do We Need Eminent Domain? An Empirical Investigation of Urban Land Assembly*, Working Paper, University of Toronto.

Burrows, Paul, 1991, "Compensation for Compulsory Acquisition," *Land Economics*, vol. 67, no. 1, pp. 49–63.

Cho, Joonmo and Iljoong Kim, 2002, "An Economic Analysis of Takings in Korea: Endogenous Probability and Announcement Effects," *International Review of Law and Economics*, vol. 22, no. 3, pp. 331–46.

Cohen, Charles, 2006, "Eminent Domain after *Kelo v. City of New London*: An Argument for Banning Economic Development Takings," *Harvard Journal of Law and Public Policy*, vol. 29, no. 2, pp. 491–568.

Cohen, Lloyd, 1991, "Holdouts and Free Riders," *Journal of Legal Studies*, vol. 20, no. 2, pp. 351–62.

Cooney, Kevin, 1996, "A Profit for the Taking: Sale of Condemned Property after Abandonment of the Proposed Public Use," *Washington University Law Quarterly*, vol. 74, no. 38, pp. 751–76.

Cypher, Matthew and Fred Forgey, 2003, "Eminent Domain: An Evaluation Based on Criteria Relating to Equity, Effectiveness, and Efficiency," *Urban Affairs Review*, vol. 39, no. 2, pp. 254–68.

Eagle, Steven, 2010, "Assembling Land for Urban Redevelopment: The Case for Owner Participation," Bruce Benson (ed.), *Property Rights: Eminent Domain and Regulatory Takings Re-Examined*, New York: Palgrave Macmillan, pp. 7–29.

Eagle, Steven, 2011, "Public Use in the Dirigiste Tradition: Private and Public Benefit in an Era of Agglomeration," *Fordham Urban Law Journal*, vol. 38, pp. 1023–89.

Ellickson, Robert, 1973, "Alternative to Zoning: Covenants, Nuisance Rules, and Fines as Land Use Controls," *University of Chicago Law Review*, vol. 40, no. 4, pp. 681–714.

Engel, Eduardo, Ronald Fischer, and Alexander Galetovic, 2005, "Highway Franchising and Real Estate Values," *Journal of Urban Economics*, vol. 57, no. 3, pp. 432–48.

Epstein, Richard, 1985, *Takings: Private Property and the Power of Eminent Domain*, Cambridge: Harvard University Press.

Finlay, Lorraine, 2010, "The Attack on Property Rights," Annual Conference of the Samuel Griffith Society.

Fischel, William, 1995, *Regulatory Takings: Law, Economics and Politics*, Cambridge: Harvard University Press.

Heller, Michael and Rick Hills, 2008, "Land Assembly Districts," *Harvard Law Review*, vol. 121, no. 6, pp. 1465–1527.

Johnson, Asmara, 2007, "Privatizing Eminent Domain: The Delegation of a Very Public Power to Private, Non-Profit and Charitable Corporations," *American University Law Review*, vol. 56, no. 3, pp. 455–514.

Kanner, Gideon, 2007, "We Don't Have to Follow Any Stinkin' Planning: Sorry about That Justice Stevens," *Urban Lawyer*, vol. 39, no. 3, pp. 529–62.

Kelly, Daniel, 2006, "The 'Public Use' Requirement in Eminent Domain Law: A Rationale Based on Secret Purchases and Private Influence," *Cornell Law Review*, vol. 92, no. 1, pp. 1–65.

Kelly, Daniel, 2009, "Pretextual Takings: of Private Developers, Local Governments, and Impermissible Favoritism," *Supreme Court Economic Review*, vol. 17, no. 1, pp. 173–236.

Kelly, Daniel, 2011, "Acquiring Land through Eminent Domain: Justifications, Limitations, and Alternatives," Kenneth Ayotte and Henry Smith (eds.), *Research Handbook on the Economic Analysis of Property Law*, Cheltenham and Northampton: Edward Elgar, pp. 344–71.

Kerekes, Carrie, 2011, "Government Takings: Determinants of Eminent Domain," *American Law and Economics Review*, vol. 13, no. 1, pp. 201–19.

Kim, Iljoong, Byung Koo Cho, Duol Kim, Sungkyu Park, Hojun Lee, and Kisang Jung, 2013, *A Law-and-Economics Study on Takings Law in Korea*, Korea Development Institute.

Kim, Iljoong, Hojun Lee, and Sungkyu Park, 2016, "Sharing Development Surplus with Landowners," Presented at the 2016 Western Economic Association International Meetings.

Kim, Iljoong and Sungkyu Park, 2010, "Eminent Domain Power and Afterwards: Leviathan's Post-Taking Opportunism," *Public Choice*, vol. 143, no. 1–2, pp. 209–27.

Kim, Iljoong and Sungkyu Park, 2012, "Private Takings as a Means of Supplying Public Goods: An Economic Analysis," *Korean Journal of Public Finance*, no. 75, pp. 63–103.

Kim, Iljoong and Sungkyu Park, 2015, "*Are Private Takings Efficient?: An Empirical Investigation*," Dept. of Economics Working Paper, Sungkyunkwan University.

Kotaka, Tsuyoshi and David Callies, 2002, *Taking Land: Compulsory Purchase and Regulation in Asian-Pacific Countries*, Honolulu: University of Hawaii Press.

Kulick, Peter, 2000, "Rolling the Dice: Determining Public Use in Order to Effectuate a Public–Private Taking: A Proposal to Redefine Public Use," *Law Review of Michigan State University-Detroit College of Law*, vol. 3, pp. 639–91.

Lanza, Steven, Thomas Miceli, C. F. Sirmans, and Moussa Diop, 2013, "The Use of Eminent Domain for Economic Development in the Era of *Kelo*," *Economic Development Quarterly*, vol. 27, no. 4, pp. 352–62.

Lehavi, Amnon and Amir Licht, 2007, "Eminent Domain, Inc.," *Columbia Law Review*, vol. 107, no. 7, pp. 1704–48.

Lum, Marissa, 2007, "A Comparative Analysis: Legal and Cultural Aspects of Land Condemnation in the Practice of Eminent Domain in Japan and America," *Asian-Pacific Law and Policy Journal*, vol. 8, no. 2, pp. 456–84.

Mangioni, Vince, 2009, "*Privatizing the 'Public Purpose Rule' in Compulsory Acquisition*," State of Australian Cities National Conference, University of Western Australia.

Merrill, Thomas, 1986, "The Economics of Public Use," *Cornell Law Review*, vol. 72, pp. 61–116.

Miceli, Thomas, 2011, *The Economic Theory of Eminent Domain: Private Property, Public Use*, New York: Cambridge University Press.

Mihaly, Marc, 2007, "Living in the Past: The *Kelo* Court and Public–Private Economic Redevelopment," *Ecology Law Quarterly*, vol. 34, no. 1, pp. 1–60.

Office of the Deputy Prime Minister (UK), 2004, *Compulsory Purchase and Compensation: Compulsory Purchase Procedure*, London: Office of the Deputy Prime Minister

Scheiber, Harry, 1973, "Property Law, Expropriation, and Resource Allocation by Government: The United States, 1789–1910," *Journal of Economic History*, vol. 33, no. 1, pp. 232–51.

Schill, Michael, 1997, "Assessing the Role of Community Development Corporations in Inner City Economic Development," *New York University Review of Law and Social Change*, vol. 22, no. 4, pp. 753–81.

Scott, Jeffery, 2003, "Public Use and Private Profit: When Should Heightened Scrutiny Be Applied to 'Public-Private' Takings?" *Journal of Affordable Housing and Community Development Law*, vol. 12, no. 4, pp. 466–90.

Shavell, Steven, 2010, "Eminent Domain versus Government Purchase of Land Given Imperfect Information about Owners," *Journal of Law and Economics*, vol. 53, no. 1, pp. 1–27.

Somin, Ilya, 2007, "Controlling the Grasping Hand: Economic Development Takings after *Kelo*," *Supreme Court Economic Review*, vol. 15, no. 1, pp. 183–271.

Somin, Ilya, 2011, "The Judicial Reaction to *Kelo*," *Albany Government Law Review*, vol. 4, no. 1, pp. 1–37.

Somin, Ilya, 2015, *The Grasping Hand:* 'Kelo v. City of London' *and the Limits of Eminent Domain*, Chicago: University of Chicago Press.

Staley, Samuel, 2010, "The Proper Uses of Eminent Domain for Urban Redevelopment is Eminent Domain Necessary?" Bruce Benson (ed.), *Property Rights: Eminent Domain and Regulatory Takings Re-Examined*, New York: Palgrave Macmillan, pp. 27–54.

Turnbull, Geoffrey, 2012, "Delegating Eminent Domain Powers to Private Firms: Land Use and Efficiency Implications," *Journal of Real Estate Finance and Economics*, vol. 45, no. 2, pp. 305–25.

Voss, Winrich, 2010, "Compulsory Purchase in Poland, Norway and Germany: Part Germany," FIG International Congress, Sydney, Australia.

Wyman, Katrina, 2007, "The Measure of Just Compensation," *University of California Davis Law Review*, vol. 41, no. 110, pp. 239–88.

8

Just Compensation in Eminent Domain in Korea: From the Perspective of Fairness

BYUNGKOO CHO*

I Introduction

The two basic requirements of eminent domain are "public use"[1] and "just compensation." Accordingly, the condemner's taking of property should be for the public use and the condemner should pay the condemnee just compensation. Even when a public project meets the requirement of public use, if the condemnees are not compensated justly, the public project should not be allowed. These basic principles of eminent domain tend to be quite similar in modern countries around the world.[2] However, in practice, the standards and methods of compensation vary considerably – this diversity is much greater than the conditions for public use. This happens due to the fact that the meaning of "being just" may be quite different depending on the circumstances, ages, countries, cultures, economic levels, social consciousness levels, etc. To put it bluntly, everyone has his or her own standard of "justness." Therefore, it is certainly not an easy task to establish an appropriate compensation system.

In this chapter I will discuss the compensation system, particularly from the perspective of fairness,[3] which is recently drawing more and more

* I would like to thank Professors Iljoong Kim, Ilya Somin, Yun-Chien Chang, Duol Kim, Hojun Lee, Sungkyu Park and Judge Kisang Jung.

1 Some countries may also use terminology such as: public necessity, public good, public interest, public purpose, etc.

2 Korean Constitution §23.3, U.S. Constitution 5th Amendment §5, German Grundgesetz §14.3, Japanese Constitution §29.3, Italian Constitution §42, Australian Constitution Section 51(xxxi), French Déclaration des droits de l'Homme et du citoyen §17, Protocol No. 1 to the European Convention on the Protection of Human Rights and Fundamental Freedoms §1, Charter of fundamental Rights of the European Union §17.1, *etc.*

3 It is not easy to define the meaning of *"fairness"* in the field of eminent domain. In this chapter, fairness implies that it should, at least, not go against the Pareto efficiency principle, and at most, distribute the *just* amount to both the condemner and the condemnees.

attention in the field of eminent domain. In Section II, I will briefly introduce the theory and practice – the theoretical, historical and legal evidence – of just compensation, and conflicts of interest related to the development projects and its compensation based on the cases of Korea, which has experienced rapid economic development for several decades. Then in Section III, I will cover the main issues concerning the compensation system such as social costs incurred by inappropriate compensation, subjective premium – whether or not to grant the condemnee a pecuniary or non-pecuniary bonus that exceeds the objective market value, and last but not least, problems in land price appraisal for compensation. By covering these issues, I will endeavor to make meaningful suggestions for a better compensation system.

II Theory and Practice of Compensation

1 *Rationales of Just Compensation*

There is no doubt that in the market economy, transaction of property based on the law of supply and demand is not only the most efficient means of exchange, but also one that is constitutional. Transactions of land are no exception. Even for public projects, it is extremely desirable for compulsory purchase to be replaced by a voluntary transaction in the real estate market. Nevertheless, eminent domain has been historically recognized and legislated in most countries, and no doubt, it is expanding due to the transition of society after the industrial revolution, which required large-scale development projects.[4] And the recent political condition whereby most governments are under increasing pressure to provide public facilities acts as another reason for the expansion of eminent domain.

These days, it is generally accepted that eminent domain starts from the historical and constitutional resolution that every property right can be defined under the law, and for the public interest the property right can be restricted to some degree – that does not harm the fundamental essence of the property right. This means that the property right is not an inviolable, sacrosanct, limitless right. In particular, the land retains the characteristics of being neither substitutable, producible, nor movable – these characteristics easily create a subjective or emotional attachment to the land – making it difficult to assess the accurate value of land, and also

[4] Melton (1996), Reynolds (2010).

cause externalities. In this respect, the land is also recognized as holding more publicness and public value than other properties. Therefore, the Constitution allows more restrictions or obligations on the land (owners).[5] Regarding the efficiency matter, from the viewpoint of law and economics, the eminent domain power is generally recognized to be a very efficient and powerful method of eliminating (potential) holdouts and reducing transaction costs. From the jurisprudence point of view, this efficiency is also well accepted.[6]

When there is a property right infringement on account of a public project, if it is considered by the law that this infringement is within the degree that the property owner should endure (inherent restriction of property rights), the condemner does not have to compensate the owner for the loss. But if this infringement crosses the line and harms the essence of the property right, then it is considered as a "special sacrifice for the public interest" and the condemner should compensate the condemnee for the loss. The constitutional obligation to protect the property right primarily means that the property right must be fully protected so the property owner can enjoy the power of "making use, gaining profit and disposing" of the property. But when property (land ownership) is taken out of public necessity, then the condemner should pay the full amount of the taken property's value. This means the Constitution allows the exchange of "full protection of property rights" with "compensation appropriate for the loss of the property". Economically, it is widely accepted that if a condemner does not have to pay just compensation, the condemner would take more property than he or she needs – the condemner does not fully internalize the cost of taking, – so this would cause inefficiency (*fiscal illusion*).[7]

To sum up, the basic principle and ideal of just compensation accompanying eminent domain has been historically, constitutionally, and legally recognized as well as from the viewpoints of economics and jurisprudence. The project runner should first try to purchase the property through the market prior to taking, then try to restrain him or herself

[5] The Korean Constitution §122: "The State may impose, under the conditions as prescribed by Act, restrictions or obligations necessary for the efficient and balanced utilization, development and preservation of the land of the nation that is the basis for the productive activities and daily lives of all citizens."

[6] Korean Constitutional Court Decision – 2007_C.C_BA 114: Achieving the legislative purpose of this taking provision, which allows the project runner to purchase the condemned property by paying the market price, is a very effective means to help the project run smoothly.

[7] Miceli (2011, p. 95).

as much as possible to proceed with the taking, and when the taking inevitably takes place, the condemner should pay the condemnee a compensation that is enough to satisfy the constitutional spirit – so, it ought to be *"just."*

2 Conflicts of Interest in Compensation

It is quite obvious that a condemnee has the incentive to take as much compensation as possible. On the other hand, a project runner generally has the incentive to reduce the compensation and the procedural cost for the project. It is common in most countries that eminent domain power may be exercised by private developers as well as the government, however, the incentives of the project runner are quite different depending on whether the project is run by the government or by a private developer.

The government tends to have an incentive to reduce arising conflicts and duration of the project operation, rather than to reduce the compensation amount itself, mainly due to political pressure.[8] Also, politicians tend to have an incentive to manipulate the development project and compensation for their own benefit. Since the execution of a development project in local areas draws national budget and stimulates the local economy, there is indeed a tendency for people to believe that the promotion of a large-scale development plan is due to the efforts of the local politician, which in the long run will benefit him or her in his popularity and becoming re-elected (Kim and Lee, 2012).

When a private developer becomes a project runner, the developer's only incentive is to earn more profit. This incentive is basically incompatible with the fundamental concern of publicness. Rather than promoting the public interest, a compulsory transfer of wealth from individual landowners to the private developer, may even cause a concentration of economic power to occur. A private developer may also try to shift the responsibility of the transaction cost for condemnee persuasion onto the government, and merely pursue the profit from the development project. If such is the case, granting private developers the prerogative of eminent domain power may create inefficiency, and inevitably private developers will show rent-seeking behavior.

[8] Severe resistance and protest against project operation cause political problems. Therefore, the government is likely to solve this problem by simply supplementing the increasing cost needed for compensation from the budget, which is comprised of the tax revenue collected from the general citizens.

Therefore, in this spiral of conflicts of interest between the persons involved, there is an urgent need to design a compensation system that can avoid inappropriate incentives and rent-seeking behavior.

3 *The Compensation System of Korea: Past and Present*

(1) Compensation System in the Past

Most countries have established and operated their own eminent domain and compensation systems. Korea was not an exception. Before adopting modern eminent domain laws, for example, during the Chosun dynasty (A.D. 1392–1897), there had been compensation standards that paid compensation according to the size and structure of houses (Kim and Kim, 2013). However, Korea adopted modern eminent domain laws which were based on continental law during the era under the colonial administration of imperial Japan. After gaining independence and in the aftermath of the Korean War, there was an urgent need to re-establish the country and to promote economic development. For this reason, from the late 1960s, it was necessary to carry out large-scale takings of property in order to build infrastructures and industrial facilities. The government fully supported these development projects by making and implementing laws to facilitate the use of eminent domain. Under this social atmosphere, Korea was able to achieve unprecedented economic development over the last several decades, and now has become the envy of developing countries.

Nevertheless, recently, the gap between the advancement of society and the backwardness of the eminent domain system often causes social conflicts and problems. In the following,[9] I will briefly mention the changes in the compensation system of Korea from the late 1960s up to now. By reviewing the compensation system of Korea, I will try to draw out some implications so that a better compensation system can be designed.

One of the important reasons that enabled the Korean economy to achieve rapid development was the consistent expansion of social infrastructure. However, with the change of social needs, the mainstream of taking and compensation also changed.

In the 1960s and 1970s, to meet the immediate needs of reconstruction after the Korean War and to pursue economic development, a quick and convenient process of taking and compensation was needed. In particular, regarding compensation, much emphasis was placed on preventing

[9] The following section is mainly based on the MOLIT report (2014).

Table 8.1. *The History of the Compensation System Modification*

Years	Main Purpose of Taking	Compensation Trend
1960s ~ 1970s	• Infrastructures • Industrial complexes • Public facilities	• Rapid & convenient process • Development surplus exclusion & rooting out speculation • Under-compensation
1980s ~ 1990s	• Industrial complexes • Housing (due to migration to cities) • Public facilities	• Rapid & convenient process • Development surplus exclusion & rooting out speculation • Under-compensation
2000s ~	• Housing • Reconstructing urban area (housing and public facility complexes) • Building new towns (administrative complex town, innovative town, company town, etc.)	• Sudden increase of total compensation amount • Fluctuant compensation standards • Process improvement (protecting procedural rights)

speculative transactions. For these purposes, the land assessment standard has gradually changed from a standard based on comparing neighboring land prices to a standard based on the "officially assessed land price" (hereafter ALP). As we can see below, ALP may easily be affected by government policy, and it is one of the main reasons of under- or fluctuant compensation.

In the 1980s and 1990s, with the rapid economic growth, industrial complex areas increased and urbanization was greatly accelerated. As a result, large-scale residential areas near big cities were urgently needed. During this period, compensation standards based on ALP were established as a principle, so that it became more convenient to assess compensation. Meanwhile, the possibility of under-compensation increased.

After the 2000s, in order to promote balanced regional development and domestic consumption, the government accelerated the construction of New Towns and the reconstruction of urban areas. Compared to other periods, during this period the total amount of compensation increased rapidly (US$7.5 billion in 2000 → US$28 billion in 2008). Due to the structural problems of ALP, the amount of compensation was overestimated as well as underestimated at times. However, the principles aimed at excluding development surplus and rooting out speculation were maintained.

To accommodate these changes, setting appropriate standards for compensation (standard land price such as ALP), diverse methods of compensation (such as bond or substitute land), and livelihood (relocation, transfer, business, etc.) compensation were adopted into the current law.

(2) Current Compensation System

Principles of Compensation The legal effect of takings (e.g. transfer of land ownership) becomes valid only after the condemner pays the condemnee or deposits the compensation amount to the court, which is determined by the (Central or Local) Land Tribunals. The Korea Land Taking and Compensation Act (hereafter KLTC) has established the principles of compensation such as the principle of a project runner's obligation to compensate, the principle of compensation in advance, the principle of compensation in cash, the principle of compensation for individuals, the principle of banning the reduction of compensation by deducting the amount of profit gains of vicinal residuary land (set-off prohibition), the principle of market value compensation, and the principle of exclusion of development surplus.[10] The most important principle is the principle of market value compensation. The compensation amount should be determined up to the level of the market price by the time of completion of negotiation between the parties, or decision by the Land Tribunal (KLTC §67 (1)).

The Standards of Assessing the Value of Condemned Land Although, as mentioned above, the land assessment standard has been changed from the standard based on comparing neighboring land prices to the standard based on ALP, the principle of market value compensation has been, at least, nominally maintained.

Since the 1970s the standard price system set up by the government has been devised and revised as a convenient method to evaluate the amount of compensation. The standard land price (the current ALP) is supposed

[10] The project runner is responsible for paying compensation (§61 of KLTC). The project runner should pay the total amount of compensation before engaging in construction (§62 of KLTC). Compensation shall be paid in cash unless there is a special clause in other Acts that stipulates otherwise (§63 of KLTC). Compensation should be made separately for the landowners (§63 of KLTC). Prohibition of set-off should be observed in compensation even when the landowner obtains various profits, such as price increases from the owner's remaining land due to the public project in question (§64 of KLTC). In calculating compensation, price changes (i.e., development surplus) arising from the public project in question shall not be taken into account (§67.2 of KLTC).

to represent the real market price. Yet, according to many studies and official opinions of the Ministry of Land, Infrastructure and Transport (MOLIT) as well,[11] it still seems insufficient to reflect the real market price. It cannot be denied that the standard price is set under the influence of government policy goals, such as preventing the increase of land prices, maintaining taxation levels, etc. Thus, it is doubtful if the

Table 8.2. *The History of Standards of Assessing Land Compensation*

Period	Actual Standard	Contents
1962–1970	Market (Trade) Price of Neighboring Lands	Individual assessment of land considering neighboring land price
1971–1981	Standard Land Price	Standard land price based on the Land Taking Act §16.2
1982–1989	Standard Land Price	Standard land price based on the National Land Usage & Management Act § 29
1989–2004	ALP	ALP[1] based on the Official Announcement of Land Price & Appraisal of Land Act[2]
2005–Present	ALP	ALP based on the Act on Public Disclosure of the Values and Appraisal of Real Estate

[1] There have been numerous land price estimation policies controlled by the government before the introduction of ALP by the Official Announcement of Land Price and Appraisal of Land Act. Examples are the standard price estimation (to calculate the amount of compensation) according to the Act on the Utilization and Management of the National Territory, market standard price (standard based on the taxation for local tax), standard price based on the inheritance tax and donation tax (national taxation standards), appraisal price based on appraisals (mainly for mortgage price estimation), etc. These land prices were each being used for compensation, taxation, and mortgage price estimation, in accordance with its original purpose. However, this caused land to have many different prices, which caused confusion. Therefore, ALP was introduced to integrate the system and manage the land price.

[2] The term "considering the neighboring land's price" was omitted by the revision of the Land Taking Act 1991, 12. 31.

[11] According to MOLIT's report (2014. 11. 14.), ALP (year 2014) still reflects only 63.3 per cent of the real market price.

market value principle is fully observed in the assessment of compensation for eminent domain. The standard has gone through many changes since 1962 as shown below.

Before 1970, considering the neighboring land price was the basic principle of land price estimation for compensation. However, after a few years, the standard price or officially assessed land price, which did not fully reflect the market value, became the standard for land price estimation. Due to this change, the transaction cost of negotiation or estimation has been decreased. However, ALP had been set at a lower price than the real land price, which increased the risk of under-compensation. Under-compensation could be considered as an efficient method contributing to rapid growth but, be that as it may, this not only induced various social costs but also went against the Constitution.[12]

In fact, compensation assessment based on the ALP system[13] has been introduced primarily in order to eliminate the speculative surplus from development projects. For this reason, the land price is calculated based on ALP, which is announced before reflecting the profit from the development project. Details of the standard may vary according to whether the land price has been changed due to the

12 Substantial analyses on the level of compensation have been made several times. In Munch (1976), it has been observed that the land in the area with a high level of land price tends to be priced higher whereas the land where the overall price is low tends to be priced lower due to the difference of the incentives for lawsuits of each taking. In Clauretie, Kuhn and Schwer (2004), it is mentioned that the calculated compensation price tends to be 17 per cent greater than the expected market value. Esposto (1996) argued that the government usually calculates the compensation price to exceed the market value in order to prevent the risk of the increase of lawsuits on compensation by the condemnee, and the delay of the public project followed by these lawsuits. In particular, Chang (2011) compared the expected fair market value to the negotiation proposal price of the condemner, demanded price of the condemnee, and the court's compensation decision price. As a result, the three prices were all found to be greater than the expected fair market value to a certain level. According to this research, the condemner has an incentive to calculate a more precise price, therefore, the price proposed by the condemner for the negotiation is most similar to the expected fair market value. Nonetheless, it is not likely to be the case for Korea due to problems of the ALP system and the certified public appraiser system, or for any other (developing) countries that are executing drastic development projects.

13 The date of announcement of the Standard Land ALP is January 1, every year. However, for this announcement, ALP of the most representative 500,000 standard lands are utilized rather than ALP of the target land, which is actually being compensated. Based on ALP of the selected standard land, the general land price increase rate between the two periods of ALP and the decision is reflected, and then the unique characteristics of the land to be taken is reflected, and after that, the amount of compensation is decided through adjustments.

announcement or notice of the public project plan. Details of the standard vary as follows:

- When the land price has been changed: When the land is acquired during the period $(B + C + D)$ after the announcement $(\tau_0{}^P)$, the compensation is calculated based on ALP announced on the date closest to the public announcement date, ALP_B (KLTC § 70.5).
- When the land price has not changed: (i) when the land is acquired through negotiation before the notice of permission of the project, compensation is estimated based on ALP, which has been announced most recently in relation to the negotiation (acquisition) date (ALP_C), (ii) when the land is acquired after the notice of permission (D), regardless of the fact that the acquiring occurred through either the negotiation after the notice or the decision of taking, ALP (ALP_D), which has been announced most recently in relation to the notice of permission date $(\tau_1{}^d)$, will be the standard for calculating the compensation (KLTC § 70.3, 70.4).

III Issues Concerning Just Compensation

1 *Emerging Problems – Social Cost*

Taking of land induces various social costs. If the resulting development benefit (B_d) is larger than the essential cost (C_e) – such as the cost for construction and cost for land compensation – needed in order to run a public project, it can be regarded as a positive public project from the economic point of view. Nonetheless, beyond the essential costs, taking of land can create a dramatic social cost due to the legislative and operational defects.

It has been quite commonly accepted that subjective value should not be included in compensation. This is not only the case in Korea, but also in many other countries. The subjective loss caused by compulsion and subjection is regarded as a cost that the condemnee must endure.[14] However, as long as there exists a characteristic of "deprivation" in the nature of taking, it is questionable whether total disregard for the subjective values is correct. There is a potential threat that an unsatisfied condemnee may become unwilling to be lawful. Also, due to disappointment, an unsatisfied condemnee may cause harm and trouble to the

[14] This can be interpreted as a limit of the property rights according to the Constitution.

society. This kind of social cost can be referred to as a "Demoralization Cost." In fact, demoralization does cause some serious problems in some countries.[15] Examples of some other possible social costs are the loss caused by excessive execution of the project despite its lack of concern for public interest which consequently brings a significantly lower benefit than expected (C_f : Cost of project failure), loss from a sudden cancellation of the project (C_c: Cost of project cancellation), and appeal procedure costs expended due to filing administrative appeals or lawsuits (C_p: Cost of legal procedure).[16]

[15] The general definition of the demoralization cost from the aspect of eminent domain can be explained as follows: this is a cost induced by the characteristic of the eminent domain to deprive the condemnee of the (property) right. At times, compensation may not be given at an adequate level satisfying the landowner, or sometimes, compensation may not be given at all. Then, the condemnee or potential condemnees become hostile towards the eminent domain policy itself and may be willing to resist the law. In that case, this becomes a social cost for the government to bear. Moreover, the demoralization cost can be easily increased since this may occur not only among current condemnees, but among those who agree with the condemnees or even potential condemnees (Michelman, 1967). As a result, in some countries where rapid growth takes place, condemnees often go against the government not only by protests but even by acts of terrorism or mass suicides.

[16] As shown in the graph below which indicates the tendency of appeals and lawsuits, the number of administrative appeals or lawsuits filed has dramatically increased. Interestingly, compared to the time (the 1970s–1980s) of rapid economic growth where under-compensations were prevalent, the numbers have increased rapidly since the late 1980s due to the growth of citizenship and democratization in Korea.

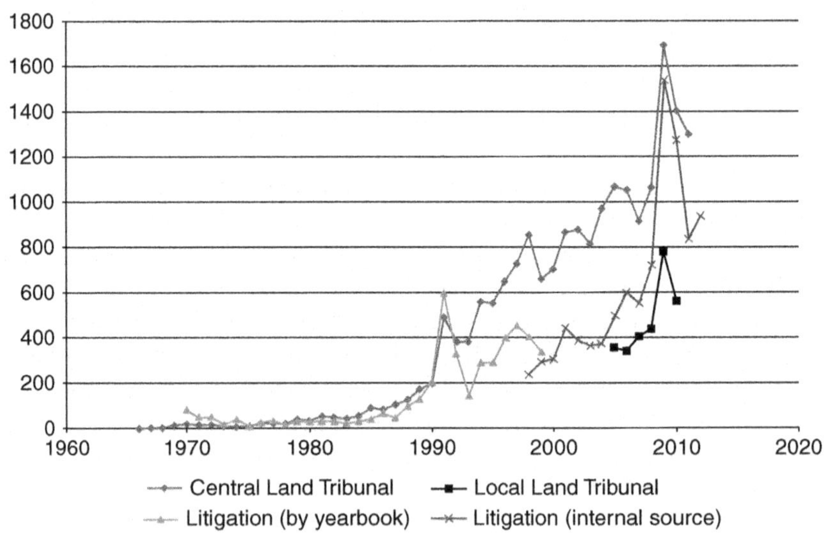

Attempts to merely reduce the project cost by lowering the compensation and disregarding the increase of other social costs may cause major social problems. Many cases of massive violence and protests by farmers who lost their land have been reported in several Asian countries undergoing rapid economic development. A few years ago, even in Korea, a 600-year-old historical building – National Treasure No. 1 – was set on fire by a person who was dissatisfied with the under-compensation of taken land. Also in Korea, some people who were dissatisfied with low business compensation and poor relocation arrangements illegally occupied a building in Seoul and threw petrol bombs that caused severe casualties.[17] Therefore, when planning a compensation policy for eminent domain, it is important to contemplate simultaneously how to reduce these social costs and also to make an efficient system.

2 *Granting of the Subjective Premium*

In most counties, the compensation is calculated and paid based on the market price standards. Related to such market price standards, the dangers of under-compensation by disregarding the subjective value as perceived by the landowner have been mentioned in many studies. According to studies such as Fischel and Shapiro (1989), Burrows (1991), and Miceli and Segerson (1994), an adequate level of just compensation may be efficiently achieved when reaching the level of social welfare maximization. However, Fischel and Shapiro (1989) and Nosal (2001) mentioned that the adequate level of compensation may be achieved at the level of market value, whereas Miceli and Segerson (1994) and Hermalin (1995) stated that the best method is to calculate the compensation independent from the market price.

Whether the compensation according to market-based pricing is sufficient depends on how one perceives subjective value. Subjective value differs greatly depending on the individual and is extremely difficult to measure accurately. As a result, in most cases, it is considered nearly impossible to include the subjective value held by landowners in compensation for the use of eminent domain. Still, considering that it is a unilateral and involuntary transaction, some legislation allows compensation that

[17] According to the National Alliance of Squatters and Evictees, which directed such situations, a total of 29 people have died related to the tearing down of buildings due to development plan implementation since 1998. Also up to 2006, over seven years, six more people either committed suicide or died due to accidents during strikes related to demolition.

exceeds the market price. This is called a subjective premium, or bonus. For example, 125 per cent of the market price of land is paid in the US state of Michigan, whereas in Indiana the compensation is made in the range of 125–150 per cent of the market price. In countries other than the US, such as in Canada (Ontario, Manitoba 5 per cent), Australia (Victoria, Western Australia up to 10 per cent), India (30 per cent), and Pakistan (15–25 per cent), the subjective premium is considered to be added to the market price (Lee, 2013).

However, when taking a closer look at the factors constituting the subjective loss, considering subjective premium as a sort of allowance or subsidy can be problematic. The factors constituting the subjective loss can be categorized as follows: The loss (L*s*) of the rational willing-seller's subjective value (e.g. attachment to the land, personal memories) due to the objective and unilateral nature of the taking process, which could have been reflected in the market transaction; the subjective loss (L*a*) due to the loss of autonomy induced by forcing of the transaction, which disables the seller from deciding when and under what condition to sell; and the subjective loss (L*o*) incurred due to the loss of opportunity to gain (speculative) surplus.[18]

The first loss (L*s*) may be considered as a subjective value loss caused by the difficulty of precise evaluation. This loss should obviously be included in the just compensation, yet, too much transaction cost is needed for the calculation. Thus, it is in fact impossible to calculate, and eventually it becomes excluded from the compensation. Therefore, if the subjective premium is acknowledged based on such reasons, then it is rather a *just compensation* of the subjective value loss rather than a *premium* or a *bonus.*[19] Comparatively, the second loss (L*a*) is derived from the land-taking system's characteristic itself. Therefore, it is a loss the condemnee must endure due to the immanent limits of property rights.[20] The above-mentioned two losses are the factors to be considered during the planning stage of the just compensation system. Compared to these two, the third loss (L*o*) is mostly induced by under-compensation bias or a speculative motive. This can lead to inefficiency, such as holdout

[18] Fennell (2004) distinguishes the uncompensated increment into three categories: subjective premium, a chance at surplus from transfer, and autonomy.

[19] However, it seems to be the case that they are choosing to provide an amount of compensation by adding a certain percentage of the objective market value, in the name of subjective "premium", because the accurate amount is difficult to identify.

[20] The accurate amount of autonomy value loss cannot be identified as well.

problems. Therefore it should be eliminated during the planning stage of the just compensation system.[21]

As I have argued above, it is appropriate for L*s* to be included in the just compensation. However, it is questionable whether compensating for L*a* or L*o* to some extent can also be possible or not. This may be considered as a discussion as to whether distributing an amount that exceeds just compensation, especially a portion of the development surplus, to the condemnees in the fairness point of view is desirable or not. Practically, I believe an appropriate amount ought to be spent in order to prevent demoralization.

Indeed, it is uncontroversial for the project runner to receive the result of the project – either the profit or the loss. The risk belongs to the project runner. Accordingly, it is not allowed for the condemnee to claim the development profit at the time of the compensation – in advance of the initiation of a project – since it is the same as demanding a not-yet-realized and unearned windfall income. The exclusion of development surplus is one of the basic principles of compensation in many countries.

However, as long as eminent domain itself intrinsically causes the loss of subjective value, which is not covered by the compensation based on the market value standard, compensating this loss does not go against the Constitution – rather, it is in accordance with the constitutional spirit. The problem lies in whether to allow compensation of subjective value loss with the development surplus. I would argue that the reason why the development surplus should be used as a reservoir of subjective value loss compensation is because people's subjective loss reaches the maximum level when they believe that they are relatively more deprived.[22] In addition, I would also argue that the realization of

[21] The boundary to distinguish these three subjective losses can be quite ambiguous since all are "subjective." Nevertheless, it shares a general stance in the law and economic point of view that compensation must be made including the actual subjective loss. On the contrary, Lee (2013) argues that providing the fixed-percentage bonus in addition to the fair market value of the land in order to give compensation for the subjective loss may result in excessive investment and the polarization of wealth and, moreover, the fair market value in eminent domain tends to be higher than the actual market price, and therefore subjective premium should not be acknowledged.

[22] Let's take a look at the reason why the principle of the exclusion of development surplus has been founded. For the condemnee to demand a yet-to-be-realized development profit is unacceptable. This is because, when demanding such profit is allowed, a dramatic increase of opportunistic behavior such as holdouts may increase, only to result in a cancellation of a public project. An additional reason is because an externality such as windfall through free-riding may occur. However, if by any chance these concerns can be eliminated, an overtly strict operation of this principle can still bring unjust

the idea of *just* compensation is eventually related to whom the profit from the land price increase from a specific development project, or the general development surplus is distributed. From this point of view, or the viewpoint of fairness, the development surplus may be distributed to the landowners who suffer from the subjective value loss and a sense of deprivation.

In reality, the total amount of profit earned from a development project is difficult to calculate precisely. Also, the level of contribution of each person concerned to the development profit is very difficult to distinguish, due to the characteristic of development projects as the profit comes from many different factors. Despite these limitations, a system to give a portion of the development profit to the condemnees is needed not only to seek economic fairness, but also to prevent potential excessive taking by the condemner.[23]

Before setting the range of compensation for the amount of subjective value loss, the objective value (market price) for the condemned land must be precisely assessed. Merely granting the subjective premium as a form of subsidy will only bring disorder to the compensation system. The subjective premium is strongly recommended under the situation where the condemnees must move out from the region due to a loss of land. These condemnees are the ones who feel the deepest subjective loss and sense of deprivation from having to leave their homes and their living bases.[24, 25]

consequences. In particular, let's take a look at the case that a development plan is set to give compensation to the condemnee of an amount similar to or below the market price of the land, while the project runner, or a private company, earns the development profit due to its possession of the right to operate the project, where it is almost certain that revenue will be generated. In the fairness point of view, the need for providing the condemnees, who must leave their homes and living base, with compensation due to consideration of their subjective value loss and the sense of deprivation can be acknowledged. In other words, if the project is likely to have no risk of loss for the project runner, and also if it is obvious that merely the development profit is to be gained by the project runner, a portion of the development profit can be paid to the condemnees to a certain degree. The degree of how large the portion of the development profit that should be given to the condemnees is decided considering many different relative factors, such as the characteristic of each public project, the degree of publicness of the project as well as the yield, which is gained by the private project runner, etc.

23 This view can also be found in Epstein (1985).

24 Subjective premium can be indirectly given through methods such as substitute land provision, tax reduction benefits, bonds, or stocks rather than being given as an actual pecuniary payment, especially when the development surplus is uncertain.

25 For more details about surplus distribution, refer to Park (2015).

3 *Assessment of Land Price*

Accurately accessing the value of the condemned land is crucial for just compensation. However, it is very difficult to ensure accuracy due to the characteristics of land. In Korea, the market value calculation method for compensation has changed from neighboring lands comparison to the ALP method. While the convenience of the assessment has been greatly increased, the problem is that the ALP method is practically unable to provide just compensation. Let us figure out the reason through Korea's appraiser system and the problem of land price calculation using the ALP standard.

Public Appraiser

The public appraiser sets the compensation price according to §68.1 of the KLTC. The professionalism and impartiality of appraisers on the issue of compensation estimation are recognized by law. However, because of the underlying risks, the compensation estimation through public appraisers may act as a factor for inducing a systematic problem in the compensation, along with the ALP standard.

In Korea, appraisal for the land compensation price is made by public appraisers (certified),[26] who are given the authority by the government, specifically, MOLIT. Korea's MOLIT, which is the ministry in charge of eminent domain, national development projects and real estate (price) policies, at the same time, also controls and supervises appraisers. Other than the calculation of the initial compensation, the appraiser is also in charge of the "Estimation of the compensation in the local or central land tribunal stage" and the "Estimation of the compensation in the stage of the lawsuit." For these two stages, the Land Tribunals and the court respectively select the public appraisers.

The most important role of the Land Tribunals is to determine the appropriate level of compensation. During the stage where the project is pushed ahead, simply an arithmetic mean of the compensation amounts calculated by two or three selected appraisers is used to decide the compensation. If a condemnee, who disagrees with the compensation,

[26] Up to 1970, only one appraiser recommended by the condemner was appointed to submit the appraisal. However, after the industrialization in the 1970s, the number increased to two. From 2003, the condemnee was also allowed to recommend one appraiser, increasing the number to three. Then in 2012, a revision was made in the KLTC that the condemner's right to recommend one of the two appraisers should be given to the governor of the city or the county – if the condemnee desires. These amendments were made out of concern for the fairness and transparency of appraisal.

makes an objection to the tribunal or files a lawsuit in the administrative court, then a second round of appraisal will be made. Even if four or five appraisers proposed similar appraisals for the first and second round of appraisals, the drawback can be overcome by a new one at the next appeal stage. However, this procedure can be a burden for the appraisers who are under the supervision of MOLIT, because when MOLIT perceives a certain compensation amount to have been calculated as excessively high, the appraisers may receive disciplinary actions such as suspension of business or revocation of licenses.

Under the current law, the appraisers are selected by the project runner and the landowners who are the actual parties involved in compensation matters. The landowner will ask for more compensation, and conversely the project runner will demand minimum compensation. Under these circumstances, it is fairly difficult for the appraisers to refuse the request made by the clients who are, in fact, the ones that pay for the appraisal. In particular, appraisers tend to be more influenced by large-scale project runners, such as local autonomous entities or the Korea Land and Housing Corporation, which repeatedly request appraisals. Thus, the incentives of these parties are inevitably included in the appraisal procedure. Therefore, there is a high possibility for the appraisal to be biased, and due to the circumstances mentioned above, under-compensation is more likely to occur.

Land Appraisal Standard

The compensation price for land is derived from the arithmetic mean of the prices calculated by two or three appraisers (at the same stage). These appraisers must follow the Land Appraisal Standard stated in §70 of the KLTC in order to eliminate development profit.

The practical method of land appraisal, which is to calculate the actual land appraisal price based on §17 of the Land Appraisal Standard, is as follows: when the land zoning, current state of usage, category of land, and the surrounding environment of a certain nearby standard land is identical or similar to the land for the project, the nearby standard land becomes the Comparative Standard Land → the ALP of the Comparative Standard Land is revised to the date of compensation according to the general land price increase rate → adjusting factors of individual estimations derived from the comparison of the target land and the comparative standard land are applied on the revised ALP → a couple of transaction cases of nearby similar lands are also considered as adjusting factors.

In particular, the "nearby land transaction case" factor differs greatly depending on the case. Moreover, these nearby land transaction cases are selected and considered solely by the appraisers without any specific rules or legal evidence. Hence, this is used in practice as a controlling or manipulating factor for the appraisers to reduce the gap between the ALP and the real market price. Thus, there are criticisms on the subjectivity of this factor as an adjusting factor in the estimation (Park, 2011). The "nearby land transaction case" factor makes it difficult for the Land Tribunals or the court to make a decision on the compensation.

Moreover, it is more difficult for just compensation to take place due to such systematic problems mentioned below regarding the standard date for the land price.

The longer period *A*, the more difficult it will be to eliminate the (expected) development profit from being reflected in the land price. Also, negativity may increase if rent-seeking behavior – such as buying the land at a low price and holding out – is shown during period *A* by the parties concerned or the insiders who monopolize the information related to the decision making of the project. When the project is officially announced under this situation, the speculative expectation for the potential profit from the development may already be projected into ALP_B. Therefore, the compensation calculated based on ALP_B may be biased, which may result in excessive compensation.[27] In this case, it fails to exclude the development surplus from the compensation, as Figure 8.1 depicts.

However, in most cases, there is a greater possibility for under-compensation when the price is set at the rate given at a certain period, not the actual transaction price or fair market price at the time when the taking takes place.

Figure 8.2 depicts the growing concern of a possible under-compensation by showing the increase of loss due to ALP, as the gap increases between the calculated land price based on ALP and the market price of the land at the point of notice of project permission. This may be resolved by reducing the gap between ALP established most recently in relation to the project permission date and the market price at the time of project permission.

[27] There is a possibility that the compensation may increase to facilitate the operation of the project, when the project is a politically emphasized by the government – in other words, when it is a project that must be carried out swiftly due to various political reasons such as if it was a part of the campaign promise of a presidential nominee or other local elections. Lee and Kim (2012) mention cases of excessive compensation made for national projects such as the Innovation City Construction Project.

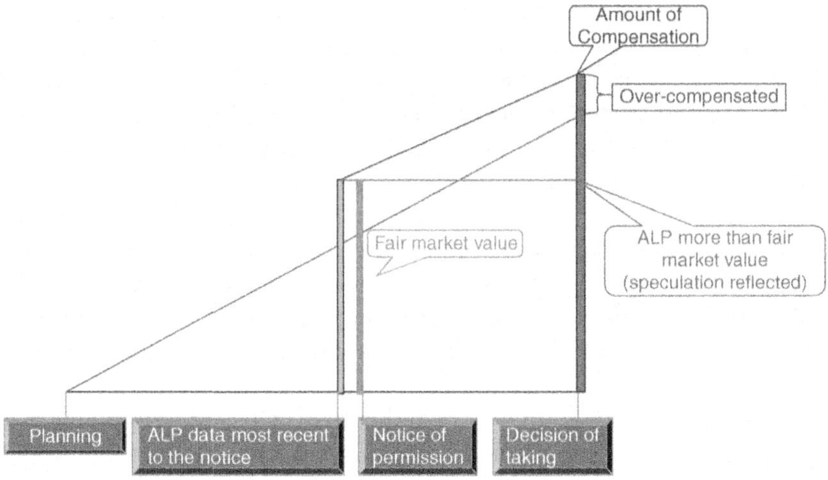

Figure 8.1.

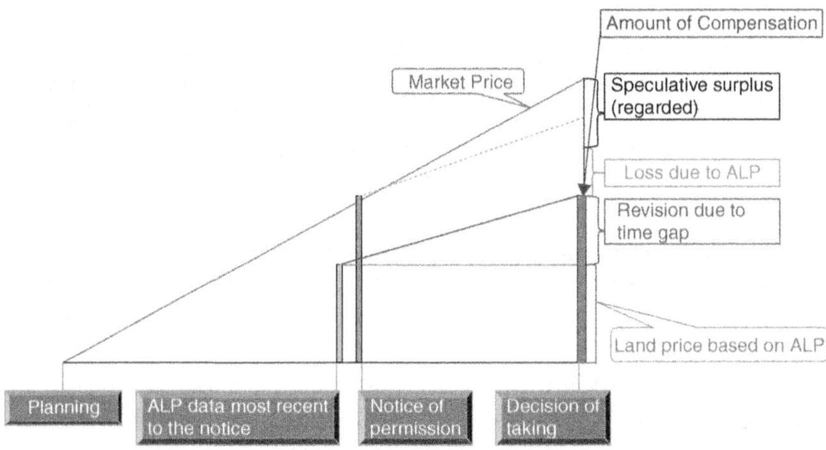

Figure 8.2.

Still, as aforementioned, various real estate and tax policies tend to force the land price to stay at a lower rate than the actual market price.[28]

In the end, the compensation based on the ALP system will become swift and efficient, yet, there are many problems which prevent the

[28] As mentioned above, the level of ALP compared to the actual land transaction cost (Realization Rate) was only 63.3 per cent in 2014.

compensation from reaching the level that is just. A compensation system in favor of the project runner has contributed to the rapid economic development of Korea, but there is growing dissatisfaction by the condemnees, which leads to demoralization. So, it seems a system that provides a just amount of compensation (fair market value) should be created, and then based on this system, a compensation system, which grants subjective premium should be discussed.

IV Conclusion

Thus far, I have analyzed various issues relating to eminent domain in Korea. In fact, eminent domain has contributed immensely and acted as a great advantage for the rapid economic development of Korea.[29] But the uniform compensation calculation system based on the ALP standard and the public appraiser system under government influence or large-scale project runners have been continuously criticized for causing unfairness in eminent domain. However, there are efforts to bring changes to the ALP system in order to resolve the problems of the previous compensation system. Also, there are gradual efforts to create a variety of compensation methods, so that projects can be executed justly and the rights of condemnees can be properly protected.

Above all, the accurate assessment of the land to be taken based on the market price is basically a stepping stone to achieve appropriate estimation of the compensation. Therefore, paying attention to the reasonableness of the Land Appraisal Policy is crucial. In order to build an optimal compensation system, considering the reduction of various social costs related to eminent domain and discussing whether to consider the subjective premium are also very crucial. These kinds of discussions will enable us to figure out the economic incentives of various parties concerned, so that we can prevent potential unfairness or dissatisfaction towards the compensation system.

References in English

Burrows, Paul, 1991, "Compensation of Compulsory Acquisition," *Land Economics*, vol. 67(1), pp. 49–63.

[29] For this reason, in many developing countries in Asia the KLTC is inspected with a view to introducing it into their own system, yet the current system, as it is, seems inappropriate for dissemination.

2011, "An Empirical Study of Court-Adjudicated Takings Compensation in New York City: 1990–2003," *Journal of Empirical Legal Studies*, vol. 8(2), pp. 384–412.

Clauretie, M. Terrence, William Kuhn and Keith R. Schwer, 2004, "*Residential Properties Taken under Eminent Domain: Do Government Appraisers Track Market Values?*," *Journal* of *Real Estate Research*, vol. 26(3), pp. 317–28.

Epstein, Richard A., *Takings: Private Property and the Power of Eminent Domain* (Harvard University Press, 1985).

Esposto, G. Alfredo, 1996, "*The Political Economy of Taking and Just Compensation*," *Public Choice*, vol. 89(3–4), pp. 267–82.

Fennell, Lee Anne, 2004, "Taking Eminent Domain Apart," *Michigan State Law Review* vol. 2004: 957–1004.

1989, "A Constitutional Choice Model of Compensation for Takings," *International Review of Law and Economics*, vol. 9(2), pp. 115–28.

Hermalin, Benjamin E., 1995, "An Economic Analysis of Takings," *Journal of Law Economics and Organization*, vol. 11(1): 64–86.

Kotaka, Tsuyoshi and David L. Callies, *Taking Land: Compulsory Purchase and Regulation of Land in Asian-Pacific Countries* (University of Hawaii Press 2002).

Lee, Brian Angelo, 2013, "Just Under-compensation: The Idiosyncratic Premium in Eminent Domain," *Columbia Law Review*, vol. 113, pp. 593–655.

Melton, Buckner, F., 1996, "Eminent Domain, Public Use, and the Conundrum of Original Intent," *Natural Resources Journal*, vol. 36, pp. 59–85.

Miceli, J. Thomas, *The Economic Theory of Eminent Domain: Private Property, Public Use* (Cambridge University Press, 2011).

Miceli, J. Thomas and Kathleen Segerson, 1994, "Regulatory Takings: When Should Compensation Be Paid?" *Journal of Legal Studies*, vol. 23, pp. 749–76.

Michelman, I. Frank, 1967, "Property, Utility, and Fairness: Comments on the Ethical Foundations of Just Compensation Law," *Harvard Law Review*, vol. 80, pp. 1165–1258.

Munch, Patricia, 1976, "An Economic Analysis of Eminent Domain," *Journal of Political Economy*, vol. 84, pp. 473–97.

Nosal Ed., 2001, "The Takings of Land: Market Value Compensation Should Be Paid," *Journal of Public Economics*, vol. 82, pp. 431–43.

Park, Sungkyu, *Distribution of Development Surplus in Takings*, paper presented at the International Conference on Shifting the Paradigm for Sustainable Development: Eminent Domain and Property Rights (Korea Development Institute, 2015).

Reynolds, Susan, *Before Eminent Domain: Toward a History of Expropriation of Land for the Common Good: Toward a History of Expropriation of Land for the Common Good* (University of North Carolina Press, 2010).

References in Korean

Kim, Duol and Iljoong Kim, *Is Just Compensation for Compulsory Purchase a Creature of Modern Constitution in Asia? Evidence from Late 18th Century Korea*, Working Paper, KLEA International Conference of Law and Economics (2013).

Kim, Iljoong, ByungKoo Cho, Duol Kim, Sungkyu Park, Hojun Lee and Kisang Jung, *A Law-and-Economics Study on Takings Law in Korea* (KDI, 2013).

Kim, Jaehoon and Hojun Lee, *Political Economy of Public Investment Projects*, KDI Policy Research Series (KDI, 2013).

Lee, Hojun and Hyungtai Kim, *Studies on Public Expropriation*, KDI, Policy Research Series (KDI, 2012).

MOLIT, *2013 Modularization of Korea's Development Experience: The Expropriation and Compensation System in Korea* (MOLIT and Korea Research Institute for Human Settlements, 2014).

Park, Sungkyu, 2011, "Eminent Domain, Just Compensation, Officially Announced Land Price, Market Value, Revision Based on Other Factors," *Journal of Korea Real Estate Analysis Association*, vol. 17, pp. 133–54.

9

Overall Due Process in Takings in Korea

KISANG JUNG

I Introduction

The order of how the project runners acquire land is composed of two steps called the "bargain purchase" and the "compulsory purchase (takings),"[1] the former being the procedural prerequisite of the latter. Viewing from the institutional aspect, there has been more emphasis on the compulsory purchase (takings), which restricts private property rights. Moreover, the Korean Constitution declares that public necessity and just compensation are necessary conditions in order to compulsorily purchase private property for executing a project (§23.3).[2] In this chapter, the takings process will be reviewed, focusing on the stages of scrutinizing whether the intended projects in Korea are indeed for public necessity.

The takings process in Korea consists of (1) the phase to grant the power of eminent domain after having confirmed that a project meets the public-interest criterion (permission of a public project), and (2) the phase to confirm the specific contents of takings and to exercise the power (decision of taking). However, this chapter will demonstrate how these procedures are institutionally insufficient to support the verification of public necessity due to theoretical and practical limitations in the law and economic perspective. Analyses on related court decisions and

1 Across different jurisdictions, takings is also known as eminent domain, condemnation, expropriation, compulsory acquisition, compulsory purchase, and land acquisition and resumption. However, "takings" and "eminent domain" will be the terminologies mainly used in this chapter.

2 §23.3 of the Korean Constitution stipulates: "Takings, use, or limitation of private property for the sake of public necessity and the related compensation shall be governed by acts, and just compensation should be paid." Many countries have a clause on eminent domain that is similar, for example, to that declared in the Fifth Amendment to the US Constitution ("Nor shall private property be taken for public use, without just compensation").

international comparison that are of direct relevance will support the demonstration.

The main point of this chapter will be as follows: if it is proven in any phase of the takings process that the project does not meet the public-interest criterion, the phase where the problem has been detected ought to be stopped and takings for the project must not be permitted – for this to be possible, all phases constituting the takings process must be closely examined to prove public necessity.

II Takings Process in Korea and Related Legal Controversies

1 *Overview of the Takings Process*

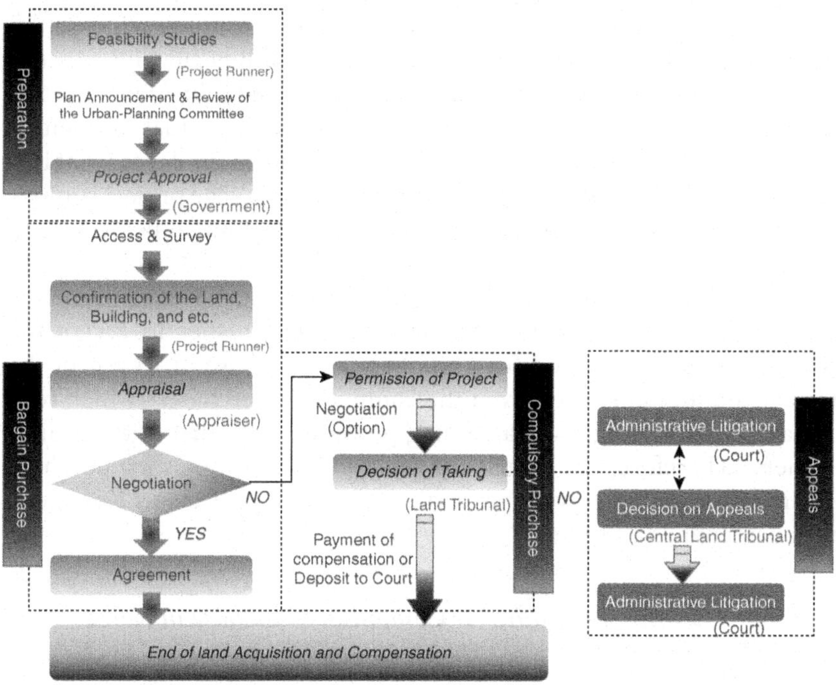

Figure 9.1. Takings Process in Korea: The Most Basic Order

2 *Nominal Procedure for Bargain Purchase*

Project runners survey lands and buildings within the target area for the public project. The procedure for bargain purchase begins when project runners notify the landowners of the overview of the public project and the compensation plan describing the timing, methods, and the procedure of the compensation (Korea Land Takings and Compensation Act (hereafter KLTC) §15.1). Project runners request the appraisal of the land for compensation to two or three certified public appraisers. The three appraisers are recommended by the provincial governor or metropolitan city mayor, the project runners, and (upon request) landowners. Project runners and landowners begin the negotiation based on the average of the three appraised values suggested by the three appraisers (KLTC §68).

Landowners are pressured to accept the given average price. This is because, if the landowners and project runners do not reach a settlement,[3] the procedure for compulsory purchase will begin immediately. In compulsory purchase, the average of the appraised values from the two or three certified public appraisers will become the actual amount of compensation. In general, the average amount will be similar to what had been originally appraised from the bargain purchase. The project runners who are expected to obtain the power of eminent domain possess more advantage to win the negotiation than landowners. Therefore, for the project runners, the incentive to reach a settlement is not immense. Eventually, the landowners can merely decide whether to accept the average amount appraised from the bargain purchase or to accept the average amount appraised from the compulsory purchase – which robs the landowners of rightful bargaining power equal to that of the project runners. Therefore, the actual influence of the compulsory purchase (takings) to acquire private properties for public projects in Korea can be considered as absolute.

3 *Dualistic Procedure for Compulsory Purchase in Korea*

The procedure for compulsory purchase is mainly composed of (1) permission of a public project and (2) decision of taking. In the former phase, the power of eminent domain is granted after scrutinizing

[3] If landowners and project runners reach a settlement, both parties make a contract, implying that compensation arrangements for the project are completed.

whether the intended project meets the public-interest criterion; and then in the second phase, the specific contents of the takings apt for the project is confirmed and the legal effect of takings occurs. As mentioned, in Korea, the granting and exercising of the power of eminent domain are separated into two phases, however, this is not unusual in comparative law. Compulsorily acquiring private property for a project can be constitutionally justified according to "la déclaration d'utilité publique" in France and "permission of a public project" in Japan. The "permission of a public project" and the "decision of taking" are merely put in a separate form due to the allocation of each of their functions, however, those two are closely inter-correlated for the sole purpose of taking. Nevertheless, the fact that the Supreme Court of Korea insists on the strict separation of the two is quite noteworthy. This can be clearly recognized in the following decisions from two Supreme Court cases in Korea. First, if the permission of a public project cannot be invalidated due to not having a high degree of illegality, in principle, it is not permitted to take legal actions for revocation of decision of taking as a follow-up administrative disposition – even if a certain degree of illegality has been found.[4] Next, if a permission of a public project has not been revoked during administrative litigation, the Land Tribunal cannot make the decision of taking, which disables the project to be carried out.[5] In other words, if the power of eminent domain is granted by the permission of a public project, the Land Tribunal will not be able to stop the procedure for compulsory purchase through the decision of taking. This shows that the permission of a public project is, in fact, the exclusive procedure for the verification of public interest. As described further, the thorough separation of the permission of a public project and the decision of taking by the Supreme Court of Korea has resulted in weakening the verification of public interest within the overall takings process.

4 *Overview of Permission of a Public Project*

(1) Function: The Verification of Public Interest

Permission of a public project is an administrative disposition granting the power of eminent domain to the project runners under the condition that it fulfills all requirements for eminent domain including the public interest criterion under the KLTC.[6] The main purpose of this is to

[4] 87_S.C._NU395, 91_S.C._NU4324. [5] 2004_S.C._DU8538. [6] 95_S.C._NU4889.

scrutinize whether a project meets the public-interest criterion well enough to constitutionally justify that private property is compulsorily acquired. Considering that takings occur in most public projects, the power of eminent domain not being granted *de facto* means the discontinuance of the project.

In Korea, §4 of the KLTC lists individual types of public projects that are permitted to use eminent domain. The goal of explicitly listing these types on the constitutional level was to apply strict principles and to prevent abuse, similar to the practice involved, for example, in the Land Takings Act in Japan.[7] This is to categorize public projects in order to roughly filter out the projects that do not meet the public-interest criterion. In other words, the projects categorized as a type of public project in this provision are only subject to the permission of a public project. More specifically, §4 of the KLTC provides detailed project types in a total of seven categories, with one extra sub-article (§4.8) as explained in the footnote below. The seven groups include a wide variety of public projects.[8]

[7] In Kim et al. (2013), this is designated as the "legislative verification of public interest." In contrast, the permission of a public project is designated as the "administrative verification of public interest."

[8] "1. Projects for the national defense and military affairs; 2. Projects to be implemented for public interests by obtaining permission, authorization, approval, designation, etc. under the related Acts, with respect to railroads, roads, airports, harbors, parking lots, public garages, cargo terminals, rail tracks, rivers, dikes, dams, canals, water supply and waterworks systems, sewerage systems, terminal sewage treatment, wastewater treatment, erosion control, windbreak, fire prevention, tide embankments, water embankments, reservoirs, irrigation and drainage canals, petroleum reservation, oil supply, waste treatment, electricity, telecommunications, broadcasting, and gas and meteorological observations; 3. Projects for office buildings, plants, research institutes, test sites, health facilities, cultural facilities, parks, arboretums, squares, athletic fields, markets, graveyards, crematories, slaughterhouses, or other public facilities to be established by central or local governments; 4. Projects for the establishment of schools, libraries, museums, and art galleries to be implemented for public interests by obtaining permission, authorization, approval, designation, etc. under the related Acts; 5. Projects for the construction of houses or creation of housing lots for the purposes of lease or transfer, which are to be implemented by central, local governments, or public institutions under Article 4 of the Act on the Management of Public Institutions, local public enterprises under the Local Public Enterprises Act, or persons designated by the State or local governments; 6. Projects for pathways, bridges, cables lines, material storages, or other accessory facilities necessary for implementing the projects under Subparagraphs 1 through 5; 7. Projects for the development of relocation complexes, such as houses, factories, etc. necessary for implementing the projects under Subparagraphs 1 through 5; 8. Projects for which properties, such as land, can be taken or used under other Acts."

The verification of public interest includes (1) the investigation on the existence and contents of the public interest that can be achieved by the project, and (2) the comparison of the public interest and the private interest related to the project. The verification process is abstract *per se*, thus the wide discretion for the permission of a public project can be acknowledged. The adequate examination on the wide discretion guarantees the optimal verification of public interest.

(2) Process

A project runner must request for a permission of a public project to the Minister of Land, Infrastructure, and Transport in order to compulsorily acquire or use the land for the public project. Then the Minister officially declares the permission after having consultations with the provincial governor or metropolitan city mayor, and hearing a variety of opinions by the Central Land Tribunal and persons concerned (KLTC §20 and 21). When the Minister declares the permission, the contents are immediately notified to the project runner, landowners, persons concerned, heads of the provincial government or the municipal government concerned, and then information such as the name of the project runner, the type of project, and the details of the land taken or used is reported to the official gazette, and finally the permission of a public project derives its validity from being reported in the official gazette (KLTC §22).

The verification of public interest by the permission of a public project is realized by the following three steps: (1) consultations with the administrative institutions concerned; (2) hearing opinions of experts in the related field; and (3) procedural participation by the persons concerned. Among these steps (3), the procedural participation by the persons concerned, indicates that the opinions of unspecified individuals on the proposed project can be heard. Thus, scrutinizing whether the project meets the public-interest criterion becomes possible through examination by unspecified individuals. This entire process is designed to minimize biases in favor of the project runners.

However, the process which enables the administrative authority to provide an explanation of the project details to the persons concerned or to hear a variety of opinions of the persons concerned – such as a public hearing – is not organized. The persons concerned can merely express their opinion by individually having access to the details of the permission of a public project by reading relevant documents displayed at the related administrative office. The fact that the persons concerned must expend a great deal of effort in order to access the details of the permission of a public project acts as a practical restriction from participating in the procedure of the permission of a public project.[9]

(3) Legal Effect

Upon the receipt of the permission of a public project, the project runner effectively obtains the power of eminent domain. This is the essential legal effect of permission of a public project. This merely grants the general authority to take private properties for the public project, thus there must be a follow-up administrative disposition (decision of taking) in order to complete the legal transfer of the specific properties to the project runner.

An amount of compensation for taken lands is calculated based on "the officially announced land price" at the time when the notice for the permission of a public project is given (KLTC §70.4). This enables the fixing of a base price for the amount of compensation, and is necessary in order to eliminate the incentive of planning an unjust gain by jumping on the public project.[10]

After the notice of the permission of a public project, acts such as changing the form and quality of the land in the area of the public project, tearing down buildings on the land, and constructing new buildings on the land are restricted (KLTC §25). This prevents landowners from hindering the public project directly or indirectly and hence, the public project can run smoothly.

5 *Overview of Quasi-permission of a Public Project*

(1) Meaning

The "permission of a public project" is an administrative disposition in order to grant the power of eminent domain to the project runner for the proposed public project. Conceptually, this precedes the "decision of taking," which completes the legal effect of taking. However, as shown in Table 9.1, the number of permissions of a public project appears to be dramatically lower when compared to the number of decision of taking

[9] In the Land Takings Act in Japan, it is stated that the details of the permission of a public project must be announced and widely spread to the persons concerned by providing business briefing sessions and public hearings (§15/14, 23).

[10] Concerning the procedure and method to calculate the amount of compensation, see Cho (2015) for a detailed explanation.

Table 9.1. *The Number of Permissions of a Public Project and Decisions of Taking Per Annum*[11]

		2000	2001	2002	2003	2004	2005	2006	2007	2008	2009	2010	2011	2012	2013	2014
Decisions of Taking per Annum	Central Land Tribunal	849	892	915	919	990	1,134	1,136	1,040	1,152	1,603	1,525	1,668	1,457	1,398	1,457
Permissions of a Public Project per Annum		29	30	17	24	11	17	8	18	9	29	23	13	14	10	15

Source: Central Land Tribunal (2010–2015), *Manual on Land Takings.*

[11] These data have been gathered from the webpage of the Ministry of Land, Infrastructure, and Transport (http://stat.molit.go.kr/), however, the statistics from the years 2000 to 2004 for the number of decisions of taking made by the Local Land Tribunals has not been released to the public.

Table 9.2. *The Number of Projects of Total Compensation above KRW 1 Billion and Permissions of a Public Project Per Annum*

	2000	2001	2002	2003	2004	2005	2006	2007	2008	2009	2010	2011	2012	2013	2014
Projects of total compensation above KRW 1 billion per Annum	1,716	1,871	2,011	2,554	2,860	3,090	3,341	3,573	4,160	4,874	3,937	3,313	3,474	3,065	3,100
Permissions of a public project per annum	29	30	17	24	11	17	8	18	9	29	23	13	14	10	15

Source: Korea Association of Property Appraisers (2015), *Inventory Data of Annual Compensation*.

for the past few years.[12] Also, as shown in Table 9.2, even the number of "projects of total compensation above KRW 1 billion per annum" is substantially more than that of the number of permissions of a public project. While we can start posing questions about the reasons why making the decision of taking for the projects without the permission of a public project has been possible, a concept of the so-called "quasi-permission of a public project" can be introduced to provide us with a detailed explanation.

The quasi-permission of a public project is to regard a particular administrative disposition stipulated in the individual Acts as the permission of a public project under the KLTC. Under the quasi-permission of a public project, project runners automatically obtain the power of eminent domain at the time their projects are approved by the heads of local governments such as mayors or provincial governors. It is thus well known that the quasi-permission of a public project is more generous for project runners.[13] Quasi-permission of a public project is a very distinct feature of the takings system in Korea, as will be mentioned later.

Ironically, the KLTC – which stipulates the permission of a public project as the original framework of the takings process – in fact, opens the gate to granting the power of eminent domain without the permission of a public project. This may be possible according to §4.8 of the KLTC. Through this provision, "projects for which properties, such as land, can be taken or used under other Acts" are included under the category of the public project – and individual Acts, other than the KLTC, can deal with eminent domain. The project runners can obtain the power of eminent domain through a particular administrative disposition stipulated in individual Acts. It means that they are able to evade the cumbersome procedures of "permission of a public project" under the KLTC. Eventually, as §4.8 of the KLTC comprehensively permitted the "takings under individual Acts," the original framework of the takings process became thoroughly distorted, as if a Pandora's box has been opened.

[12] It is quite difficult to explain the number of decisions of taking, which surpassed that of the permissions of a public project by several ten-folds, even when considering the possibility of the abundance of land and buildings within the area of the proposed project as well as the understanding of the legal relations that lead to having many decisions of taking for a single permission of a public project.

[13] As explained later, this alternative option has induced excessive takings which cannot be justified based on the public-interest criterion and so would not have been permitted if they had undergone the process of the permission of a public project under the KLTC.

As a result, most of the project runners were able to take private properties even without the strict procedures of permission of a public project under the KLTC through the quasi-permission of a public project, and this has weakened the verification of public interest in the takings process.

(2) Regulation Format

The format stipulating the quasi-permission of a public project in the individual Acts is uniform. The format is explained as "When ***X*** (a particular administrative disposition) is given, it is deemed that the permission of a public project stipulated in §20.1 and §22 of the KLTC exists," of which ***X*** includes administrative dispositions such as the approval announcement of project planning made according to the provisions of individual Acts. For example, the Aviation Act §98.2 stipulates that: "When there is an approval announcement of an airport development project, it is deemed that there is a permission of a public project by §20.1 and §22 of the KLTC." Here, the above-mentioned approval announcement of an airport development project is ***X***. The administrative dispositions in the ***X*** are sorted broadly into three groups, namely: (1) designation announcement of project planned area or approval announcement of project planning in the stage where the project planning is publicly announced; (2) approval announcement of project implementation in the stage where details of the project are confirmed; and (3) administrative dispositions unique to the individual projects, for example, designation of route under §13.2 of the Act on the Rearrangement of Roads in Agricultural and Fishing Villages.

(3) Status of Current Legislation

The provision of the KLTC with respect to the takings process shall apply in takings for development projects under many other Acts. As many as 100 individual Acts, besides the KLTC, deal with eminent domain in Korea.[14] This number is equivalent to about 8 per cent of the total number (1,280) of all Acts in Korea, as of 2014. Out of the 100 Acts, 54 are concerned with urban development, regional and industrial development, and development for specifically designated projects.[15] The

[14] According to the first-time examination of all substantive laws provided by the website of Korean Laws (www.law.go.kr) of the Ministry of Government Legislation, Kim et al. (2013) found that takings were being allowed in 100 individual Acts, as of June 2013.

[15] The first category includes 13 Acts such as the Urban Development Act and the Act on the Promotion of Housing Site Development; 32 laws in the second category include the

remaining 46 Acts are related to the provision of infrastructures and various government-use facilities such as military sites and the buildings of central and local governments, and to environmental protection or disaster prevention.[16]

Out of the 100 Acts, only 19 borrow provisions on the requirement for permission of a public project and its procedure under the KLTC. In the remaining 81 Acts, administrative disposition considered as permission of a public project is stipulated. Since the scope of the projects covered by the Acts (81)[17] which adopted the quasi-permission of a public project is much broader than that of the projects covered by the Acts (19)[18] which did not adopt the quasi-permission of a public project, project runners mostly use the quasi-permission of a public project. Permission of a public project, which is a critical filtering process, is hardly used in Korea these days.

(4) Stance of the Constitutional Court of Korea on Quasi-permission of a Public Project

The Constitutional Court of Korea stated in the 2006_C.C_HEONBA79 case and the 2010_C.C_HEONBA114 case, that quasi-permission of a public project does not go against the due process of law, the principle of just compensation, and the principle of equality, nor does it infringe on private property rights. This is to say that the verification of public interest does not necessarily have to be done through the procedure of permission of a public project under the KLTC, and, going through the procedure of permission of a public project under the KLTC once again even after having gone through the procedure of an administrative disposition is regarded as a permission of a public project under the individual Acts, which is nothing more than an overlapping procedure.

Special Act on Enterprise Cities and the Industrial Location and Development Act. There are nine laws belonging to the third category, with a representative example being the International Contest Support Act.

16 22 infrastructure-related laws include the National Land Planning and Utilization Act. An important example of the eight laws concerning government-use facilities is the National Defense and Military Installations Projects Act; and the Natural Environment Conservation Act is an important example of the 16 environment/disaster-related laws.

17 For example, the National Land Planning and Utilization Act, Urban Development Act, Act on Maintenance and Improvement of Urban Areas and Dwelling Conditions for Residents, Water Supply and Waterworks Installation Act.

18 For example, the Tourism Promotion Act, and Ground Water Act.

However, despite the strict procedures of permission of a public project for verification of public interest under the KLTC, permitting the administrative disposition regarded as the permission of a public project by the individual Acts is, *per se*, merely an attempt to bypass the strict procedures under the KLTC. This is because, if both procedures totally overlap with each other, there would have been no reason for the quasi-permission of a public project to be made. Thus, the permission of a public project for scrutiny on the public interest cannot be substituted with a different administrative disposition. The verification of public interest must be fulfilled by the procedure of permission of a public project solely created for the verification purpose.

6 *Overview of Decision of Taking*

(1) Function

When a project runner – who obtains the power of eminent domain by the permission of a public project or quasi-permission of a public project – does not reach a settlement over land purchase with the landowners, the project runner will compulsorily purchase the land through the decision of taking by the Central Land Tribunal or the Local Land Tribunals. According to §50 of the KLTC, the contents of the decision includes: (1) the area of land to be taken; (2) the amount of compensation; and (3) the effective date of the taking. The decision of taking has two functions. One is to confirm the details of taking in order to bring the taking into effect ((1) and (3)), and the other is to determine the amount of compensation ((2)). In other words, the decision of taking is an administrative disposition that completes the legal transfer of the properties to the project runner by ordering the final amount of compensation determined by the reports made by two newly appointed appraisers.

However, in practice, the former function was weakened, and this merely degraded the decision of taking to become a mechanical process used in determining the amount of compensation. There have been no documented cases where the Central Land Tribunal or the Local Land Tribunals refused to make the decision of taking upon the request by a project runner. Under any situation if the Land Tribunals conclude that a project does not meet the public-interest criterion, they cannot refuse the decision of taking itself. This is because, as aforementioned, if a permission of a public project is not revoked by an administrative lawsuit, the Land Tribunals will not be able to make the decision of taking, which disables the running of the project.[19]

Nonetheless, it is inappropriate to dismiss the decision of taking as a passive process which mechanically exercises the power of eminent domain. Compulsorily purchasing private properties for the project can be constitutionally justified only when a project meets the public-interest criterion. Thus, the verification of public interest must be conducted throughout the takings process. Therefore, the Land Tribunals must also be able to refuse the decision of taking for project which does not meet the public-interest criterion.

(2) Process

If a settlement over property purchase cannot be reached between the project runner and the property owner, the project runner can request for the decision of taking at the Central Land Tribunal or the Local Land Tribunals[20] (KLTC §28.1). Since project runners cannot directly exercise the power of eminent domain, Land Tribunals with expertise and neutrality carry out the decision of taking. The Land Tribunals scrutinize and hear opinions on the legitimacy of the relevant request and make the decision of taking in written letter format within 14 days of the commencement of the hearing. The contents of the decision letter excluding the compensation part merely has "the date to bring the taking into effect." This shows that the Land Tribunals turn away from verifying public interest.

At the date to bring the taking into effect, project runners acquire the title to the relevant properties, and the pre-existing rights on the properties are all extinguished (KLTC §45.1). The project runner must pay the determined amount of compensation to the property owner before the date (KLTC §40.1). The property owner must also deliver the relevant property to the project runner before the date (KLTC §43).

The project runner or the property owner can file an objection on the decision of taking to the Central Land Tribunal (KLTC §83). Once the Central Land Tribunal makes the conclusion that the decision of taking is

[19] The aforementioned decision; 2004_S.C._DU8538.

[20] The Central Land Tribunal is in charge of the decision of taking for projects executed by the nation, city or province, and projects involving land, or taking of things other than land, which covers two or more cities or provinces; whereas the Local Land Tribunals are in charge of the decision of taking for all of the other projects (KLTC §51). There is one Central Land Tribunal and there are 16 Local Land Tribunals, which are composed of government officials, attorneys, judges, professors, and appraisers.

illegitimate, the decision may fully or partially be revoked or the amount of compensation may be adjusted (KLTC §84.1). The Central Land Tribunal makes the Decision on Appeals regardless of the agency that made the decision of taking (the Central Land Tribunal or the Local Land Tribunal). The project runner or the property owner can bring litigations to the Administrative Courts for the revocation of the decision of taking or decision on appeals (KLTC §85).

III Comparative Survey on the Takings Process

1 *The US State of California*

Each individual state has its own takings process in the United States. The state of California has a dualistic process of taking. Private property shall be taken by eminent domain only when there is a public use (California Code of Civil Procedure §1230.030). The government agency must adopt a formal resolution, also known as the Resolution of Necessity to acquire the property before commencing an eminent domain proceeding in court. The resolution of necessity must be adopted at a public hearing (California Code §1245.220). Thereafter, the eminent domain action is filed in court. If a settlement cannot be reached between the owner and the government agency, trial regarding the eminent domain action takes place before a jury which determines a fair market value of the subject property. When the judgment is entered, the government pays compensation within 30 days following the entry of judgment and the title to the relevant property is transferred to the government by the court.[21]

2 *Germany*

If a settlement over property purchase cannot be reached between the property owner and the project runner, the project runner will make the request of taking to the local government, and the local government will send a request letter and an opinion report to the Expropriation Agency (*Enteignungsbehörde*) (Construction Act §105).[22] If the project runner reaches a settlement through bargaining with the property owner, the legal effect of taking occurs as mentioned in the settlement. If a

[21] For more details, see http://eminentdomain.uslegal.com/state-laws-on-eminent-domain/california/.

[22] The Construction Act (Baugesetzbuch) defines the takings process (*Enteignungsverfahren*) from §104 to §122 in Chapter 5 (Expropriation; *Enteignung*).

settlement is unable to be reached, the Expropriation Agency makes the decision of taking (*Enteignungsbeschluß*) (Construction Act §112, §113). The project runner pays compensation according to the decision of taking. The title to the relevant property is transferred to the project runner by "the order of execution" of the decision of taking (*Ausführung des Enteignungsbeschlusses*; Construction Act §117).

3 *France*

The takings process in France is composed of the administrative phase (*la phase administrative*) and the judicial phase (*la phase judiciaire*). In the administrative phase, permission of a public project (*déclaration d'utilité publique*) is given by a ministerial ordinance or a provincial ordinance (Expropriation Act[23] §L11-2[24]). It shows that the project meets the public-interest criterion. When the property to be taken is decided through a field investigation, the governor will send notice to the property owner (*arrêté de cessibilité*; Expropriation Act §L11-8). A property owner who objects to the above administrative dispositions can bring an action to the Administrative Courts.

In the judicial phase, the Expropriation Court (*juge de l'expropriation*) makes the decision of taking (*L'ordonnance d'expropriation*). All of the rights relating to the relevant property are extinguished according to the decision of taking, and the project runner acquires the title to the property (Expropriation Act §L12). In addition, the Expropriation Court determines the amount of compensation (Expropriation Act §L13). Actions can be brought to the Cour de Cassation[25] when the property owner wants to file an objection against the decision of taking, whereas litigation can be brought to a court of appeals when the property owner is willing to file an objection against the determined amount of compensation.

4 *Japan*

Bargaining between the project runner and the owners also takes place in Japan in order for the project runner to acquire the properties necessary

[23] In France, the Expropriation Act (*Code de l'expropriation pour cause d'utilité publique*) defines the takings process.

[24] For important projects, permission of a public project can be given due to the order of conseil d'etat.

[25] Cour de Cassation is the Supreme Court of France in civil action.

for the project. If a settlement cannot be reached between the property owner and the project runner, the project runner requests the Minister of Land and Transport or a governor for the permission of a public project (Land Takings Act §18). The Minister or the governor will give permission of a public project after hearing the opinions of the persons concerned and participating in public hearings (Land Takings Act §16, §17, §20).[26] The persons concerned will obtain the information about the project during project information sessions and public hearings. Thereafter, a project runner requests the Land Tribunal for the decision of taking (Land Takings Act §39). The Land Tribunal decides "the date to bring the taking into effect" by the decision of taking. On that date, the project runner acquires the title to the property taken and the property owner loses it (Land Takings Act §101).

5 *Comparative Analysis*

The procedure for compulsory purchase in Korea has the dualistic structure consisting of the permission of a public project and the decision of taking. The power of eminent domain should be exercised cautiously to minimize any infringement on private property (Epstein, 1985). The permission of a public project prevents the abuse of eminent domain as a part of the eminent domain proceeding, aiming for the verification of public interest. This is the very purpose of the dualistic procedure. As aforementioned, the dualistic procedure for compulsory purchase can be found in several other countries as well. From the takings systems of these countries, we can find a few things worth noting.

First, the property owner and persons concerned get the chance to gain more information about the project. They can obtain detailed information on the necessity of taking through project information sessions, public hearings, and advance notices that enables them to actively participate in the takings process. They can submit opinions on the permission of a public project, and also protest against permission of a public project or decision of taking. The general release of detailed information

[26] In order to give the permission of a public project, the Minister of Land and Transport or a governor must find: (1) that the project is included in the scope of projects stipulated in §3 of the Land Takings Act; (2) that a project runner has the intent and ability to carry out the project; (3) that the project plan contributes to the reasonable use of land; and (4) that the project has public necessity to acquire land (§20 of the Land Takings Act).

about the project substantially guarantees the procedural rights of the property owner and persons concerned.

Second, many countries have an eminent domain proceeding in court. After the permission of a public project takes place, an eminent domain proceeding in court commences. This means that a judicial review on the necessity of taking comprises one phase of the procedure for a compulsory purchase. Judicial examinations on the executive's leading role during the procedure for compulsory purchase contribute in preventing takings that do not meet the public-interest criterion, also referred to as excessive takings.

Third, the quasi-permission of a public project is a very distinct feature of the takings system in Korea. In other countries, there are unified provisions on the procedure for compulsory purchase. It is extremely rare to enact an individual law, which permits eminent domain – as an exception to the general law on eminent domain. Even though such an individual law exists, it borrows provisions from the general law in regard to the procedure for compulsory purchase. Therefore, it can be officially acknowledged that the project meets the public-interest criterion only by the permission of a public project. Methods to commence the proceeding for compulsory purchase without the verification of public interest by the permission of a public project thus institutionally do not exist.

IV Critical Perspectives on the Takings Process in Korea

1 *Possibility of Constitutionally Unjustifiable Takings*

The project runner has the incentive to push ahead with the projects outside the boundary of the public-interest criterion by permission of a public project. The project runner who wishes to earn as much profit as possible from the project may put public interest outside the area of concern. The permission of a public project prevents unjustifiable takings (excessive takings), which may occur due to the incentives mentioned above.

When the systems for the verification of public interest become more inadequate, the possibility increases for the project runner to unjustly take the land through projects that do not meet the public-interest criterion. Let's say P is the profit the project runner can gain from the project, X is the probability of discontinuance of a takings process of the project to occur as it is verified that the project does not meet the public-interest criterion, and L is the loss of the project runner caused from being unable to continue running the project since the permission of a public project was not given because the project did not meet the public-interest criterion from the beginning. When the expected profit ($= P \times (1 - X)$) happens to be larger than the expected loss ($= L \times X$), the project runner would want to proceed with the takings process even for the project that does not meet the public-interest criterion. Therefore, as X becomes greater, the probability to take the private property for the project that does not meet the public-interest criterion will become smaller, and, as the verification of public interest is done more widely, X will be bigger in general.

However, the Supreme Court of Korea takes the stance that, in principle, the procedure for compulsory purchase can be ceased when it is verified that the project does not meet the public-interest criterion only in the phase of permission of a public project.[27] According to the above stance, unless the permission of a public project is considered invalid due to a high degree of obvious illegality, even though it has been verified in the phase of decision of taking that the project does not meet the public-interest criterion, the procedure for compulsory purchase cannot be ceased. Thus, the decision of taking has been merely degraded to become a mechanical procedure to determine the amount of compensation. In other words, in substance the verification of public interest cannot be done in the phase of decision of taking. As a result, the scope for verification of public interest is narrowed down, and X is decreased.

2 *Possibility of Evading the Verification of Public Interest*

The overall process of permission of a public project focuses on gathering opinions from experts and persons concerned on whether the project meets the public-interest criterion. The Minister can obtain information for the verification of public interest from the gathered opinions in this way. However, since the process demands substantial time and strict formalities, the project runner has an incentive to skip all or parts of the process. The project runner wants to take properties without cumbersome procedures. Their wish comes true by the quasi-permission of a public project.

[27] See the Supreme Court Decisions explained in Somin, Chapter 2, this volume.

The purpose of the quasi-permission of a public project is to grant a legal effect of permission of a public project to another administrative disposition, and the procedure for verification of public interest is not borrowed from the permission of a public project under the KLTC. Different from other countries, the permission of a public project is not a requisite for takings in Korea. The project runner can take properties by using the quasi-permission of a public project even without the permission of a public project. This, *per se*, means the weakening of the verification of public interest. This is because the quasi-permission of a public project is a part of the takings system created in order to take properties without going through the strict procedure of the verification of public interest. In fact, it is not surprising that project runners take properties by using the quasi-permission of a public project for most of the public projects carried out in Korea.[28]

3 *Possibility of Encouraging Opportunism by Project Runners*

According to §30.1, §31.1 and §37.2 of the Act on Support for the 2018 Pyeongchang Winter Olympics and Winter Para-Olympics, the governor of Gangwon province is authorized to run the project including installing and utilizing facilities for the above-mentioned events, and the governor is authorized to give administrative disposition (the permission of project plan), which is considered as the permission of a public project. In other words, the project runner grants the power of eminent domain to itself. These irrational provisions can be found in Acts enacted for preparing large-scale state occasions. This can be considered as a result of carelessness towards the verification of public interest focusing only on the smooth preparation of national events. The power of eminent domain – which the project runner has granted itself – does not have procedural legitimacy from the perspective of the verification of public interest. Eminent domain by unchecked power can invade the property rights of individuals. Therefore, it cannot be constitutionally justified.

[28] As already shown in Table 9.1, there have only been around 20 occurrences per annum during the last few years that the project runners took properties by the permission of a public project under the KLTC.

V Concluding Remarks with Policy Prescription

1 *Emergence from Radical Dualism*

The permission of a public project is the phase that grants the power of eminent domain, and the decision of taking is the phase that allows such power to be exercised. Both require the project to meet the public-interest criterion as an ontological presupposition. Even though the permission of a public project is given, if it is found that the project does not meet the public-interest criterion in the phase of the decision of taking, the procedure for compulsory purchase must be stopped because, according to §23.3 of the Korean Constitution, taking private property for projects without the basis for public necessity is constitutionally not permitted. Dividing of the two in function does not necessarily mean the institutional severance of the two. Both must be integrated closely in the overall takings process.

The Supreme Court of Korea has adhered to the radical dualism of permission of a public project and decision of taking. According to this view, the verification of public interest is exclusively done by the permission of a public project. In principle, this view derives the dogmatic conclusion that the takings process for projects without public necessity cannot be stopped in the phase of decision of taking. But the Supreme Court of Korea has recently made a significant decision on the abuse of eminent domain.[29]

> Considering the spirit of §23 of the Korean Constitution that a property of individual can be taken to a minimum in inevitable cases, continuing with the procedure of compulsory purchase even though the project had lost the public necessity after the permission of a public project is, in short, an abuse of eminent domain which cannot be permitted.

2 *Phase-out of Quasi-permission of a Public Project*

Quasi-permission of a public project, which excludes the general procedures of the verification of public interest, damages the foundation of the takings system. Therefore, the quasi-permission of a public project should be abolished. However, in reality, if it is difficult to fully abolish the quasi-permission of a public project all at once due to the fact that most of the projects are run already based on the quasi-permission of a public project, the quasi-permission of a public project should, at least,

[29] 2009_S.C._DU1051.

be phased out. Since the KLTC stipulates the general procedures of takings for public projects, providing special provisions on the takings process in the individual Acts for particular national events or specific national projects must be avoided. Even if the individual Acts give the provisions on takings in order to supplement the contents, which the KLTC does not stipulate, the provisions of the KLTC regarding the takings process must be followed.

3 *Institutional Escape from Opportunism by Project Runners*

Under the individual Acts, if the project runner is the administrative agency, which makes the administrative disposition regarded as a permission of a public project, then we cannot expect that the verification of public interest will be done properly. As aforementioned, the quasi-permission of a public project must be phased out, and also, an immediate legislative improvement to eliminate the practice of the project runner granting the power of eminent domain is sorely needed. In the hope of contributing to the improvement of the provisions, I would propose that, in cases when both statutes overlap, the Minister of Land, Infrastructure, and Transport makes the administrative disposition regarded as the permission of a public project.[30]

References

Central Land Tribunal, 2010–2015, *Manual on Land Takings*, Central Land Tribunal

Cho, Byungkoo, 2015, "Just Compensation in Eminent Domain in Korea: From the Perspective of Fairness," *International Conference Material*, Korea Development Institute, pp. 136–64.

Epstein, A. Richard, 1985, *Takings: Private Property and the Power of Eminent Domain*, Cambridge, M.A.: Harvard University Press.

Kim, Iljoong, Byungkoo Cho, Duol Kim, Sungkyu Park, Hojun Lee and Kisang Jung, 2013, *A Law-and-Economics Study on the Takings Law in Korea*, Korea Development Institute (in Korean).

[30] According to §17 of the Japan Land Takings Act, in principle, the governor who has jurisdiction over the project area has the authority over permission of a public project, and the Minister of Land and Transport has the authority in cases when the governor is the project runner.

10

Distribution of Development Surplus in Takings*

SUNGKYU PARK

I Introduction

Takings for private economic development have a long history.[1] Recently, the use of eminent domain power for this type of development has been increasing. Many developed countries (e.g., the United States, the United Kingdom, Germany, etc.) stipulate this in law. This especially affects developing countries. Many developing countries aggressively pursue methods to permit eminent domain power in order to achieve rapid economic growth by encouraging private capital investment.[2]

Normally, when a development project starts and if it is completed successfully, social welfare increases. The net value increased through the development is referred to as the "development surplus." Such a surplus is achieved by inputting the factors such as land, labor, and capital. Land is the main factor and a large part of the development cost. Under the market economy, private developers must acquire land through voluntary exchange. But, if the eminent domain power is acknowledged, a developer can compulsorily acquire land at a lower prices without the landowner's consent. Thus, a reduction in development cost becomes possible for private developers.

Development surplus is created through a contribution made by developers, landowners, and the government. Then, how do we distribute development surplus? Despite many studies on takings, only a few studies have been conducted on this issue. Traditionally, the government and most scholars did not pay much attention to the distribution of development

* I am indebted to Professor Iljoong Kim and Dr. Hojun Lee for helping with the theoretical illustrations as well as their constructive suggestions in general.

[1] New Hampshire Mill Act, 1868 N.H. Laws of the U.S.

[2] Eminent domain is often introduced to support private development together with tax exemption, deregulation, infrastructure provision by local government, and the transfer of state-owned land at lower prices. A typical Act of private capital investment is the Special Act on Enterprise City Development in Korea.

surplus while they argued about the necessity of sacrificing landowners for efficient development. Thus not even a small portion of the surplus was distributed to the landowners. Also, they emphasized that measurement of development surplus is very difficult and it is restituted properly in the form of new job and tax revenue for the public. These claims are partially correct.

However, this argument seems like an excuse in terms of fairness. Zero distribution of development surplus to landowners is disproportionate compared to the degree of contributions. Moreover, under this distribution standard, the incentives of developers might be distorted. The distribution standard of development surplus may be a huge issue in terms of efficiency. The purpose of this chapter is to examine the fairness and efficiency of this issue.

The order of the chapter is as follows. Section II outlines what are takings for economic development and how the development surplus is generated. Section III deals with the issue of how development surplus is distributed. I will discuss the possible distribution criteria followed by a review of the distribution principle in Korea. In Section IV, I will discuss why some development surplus should be distributed to landowners in fairness and efficiency. Also, I suggest a simple theoretical model and empirical examination. Section V will conclude with policy implications.

II Creation of Development Surplus

1 *Takings for Economic Development*

Investment for economic development requires a lot of land. Many countries permit developers' compulsory purchase of other private properties based on eminent domain power. These are called Economic Development Takings (hereafter, *EDT*).[3] Development projects can be classified into two categories: infrastructure projects to build public goods (e.g., roads, railways, harbors, airports, and electricity) and regional development projects to build non-public goods (e.g., towns, industrial complexes, and tourism complexes). The former will be referred to as EDT^{PG}, while the latter as EDT^{NPG}. EDT^{PG} is more public than EDT^{NPG} in

[3] Cohen (2006) and Somin (2007; 2008) stated the act of transferring the condemned land by using the eminent domain power to private developers as EDT. However, in this chapter, takings by all economic development purposes are broadly defined as EDT.

terms of publicness. However, it is very difficult to accurately define the degree of publicness of individual development projects.[4]

The EDT^{NPG} expanded significantly by economic progress. The main reason is that the concept of public use requirement is ambiguous and that it has been expanded (Bell, 2009, p. 522).[5] As development competition grew intense across countrys and throughout regions, the scope of economic development projects through takings expanded in the name of economic growth and Korea was no exception.

Korea is one of the countries in the world where EDT^{NPG} is most widely accepted. Despite the possibility of unconstitutionality, the government expanded *EDT*. First, Korea permits the use of eminent domain power in the Korea Land Takings and Compensation Act (hereafter, KLTC) and 100 other Acts: 54 among those are focused on pure economic development.[6]

Second, developers (project runners in Korea) can pick and choose from several Acts which are most beneficial to them, even if the type of project is the same.[7] Moreover, there are Special Acts to simplify the takings procedure in order to achieve rapid progress in some projects.[8]

Third, transferring the condemned land by public entities to private developers is widely accepted. Bell (2009) and Kim and Park (2014) refer to such takings as public–private takings. These types of takings appear mainly in urban developments and industrial complex

[4] Public development projects (e.g., road, railroad, etc.) create great economic benefits. However, in reality, their economic benefits are not great in most cases. In some cases, economic benefits are zero or negative (–). The most exemplary is the construction of a military airport for national defense. The government conducts such development projects but private developers do not pursue such developments. The discussion below deals with development projects with low publicness but high benefits.

[5] Bell (2009) argues that, in the United States, the concept of public use has expanded from public ownership to public interest. Examples can be found from how various economic development projects such as creating new jobs or generating tax revenues, which are considered as public projects.

[6] The 54 Acts can be classified into groups of 13 urban development Acts, 32 regional and industrial development Acts, and nine Acts for the development of specifically designated projects.

[7] The entity that exercises the eminent domain power, or the condemner in Korea, is the project runner. And, as for laws on development for supplying land for housing, there exists the Urban Development Act, the Act on the Promotion of Housing Site Development, the Special Act on Construction of Bogeumjari Housing, etc.

[8] Special Act on the Simplification of Procedures for Approval and Permission for an Industrial Complex.

establishments. Public–private takings have been much debated in many countries, but not in Korea.[9]

Fourth, private entities can be condemners that directly use eminent domain power. Kim and Park (2014) refer to such takings as "direct private takings." In Korea, 49 Acts stipulate direct private takings. In most private takings, developers can condemn all lands. However, in some cases, the private project runner has to acquire some of the land in advance through voluntary market transactions before being allowed to exercise the eminent domain power.[10] Typically, the project runner has to acquire two-thirds of the land in advance through market transactions, and then it must obtain consent from half of all landowners.

2 *Creation of Development Surplus*

If a development project by takings is processed successfully, economic surplus is generated. This is referred to as "development surplus" (π). π is defined as the net economic value increased by the development project broadly. The compensation for landowners, the project runner's investment cost, and the government's support are not included in π.[11] The size of development surplus is diverse depending on the project area, development type, strength of land use regulation, etc. Sometimes, development surplus may be zero or negative due to the changing economic situation in process. But, in most cases, these projects

9 Refer to *Poletown Neighborhood Council v. City of Detroit* [304 NW2d 455, Mich 1981] and *Kelo v. City of New London* in the United States; *Boxberg* [BVerG, 1 BvR 1046/85] in Germany; *Elizabeth Pascoe v. First Secretary of State* [EWHC, 2356, 2006] in the United Kingdom; and *Parramatta City Council v. R and R Fazzolari Pty Ltd* and *Parramatta City Council v. Mac's Pty Lt* [132, NSW, 2008] in Australia.

10 49 Acts (of 54 economic development Acts) state that private entities can directly use the eminent domain power. 20 among those define these conditions.

11 In general, compensation is based on the fair market value of private condemned property. This standard is applied in many countries. But, in this chapter, compensation indicates the payment paid to the landowner based on the just compensation clause in the Constitution. So, I assume that landowners' subject value is properly reflected in compensation. Investment cost means the expenses for construction (e.g., planning, approval or permission fee, and fee of cadastral survey and appraisal). Government's supports are mitigation of land-use regulation, infrastructure provision by local government, and the transfer of state-owned land at lower prices. These supports return to government by the form of property tax, development charges, and forced donation of public land (e.g., roads, parks).

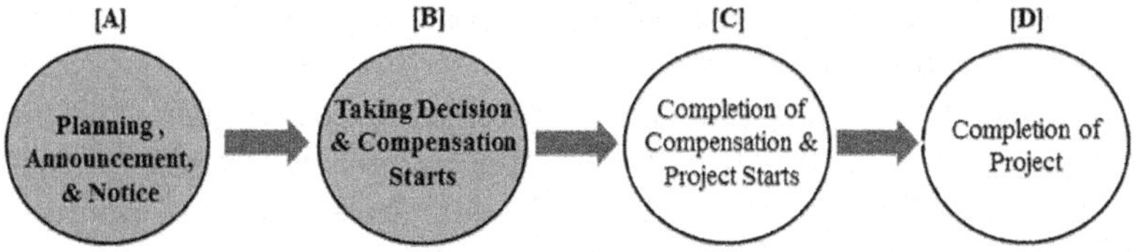

Figure 10.1. The General Sequence of the Takings Procedures

are cancelled or their development size becomes reduced significantly. So, I will consider only the cases in which π is positive ($\pi > 0$).

Development surplus is broadly created through the following steps. The takings procedures for a project are usually conducted in the following order as shown in Figure 10.1.[12]

The following are the reasons why property values rise due to takings: land assembly, project runner's investment, and various support from the government. First, development surplus is created through land assembly (Krier and Serkin, 2004, p. 870). Generally, development surplus is maximized at one time when there is a proper size of land assembly in EDT^{PG} and it gradually increases as more parcels are combined in EDT^{NPG} (Fennell, 2004, pp. 973–74).[13]

Second, the project runner invests massive capital from the planning step to the completion step. The amount of money spent on such investments varies from millions to billions of dollars according to the type and size of development project. Such capital investments naturally raise the economic value of properties.

Third, government support such as speedy approval, infrastructure provision, and temporary tax cuts contribute to create surplus. To initiate a project, the project runner must undergo various and complicated approval processes stipulated by the Act (e.g., permission to cut down forests for other uses, environment impact test, and permission for construction).

12 Procedure [A] involves planning, obtaining approvals from agencies in charge, and announcing the plan to landowners and the public. The decision for taking is made and compensation starts in Procedure [B]. Compensation is completed and construction begins in Procedure [C], and the construction of the intended public project is finalized in Procedure [D].

13 The relationship between land value and parcel size would be S-shaped in a market economy. Many scholars found the existence of an S-shaped value-size curve (Colwell and Sirmans, 1978, Thorsnes and McMillen, 1998; Guntermann et al., 2015).

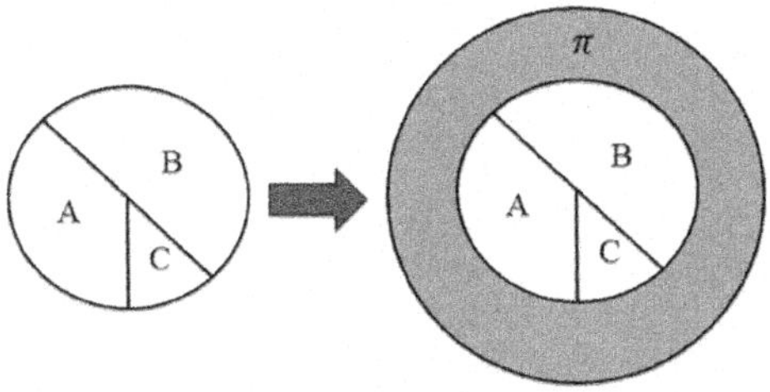

Figure 10.2. Creation of *DS*

In conclusion, development surplus is a result of the collective contribution of landowners, project runner, and the government. Let us assume that π (or *DS*) is created by some development project. From Figure 10.2, let us assume *A* is the contribution from landowners (condemned land), *B* is the contribution from project runners (investment), and *C* is the contribution from local government (policy support). How should π be distributed? I will discuss this issue in Section III in more detail.

III Distribution of Development Surplus

1 Distribution Criteria

Various criteria exist concerning how to distribute π. Epstein was probably the first scholar who took the issue of distributing π seriously. Merrill (1986, pp. 1574–75) suggested a few representative examples based on Epstein (1985). However, he did not examine their characteristics, including the merits and demerits. Subsequent work on this issue has also been scarce. Therefore, an attempt to explain these criteria from an economic perspective may contribute to describing the methods for the distribution in more detail.

First, let us have a look at the Pareto Criterion. Under this criterion, any distribution of π would be justified so long as everyone kept, at least, the original contributions of their own property (*A*, *B*, and *C* in Figure 10.2). Thus, π can be distributed to any of the persons involved – such as landowners, project runner, or even the government. Technically, there may be numerous ways to distribute π to meet these criteria.

The second is the equal or difference distribution. In equal distribution criteria, π is distributed equally among parties regardless of their contributions. Equal distribution of π would be a slight variant which is

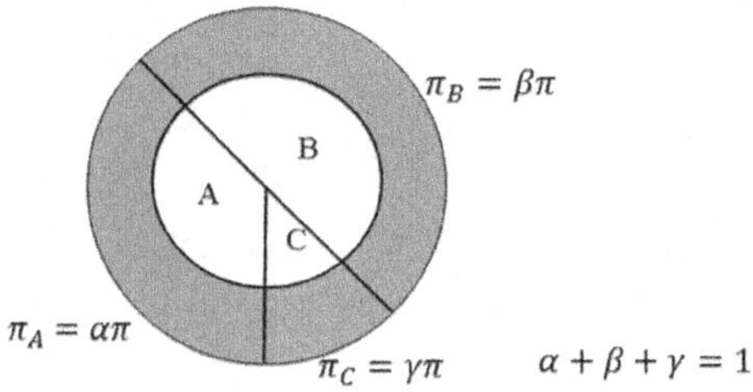

Figure 10.3. Epstein's View on Distributing *DS*

giving more to the landowners who are generally in the weakest position. Merrill (1986, p. 1574) called this the Rawl's difference principle.

The third is the proportional distribution. Epstein (1985, p. 4) argued that surplus created by the action (the outer ring in Figure 10.2) should be divided among individuals in accordance with the size of their original contributions because property is a natural right. Merrill (1986, p. 1575) called this the "Epsteinian proportionality rule."

The social contract tradition suggests a possible justification for this proportionality rule, which is "consent" (Merrill, 1986, p. 1561). As shown in Figure 10.3 above, the Epsteinian Criterion concerning the division of π can be depicted as follows. α, β, and γ indicate the share of landowners, the project runner, and the government, respectively, under the condition that $\alpha + \beta + \lambda = 1$. According to this criterion, landowners receive an extra amount above just compensation. Let us define, the proportion for landowners under the Epsteinian Criterion as $\alpha^e = A/(A + B + C)$.[14]

Some scholars discuss Epstein's so-called 50 per cent bonus compensation of the fair market value in terms of just compensation.[15] This is related to A inside the inner circle in Figure 10.3. However, he seems to be focusing mainly on the distribution of surplus as well as on the under-compensation bias in the scheme of fair market value compensation. In fact, he introduced discussions on the 50 per cent bonus compensation mostly when he explained how to distribute the surplus. All in all, to

[14] The proportions for the project runner and the government can be defined as $\beta^e = B/(A + B + C)$ and $\gamma^e = C/(A + B + C)$, respectively.

[15] Epstein's 50 per cent bonus compensation tends to be frequently mentioned during discussions on just compensation. The idea of the bonus system can be found in Fennell (2004), Heller and Hills (2008), Kelly (2006), Krier and Serkin (2004), Bell and Parchomovsky (2007), Lehavi and Licht (2007), Serkin (2007), and Wyman (2007). In reality, a few US states (Michigan, Kansas, etc.) choose to follow similar methods.

Epstein, the 50 per cent bonus might have originated from both accounts, knowing that the fair market value scheme can never overcome the under-compensation bias.

Eventually (despite the "proportionality rule"), even Epstein acknowledged the inevitability of the estimation to be based on the market value in reality. However, what Epstein really wanted to emphasize was that the development surplus must be reflected in the estimation for compensation.[16] In the same context, Merrill (1986), Kowal (2006), and Williams (2009) argued for "Restitutionary Compensation" and Krier and Serkin (2004) argued for "Gain-based Compensation."

2 *Distribution of DS in Korea:* $\pi_A = 0$

In this section, I will discuss the type of development surplus distribution standard used in Korea. The KLTC prohibits the landowner from earning development surplus, in principle. This is the "Principle of Prohibiting the Condemnee from Sharing in the *DS*."[17] According to this principle, from Figure 10.4, $\alpha = 0$ and π_A is shared by the project runner and the government. That is to say, the project runner and the government take an additional surplus of $\pi_B{}' = (\alpha_1 \pi_A)$ and $\pi_C{}' = (\alpha_2 \pi_A)$ each, as shown in Figure 10.4. Although the project has been executed due to unilateral transfer, since the compensation (A) has been made to the landowner, many Korean scholars insist that $\pi_A = 0$. The Constitutional Court also consistently makes judgment that $\pi_A = 0$ is constitutional.[18] This distribution standard of Korea can be considered as the Pareto Criterion.

In Korea, π_C and $\pi_C{}'$ are called the "Restitution of Development Surplus." Many scholars insist that the restitution of development surplus to government must be strengthened. However, (unlike π_B or $\pi_B{}'$) π_C and $\pi_C{}'$ are set according to the Act (e.g., Property Tax Act, Development

[16] "Epstein is correct in that the current opportunity cost formula for determining the measure of compensation ignores two important elements of value: *the social surplus generated* by the taking and *the consumer surplus* that the condemnee attaches to the property." (Merrill, 1986, p. 1571, emphasis added).

[17] This is stated in §67.2 of the KLTC. This principle means that appraisers should exclude the land price increment that has occurred between the timing of plan announcement and the taking decision in measuring the compensation.

[18] Cases in which the Constitutional Court held the "Principle of Prohibiting the Condemnee from Sharing the *DS*" are 2006_C.C_BA79, 2008_C.C_BA112, 2009_C.C_BA142, and 2008_C.C_BA102. This view has been widespread among Korean law scholars.

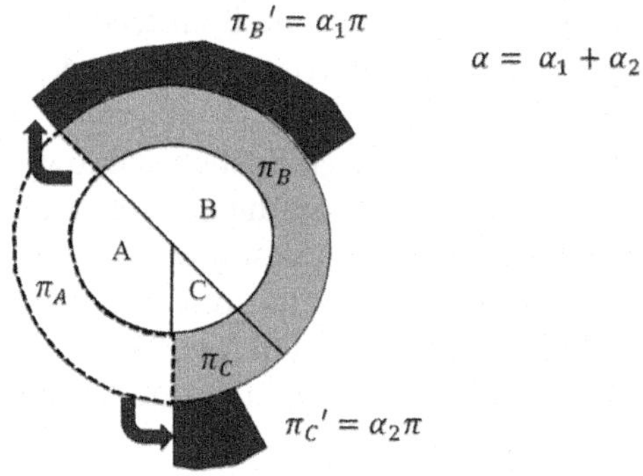

Figure 10.4. Distribution of the *DS* in Korea

Surplus Restitution Act, etc.).[19] Moreover, the restitution system is not working properly. The project runner is exempted from payments such as property tax, capital gains tax, and charges for development within the special district (e.g., the non-metropolitan area).[20] So, through ordinance, local governments mandatorily require developers to build such public facilities as roads, parks, schools, etc. and force them to donate the completed facilities back to local governments free. However, such donation of public facilities takes up less than 10 per cent of the developed land. As a result, a large portion of development surplus is distributed to project runners.

IV Economic Perspectives of Distribution of *DS*

1 *DS Distribution to the Landowners for Fairness and Efficiency*

Let us assume the following three conditions. First, the degree of publicness differs according to individual projects in which the eminent domain power is exercised. Here, I assume that the development projects are EDT^{NPG}. Second, development surplus has a positive value ($\pi > 0$). Moreover, the incentives of the landowners and the project runner will differ according to how the development surplus is distributed. Third,

[19] This is imposing tax or a charge for the development. The local government imposes property tax, capital gains tax, and charges for development onto the project runners.

[20] This is donating a part of the developed land to the government. This forced donation is used in cases when constructing roads or parks within the development project area at the expense of the project runner. These are eventually included as an asset of the government.

the landowners were able to be justly compensated. This means that a reasonable level of subjective value has been reflected in the amount of compensation. That is to say that, *A* in the small circle in Figure 10.3 has been met.[21]

Certainly, there exist limitations in that subjective values are difficult to measure. For this reason, as explained in Section III, the idea of giving bonuses in addition to the fair market value has been suggested. I argue that a portion of the development surplus should be distributed to the landowners for fairness and efficiency even though the subjective value has been included in the compensation.[22]

Let us look at takings in terms of fairness. How to define fairness varies by scholars. Epstein (1985, p. 5; 2011, p. 107) argues that there must be no change in the state of landowners.[23] In his mind, unfairness means when disproportionate loss occurs to the landowners. This can be considered in the following two aspects. First, during the takings process, the autonomy of the landowner is confiscated. The autonomy indicates the right of the landowner to be able to autonomously decide whether to sell and when to sell. The importance of autonomy and the necessity for compensation can be found in Fennell (2004; 2013), Wyman (2007), and Lee (2013).

21 There has been much controversy among scholars over the third assumption. Fischel (1995), Miceli and Segerson (2000), Nosal (2001), and Miceli (2011) argue that the fair market value compensation should exclude the subjective value. Many countries choose such a standard in appraising the compensation. In contrast, Epstein (1985) and Merrill (1986) argue that when subjective values of landowners are not reflected in the compensation, an under-compensation bias will occur. The risk of excessive takings will be increased as a result. Recent discussions on subjective value compensation can be found in Fennell (2004), Krier and Serkin (2004), Somin (2007), Heller and Hills (2008), Bell and Parchomovsky (2010), Chang (2013), and Lee (2013).

22 A few scholars are concerned with the risk of overcompensation and opportunistic behaviors (e.g., inefficient overinvestment, rent-seeking behaviors such as lobbying for condemnation) by landowners in subjective value compensation (Fennell, 2004, p. 993; Somin, 2007, pp. 215–16). Such suspicion is partially a persuasive argument. But, in Korea, the former can be administratively regulated by prohibiting investment activity after the taking decision, and the latter being difficult to be achieved due to the fact that a well-organized political lobbying group is not easily formed. Therefore, what has been mentioned above seems to be undue concerns.

23 "The requirement of just compensation assures that the state will give to each person a fair equivalent to what has been taken" (Epstein, 1985, p. 5). "State Coercion should be used to overcome the barriers of high transaction cost by seeking . . . to leave those persons subjected to the state's coercive power at least as well off after its imposition as they were before." (Epstein, 2011, p. 7)

Second, in the coercive transfer by takings, the landowners lose the chance to gain some surplus from voluntary market transactions. Here, surplus may be defined to have been created when a transfer of land occurs from those who evaluate the value as being lower to those who evaluate the value as being higher. In fact, the landowners normally expect to share the surplus from the development project. This is because, if a coercive transfer does not take place, the landowner will be able to suggest a higher price to gain a portion of the development surplus. Forced property transfer due to takings deprives landowners of such chances and results in the disproportionate loss only to the landowners. Eventually, π_A in Figure 10.3 should be greater than 0 in terms of fairness. Similar views can be found in Fennell (2004), Krier and Serkin (2004), Kowal (2006), Householder (2007), Wyman (2007), and Lee (2013).

Next, let us take a look at takings in terms of efficiency. Main discussion is whether distributing some development surpluses to the landowners ($\pi_A > 0$) produces a more efficient result than not doing so ($\pi_A = 0$). A more socially efficient result may be achieved when π_A would be greater than 0 due to the following reasons. First, a positive value of π_A will contribute to deter the rent-seeking behavior of the private developer. In several countries (e.g., the United States, the United Kingdom, Germany, and Korea), the private developer can be a condemner (Kim and Park, 2014). The private condemner has the incentive to maximize profit. The π_B is more than $\beta\pi$ of Figure 10.3 in $\pi_A = 0$. Under the system of inadequate public oversight on the private condemner, various opportunism (e.g., *the adverse selection problem*) may occur as mentioned in Kim and Park (2014).[24] In other words, the private condemner will participate in the project without sufficient preparation. However, when $\pi_A > 0$, *ceteris paribus*, the private condemner will be more cautious when analyzing the cost and benefit of the development project. As a consequence, the probability of inefficient takings will be reduced.[25]

[24] Merrill (1986, p. 86), Kochan (1998), and Fennell (2004, p. 978) suspect that inefficient rent-seeking behavior may occur when a project runner takes too large a portion of the development surplus.

[25] A similar sense can be found in Gillette (2005) and Wyman (2007). "A requirement that just compensation include some sharing of the upside risk of a project with condemnees may reduce undue optimism and thus induce a more meaningful comparison of the costs and benefits of a proposed economic development." (Gillette, 2005, p. 21) "Some proponents of sharing the gains with takees propose this sharing to promote efficient government decisions about takings." (Wyman, 2007, p. 259)

This is in the same vein as how increased compensation decreases inefficient takings.[26] Kim and Park (2014) suggest the post-taking inefficient indexes (e.g., cancellation and change in the project runner). They argued that inefficient results would incur because of the private developers' rent-seeking behaviors.[27]

Second, a positive value of π_A will decrease the socially inefficient cost of the takings disputes. The dispute resolution process varies by country. It is undoubtedly true that a great amount of cost (e.g., legal and appraisal fees) will be spent for administrative or judicial dispute settlement.[28] Perhaps generous compensation is one way to reduce the probability of conflict occurrence. When the publicness of development project is ambiguous and the condemner is a private entity, the demoralization cost of the landowners will be greater. Krier and Serkin (2004, p. 867) argue that development projects of a lower publicness should have a bigger value of π_A.

Third, a positive value of π_A will provide incentives to the landowners to monitor the project if some of the development surplus is distributed to landowners at the completion of the project. Most discussions on the distribution of development surplus assume that compensation would be completed before the start of the project. However, it is difficult to accurately measure the development surplus at the beginning. As an alternative solution, a method of distributing a portion of development surplus to landowners after the completion of the project can be considered.[29] For such cases, the landowners will have a strong incentive to monitor the project runner's activities. Such monitoring will deter the rent-seeking behaviors of the project runner (e.g., *moral hazard*).[30]

[26] "Increased compensation levels will significantly reduce the incidence of economically inefficient takings for development purposes." (Somin, 2007, p. 217)

[27] This index will be applied in the rough empirical examination which will be discussed later.

[28] In Korea, the appeal process in takings is divided decision on appeals through the Land Tribunal and administrative litigation through court. Around 3,000 or more decisions and 800 or more cases related to compensation are filed every year.

[29] Such method is to have both the landowners and the project runner sign a sort of option contract at the time of compensation. Although this does not exactly match the development surplus distribution, paying compensation in the form of giving back the developed land after the completion of the project is used in Korea. This is called alternative land compensation. This system was legislated in 2007 and approximately 1 per cent of the overall compensation is paid using this system in Korea.

[30] This is to monitor behaviors such as irregular delay of projects or transferring the development right to other developer. These activities arise due to the inadequate oversight of government.

Similar views can be found in Kim and Park (2010) dealing with the economic function of repurchase rights.

2 *Theoretical Model in Distribution of DS for Landowners*

Let us extend the theoretical model in Lee (2015) where there are two landowners ($A1$ and $A2$) and a project runner (*PR*) to the typical eminent domain system in Korea. According to the KLTC, while *PR* bargains with landowners, *PR* should offer the price determined by appraisers who exclude the expected development surplus in measuring the fair market value of the condemned property. I will define ${P_{Ai}}^{PR}(> 0)$ as the amount of compensation for landowner Ai.

According to the KLTC, when a landowner Ai rejects the offer ${P_{Ai}}^{PR}$, *PR* could move on to the compulsory purchase stage in most cases. Therefore, regardless of whether a landowner accepts the offer, his land is condemned by *PR*. When *PR* condemns the land and develops a project, then *PR* gets $\sum V_{Ai} + b - c - \sum {P_{Ai}}^{PR}$. Where V_{Ai} is the landowner Ai's subject value of his land, $\sum V_{Ai} + b$ is the socio-economic benefit of the project, and c is the socio-economic cost of the project. Then landowner Ai's payoff is always ${P_{Ai}}^{PR} - V_{Ai}$.

Figure 10.5 describes the brief game structure under the KLTC. Regardless of the willingness of landowners to sell, the lands are condemned as long as the project has been approved for compulsory purchase by the government. Under the circumstances, it is not surprising that most landowners accept *PR*'s offer at the initial bargaining stage, which is one of the equilibria of the game.

Although *PR* could condemn private land, it takes time to implement the project successfully and enjoy the development surplus (π) from it. Depending on the effort of *PR* to implement the project as scheduled, the time when π is realized changes. As the surplus is realized later, the present value of it should be discounted. So, we consider the case when π is discounted by a factor which is affected by the effort of *PR*. Let us suppose that π from the project, $\sum V_{Ai} + b - c - \sum {P_{Ai}}^{PR}$, is given. We also define the level of effort by *PR* as $e \in (0, \infty)$, the discount factor as a function of the effort by *PR* as $\delta(e)$, and the disutility or cost of the effort as a function of the effort, $\gamma(e)$. Then, the objective function of *PR* can be described as follows.

$$\delta(e)\pi - \gamma(e), \text{ where } 0 \leq \delta \leq 1.$$

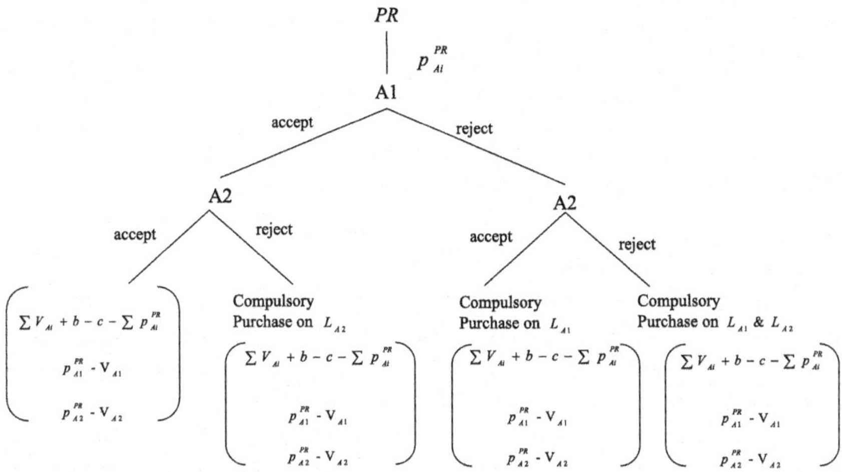

Figure 10.5. Game Structure in Eminent Domain
Note: a variant of Lee (2015, Figure 10.1)

Here are the assumptions on the discount factor, $\delta(e)$, and the disutility function, $\gamma(e)$.

Assumption 1. $\delta'(e) > 0$, $\delta''(e) < 0$, $\gamma'(e) > 0$, and $\gamma''(e) > 0$.[31]
We assume that the discount factor function, $\delta(e)$, is an increasing function of the effort and is concave. This implies that *PR* can realize the development surplus earlier as she puts more efforts in project implementation and that the marginal effect of a unit of effort to shorten the implementation period decreases. By Assumption 1, the objective function of *PR* is a concave function of *e*. Given the objective function, *PR* chooses her effort level. By the concavity of the objective function, the optimal effort level e^* uniquely exists.

Now we consider the case when some portion of π is distributed to landowners. By distributing some portion of π to the landowners, *PR* could induce cooperation from landowners and shorten the project implementation period. When we define θ as the portion of π to *PR*

[31] It is natural that we assume that the effect by *PR* is positive, but the marginal effect decreases as the level of effort increases. Also, the convex disutility function assumption is one of the common assumptions in the literature. Therefore, δ is assumed to be an increasing and concave function of *e*, and the disutility function is assumed to be an increasing and convex function of *e*.

and the portion of π to landowners is $(1-\theta)$, then the objective function of *PR* is as follows.[32]

$$\theta\delta(\theta, e)\pi - \gamma(e), \text{ where } \theta \in (0,1)$$

Given θ, *PR* chooses her unique effort level, e^*, to maximize her objective function as shown in the following Lemma.

Lemma 1. For any given θ, there exists a unique e^*.
<Proof> See the Appendix.
We assume that *PR* could increase δ with the same level of effort by increasing the portion of π to the landowners. It is natural to assume that landowners become more cooperative to the project implementation as more portion of the economic surplus is given to them.

Another key assumption of the model is about the cross partial derivative. We assume that the marginal effect of effort to shorten the project period increases as the landowners get a greater portion of the surplus and become more cooperative. So, as the amount of the portion of π given to landowners increases, the marginal effect of *e* on δ increases, that is $\delta_{e\theta} < 0$. Moreover, it is reasonable to assume that the marginal effect of the *PR*'s effort on landowners' cooperation decreases as their share increases. As the share of landowners increases, the marginal effect of increasing another share to them decreases. So, I assume that $\delta_{e\theta\theta}$ is negative.

Assumption 2. For any $\theta \in (0,1)$, $\delta_\theta \in (-\infty, 0)$, $\delta_{e\theta} \in (-\infty, 0)$, and $\delta_{e\theta\theta} \in (-\infty, 0)$.

The following assumption is to make the model more meaningful. As θ is close to 1, which means that the share given to the landowners is small, the absolute value of the cross partial derivative of δ with *e* and θ is large, and dominates the value of the derivative of δ with *e*. In other words, the degree of increasing marginal effect of *e* on δ is very large when the landowners' share is close to zero.

Assumption 3. $\lim_{\theta \to 1} \delta_e + \theta\delta_{e\theta} < 0$.

Proposition 1. There exists $\hat{\theta}$ that satisfies $\frac{de^*(\theta)}{d\theta}$ and has a negative value if and only if $\theta \in (\hat{\theta}, 1)$.

[32] In this subsection, I assume that $\pi_C = 0$ in Figure 10.3 for convenient discussion. Although $\pi_C > 0$, the portion of π to government are generally fixed by the related acts in Korea. Moreover, π_C is not affected by the project runner's effort. So, π_C is excluded in this theoretical model.

<Proof> See the appendix.
The proposition means that, in a region, the *PR* induces more effort as the share to him decreases. This is because as a *PR*'s share of π decreases, the effect of effort to shorten the project implementation period by drawing the landowners' cooperation increases. However, if *PR*'s share becomes too small, then it is hard to give *PR* incentives to induce his effort as his benefit from shortening the period is too small.

Therefore, comparing with the case where all π is given to *PR*, if we picked an appropriate portion for landowners, we can induce more effort from *PR*. Eventually, stronger cooperation from landowners and a shorter project period decrease efficiency loss during the project development.

In this model, I define a social welfare function (*SWF*) as the sum of net benefits of all participants, *PR*, *A*1, and *A*2 as below.

$$SWF(\theta, e) = \theta\delta(\theta, e)\pi - \gamma(e) + (1-\theta)\delta(\theta, e)\pi - \sum V_{Ai} + \sum P_{Ai}^{PR} < 0$$

$$= \delta(\theta, e)\pi - \gamma(e) - \sum V_{Ai} + \sum P_{Ai}^{PR} = \delta(\theta, e) - \gamma(e) + K$$

A social planner considers the social welfare function while *PR* considers his objective function. So, as shown in Lemma 2, the optimal level of effort for maximizing *SWF*, given θ, is greater than that of maximizing *PR*'s objective function.

Lemma 2. For any given $0 < \theta < 1$, $e^* < e_{FB}$
Where $e^* = argmax\ \theta\delta(\theta, e)\pi - \gamma(e)$ and $e_{FB} = argmax\ SWF(\theta, e)$.
<Proof> See the appendix.
Due to the information asymmetry and the hidden action problem from *PR*'s choice on his effort level, it is natural to assume that the effort level is chosen by *PR* to maximize *PR*'s objective function given θ chosen by a social planner to maximize the social welfare function. Therefore, let us consider the case where the social planner chooses θ when $e^*(\theta)$ is chosen by *PR*. Then the social planner's problem given *PR*'s incentive compatibility condition is as follows.[33]

$$\underset{\theta}{Max}\ \delta(e^*(\theta, e), \theta)\pi - \gamma(e^*(\theta))\ (SP)$$

s.t. $e^* = argmax\ \theta\delta(\theta, e)\pi - \gamma(e)\ (IC_{PR})$

[33] As described in Lemma 2, the effort level chosen by *PR* is different from the level to maximize the social welfare function. In this sense, the solution of the social planner's problem gives the second-best result.

We find an interesting feature, as explained in Lemma 3, such that the optimal level of θ does not vary in the characteristics of the disutility function of *PR*.[34]

Lemma 3. The characteristics of the disutility function $\gamma(e)$ does not affect the social planner's optimal choice of θ.
<Proof> See the Appendix.
It then follows Proposition 2, which suggests that the socially optimal portion of π to landowners is positive. Therefore, under certain assumptions that are not extreme, giving a positive portion of the development surplus to landowners is socially more efficient than giving none. This result is mainly from the assumption that the marginal effect of effort to shorten the project period increases as the landowner gets a greater portion of the surplus and becomes more cooperative. Even if *PR* loses some portion of the surplus, he exerts more effort to shorten the project implementation period, which increases the efficiency of project implementation.

Proposition 2. $\theta^* < \hat{\theta} < 1$
Where θ^* solves (SP) given (IC_{PR}), and $\frac{de^*(\theta)}{d\theta} < 0$ if and only if $\theta \in (\hat{\theta}, 1)$.
<Proof> See the Appendix.
Now let us add another case where there are two types of project runners (say *g* type and *b* type) and each has a different disutility function. One developer can relatively easily handle the dispute or obstacles during the project implementation, and the other cannot. Suppose one developer has a lower disutility function than the other, that is $\gamma_g(e) < \gamma_b(e)$ for all *e*. Then, given θ^* chosen by the social planner,[35] the net benefit of *g* type, $\theta^*\delta(e_g{}^*(\theta^*), \theta^*)\pi - \gamma_g(e_g{}^*(\theta^*))$, is greater than that of *b* type, $\theta^*\delta(e_b{}^*(\theta^*), \theta^*)\pi - \gamma_b(e_b{}^*(\theta^*))$. Suppose *PR* has an outside option so that, if *PR* did not participate in developing the project, *PR* could get alternative benefits, $\overline{U}$ from another financial investment.

If the outside option $\overline{U}$ is between two net benefits so that *g* type's net benefit is greater than $\overline{U}$ while *b* type's is less than $\overline{U}$, then only *g* type developers will join the project implementation. In this sense, developers with poor ability to handle the challengers during the implementation

[34] This feature is quite similar to the envelop theorem. While $e^*(\theta)$ is not maximizing the social planner's objective function but *PR*'s, the objective functions of the social planner and *PR* are very similar. That is why we have a result similar to the result of the envelop theorem.

[35] As in Lemma 3, the optimal θ is determined regardless of the type of *PR*.

can be screened. Therefore, we can improve the social efficiency by excluding the developers with poor ability in this case.

3 *Distribution of DS and efficiency*

From the above theoretical model, a socially more efficient result will be brought under a positive π_A ($\theta < 1$ in the model). What would be the most desirable level of π_A^*? In reality, the publicness of projects is different and the types of project runners are various from the public to the private. Under such a situation, it is very difficult to figure out the most desirable level. Nonetheless, several second-best alternatives can be suggested. First is to add a certain bonus on the fair market value, suggested by Epstein (1985), Merrill (1986), and Fennell (2004).[36] Second is to suppose the standard for measuring the fair market value as the highest and best use of the land at the time of the development completion rather than at the time of compensation, as suggested by Krier and Serkin (2004, p. 873). Third is to buy a certain portion (e.g., more than 1/2 or 2/3) of the overall planned land by voluntary market transaction, and acquire the rest of the land compulsorily through eminent domain power such as is the case in Korea.[37]

Under the above third alternative, the condition for using the eminent domain power is established in several types. A typical type is acquiring two-thirds of the land in advance through market transactions. Seventeen Acts (e.g., Urban Development Act) stipulate such a condition. During the voluntary negotiation of landowners and developer, some portion of future development surplus will be transferred to the landowners. The empirical examination below shows whether a more efficient result is derived under the condition.

It is difficult to find an empirical study on whether distributing the development surplus to landowners ($\pi_A > 0$ in Figure 10.3) will derive a more efficient result. I will roughly compare the relative efficiency by comparing two development project cases where some portion of

[36] Lee (2013) suggested providing additional amounts of compensation in fixed dollar amounts. Meanwhile, Fennell (2004) and Bell and Parchomovsky (2007) suggested compensation through self-assessment valuation. However, these methods are only suggested as an idea.

[37] Such a method is used when a private entity executes a project by using eminent domain power. Nonetheless, there exists a limitation as it can be applied only when the project runner is a purely private entity, and it is applied in only 20 Acts. This is also related to the argument that condemnees' holdout problems may not be serious in reality, as mentioned in Benson and Brown (2010), and Shavell (2010).

development surplus is transferred to the landowners and in the other, where a portion of development surplus is not transferred to the landowners.

For urban development projects under the Urban Development Act, a private developer has to buy in advance two-thirds of the planned land through voluntary negotiation before using the eminent domain power. Formally or informally, the landowners will get to know about the development plan, and expect the development surplus to be reflected in the transaction price. The developer estimates in advance the prospective scope of the development surplus and will participate in the negotiation based on this estimation. In the process of negotiation, some portion of development surplus is included in the transaction price.[38] A positive π_A will be realized. From the field experts' survey, the real transaction price tends to be decided at above 30–50 per cent of the fair market value. Meanwhile, for industrial complex construction projects under the Industrial Location and Development Act, the total of planned land can be condemned by the project runner without any negotiation. $\pi_A = 0$ occurs in land transfer.

Urban development and industrial complex construction are not exactly identical in their characteristics. However, two projects have several similarities. First, they are low publicness projects only for regional development. These are spread widely all over the country. Second, a private project runner may become a condemner to use the eminent domain power in both projects. Moreover, the proportion of private project runner is quite high. Third, the project procedures are similar, and mostly the development cost is funded through resale to other private entities.

Kim and Park (2014) suggested post-taking irregularities (cancellation or change in project runner, *CoC*) as inefficiency index.[39] This index is related to $\gamma_b(e)$ in Proposition 2. The sample period is from 2003 to 2010. During this period 126 industrial complex development projects and 46 urban development projects have been run by private developers. Among the 126 industrial complex development projects, there were 15 cancellations and 23 changes in project runner. The rate of *CoC* was 30.2 per cent. During the same period, in the urban development projects,

38 When acquiring two-thirds of the planned land through negotiation is completed, the remaining one-third of the land will be affected by the eminent domain power due to the permission of public project. In takings, the development surplus is not included in the compensation.

39 Generally, cancellation of project makes sunk pre-investments by the project runner and local government. Change in project runners causes delay of development projects.

Table 10.1. *Irregularities in Urban Development and Industrial Complexes Projects*

	Total (A)	Cancellation (B)	Change in Project Runner (C)	B+C [(B+V)/A,%]
Industrial complexes ($\pi_A = 0$)	126	15	23	38 (30.2)
Urban development ($\pi_A > 0$)	46	3	2	5 (10.9)

among the total of 46, there were 3 cancellations and 2 changes in project runner. The rate of *CoC* was 10.9 per cent. The *CoC* rates in Table 10.1 indicate that the rate of industrial complex projects is about three times higher than that of urban development projects.

These statistics are hardly regarded as definite evidence to prove that relatively fewer inefficient cancellations or changes in project runners will occur when $\pi_A > 0$. Several other factors can affect irregularities, including the characteristics of individual projects, type of project runner, regional location, and time, etc. Despite the limitations of the data and analysis method, it is noteworthy that a dramatically large difference between the rate of *CoC* for development projects of $\pi_A > 0$ and $\pi_A = 0$ has been detected. More rigorous studies appear to be warranted with a variety of detailed proxies.

V Conclusion

Many countries including Korea prohibit distribution of development surplus to the landowners in principle.[40] While the publicness became more ambiguous and scrutiny of the publicness became imperfect, should such a principle be maintained? Should such a rule be applied even when the condemner is a private developer?

[40] It is called the "Principle of Prohibiting the Condemnee from Sharing the *DS*" in Korea and "The Pointe Gourde and San Sebastian Principle" in the United Kingdom The Food and Agricultural Organization (FAO) (2008, p. 54) also recommends similar points of view in principle.

These questions make us rethink the distribution of the development surplus.

A few scholars have proposed that landowners should receive extra compensation above the fair market value, to be compensated for the landowners' loss of autonomy and potential surpluses from trade as well as subjective value. In terms of fairness, there is no doubt that it is unfair when the landowners cannot take any of the development surplus ($\pi_A = 0$). The lower the publicness, or when the project runner is a private developer, the larger the unfairness problem will grow.[41]

In this study, the main focus is not about fairness, but about efficiency. The incentives of project runner and landowners differ according to what kind of compensation system is legislated. Their activities will be affected according to what standards of development surplus distribution are applied. Such a change of incentives ultimately affects social efficiency as well.

I believe a more socially efficient result will be derived when $\pi_A > 0$ than when $\pi_A = 0$. $\pi_A > 0$ will contribute to deter opportunistic behavior (e.g. adverse selection) of project runners. Also, it will mitigate the conflicts related to takings and compensation, which will result in the reduction of inefficient dispute resolution costs. If an *ex post* development surplus distribution is applied, it can also enable the landowners to monitor the development process.

It is very difficult to actualize $\pi_A > 0$ in reality. As a second-best alternative, the bonus compensation system can be considered, for which a few scholars including Epstein (1985) have argued. In fact, several states in the United States (Michigan, Kansas, etc.) have chosen similar methods after the *Kelo* case.[42] Also, the method to make the decision for the highest and best use at the time of the development completion as suggested by Krier and Serkin (2004) and to make the voluntary market transaction on some portion of the land (used in Korea) seems to be an alternative that should also be considered.[43]

41 Because of this, FAO (2008, p. 12) recommends that development surplus should be included in the compensation through strict publicness examination for eminent domains for private development.

42 Even in the state of Kansas, for takings of purely private development purposes, the compensation should be made at 200 per cent of the fair market value in some cases (Wyman, 2007, p. 257).

43 As suggested by Somin (2007), I also see the possibility of inefficient overinvestment risk and the possibility of rent-seeking by landowners due to over-compensation. However, in reality, it also seems that the concern will not be as serious as they think it to be, and also the rent-seeking possibility of the project runner may be greater.

Appendix

<Proof of Lemma 1>

By Assumption 1, e^* satisfying *F.O.C.* does uniquely exist.

$$(F.O.C.)\ \theta\delta_e(\theta, e^*)\pi = \gamma_e(e^*)\ .Q.E.D.$$

<Proof of Proposition 1>

By Implicit Function Theorem, $\frac{de^*(\theta)}{d\theta} = -\frac{\partial I/\partial\theta}{\partial I/\partial e}$, where $I \equiv \theta\delta_e(\theta, e)\pi - \gamma_e(e)$.

$$\frac{de^*(\theta)}{d\theta} = -\frac{\partial I/\partial\theta}{\partial I/\partial e} = -\frac{[\delta_e(\theta, e) + \theta\delta_{e\theta}(\theta, e)]\pi}{\theta\delta_{ee}(\theta, e)\pi - \gamma_{ee}(e)}$$

So, $\frac{de^*(\theta)}{d\theta} < 0$ if and only if $\delta_e(\theta, e) + \theta\delta_{e\theta}(\theta, e) < 0$. $\lim_{\theta\to 0}\delta_e(\theta, e) + \theta\delta_{e\theta}(\theta, e) > 0$ by Assumption 2 and $\lim_{\theta\to 1}\delta_e + \theta\delta_{e\theta} < 0$ by Assumption 3. As $\delta_e(\theta, e) + \theta\delta_{e\theta}(\theta, e)$ is a continuous function, there exists θ that satisfies $\delta_e(\theta, e) + \theta\delta_{e\theta}(\theta, e) > 0$. Moreover, the partial derivative of $\delta_e(\theta, e) + \theta\delta_{e\theta}(\theta, e)$ with θ is 2 $\delta_{e\theta}(\theta, e) + \theta\delta_{e\theta\theta}(\theta, e)$ which is negative by Assumption 2. Therefore, there is a unique $\hat{\theta} \in (0, 1)$ that satisfies $\delta_e(\hat{\theta}, e) + \hat{\theta}\delta_{e\theta}(\hat{\theta}, e)$ equals to zero, which means $\delta_e(\theta, e) + \theta\delta_{e\theta}(\theta, e) < 0$ if and only if $\theta \in (\hat{\theta}, 1)$. *Q.E.D.*

<Proof of Lemma 2>

F.O.C. for maximizing *PR*'s objective function is $\theta\delta_e(\theta, e)\pi - \gamma_e(e)$ while *F.O.C.* for maximizing *SWF* is $\theta\delta_e(\theta, e)\pi = \gamma_e(e)$. For $\theta < 1$, *PR*'s *LHS* is less than *SWF*'s *LHS*. Therefore, $\theta\delta_e(\theta, e_{FB})\pi < \gamma_e(e_{FB})$. As *LHS*s are decreasing functions of *e* and *RHS*s are increasing functions of *e*, $e^* < e_{FB}$. *Q.E.D.*

<Proof of Lemma 3>

$\frac{dSWF}{d\theta} = [\delta_\theta + \frac{\partial\delta}{\partial e}\frac{de}{d\theta}]\pi - \gamma_e\frac{de}{d\theta} = [\delta_\theta + \frac{\partial\delta}{\partial e}\frac{de}{d\theta} - \theta\frac{\partial\delta}{\partial e}\frac{de}{d\theta}]\pi = [\delta_\theta + (1-\theta)\frac{\partial\delta}{\partial e}\frac{de}{d\theta}]\pi$, by ($IC_{PR}$). Therefore, the slope of *SWF* is not affected by $\gamma(e)$. While the maximum level of *SWF* is affected by $\gamma(e)$, the optimal value of θ is determined regardless of the characteristics of $\gamma(e)$. *Q.E.D.*

<Proof of Proposition 2>

$\frac{dSWF}{d\theta} = [\delta_\theta + (1-\theta)\frac{\partial\delta}{\partial e}\frac{de}{d\theta}]\pi$ by Lemma 4. If $\theta > \hat{\theta}$, $\frac{dSWF}{d\theta} < 0$. For all $\theta > \hat{\theta}$, $SW(\theta) < SW(\hat{\theta})$. So, $\theta^* \leq \hat{\theta}$. Also, $\frac{dSWF}{d\theta}|_{\theta=\hat{\theta}} = \delta_\theta\pi < 0$. Therefore, for some $\varepsilon > 0$, $SWF(\hat{\theta} - \varepsilon) > SWF(\hat{\theta})$. *Q.E.D.*

References

Bell, Abraham, 2009, "Private Takings," *University of Chicago Law Review*, vol. 76, no. 2, pp. 517–85.

Bell, Abraham and Gideon Parchomovsky, 2007, "Takings Compensation Private," *Stanford Law Review*, vol. 59, pp. 871–906.

Bell, Abraham and Gideon Parchomovsky, 2010, "The Hidden Function of Takings Compensation," *Virginia Law Review*, vol. 96, pp. 1673–1725.

Benson, Bruce and Matthew Brown, 2010, "Eminent Domain for Private Use: Is It Justified by Market Failure or an Example of Government Failure," in Benson, Bruce (ed.), *Property Rights: Eminent Domain and Regulatory Takings Re-Examined*, NY: Palgrave Macmillan.

Chang, Yun-Chen, 2013, *Private Property and Takings Compensation: Theoretical Framework and Empirical Analysis*, Northampton MA: Edward Elgar.

Cohen, Charles, 2006, "Eminent Domain After *Kelo v. City of New London*: An Argument for Banning Economic Development Takings," *Harvard Journal of Law and Public Policy*, vol. 29, no. 2, pp. 491–568.

Colwell, F. Peter and C. F. Sirmans, 1978, "Area, Time, Centrality and the Value of Urban Land," *Land Economics*, vol. 79, no. 1, pp. 514–19.

Epstein, A. Richard, 1985, *Takings: Private Property and the Power of Eminent Domain*, Cambridge, MA: Harvard University Press.

Epstein, A. Richard, 2011, *Design for Liberty: Private Property, Public Administration, and the Rule of Law*, Cambridge MA: Harvard University Press.

Fennell, Lee Anne, 2004, "Taking Eminent Domain Apart," *Michigan State Law Review*, vol. 2004, pp. 957–1004.

Fennell, Lee Anne, 2013, "Just Enough," *Columbia Law Review*, vol. 113, pp. 109–22.

Fischel, A. William, 1995, *Regulatory Takings: Law, Economics, and Politics*, Cambridge MA: Harvard University Press.

Food and Agriculture Organization, 2008, *Compulsory Acquisition of Land and Compensation*, Rome: United Nations

Gillette, P. Clayton, 2005, "*Kelo* and the Local Political Process" *Hofstra Law Review*, vol. 34, pp. 13–22.

Guntermann, L. Karl, Alex R. Horestein, Federico Nardari, and Garth Thomas, 2015, "Parcel Size and Land Value: A Comparison of Approaches," *Journal of Real Estate Research*, vol. 37, no. 2, pp. 281–319.

Heller, Michael and Rick Hills, 2008, "Land Assembly Districts," *Harvard Law Review*, vol. 121, no. 6, pp. 1465–1527.

Householder, A. Benjamin, 2007, "*Kelo* Compensation: The Future of Economic Development Takings," *Chicago-Kent Law Review*, vol. 82, no. 2, pp. 1029–61.

Kelly, B. Daniel, 2006, "The Public Use Requirement in Eminent Domain Law: A Rational Based on Secret Purchase and Private Influence," *Cornell Law Review*, vol. 92, pp. 1–66.

Kim, Iljoong and Sungkyu Park, 2010, "Eminent Domain Power and Afterwards: Leviathan's Post-Taking Opportunism," *Public Choice*, vol. 143, pp. 209–27.

Kim, Iljoong and Sungkyu Park, 2014, "Are Private Takings Efficient?: An Empirical Investigation," Department of Economics Working paper, Sungkyunkwan University.

Kochan, J. Donald, 1998, "Public Use and Independent Judiciary: Condemnation in an Interest-group Perspective," *Texas Review Law and Politics*, vol. 3, pp. 49–116.

Kowal, Tim, 2006, "The Restitutionary Approach to Just Compensation," *Chapman Law Review*, vol. 9, pp. 463–92.

Krier, James and Christopher Serkin, 2004, "Public Ruses," *Michigan State Law Review*, vol. 2004, pp. 859–75.

Lee, Brian, 2013, *Just Under-compensation: The Idiosyncratic Premium in Eminent Domain*, Legal Studies Research Paper no. 339, New York: Brooklyn Law School

Lee, Hojun, 2015, "*Public Interest Criteria and Korea's Scrutiny System*," Paper presented at the International Conference on Shifting the Paradigm for Sustainable Development: Eminent Domain and Property Rights, Korea Development Institute.

Lehavi, Ammon, and Amir N. Licht, 2007, "Eminent Domain Inc.," *Columbia Law Review*, vol. 107, pp. 1704–48.

Merrill, Thomas, 1986, "Rent Seeking and the Compensation Principle," *Northwestern University Law Review*, vol. 80, pp. 1561–90.

Miceli, J. Thomas, 2011, *The Economics Theory of Eminent Domain: Private Property, Public Use*, New York: Cambridge University Press.

Miceli, J. Thomas, and Kathleen Segerson, 2000, "Takings," Boudewijn Bouckaert and Gerrit de Geest (eds.), *Encyclopedia of Law and Economics*, Cheltenham: Edward Elgar.

Nosal, Ed, 2001, "The Taking of Land: Market Value Compensation Should Be Paid," *Journal of Public Economy*, vol. 82, pp. 431–43.

Serkin, Christopher, 2007, "Local Property Law: Adjusting the Scale of Property Protection," *Columbia Law Review*, vol. 107, no.4, pp. 883–948.

Shavell, Steven, 2010, "Eminent Domain versus Government Purchase of Land Given Imperfect Information about Owners," *Journal of Law and Economics*, vol. 53, pp. 1–27.

Somin, Ilya, 2007, "Controlling the Grasping Hand: Economic Development Takings after *Kelo*," *Supreme Court Economic Review*, vol. 15, pp. 183–271.

Somin, Ilya, 2008, "The Politics of Economic Development Takings," *Case Western Reserve Law Review*, vol. 58, no. 4, pp. 1185–98.

Thorsnes, Paul and Daniel, P. McMillen, 1998, "Land Value and Parcel Size: A Semi-parametric Analysis," *Journal of Real Estate Finance and Economics*, vol. 17, no. 3, pp. 233–44.

Williams, C. Matthew, 2009, "Restitution, Eminent Domain, and Economic Development: Moving to a Gains-Based Conception of the Takings Clause," *The Urban Lawyer*, vol. 41, no. 1, pp. 183–216.

Wyman, Katrina, 2007, "The Measure of Just Compensation," *University of California Davis Law Review*, vol. 41, pp. 239–88.

11

Takings, Disputes, and Resolutions in Korea: A Quantitative Review

DUOL KIM

I Introduction

Eminent domain is a power of government, which is used for the welfare of the public, but only by sacrificing one of the most basic principles of a free and democratic society: the property rights of landowners. The power, therefore, should be used only when it is inevitable, and careful and thorough considerations should be made before it is exercised, and the whole process should be transparent and legitimate.

The Korean government, like any other, has implemented laws and institutions concerning compulsory purchase that limit the abuse of power and protect the condemnees. But the existence of these systems is one thing, and their functioning is another. Diagnosing the actual operation of the whole system and proposing relevant prescriptions, therefore, are indispensable to make the institution work as planned.

This chapter deals with the latter part of the whole process; disputes arising from compulsory purchases and the institutional setup for resolving conflicts of interest. When the government makes an offer for the purchase of land, even if the landowner admits the inevitability of the sale of the land, she can be discontent with the offer from the government. As the government is a party to the conflict, unlike in usual civil disputes, it is hard to design a resolution process that the landowners regard as impartial. If such a system does not exist or if it does not work well even if it exists, it can harm the legitimacy of the government, which is the fundamental basis of the state.

In this chapter, I examined how the dispute resolution system on land takings is designed and how it works in Korea. Like any other country, the Korean system is not perfect. It is not mainly because the design of the system written in the law is flawed but because the operation of the system does not follow the spirit of the law. Using available statistics, I will show how the dispute resolution system works and what the main problems are, and then I will suggest some possible remedies. This empirical analysis can contribute to the improvement of the compulsory purchase system in Korea.

For this, I will first introduce Korea's system of dispute resolutions (Section II). And then, I will review the origin of the disputes (Section III). Based on that, I will examine the incidence of disputes and how they are dealt with (Section IV). Lastly, I will make concluding remarks with some policy suggestions (Section V).

II Process of Dispute Resolution

The first modern takings Act of Korea was the Rule on Land Taking, which was introduced in 1911 by the Japanese governor-general. After the Liberation in 1945, the Korean parliament replaced the colonial rule by the Takings Act in 1962. This law provided rules on almost every aspect of the land-taking process. Since then the law has been revised several times. However, the basic structure of the principles, processes, and institutions described in the original law has continued so far.[1]

According to the Takings Act, the government can exercise the power of eminent domain and take lands from landowners in two ways: negotiation and compulsory purchase (Figure 11.1). When the government decides to expropriate lands for public purpose, the Central Land Tribunal (CLT) within the Ministry of Land, Infrastructure and Transport first tries to purchase the land from the landowners via negotiation. If they reach an agreement, the land will be purchased. Nonetheless, if they fail to do so, the CLT proceeds to compulsory purchase; the CLT reviews the case, sets the price and sends the notice to the landowner, and then takes possession of the land.

If the condemnee agrees to the price offered in the compulsory purchase, then the government purchases the land accordingly. If not, the condemnee can appeal to the CLT. The CLT reviews the case, and adjusts and proposes a new price. If the condemnee accepts it at this stage, the process will be completed. However, if she does not agree, she may choose to go to the administrative court.

[1] The discussion below will be based on the most recent version of the law (#12471, enacted on March 18, 2014). Otherwise, I will denote the source.

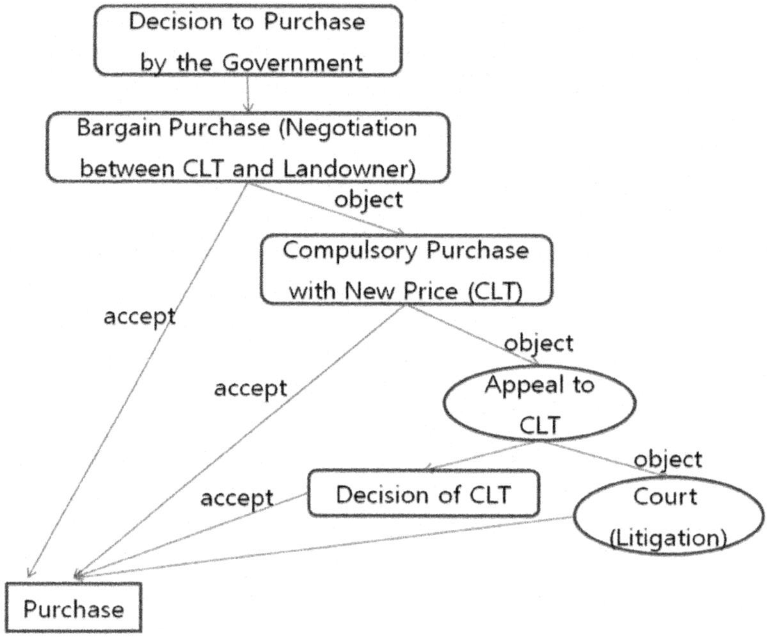

Figure 11.1. Process of Compulsory Purchase, Negotiation and Appeals: Illustration
Source: Takings Act and CLT website

According to the above description of the whole process, it seems that the condemnee has several opportunities to request for reconsideration by the government and the system seems to work in protecting the property rights of the landowner. However, in the real world the institutions or processes described in the law might work differently. Does the dispute resolution system work according to the spirit of the law? If not, what causes such discrepancies? Answering these questions requires the analysis of data, and this is done below.

III Origins of Disputes: A Quantitative Review of Takings in Korea

Before anatomizing the dispute resolution system itself, I will first examine the source of disputes, that is, the general aspects of takings in Korea such as their incidence, size, the usage of purchased land, amount of compensation and so on.

In Korea, two entities can exercise the power of eminent domain: the central government and municipalities. As the municipalities generally do not regularly report statistics on their compulsory purchases, unfortunately, I cannot examine their practice. The discussion below, therefore, will focus on the compulsory purchases by the central government, and will add information on the takings by municipalities if possible.

A Size

In 2011, the central government of Korea purchased 120 km^2 using the power of eminent domain (Table 11.1). This is twice as large as Manhattan Island, New York.[2] If we look at the trend for the last three to four decades, this was around the annual average (Figure 11.2). From 1976 to 2011, the central government has purchased 5,384 km^2 in total, and the average purchase per year was 150 km^2.[3]

According to Figure 11.2, land purchases have been done with some fluctuations. Three peaks are worth mentioning; two spikes in the 1990s are related to the construction of new cities in the Seoul metropolitan area. The big jump around 2006 comes from the construction project of Sejong City, the new administrative capital. They imply that unusual increases of expropriation originated from housing projects to ameliorate overcrowding in the capital Seoul. Otherwise, the government projects requiring compulsory land purchases have been done roughly at the same level during the last three to four decades.

The total amount of compensation for the condemned land was KRW14.5 trillion in 2011. As reported in Table 11.1, this is about double the average level of compensation from 1976 to 2011. This is because the total amount of compensation has steadily increased during the last four decades (Figure 11.3). Even if we measure the real value after controlling for inflation, this steady increase is still evident.

Linking Figure 11.2 with Figure 11.3, we can expect that compensation per unit area has gone up from 1976 to 2011. Figure 11.4 confirms this inference. Both the nominal and the real value of compensation per unit area have increased steadily. Especially, if we compare the 1990s and the 2000s, the compensation per unit area has almost tripled in terms of the nominal value and doubled in terms of the real value.

2 The area of Manhattan Island is 59 km^2.

3 5,384 km^2 is about nine times larger than Seoul (605.3 km^2) and three times larger than Jeju Island (1849.2 km^2).

Table 11.1. *Size of Condemned Land and Compensation in Korea*

			Average		Cumulative Total	
		2011	1976–2011	2001–2011	1976–2011	2001–2011
Area (km^2)		120.1	149.6	173.4	5,384.3	1,907.3
Amount (billion won)	Nominal	14,531.0	7,573.7	16,542.4	272,652.7	181,966.1
	Real	12,735.3	8,907.5	15,985.2	320,669.7	175,836.9
Compensation per km^2 (billion won)	Nominal	121	50.6	95.4	–	–
	Real	106	59.6	92.2	–	–
Relative to GDP (%)		1.2	1.6	1.7	–	–
Relative to government spending (%)		5.3	8.8	7.9	–	–

Note: GDP deflator is used for real value, and the base year is 2005.

Sources: Statistics Korea; Ministry of Land, Infrastructure and Transport, *Statistical Yearbook*; Onnara Real Estate Portal.

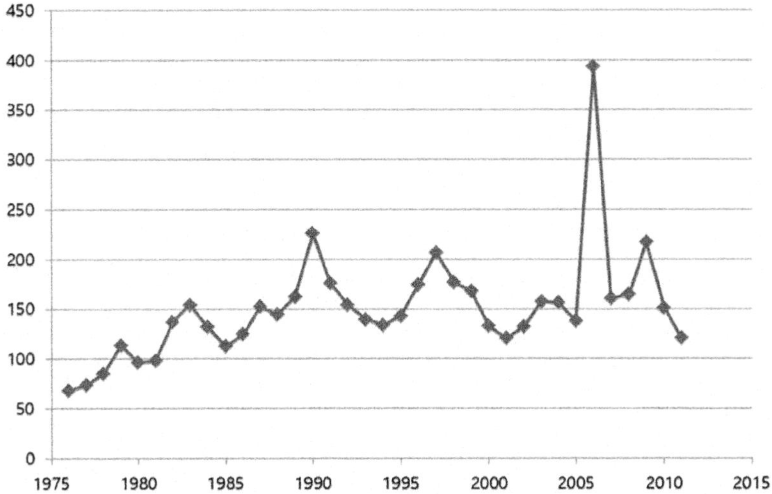

Figure 11.2. Condemned Area by the Central Government (unit: km^2)
Source: see Table 11.1.

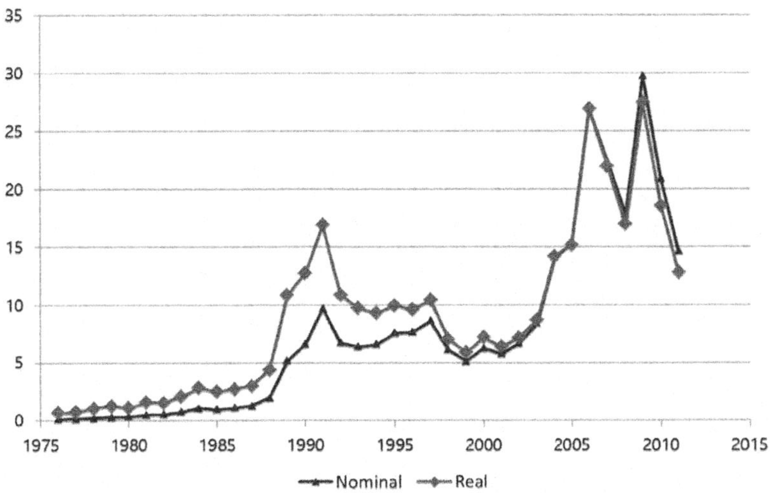

Figure 11.3. Amount of Compensation for Condemned Land (Trillion Won)
Source: see Table 11.1.

Considering the size of the Korean economy or the Korean government, the amount of compensation for takings has been significant. Figure 11.5 shows the ratio of compensation to GDP and government expenditure, and the compensation, on average, is 1.5 per cent to 2.0 per cent of the

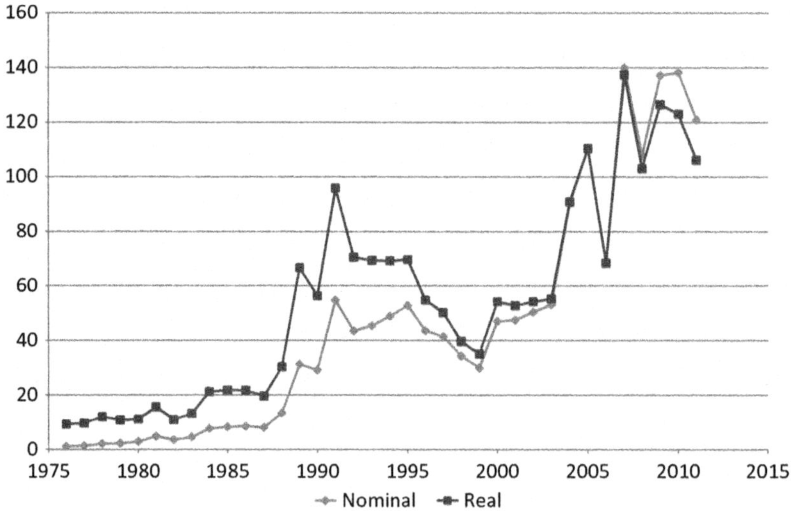

Figure 11.4. Amount of Compensation Per Unit Area (Thousand Won/m^2)
Source: see Table 11.1.

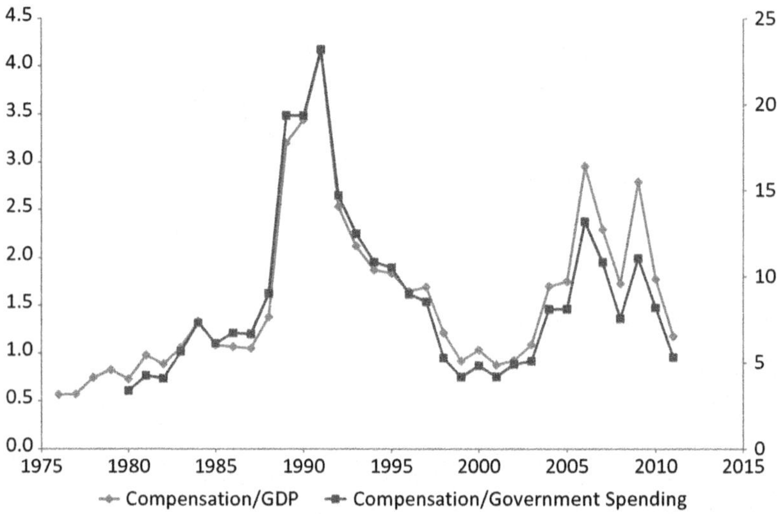

Figure 11.5. Size of Compensation Relative to GDP and Government Spending (%)
Note: The left and right axis show compensation relative to GDP (%) and compensation relative to government spending (%) respectively.
Source: see Table 11.1.

total GDP or 5 per cent to 10 per cent of the government expenditure throughout the period.

Noteworthy is the big surge around 1990 and the mid-2000s, which is related to the big construction projects mentioned earlier. The amount of compensation reached 25 per cent of total government expenditure in the early 1990s and 15 per cent in the late 2000s. In particular, the large payments in the late 2000s have left a huge burden on the Korean government, at least implicitly, as the debts are on the balance sheet of the Korea Land and Housing Corporation, a public enterprise that performed the project.

B *Usage of Condemned Land*

So, for what purpose has the Korean government taken the land? The most common reason for takings all around the world is to build public goods such as roads, military facilities, dams, and utilities. A distinctive aspect of Korea is that the government has exercised power beyond these classical areas. The government has actively taken lands for housing projects and the building of industrial complexes.

During the 1970s and 1980s, the rapid expansion of Seoul and other large cities caused a severe housing shortage. The Korean government tried to resolve this problem by providing multi-floor apartment complexes with thousands of units. For this, the government purchased land, removed the tenants, and then re-sold the land to construction companies to build apartment complexes. Construction of new cities near metropolises was done in a similar manner.

During the same period, the Korean government also expropriated lands for constructing industrial complexes. For accommodating the construction of manufacturing facilities, the Korean government declared "industrial complex regions" in certain areas. Then, the government constructed basic infrastructure for factories, and rented out or sold the land in pieces to companies that met the conditions.

Table 11.2 shows the patterns of compulsory purchases according to land usage. In 2011, 90 km^2, about 75 per cent of the total purchased land was used for five major areas: Transportation, housing, water, defense, and industry. The largest out of these were housing and transportation. Even if we measure the share using the amount of compensation, the relative importance does not change much.

Figure 11.6 shows the long-term trend of land usage expressed as a share. In terms of area, the land for transportation, such as construction

Table 11.2. *Size of Condemned Land and Compensation*

			Average		Total	
		Year 2011	1976–2011	2001–2011	1976–2011	2001–2011
Area (km^2)	Five major areas	91.2	122.4	140.6	4407.8	1547.1
	Road, railroad	30.8	49.7	71.4	1788.8	785.9
	Housing	24.5	20.1	32.3	724.7	355.5
	Water	17.9	20.1	17.2	722.4	188.9
	Defense	6.0	21.0	9.4	754.4	103.6
	Industry	12.1	11.6	10.3	417.4	113.2
	Others	28.9	27.1	32.7	976.5	360.2
	Total	120.1	149.6	173.4	5384.3	1907.3
	Share of the five major areas	76.0			81.9	81.1
Amount (Nominal, Trillion Won)	Five major areas	12.4	6.3	13.5	225.3	148.7
	Road, railroad	2.8	1.9	3.5	68.4	38.8
	Housing	7.6	3.5	8.1	124.6	89.6
	Water	0.7	0.3	0.5	9.9	6.0
	Defense	0.2	0.1	0.2	4.0	2.1
	Industry	1.2	0.5	1.1	18.4	12.3
	Others	2.1	1.3	3.0	47.4	33.2
	Total	14.5	7.6	16.5	272.7	182.0
	Share of the five major areas	85.6			82.6	81.7

Source: see Table 11.1.

(a)

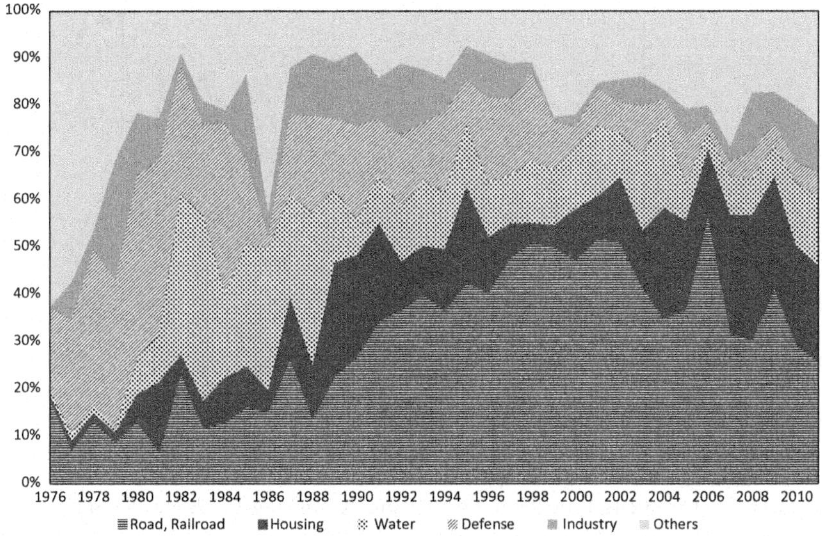

(b)

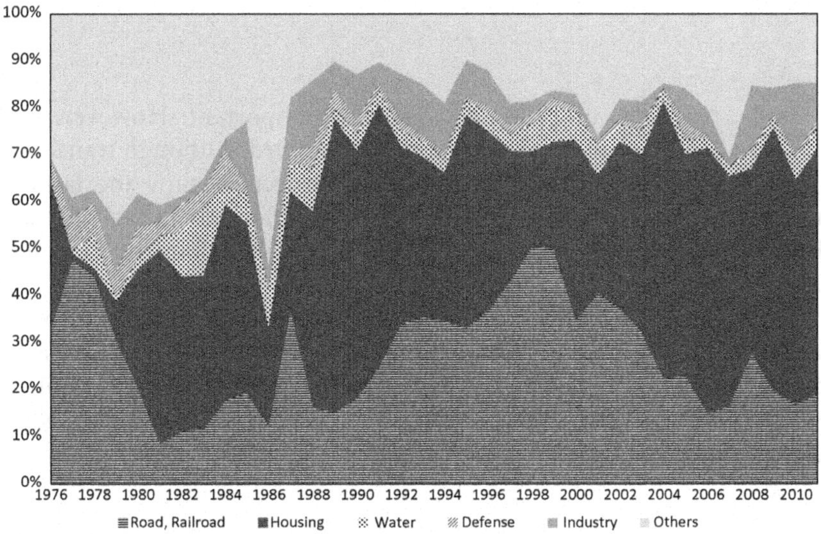

Figure 11.6. Proportion of Takings by Project Type (%)

(A) Area

(B) Amount of compensation

Source: see Table 11.2.

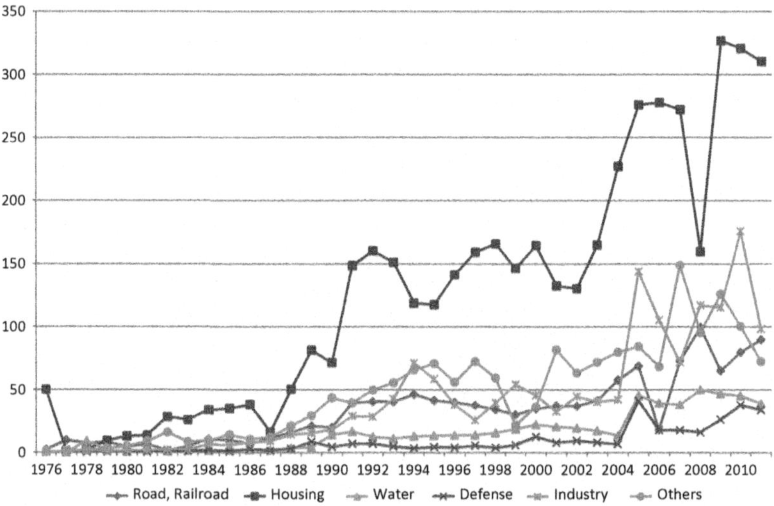

Figure 11.7. Compensation Per Unit of Land According to Usage (Thousand Won/m^2)
Source: see Table 11.2.

of roads, freeways, or railroads, was most important. However, the amount of compensation shows a different pattern. Although transportation is considered important, housing projects occupy the largest share. This pattern can be explained by the difference in land prices. The land for housing was usually more expensive than the land for transportation.

The difference in land prices based on their usage can be seen more clearly in Figure 11.7, which shows compensation per unit of land according to usage. The lowest is condemned lands for military facilities and lands for water facilities. The price of land for housing was far higher than the others.

C Summary

The Korean government has expropriated a large amount of land during the last four decades, and the overview so far reveals some intriguing characteristics. The most distinctive might be that the exercise of eminent domain power was closely related to economic development. According to the size of purchased land and the amount of compensation, the most important reason to use the power of eminent domain was to facilitate economic development by supplying more houses and more factories promptly, rather than to construct the classical public goods. It is not possible at this time to say how the Korean experience differs from those of developed countries or whether it is similar to the experiences of developing countries. It is even difficult to infer whether this pattern may cause more disputes or not. An international comparative study would give the answer to these questions and provide valuable policy lessons.

IV Disputes from Compulsory Purchase

A Compulsory Purchase

As described in Section II, when the government expropriates land, the CLT first negotiates with the landowner. When the negotiation fails, the CLT proceeds to compulsory purchase. This means that the occurrence of disputes is primarily determined by two factors: The amount of land expropriated and the ratio of compulsory purchases out of the total amount of expropriated land.

In 2011, about 75 per cent to 80 per cent of condemned land was purchased via negotiation, and the remaining 20 per cent to 25 per cent was purchased through compulsory purchase (Table 11.3). The share of compulsory purchase in 2011 is twice as high as the average from 1976 to 2011. This is because the share of the land taken by compulsory purchase has increased steadily for the past ten years (Figure 11.8). The ratio of the amount of compensation also shows a similar pattern; the ratio remained about 10 per cent before 2000, but it has increased to 20 per cent by 2011.

This pattern, however, should be interpreted very carefully. During the 1970s and 1980s when Korea was under an authoritarian regime, "negotiation" in the expropriation was not made between citizens assured of their rights and a government fully constrained by the rule of law. Condemnees were not able to easily reject the conditions proposed by the government, nor were they able to try to bargain.[4] In other words, the rising share of compulsory purchase in the 2000s reflects the condemnees' enhanced freedom to say "no" to a government decision.

Although we take this factor into account, the rising trend even throughout the 2000s strongly suggests a possibility that the CLT might

[4] A recently finalized case on the expropriation for Kuro Industrial Complex in the 1970s is a good example: February 20, 2014, Chosun Ilbo.

Table 11.3. *Compulsory Purchase According to Procedure*

			Average		Cumulative Total	
		2011	1976–2011	2001–2011	1976–2011	2001–2011
Area (km^2)	Negotiation	95.0	137.0	150.9	4,933.5	1,659.4
	Decision	25.1	12.5	22.5	451.7	247.8
	Total	120.1	149.6	173.4	5,384.3	1,907.3
Amount (billion won, nominal)	Negotiation	11,040.6	6,537.7	14,118.6	235,358.7	155,304.4
	Decision	3,490.3	1,036.1	2,423.8	37,299.8	26,661.7
	Total	14,531.0	7,573.8	16,542.4	272,658.4	181,966.1

Source: CLT website.

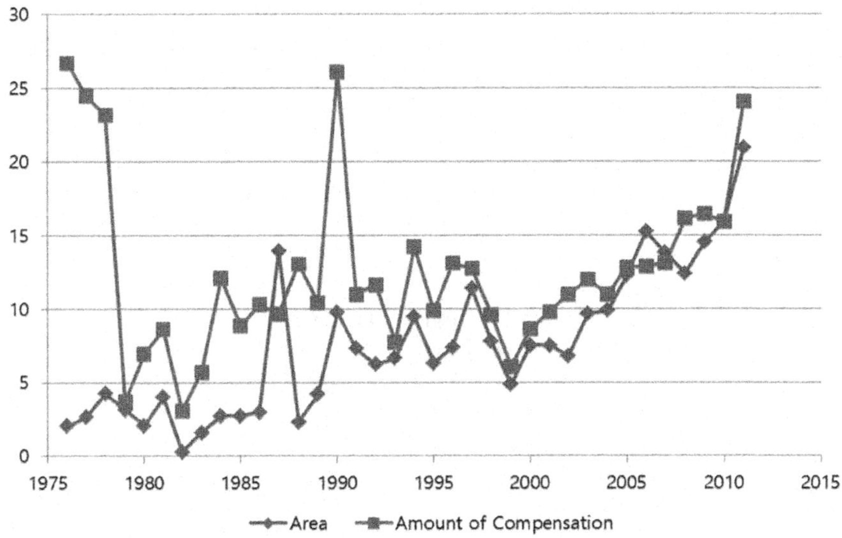

Figure 11.8. Share of Land Taken by Compulsory Purchase (%)
Source: see Table 11.3.

not work as desired; the condemnees are more and more discontented with the conditions proposed by the government during negotiations, and the government cannot avoid using compulsory purchase, that is, to determine the price unilaterally and purchase compulsorily.

B Appeal

When the CLT takes the lands via compulsory purchase, discontented condemnees can appeal in basically two sequential steps. First, the condemnees can appeal to the CLT and request a new decision. Then, the CLT reviews the appeal and revises or reaffirms its decision. Second, if the condemnees still disagree with the decision, they can go to the administrative court.[5]

Table 11.4 shows the patterns of appeal and decision by the CLT and litigation. In 2011, there were 1,303 appeals and rulings by the CLT, of

[5] There are other alternatives to settle disputes, such as appealing to institutions like the National Human Rights Commission of Korea, writing letters to the president, or involving the mass media. The number of cases that go to these institutions, however, is much lower, and these institutions are much less effective in solving the problem than the CLT or the courts.

Table 11.4. *Appeals to Land Tribunals and the Court*

		CLT		Municipal Land Tribunal	Court
		Appeal	Decision	Decision	Litigation
		2006	2011	2010	2011
Cases			1,303	562	840
Area		2,199	11,363	–	–
Compensation		524,808			
Appeal/non-negotiated purchase	Cases		85.9	42.2	–
	Area	3.7	22.2		–
	Compensation	15.2			

Source: CLT website and the Supreme Court.

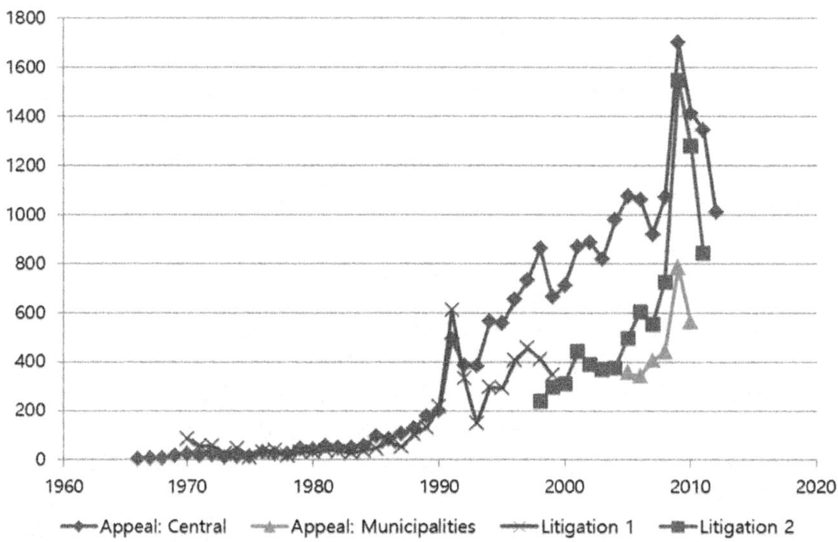

Figure 11.9. Appeals and Litigation against Compulsory Purchase (Unit: Number of Cases)
Sources: See Table 11.4.

which about 85 per cent were compulsory purchases. This means that most of the condemnees were discontent with the conditions of compulsory purchase. During the same year, there were a total of 840 actions. It is difficult to link the two numbers directly, but it suggests that the majority of condemnees continue to bring the issue before the court even after compulsory purchase by the CLT to amend the conditions under which the takings has been carried out.

Figure 11.9 shows the number of appeals to the CLT and the court during the last four to five decades. It appears that the appeals against compulsory purchase have increased consistently. The fall after 2009 does not imply the start of a declining trend but rather a return to normal growth after a surge of appeals related to the construction of Sejong City.

C *Sources of Growth of Appeal*

Then, why have the appeals increased? Although preliminary, I can provide a very tentative answer using a simple decomposition analysis. The amount of condemned land (CL) is expropriated either by negotiation (N) or by compulsory purchase (CP).

$$CL \equiv N + CP$$

The ratio of total appeal (AP) to total purchase ($\lambda \equiv AP/CL$) is influenced by two factors. One is how the purchase is made, that is, the share of compulsory purchase out of total condemnation ($\mu \equiv CP/CL$). The other is the response to the content of the compulsory purchase, that is, the total appeal out of compulsory purchase ($\beta \equiv AP/CP$). This means that:

$$\lambda = \mu \cdot \beta$$

If the growth of λ comes mainly from growth of μ, it means that the increase of compulsory purchase itself is the source of the problem. Otherwise, the operation of the compulsory purchase might be less and less acceptable to condemnees, and this might raise β and then λ.

Focusing on the 2000s, β is relatively stable (Figure 11.10). However, as seen in Figure 11.8, μ has risen. This implies that the rise of disputes in Figure 11.9 came from the rise of μ, that is, that the government increased the purchase of land via compulsory purchase, that is, the government progressively finalized negotiations without full agreement from the condemnees.

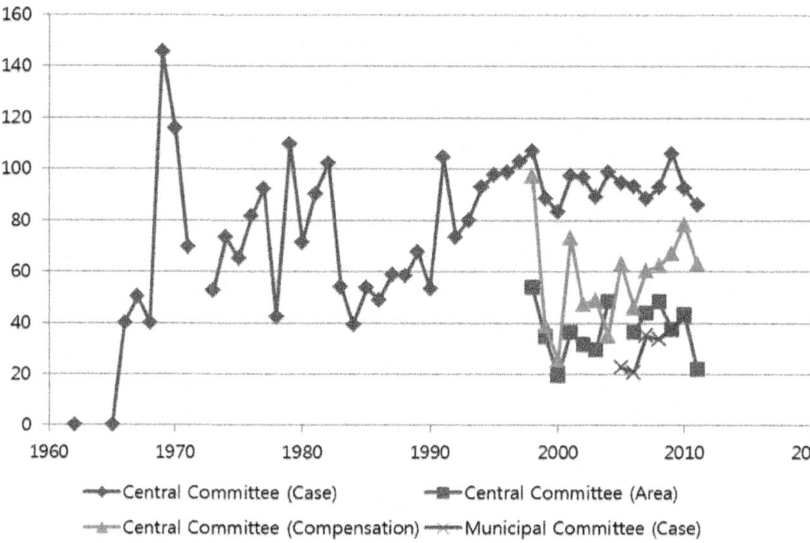

Figure 11.10. Ratio of Total Appeal out of Compulsory Purchase (μ,%).
Sources: See Table 11.4.

Of course, this result should be interpreted carefully. More detailed data can help to understand this pattern. But it is apparent that further effort should be made at the negotiation stage to obtain agreements from the landowners when exercising the power of eminent domain. To clarify the meaning of this pattern, we need to look inside the CLT.

V Dispute Resolutions by the CLT

In Korea, the CLT should exercise compulsory purchase and review appeals against compulsory purchase. According to the law first enacted in 1962, the CLT was organized as a committee without full-time staff; the committee consisted of five non-permanent members who were experts on takings (Table 11.5).[6]

Since then, there have been several important changes regarding the structure and operation of the CLT, and two are worth mentioning. First, the CLT became a permanent organization with about 30 full-time staff in 1990.[7] Second, the number of committee members has been extended

[6] Land Takings Act.

[7] Land Takings Law (#4231, July 8, 1990). Actual establishment of the permanent organization was completed in April 1991.

Table 11.5. *Organization of the Committee of CLT*

	Total	President	Committee Member
1962–1971	5	1	4
1971–1981	7	1	6
1981–2003	9	1	8
2003–present	20 and below	1	Below 20

Source: Takings Law.

and meetings have been held more frequently. In 2003, the law specified that the number of committee members should not exceed 20. The number of committee members grew to 14 in 2014. Not every member attends every meeting; according to the law, the chair appoints seven members to attend per meeting.[8]

To understand why there are so many appeals against compulsory purchase, we need to anatomize the CLT; how the committee reviews information, exchanges opinions, and makes decisions in detail. However, this is impossible due to the lack of disclosed data. However, we can make an inference using an important clue from the homepage of the CLT. The CLT once disclosed a full list of cases reviewed at each meeting from 2009 to 2012. Using this data, we can figure out the caseload of each meeting, and this can provide information, although limited, on how decisions are made within the committee.

Table 11.6 summarizes this data. From 2009 to 2012, the committee met 66 times, and made decisions on 12,571 cases including compulsory purchase and related appeals. From this, it can be deduced that an average of 190 cases have been reviewed per meeting. As the amount of time spent per meeting is unknown, it is hard to figure out how much time had been spent for each case on average. However, it is clear that the committee members were unable to spend enough time to review all these cases.[9]

Intriguing are the changes in the number of gatherings and the amount of work done at each meeting. In 2009, the gathering was almost twice per

[8] Land Takings Law, Article 52 section 6.

[9] If a full day or eight hours was spent for a meeting, it would mean that the committee devoted three minutes per case.

Table 11.6. *Number of Cases Dealt with by the Committee in, 2009–2012*

		Number of Cases				
Year	Number of Meetings	Compulsory Purchase	Appeal	Others	Total	Average Cases per Meeting
2009	23	1,612	1,697	409	3,718	161.7
2010	17	1,513	1,405	320	3,238	190.5
2011	15	1,592	1,319	332	3,244	216.3
2012	11	1,188	905	278	2,371	215.5
Total	66	5,905	5,326	1,339	12,571	190.5

Source: Homepage of the CLT.

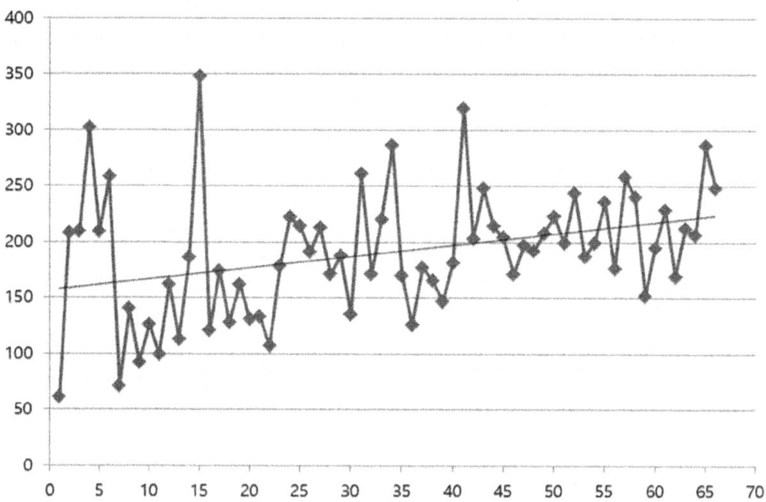

Figure 11.11. Number of Cases Reviewed by the CLT at Each Meeting from 2009 to 2012 (Unit: Case)

Note: The figure can be read as follows. From 2009 to 2012, 66 meetings were held. They were numbered according to time, and the X-axis represents them. Y-axis shows the number of cases reviewed at each meeting. I have shown the date of each meeting and detailed statistics for the year 2011 as an example.

Source: CLT website.

month. However, it has decreased to once a month by 2012. For the same period, the number of cases has also declined. However, it was not as much as 50 per cent. This means that the caseload per meeting has increased by about 30 per cent (Figure 11.11).

Of course, the members could carefully and thoroughly review the case before coming to the meeting, and they could reach an agreement instantly. However, the position of committee member is not a full-time one, and the appeal cases probably were not typically easy. This inference leads us to worry that the appeals by condemnees might not be reviewed carefully. This can be one of the most important reasons why significant compulsory purchases are not accepted by the condemnees and the majority of the appeal cases go to the administrative court.

VI Conclusion

The Korean government has expropriated a large amount of land during the last four to five decades. The Takings Law stipulates that institutions and procedures including the CLT should be established to protect the rights of condemnees. This chapter has shown, although very tentatively, that the CLT may not work as the law suggested. In the 2000s, the CLT tended to be less careful and less patient in negotiating with the condemnees and to hasten towards compulsory purchase; when condemnees appealed against the decision, the CLT did not seem to spend enough time or make enough effort in reviewing the case. This has caused an increased number of appeals both to the CLT and the administrative court.

This pattern might have originated from a desire to achieve rapid economic growth in the 1970s and the 1980s. The lack of government resources for adequate compensation might also reinforce this custom. However, the Korean economy has grown successfully since then. Therefore, aligning with the changing times, the government ought to behave differently. More emphasis should be placed on the protection of constituents' property rights in exercising the power of eminent domain. Policymakers should be aware that reckless expropriation can harm the legitimacy of the state and cause catastrophic results.

Appendix

Number of Cases Dealt with by the Committee in 2011

Order	Date	Total	Compulsory Purchase	Appeal	Others
1	January 21	319	137	157	25
2	February 18	203	81	96	26
3	March 11	248	123	104	21
4	April 1	214	105	85	24
5	April 22	204	95	89	20
6	May 13	171	87	73	11
7	June 3	197	114	67	16
8	June 24	192	101	66	25
9	July 15	208	98	91	19
10	August 12	223	119	77	27
11	September 2	199	109	72	18
12	October 7	244	115	101	27
13	October 28	187	91	71	25
14	November 18	199	91	90	18
15	December 16	236	126	80	30

Source: CLT website.

References

Central Land Tribunal, http://clt.molit.go.kr/intro.do
Statistics Korea, http://kosis.kr (source for some tables in this chapter)
Ministry of Land, Infrastructure and Transport, *Statistical Yearbook*
Onnara Real Estate Portal, www.onnara.go.kr
Supreme Court, *Yearbook of Judicature*

Conclusion

ILJOONG KIM, HOJUN LEE AND ILYA SOMIN

The chapters in this book have reviewed a variety of eminent domain systems around the world, focusing on the Six Pillars. It is difficult to make sweeping generalizations about such a wide range of systems. Nonetheless, there are at least four important lessons that we can tentatively draw from the evidence. These include the relationship between economic development and protection for property rights, the prevalence of abusive takings in many countries, the need to limit official discretion in order to prevent such abuses, and the growth of popular opposition to condemnations that seem to victimize ordinary people for the benefit of powerful interests.

There is a clear relationship between a nation's level of economic development and the degree of protection for property rights against takings. In many developing countries, property rights get little or no effective protection. There are multiple reasons for this trend, including weak legal institutions and ineffective constitutional constraints on government power. Protection against takings is stronger in more advanced nations, such as Germany, some other states in the European Union, and the United States.

But strong protection for property rights is far from universal even in wealthy nations. As the chapter on the United States suggests, the federal Supreme Court has done very little to limit condemnations in recent decades, though things are different in many states. South Korea and Taiwan have now attained the same level of economic development as many Western states.[1] Nonetheless, these two nations have experienced serious problems with eminent domain abuse, which their legal systems

[1] Taiwan's per capita GDP, estimated by the purchasing power parity method, for example, is comparable to such nations as Germany and Canada, and higher than France, Italy, the United Kingdom, and Spain. South Korea's is similar to that of Italy, Spain, and New Zealand. See International Monetary Fund, World Economic Outlook Database, available at www.imf.org/external/pubs/ft/weo/2015/02/weodata/index.aspx.

have had difficulty controlling. As discussed below, we believe that increased public awareness of property rights and opposition to eminent domain abuse may lead to institutional reforms in these countries.

Our second major conclusion is that, in a wide range of legal systems, eminent domain is often used for the benefit of powerful private interest groups, and often in ways that harm the economy more than they benefit it. This is a particularly severe problem in developing nations, which have weak legal institutions. The tragedy there is particularly great in light of the fact that modern development economics strongly suggests that protection for property rights, far from impeding development, is actually a crucial mechanism for spurring economic growth, especially growth that benefits the poor.[2] But large-scale eminent domain abuse persists even in many wealthy nations covered in this volume, such as the United States, Korea, and Taiwan.

Influential private interests can sometimes "capture" the political process and lobby for condemnations that transfer property to them, at the expense of both the owners and the general public. In many cases, the public has difficulty curtailing such takings, perhaps because voters do not understand what is happening, or lack the knowledge needed to assess the effectiveness of takings in promoting development.[3] Such abuses turn out to be extremely difficult to control, even in otherwise well-developed legal systems.

This naturally brings us to our third conclusion: the establishment of strong legal institutions is not by itself sufficient to prevent abusive condemnations. Nations such as South Korea, Taiwan, and the United States have effective systems of judicial review and the rule of law, yet still have serious problems with the use of eminent domain.

In order to curtail eminent domain abuse more effectively, it is also essential to impose tight limits on the discretion of condemning authorities. Otherwise, they will often be vulnerable to capture by private interests, and will tend to ignore the harm inflicted on the victims of eminent domain, most of whom lack significant political influence.

[2] On the importance of property rights for economic development, see, e.g., Robert D. Cooter and Hans-Bernd Schäfer, *Solomon's Knot: How Law Can End the Poverty of Nations* (Princeton University Press, 2012), ch. 6; Hernando De Soto, *The Mystery of Capital: Why Capitalism Triumphs in the West and Fails Everywhere Else* (New York: Basic Books, 2000), pp. 49–63.

[3] On the role of voter ignorance in facilitating abusive takings, see Ilya Somin, *The Grasping Hand: Kelo v. City of New London and the Limits of Eminent Domain* (University of Chicago Press, 2015), ch. 3.

There are a variety of different strategies for limiting official discretion. The contributors to this volume do not all agree on which would be the most effective.[4] In their respective chapters on South Korea and the United States, Hojun Lee and Ilya Somin contend that the best approach is judicial enforcement of tighter public interest or public use limitations on takings.[5] Hans-Bernd Schäfer contends that this approach has been effective in limiting abusive takings in Germany.

By contrast, Yun-chien Chang contends that this strategy is unlikely to work in Taiwan, and that it might be better to pursue stronger procedural restrictions on takings. Instead of limiting the purposes for which property can be condemned, this strategy would require the government to go through more stringent procedural hurdles before a taking can be approved, thereby enabling more thorough consideration of potential costs and benefits. Such deliberation may give opponents an opportunity to expose flaws in the development plan underlying the proposed taking.[6]

Other scholars have proposed such strategies as increasing compensation for owners of condemned property, giving community residents a greater say in condemnation decisions, adopting special protection for homes, and imposing heightened judicial or administrative scrutiny on takings that transfer property to private parties.[7] It is possible that no one approach will be right for every nation. The optimal mix of strategies for limiting the use of eminent domain might vary from country to country, or even between different jurisdictions in a federal system. But scholars, policymakers, and ordinary citizens in many countries should at least recognize that they have a common problem, and look for better ways to address it.

Our final observation is that political conflict over the use of eminent domain has gradually emerged in a wide range of countries. In the United States, this is most evident in the massive public backlash triggered by the *Kelo* case, and continuing controversy since then.[8] Similar conflicts have arisen in Korea, Taiwan, and even authoritarian mainland China, where millions of people have been forcibly displaced by development projects.[9]

One of the co-editors of this volume (Somin) was invited to teach at a Chinese university in the summer of 2014, primarily because of his

[4] For an overview of a wide range of approaches, see Somin, *Grasping Hand*, ch. 8.

[5] See also ibid., chs. 3 and 8.

[6] For a critique of similar proposals in the American context, see ibid., pp. 209–12.

[7] For analysis of these and other approaches, and citations to relevant literature, see ibid., ch. 8.

[8] See Chapter 2, in this volume.

[9] Somin, *Grasping Hand*, pp. 244–45.

work on eminent domain in the United States. He was surprised by the notable similarities between the American and Chinese debates over takings, despite the many differences between the two societies.[10]

The eminent domain system of development-oriented countries such as Korea and Taiwan might potentially have contributed to their rapid early economic growth, though it is also possible they would have done even better with stronger protection for property rights. Regardless of its past record, however, largely unconstrained use of eminent domain is increasingly incompatible with citizens' enhanced awareness of property rights and greater empowerment in the wake of the rise of democracy and societal liberalization. Increasing wealth and education may also make it easier for civil society to mobilize in opposition to takings.

As in Korea, very serious conflicts between condemners and condemnees have arisen in a variety of developing countries most notably Asian states such as China, Vietnam, Indonesia, Malaysia, the Philippines, Thailand, Cambodia, Laos and others. Officials in many of these countries often view Korean institutions as a model to follow in promoting their own economic development. There may indeed be valuable lessons to be learned from Korea's experience. But one of them is that developing nations would do well to tighten restrictions on the use of eminent domain.

Although we have tried to draw some general conclusions, we are well aware that each country has a distinctive history, political ideology, degree of adherence to the rule of law, community norms, stage of economic development, land use patterns, dissemination of information, and so on. It is unlikely that the same exact approach to eminent domain policy will work for all.

Still, there are some striking general patterns that recur in a variety of different nations, including the challenge of constraining eminent domain abuse, and the social conflict that it causes when left largely unrestricted. We suggest that at least some convergence in policy solutions to these problems may well be necessary. We conclude this volume with three additional suggestions that may help promote useful reform.

First, the developing nations analyzed in this volume could benefit from improvements in the basic structure of property rights. These

[10] This experience is described in Ilya Somin, "The Conflict Over Takings and Property Rights in China and its Parallels to that in the United States," *Washington Post*, Aug. 8, 2014, available at www.washingtonpost.com/news/volokh-conspiracy/wp/2014/08/08/the-conflict-over-takings-and-property-rights-in-china/.

include increasing the availability of up-to-date information on the ownership of existing rights.[11] Legally delineating *who owns what* is an essential task. An improved system for assessing land values is also important so that such information can be disseminated to promote market transactions.

Making it easier to voluntarily transfer land is both valuable in itself, and may reduce the incentive to resort to the use of eminent domain to solve assembly problems. In some cases, it might be hard for developing nations to rapidly accomplish these tasks on their own. International cooperation and knowledge-sharing with more developed nations might help accelerate the process.

Second, emerging economies should do more to tackle the widespread practice of abusive takings that is prevalent in all too many societies. This can also help stave off the growing social and political conflicts over the use of eminent domain that have arisen in numerous countries. As already discussed, it is important to find effective ways to tighten controls over the discretionary use of eminent domain.

Ultimately, public officials are people just like the rest of us. They are tempted to use their power to promote their own self-interest and that of politically influential groups, often at the expense of protecting the property rights of the politically weak. Once such practices become institutionalized, they can incentivize additional lobbying and interest group pressure, which in turn leads to even more harmful takings. Reforms are needed to break this vicious cycle. That need is not limited to poor nations alone. As we have seen, even economically advanced states such as Korea, Taiwan, and the United States have experienced similar problems.

Third, much of the analysis of eminent domain in this volume is also relevant to the issue of "regulatory takings": cases where the government constrains property rights without formally transferring possession. Like the use of eminent domain, regulatory takings can often undermine the security of property rights severely, and victimize the politically weak.

There is also evidence that officials sometimes attempt to substitute regulatory takings for physical takings in order to avoid having to pay compensation. Consequently, the issue has led to significant political conflict in many countries, though not yet on the same scale as the struggle over eminent domain.

And, as with eminent domain, there is great disagreement among experts as to how best to deal with this issue. We hope to pursue the

[11] The importance of this point is also stressed in De Soto, *The Mystery of Capital*.

parallels between the two issues in greater detail in future work. In both cases, an international comparative approach might help shed new light on the subject.

We hope that this volume has helped achieve a better comparative understanding of eminent domain around the world. But there is much room for future research. Scholars can use our framework to analyze condemnations in nations that have not been included in this volume. There is also great need for comparative evaluation of the effectiveness of various reform strategies for reining in abusive takings. The "despotic power" of eminent domain may be an essential, or at least unavoidable attribute of legal systems "that exists in every country."[12] But that is all the more reason to study the ways in which such despotism might be limited and constrained.

[12] *Vanhorne's Lessee v. Dorrance*, 2 U.S. (2 Dall.) 304, 311 (1795).

INDEX

Lightning Source UK Ltd.
Milton Keynes UK
UKOW05n2125070517
300649UK00016B/462/P

9 781107 177291